Horror on the Stag

Horror on the Stage

Monsters, Murders and Terrifying Moments in Theater

Amnon Kabatchnik

McFarland & Company, Inc., Publishers
Jefferson, North Carolina

This book has undergone peer review.

Library of Congress Cataloguing-in-Publication Data

Names: Kabatchnik, Amnon, 1929– author.
Title: Horror on the stage : monsters, murders and terrifying moments in theater / Amnon Kabatchnik.
Description: Jefferson, North Carolina : McFarland & Company, Inc., Publishers, 2023. |
Includes bibliographical references and index.
Identifiers: LCCN 2023013507 | ISBN 9781476675558 (paperback : acid free paper) ∞
ISBN 9781476646237 (ebook)
Subjects: LCSH: Horror in literature. | Horror in the theater. | Horror plays—History and criticism. |
BISAC: PERFORMING ARTS / Theater / History & Criticism | LITERARY CRITICISM /
Horror & Supernatural
Classification: LCC PN56.H6 K33 2023 | DDC 809.9164—dc23/eng/20230512
LC record available at https://lccn.loc.gov/2023013507

British Library cataloguing data are available

ISBN (print) 978-1-4766-7555-8
ISBN (ebook) 978-1-4766-4623-7

Front cover: Lucy (Joanna Miles) is attacked by the Vampire (Frank Langella)
in a 1967 Berkshire Theatre Festival production of *Dracula*
(photograph by Friedman-Abeles, New York Public Library of the Performing Arts)

Printed in the United States of America

*McFarland & Company, Inc., Publishers
Box 611, Jefferson, North Carolina 28640
www.mcfarlandpub.com*

For Adi and Jerry
Edan and Jennifer

Table of Contents

Acknowledgments   viii

Preface   1

Introduction: Terrifying Moments in Theater History   3

1. Supernatural Monsters   75

2. Real-Life Monsters   128

3. Harrowing Adaptations   139

4. Musical Monsters   188

5. Psychotics   215

6. Sherlock Holmes vs. Creatures of Horror   230

Appendix 1. Birth of the Gothics   245

Appendix 2. The Grand Guignol   248

Chapter Notes   251

Bibliography   264

Index   265

Acknowledgments

In my pursuit of old, out-of-print manuscripts and rare pictures related to the genre of stage horror, I render thanks to the librarians of the New York Public Library for the Performing Arts at Lincoln Center Plaza, Manhattan (especially Rod Bladel and John Calhoun), and to Paul Friedman at the General Research Division of the New York Public Library.

For photographs, my deep appreciation goes to Jeremy McGraw, Photograph Librarian, Billy Rose Theatre Division, the New York Public Library for the Performing Arts; Thomas Lisanti, Manager of the Permissions & Reproduction Services at the New York Public Library; Daniel Boland, Sales Associate at Getty Images; Sue Grinols, Director of Photo Services and Imaging at the Fine Arts Museums of San Francisco; Amy Langton of the Dramatic Publishing Company; Patricia Kelley Schultz, sister of playwright Tim Kelly; Penelope Wallace, the late daughter of author Edgar Wallace; Friedman-Abeles; Vandamm Studio; photographers Martha Swope, Fred Fehl, Christopher J. Frith, and Alfredo Valente.

A special salutation to Eleanor Bader of Brooklyn, New York; Helga Schier of Santa Monica, California; and Rebecca de Juan of Madrid, Spain, who in various ways made this project possible.

Preface

When, in October 2018, I visited the Public Library for the Performing Arts at Lincoln Center, New York, New York, to conduct research for this book, I was surprised to hear a veteran librarian state that he was not aware of any plays featuring werewolves, mummies, or zombies. I assured him that such plays exist and further explained that I have many in my private collection of theatrical materials. I then checked the library's files and, sure enough, aside from data on Dracula and Frankenstein productions, I couldn't find any information on dramas with these monstrous characters.

Many of the plays discussed in this volume are little known and out of print, so I have taken the liberty of expanding the description of their plots and have sprinkled them with samples of dialogue.

Terrifying moments were scattered in the plays of Ancient Greece, where Aeschylus, Sophocles, and Euripides thrilled the Athenians with shocking yet wrenching poetic tragedies. Horrific elements were inserted in dramas produced in Ancient Rome, with Seneca's *Thyestes* (60 CE) climaxing in one of the most horrifying images in theater history: at a royal banquet, a father unknowingly feasts on the limbs of his murdered sons. And there was no let-up of horror on the stage during the Middle Ages, Elizabethan and Jacobean periods, or the seventeenth, eighteenth, nineteenth, and twentieth centuries.

For this book, I've identified dreadful, macabre incidents in plays of the supernatural (featuring various creatures of the night); in plays about real-life monsters (Lizzie Borden, Jack the Ripper); in plays adapted from literary sources (*Dr. Jekyll and Mr. Hyde*, *The Turn of the Screw*, *The Phantom of the Opera*, and others); and in plays highlighted by cruel murders, brutal rapes, grisly mutilations, and other heinous crimes that trigger overwhelming fear. To justify shocking climaxes, I invariably related the events leading up to them. Greed, lust, jealousy, revenge, sadism, mental disorder, and sometimes pure evil were the causes of dreadful acts.

To preserve the historical perspective, I have kept offensive elements intact and did not edit or revise incidents of chauvinism, bigotry, racial prejudice, homophobia, or anti–Semitic slurs. (These transgressions of the plays must be seen in their era's context and should not be confused with my beliefs.)

I hope that this labor of love will ignite interest in these dark plays—all of which deserve renewed scrutiny and revival.

Introduction:
Terrifying Moments
in Theater History

Ancient Greek Theater

The first unnerving moment in theater history occurred when an Ancient Greek audience entered the Athens arena for a production of Aeschylus's *Prometheus Bound* (c. 480 BCE) and saw Prometheus, the Titan, chained to a cliff, an iron wedge through his breast, a girdle around his hips, and shackles on his feet with fetters of brass. The cliff was of enormous height, and the figure of Prometheus dangling high above the orchestra must have been a chilling sight, setting a dark mood for the ensuing action of the play.

The tragedy *Prometheus Bound* also introduced the first stage assassin: Zeus, King of Olympus, who, with his thunderbolt, dispatched Prometheus to Hades for having stolen fire from the gods and given it to humans.

In 463 BCE, Aeschylus (525–458 BCE) wrote and presented *The Danaid Tetralogy*, the first play about a mass murder. The story, set in Egypt, is about the 50 daughters of Danaus who murdered their 50 cousins on their wedding night to escape incestuous marriage. Their case was the first recorded courtroom drama. The goddess Aphrodite arrives and mediates neutrality between sides for the "sacred marriage of Heaven and Earth."

Aeschylus then offered the first theatrical domestic murder in *The Oresteia* (458 BCE), a trilogy that begins with the killing of Agamemnon, King of Argos, by his wife, Clytemnestra, and her lover, Aegisthus. The queen, irate at her husband for returning from the Trojan War with his lover Princess Cassandra, throws a fishnet-like robe around Agamemnon, strikes him three times with an axe, and rejoices as his blood spurts. The feud passes from generation to generation, culminating in the revenge homicide of Aegisthus and Clytemnestra by her children, Orestes and Electra.[1]

The next great Greek playwright, Sophocles (496–406 BCE), wrote a cycle of macabre tragedies. *Women of Trachis*, aka *The Trachiniae* (c. 450 BCE), depicts four murders perpetrated by Heracles, the legendary hero. At the end, he himself is killed. His wife Deianeira decides to send Heracles a potion that she mistakenly believes will keep him from loving other women. She dyes a robe with the potion, places it in a casket, and sends it as a gift, "to my absent master." Her son Hyllos arrives a little later and accuses Deianeira of murdering his father. Heracles has donned the robe: "It clung to his ribs … pain tore at his bones—and then the venom sank its fangs into him, gorging on his flesh."

3

Sophocles' *Ajax* (c. 444 BCE) takes place during the Trojan War. It portrays how, following the death of the great Greek hero Achilles, Ajax coveted Achilles' armor, thus receiving recognition as the new greatest hero. However, the army's leaders, the brothers Agamemnon and Menelaus, rule that the armor should go to Odysseus, a Greek commander. Furious, Ajax plots to kill Agamemnon and Menelaus at the dead of night. But Athena, the goddess of war and wisdom, arrives and casts a spell over him. As a result, Ajax tortures and slaughters a herd of livestock, believing that the animals are his fellow leaders. Tecmessa, Ajax's harlot, exits from his tent and relates how Ajax roped together "carcass corpses,

The revenge slaying of Aegisthus in *The Oresteia*, 458 BCE (artist: Pellissier & Allen, 1900s; The New York Public Library for the Performing Arts).

blood-drenched offerings by his own hand slaughtered." Tecmessa unveils the tent, and Ajax is revealed surrounded by dead animals, provoking mockery by all. His madness evaporates, and Ajax realizes what he has done. "The gods hate me," he says. "The Greeks hate me. The very plains of Troy hate me too." He flings himself upon his sword. This is the earliest occurrence of lethal action on stage that is not described by a messenger but actually witnessed by the audience.

Sophocles' *Antigone* (c. 442 BCE) introduces a Theban princess who challenges the decree of King Creon and at dusk buries her rebellious brother who had died on the battlefield, his body to be devoured by wild animals. Creon sentences Antigone to be buried alive in a cave.[2]

Sophocles' *Oedipus the King* (c. 429 BCE) is perhaps the first staged whodunit. King Oedipus investigates the cause of an epidemic that is consuming the city of Thebes. During the interrogation of witnesses, Oedipus admits that he had unwittingly killed his father—an irate old man who had attempted to trample him with his chariot—and had married his mother, Jocasta, queen of Thebes. Horrified by the startling resolution, Oedipus claws out his own eyes.[3]

Unlike his predecessors, the playwright Euripides (480s–406 BCE) painted legendary heroes as ordinary, flawed people and expressed doubt about the "divine justice" of the gods. His masterpiece, *Medea* (431 BCE), the tragedy of a woman scorned, is arguably the best of the lot. When Jason, Medea's lover, plans to marry the daughter of the king of Corinth, jealousy motivates Medea to fatally stab her and Jason's two sons on the roof of the palace. She throws their bodies at Jason's feet "to vex" his heart and escapes the city in a chariot drawn by dragons.[4]

In Euripides's *The Bacchae* (405 BCE), King Pentheus of Thebes rejects the divinity of Dionysus, the god of wine, who then goads the devoted women of Thebes to exact

The tyrant Creon (Philip Bosco) and his rebellious niece (Martha Henry) in a scene from the Lincoln Centre Repertory production of *Antigone*, 1971 (photo by Martha Swope, The New York Public Library for the Performing Arts).

revenge. A horde of inebriated, raging women descend Mount Cithaeron, rip to shreds a herd of grazing cows, and continue their rampage against the king, seizing him, tearing his limbs, and stripping the flesh from his body: "One and all, with blood-bespattered hands, they played ball with the flesh of Pentheus."

Antigone (Martha Henry) is led by two masked guards to be imprisoned in a dark cave (photo by Martha Swope, The New York Public Library for the Performing Arts).

Medea (Irene Papas) exhibits her brother's decapitated head before throwing him to the sea in the play *Medea*, Circle in the Square (Uptown), 1973 (photo by Martha Swope, The New York Public Library for the Performing Arts).

Ancient Roman Theater

The ancient Roman dramatists borrowed heavily from the Greeks. *The Rope* (c. 211 BCE) by Titus Marcius Plautus (c. 254 BCE–184 BCE), set in a town on the northern coast of Africa, is an early play featuring the melodramatic motif of long-lost children whose true identities are revealed before the final curtain. The complex plot includes the kidnapping of a baby by pirates and the discovery of a casket containing evidence of identification. Plautus's *The Haunted House* (c. 200 BCE) is arguably the first work to present a house inhabited by spirits of the dead.

It was the Roman Lucius Annaeus Seneca (c. 4 BCE–65 CE) who introduced graphic violence to the stage proper. In *Mad Hercules* (c. 54 CE), the goddess Juno causes the admired hero to lose his faculties, and, stupefied, he uses his strength to crush the bones of his three children. When his wife, Megara, tries to protect them, Hercules fractures her head with a heavy club, splitting her skull from her body.

In *Phaedra* (c. 60 CE), Seneca defied the predominate belief that the gods command all action and presented a pioneering psychological doctrine about the ruinous force of improper love. Phaedra, wife of Theseus, king of Troezen, falls in love with her stepson, Hippolytus. When Theseus is away on a mission, Phaedra confesses her feelings and asks Hippolytus to take his father's place as Theseus will likely never return from the underworld he has been visiting. Hippolytus rejects the offer angrily, remarking, "Woman is the root of all evil." When Theseus returns, Phaedra follows her nurse's advice, "Crime must be hidden by crime," and accuses Hippolytus of rape. Theseus asks his father, Neptune, Lord of the Oceans, to kill Hippolytus. A messenger recounts that as the prince was galloping in his chariot, a tidal wave arose toward the coastline. A monstrous bull emerged from the water causing the horses to flee, and Hippolytus becomes entrapped in the harness. "Hippolytus bloodied the countryside," says the messenger. "His shattered skull bounced down the rocks, and thorns tore off his hair.... At last a charred branch from a tree-trunk pierced him right in the middle of his groin.... The thickets cut the half-dead corpse.... Parts of the body were stuck to every tree."

In Seneca's violent *Thyestes* (c. 60 CE), Atreus, King of Argos, avenges the seduction of his wife by his younger brother Thyestes. He invites Thyestes to a banquet and coaxes his three children to a grove behind the palace, where he fatally stabs them and chops their bodies into pieces. At the festivity, Thyestes is seated at the table in gala dress, inebriated, not realizing that he drank wine mingled with his children's blood. Atreus then unfolds a covered platter, revealing the heads of Thyestes' sons. "Enjoy them," chuckles Atreus. "Kiss them, share your embrace out of all three." When the mourning father requests a proper burial for his sons, Atreus informs him that he has just eaten them and describes with relish how he himself had committed the murders and cooked the meat.

The death of the Roman playwright Lucius Annaeus Seneca, 4 BCE–65 CE, who was forced to commit suicide for alleged conspiracy against Emperor Nero (artist: Simon François Ravenet II, 1768; Fine Arts Museums of San Francisco).

Thyestes was translated into English in 1560 and served as a model for many revenge tragedies that followed, including Thomas Kyd's *The Spanish Tragedy* (1587); William Shakespeare's *Titus Andronicus* (c. 1594) and *Hamlet* (c. 1600); John Marston's *Antonio's Revenge* (1600) and *Malcontent* (c. 1603); George Chapman's *Revenge of Busy D'Ambois* (c. 1611); and John Webster's *The Duchess of Malfi* (c. 1612).

Middle Ages Theater

The grim motifs of *Orbecche* (1541), by the Italian playwright Giovanni Battista Giraldi (1504–1573), are jealousy, vengeance, and the lust for power. Orbecche is the daughter of Sulmone, king of Persia. At a young age, she secretly married Oronte, a lowly member of the court, and they have two children. The king finds out that his daughter married a poor commoner and vows to wipe the stain that has besmirched "his family, his honor, and his crown." The father of her children will die, but Orbecche's punishment will be worse—she will have to go on living after observing the annihilation of her family. Sulmone tells Oronte mockingly that he will become his successor. Then Oronte's hands are chopped off with a sharp knife. Oronte's children are brought in, and he begs the king to spare them. The king's henchmen stab one of the children in the chest and cut the throat of the other. Then they kill Oronte, placing his head and the children's corpses in a salver covered with black silk. Orbecche is summoned, and the king, with presumed affection, promises her a "wedding gift." He invites his daughter to lift the silk cloth. She does so and cries in anguish at the dreadful sight. A month or two pass. Orbecche keeps the knives that were used to kill her children. She approaches the king, pretending to reconcile with him, then suddenly stabs him. Fatally wounded, Sulmone retreats to the wings, where Orbecche chops off his head, then comes back holding the bloody skull. She cries, then pierces herself.

The Israelite King Herod was a knave and a scoundrel in many medieval plays. In *Herod the Great* (c. 1554), by the anonymous English Wakefield Master, the court's counselors prophesy that a king will ascend in the future from Bethlehem—born to a maiden "who has never sinned." Herod dispatches his knights to Bethlehem with an order to assassinate all boys who are two years old and younger. In several brief scenes, we see the knights grabbing a child from his mother's arms and stabbing him to death. The women wail, "Murder.... Alas for shame and sin!" then leave, bearing their slain children.

The Killing of Abel (latter part of the 15th century) by the Wakefield Master is influenced by the tale in the Book of Genesis that describes the first murder. Cain and Abel, sons of Adam and Eve, are the protagonists. Abel, a shepherd, urges his brother, a crop farmer, to offer a sacrifice to God, as "it is the custom of our law." Cain reluctantly consents. The two of them approach the altar. Abel offers a sheep, and the fire blazes brightly. Cain offers ten small sheaves. His offering does not burn. "Me thinks God is not my friend," says Cain angrily and assaults Abel with a jawbone. Abel tumbles, muttering, "Vengeance, vengeance, vengeance, my Lord!/ For I am slain, and not guilty." He dies. God's thundering voice is heard, questioning Cain about the location of his brother. Cain withholds any information, and God makes a mark on his forehead—the sign of a murderer; he has been labeled for eternal shame.

Elizabethan Theater

Christopher Marlowe (1564–1593) was twenty-three years old when he wrote *Tamburlaine the Great* (1587), in which a powerful ruler leads his barbaric forces across Asia. The play contains numerous horrific moments. The defeated emperor of Turkey and his wife, imprisoned in a cage, kill themselves by bashing their heads against the bars. While educating his sons in matters of war, Tamburlaine cuts off his own arm, telling the boys, "A wound is nothing, be it ne'er so deep, blood is the god of war's rich livery." Tamburlaine kills his son Calyphas for staying behind during a campaign, and the Babylonian king is hanged, his corpse used for shooting practice. When *Tamburlaine the Great* was produced by London's Old Vic in 1951 under the direction of Tyrone Guthrie with Donald Wolfit in the title role, critic Harold Hobson reported in the *Christian Science Monitor* (September 29, 1951), "The play is packed with horrors which were preserved from becoming ridiculous by becoming revolting." But the reviewer perceived it as "the most tempestuous, wildest, most frantic play in the English language."

Marlowe's *The Tragical History of Doctor Faustus* (c. 1588) is the first magnum opus of the Faust-Mephistopheles myth, wherein a scientist trades his soul to the devil to gain sorcery powers. Faustus finds himself the master of medicine, law, and theology—and is still unfulfilled. He is drawn to black magic. A Good Angel and an Evil Angel appear, each trying to sway him,[5] as Mephistopheles, a demon spirit, makes an entrance. He will surrender his soul to Lucifer, says Faustus, if he's granted 24 years to live "in all voluptuousness." They seal the bargain with Faustus's blood, and in celebration, Lucifer solicits a soiree of the seven deadly sins.[6] Faustus embarks on a life of debauchery and crime. When eventually death draws near, he pleads desperately for additional time. But at the strike of midnight, demons go through a heavy storm and carry Faustus off to Hell.[7]

At the climax of Marlowe's *The Jew of Malta* (c.1589), the title character, the merchant Barabas, is pushed into a cauldron, dying in pain. His last words are, "Damned Christians, dogs, and Turkish infidels!"

Edward II (c. 1592), considered to be Christopher Marlowe's triumph, portrays the turbulent life of the fourteenth-century king of England whose homosexual love led to deadly royal intrigue. Arrested after a coup engineered by his estranged wife, Queen Isabella, the king is taken to Berkeley Castle, where he is placed in a vault with mud up to his waist. Eventually Edward is killed by a professional assassin named Lightborn, who plunges a red-hot spit into his guts. Lightborn is one of a number of hired executioners who plays an important role in Elizabethan and Jacobean plays.[8]

Arguably the most popular play of the 16th century, *The Spanish Tragedy* (1590) by Thomas Kyd (1558–1594) tells a sensational story of murder and revenge, complete with ghosts, palace intrigue, kidnapping, ransom money, and eight violent deaths. The last scene consists of a play within a play performed at the royal court of Spain, in which Hieronimo, a general, actually stabs the murderer of his son in front of the horrified spectators. Kyd was guided by the plays of the Roman playwright Seneca, who considered the passion for revenge paramount to his works. In turn, *The Spanish Tragedy* became the prototype for future Elizabethan dramas, and its bloody elements paved the way for the Grand Guignol effects in Jacobean tragedies.

Arden of Faversham (1592), written by an anonymous Englishman toward the end of the 16th century, is the earliest known play based on a real-life domestic murder.

Thomas Arden's young wife, Alice, characterized as "tall, and well favoured of shape and countenance," falls in love with Thomas Mosby, an employee in the household of a neighbor. Alice hires a notorious ruffian, Black Will, to do her bidding. During a stormy night while Arden is playing backgammon with Mosby, Black Will emerges from a closet and twists a towel around Arden's neck, strangling him. To ensure Arden's death, Mosby then hits him with a pressing iron, Black Will cuts his throat, and Alice stabs him with a knife several times. The culprits are caught and brought to justice.

Antonio's Revenge (1600) by John Marston (1576–1634) centers on Piero Sforza, Duke of Venice, a cold-blooded tyrant who has left a trail of corpses on his route to gain power. Piero is now determined to prevent the marriage between his daughter Mellida and her beloved Antonio, a young courtier. The duke

John Barrymore as Shakespeare's no-bars villain *Richard III*, Plymouth Theatre, New York City, 1920 (photo by Vandamm Studio, The New York Public Library for the Performing Arts).

plans to marry her to Galleazzo of Florence to form a formidable political alliance. The curtain rises in the dead of night. Duke Piero and his henchman, Strozzo, have just killed Antonio's friend, Felice, and set the body in Mellida's room to make it seem as if she has been unfaithful. Piero's next victim is his own henchman, who, with a pang of conscience, refuses to defame Mellida. Piero, enraged, strangles Strozzo with a cord. During a banquet, Antonio and several friendly lords confront Piero and cut out his tongue. In a nod to Seneca's *Thyestes*, Antonio unwraps a platter that holds the limbs of Piero's child, Julio. Antonio roars, "This is for my father's blood!" and stabs Piero. "This is for my

Dungeon set by Robert Edmond Jones for *Richard III*, Plymouth Theatre, New York City, 1920 (photo by Vandamm Studio, The New York Public Library for the Performing Arts).

son!" yells another lord who stabs Piero. They all surround Piero with their swords and pierce him to death.

William Shakespeare (1564–1616) wrote a series of plays drenched with treachery, bloodshed, and horror. In *The Tragedy of King Richard the Third* (c. 1593), the hunchbacked, power-hungry Richard, Duke of Gloucester, eliminates anyone who stands in his way. He sends two assassins to lock the Duke of Clarence, his brother and political rival, in the notorious Tower of London, where they stab him and drown him in a keg of wine. Richard then spreads the rumor that King Edward's two young sons are illegitimate and therefore have no rightful claim to England's monarchy. He persuades the boys to reside at the Tower of London in a section used as royal quarters. He then hires a skilled hitman, James Tyrell, to murder both children. Notwithstanding Edmund in *King Lear*, Iago in *Othello*, and Cassius in *Julius Caesar*, Richard is the most amoral and malevolent—albeit

William Shakespeare, England, 1564–1616 (artist: George Vertue, 1719; Fine Arts Museums of San Francisco).

witty, hypnotic, and engaging—among Shakespeare's gallery of smiling villains.[9]

Shakespeare's *Titus Andronicus* (c. 1594) pictures cruel rape, inhumane mutilation, and a series of graphic murders. The instigator of the chilling deeds is Tamora, a war captive who seeks to avenge the defeat of her army, the Goths, and the killing of her son by the sons of the Roman General Titus Andronicus. The Moor Aaron, Tamora's lover, is willing to aid her. During a hunt in the woods, Tamora's sons, Chiron and Demetrius, drag Lavinia, Andronicus's daughter, deep into the forest; rape her; and slash her tongue and arms so that it will be impossible for her to speak or write about what has happened to her. The two scoundrels then slay Bassian, the emperor's brother, and throw his body into a pit. Tamora convinces Emperor Saturninus that his brother was killed by Andronicus's sons, Martius and Quintus. Aaron tells Andronicus that his sons will be released if a member of Andronicus's family will sever his hand and send it to the court. Andronicus gets an axe and directs Aaron to chop off his hand. However, soon a messenger enters with the decapitated heads of Martius and Quintus.

Simultaneously, Lavinia finds a way to disclose her sexual violation. She takes a stick in her mouth and drags it across the sand to write "Stuprum ['rape' in Latin], Chiron,

Demetrius." It is now Andronicus's turn to vow revenge. At an opportune moment, he slashes the throats of Chiron and Demetrius with a knife and tells the doomed brothers that he plans to shred their bones to dust and blend them into a sweet treat to be offered to their mother at a royal feast. During the festivity, Andronicus stabs Lavinia ("because she was enforced, stained, and deflowered"), then reveals to the shocked guests that they have dined on the remains of the two abusers. He then stabs Tamora. Saturninus stabs him. Lucius, Andronicus's remaining son, stabs Saturninus.

A scene from *Richard III* (ca. 1593), in which the two young princes of England are murdered in their sleep (engraver: Frances Legat, 18th–19th century; Fine Arts Museums of San Francisco).

Kate Mulgrew as Tamora and Keith David as Aaron, the lover-villains of *Titus Andronicus*, Delacort Theater, New York City, 1989 (photo by Martha Swope, The New York Public Library for the Performing Arts).

Aaron's punishment is to be buried breast deep and left to die slowly of starvation.[10]

Based on events that took place in ancient Rome, Shakespeare's *The Tragedy of Julius Caesar* (c. 1599) chronicles the murder of a soon-to-be emperor. Despite a worrisome premonition from his wife Calpurnia that she had a nightmare about graves and advice from a soothsayer not to appear in public that day, Julius Caesar leaves home during a raging storm. He goes to the capital where a band of conspirators encircles him and stabs him repeatedly. Bleeding profusely, Caesar falls to the ground, whispers, "Et tu, Bruté?" and dies.

In the first scene of Shakespeare's *Hamlet* (c. 1600), the title character, a young Prince of Denmark, returns home to discover that his father has been murdered and the new king, his uncle Claudius, has married Queen Gertrude, Hamlet's mother. Based on a conversation with his father's ghost, Hamlet has strong suspicions as to the identity of the murderer and, on a quest to unearth foolproof evidence, concocts a "mousetrap" scheme that introduces the first literary psychological shock that coerces a murderer—Claudius—to confess. The denouement is one of the bloodiest in the annals of

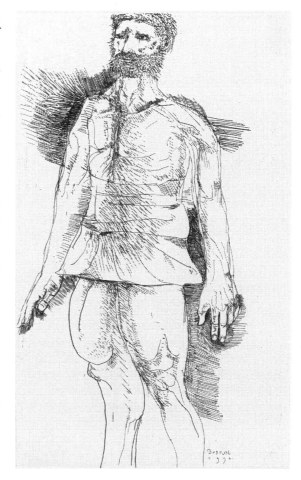

A drawing of Titus Andronicus in uniform (artist: Leonard Baskin, 1970; Fine Arts Museums of San Francisco).

The ghost of Hamlet's father appears before him and his friends Horatio and Marcellus, divulging that he was poisoned (engraver: Robert Thew, 18th–19th century; Fine Arts Museums of San Francisco).

the theater. When Prince Hamlet and Laertes, a courtier who blames Hamlet for the suicide of his sister Ophelia, meet in a Danish palace for a presumed fencing exhibition, Hamlet is not aware that his opponent intends to use a venomous foil. Just in case, King Claudius prepares a deadly cup of wine. During the match, Queen Gertrude drinks to Hamlet's health from that cup. Laertes leaps and wounds Hamlet. Hamlet, infuriated that he has been punctured by a naked edge, grasps Laertes's saber and slashes him. At that moment the queen moans, "The drink, the drink! I am poisoned!" and dies. Laertes whispers, "Hamlet, thou art slain; no medicine in the world can do thee good ... thy mother poisoned ... the king is to blame." Hamlet rapidly pierces Claudius with the poisoned saber. His last words are, "The rest is silence."[11]

"Alas, Poor Yorick." Richard Burton in the graveyard scene of *Hamlet*, 1964 (photo by Friedman-Abeles, The New York Public Library for the Performing Arts).

William Shakespeare's *Othello* (c.1604) introduces the crowning villain, Iago, an ensign in the army who does not forgive Othello, the Moorist governor of Venice, for bypassing him and elevating Michael Cassio to the coveted position of lieutenant. Iago instigates a fight between Cassio and another officer, and Othello relieves him of his post. Iago then suggests to Cassio that he ask Othello's wife, Desdemona, to intervene on his behalf. Iago arranges for Othello to observe a meeting between Cassio and Desdemona and slyly plants in his mind a seed of jealousy: "Oh, beware, my lord, of the green-eyed monster." Following another maneuver by Iago in which he deposits Desdemona's handkerchief on Cassio, Othello enters Desdemona's bedroom, rejects her terrified pleas, and smothers her with a pillow.[12]

Iago (Christopher Plummer, right) manipulates Othello (James Earl Jones) in the Broadway revival of *Othello*, Warner Theatre, 1981 (photo by Martha Swope, The New York Public Library for the Performing Arts).

Shakespeare's *Macbeth* (1606) opens on an unnerving note near a battlefield in Scotland. During stormy weather, three witches—hideous and repulsive—encounter Macbeth, a Scottish general. "Fair is foul, and foul is fair," they guffaw and plant in Macbeth's mind the fancy that he is destined to become king. Together with his wife, the ambitious Lady Macbeth, he embarks on the midnight murder of a monarch, the liquidating of competition, and the assassination of children—ending up with his own decapitaton.[13]

King Lear (1606) introduces two monstrous daughters, Goneril and Regan, who divide the kingdom of an old monarch, treat him cruelly, and come to a harsh fate themselves through the liaison of their shared lover, archvillain Edmund, the bastard son of the Earl of Gloucester. Goneril and Regan kill one another—one by poison, the other with a dagger.[14]

Othello (Paul Robeson) realizes in anguish that he wrongly smothered his wife Desdemona (Uta Hagen), Theatre Guild, New York, 1943–44 (photo by Vandamm Studio, The New York Public Library for the Performing Arts).

Coriolanus (1608) is based on the life of a Roman warrior, Caius Mercius Coriolanus, whose vanity and contempt toward the working class caused his collapse. Led by jealous, wicked tribunes, Coriolanus is exiled from Rome. He vindictively returns as the general of an armed force to overthrow the city, only to be surrounded, stabbed, and trampled to death by a flock of betrayers.

The characters of *Pericle, Prince of Tyre*

Richard Burbage, England, 1567–1619, the actor who was the first to play Richard III, Hamlet, Othello and Macbeth, among other Shakespearean characters (n.d.; Billy Rose Theatre Division, The New York Public Library for the Performing Arts).

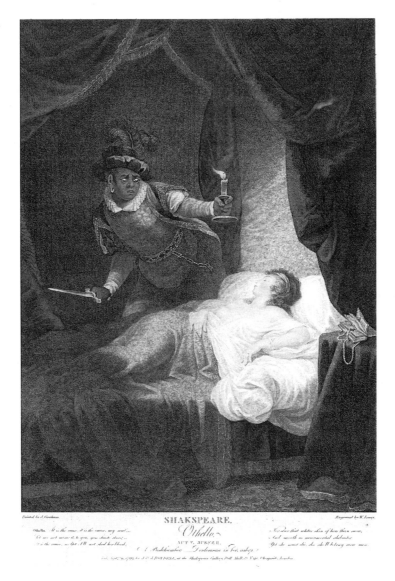

SHAKSPEARE.
Othello.
ACT V, SCENE II.

Wrongly suspecting his wife of infidelity, Othello kills Desdemona (engraver: William Leney, 18th–19th century; Fine Arts Museums of San Francisco).

(c.1608) include a tyrannical king who initiates an incestuous relationship with his daughter; an envious governor's wife who plots the killing of a beautiful 14-year-old girl; a prince who finds himself in mortal danger; professional assassins; and ferocious pirates. The play is the first to originate a Mad Scientist who revives a deceased queen and howls, "She is alive!" many years before *Frankenstein*.

The plot of *Cymbeline* (c. 1609) unfolds with seemingly unrelated topics—royal conspiracy, the abduction of children, larceny in the dead of night, an idyllic romance shattered by a con man, an attempted murder with a poisonous vial, and long-lost sons—all interwoven skillfully by the maestro. Among the vicious characters is a nameless queen, who is a crafty assassin, and her son, who follows in his mother's footsteps with menacing flair.

The three Witches who incited Macbeth to treachery and murder (artist: Henry Fuseli, ca. 1783; Wallace Division Collection, New York Public Library).

Maurice Evans as Macbeth and Judith Anderson as Lady Macbeth in *Macbeth*, National Theater, New York City, 1941 (photo by Fred Fehl, The New York Public Library for the Performing Arts).

Jacobean Theater

Some years ago, the elderly duke of a nameless Italian province raped Gloriana, the beloved of Vindice, causing her to commit suicide. Now Vindice, the protagonist of Cyril Tourneur's (1575–1626) *The Revenger's Tragedy* (1606), finds an ingenious, albeit far-fetched, method of murdering the duke. Disguised as a pander, he promises the lusty nobleman that he will procure a beautiful young girl for him. The tryst will take place secretly in a dark cottage. Vindice camouflages Gloriana's skull and smears its lips with poison. The duke kisses the "girl"—and dies in agony.

The Rape of Lucretia (1607) by Thomas Heywood (1574–1641), based on a legendary case in the history of ancient Rome, depicts in detail a rape scene and its repercussions. Sextus Tarquinius, the wild son of the last emperor of Rome, meets Lucretia Collatine, the beautiful wife of a consul. Aware the husband is away in a military camp, Sextus dismounts at Lucretia's house and asks to be sheltered for the night. Later, he clandes-tinely enters her bedroom and pulls back a curtain to reveal the naked woman. Trembling, Lucretia begs Sextus "not to wreck a woman's chastity," and says that she would rather die. He tells her that he would murder one of her grooms and place them both, grasped arm in arm, on her bed. The perception of having committed adultery with a lowly slave would have brought dishonor to Lucretia's family, so she yields. The next day, Lucretia, dressed in black, gathers her relatives, tells them what happened, picks up a dagger, and plunges it into her heart.[15]

A Yorkshire Tragedy (1608), by an unknown English play-wright, reenacts the real-life case of Walter Calverley of Yorkshire. In an early scene, his wife Griselda addresses the audience with a solilo-quy in which she laments her husband's vices of "dice, and voluptuous meetings, and mid-night revels." Hostile and irri-table, Walter Calverley enters and shouts that his sons are bastards, begot from his wife's

THE RAPE OF LUCRECE.

Her wrongs to us, and by this bloody knife,
We will revenge the death of this true wife.

Page 988.

Following the rape of Lucretia by the son of Rome's emperor and her ensuing suicide, Lucretia's brother and husband vow revenge (artist: Alexander Anderson, 18th–19th century; Fine Arts Museums of San Francisco).

adulterous affairs. He fatally stabs his eldest son, then slashes a baby held in his wife's arms. He intends to pierce her, but a servant rushes in and restrains him. Calverley flees on horseback. The servant believes that his crazed master is en route to kill the third child. Pursuers find Calverley on a road outside Yorkshire, where he has been thrown from his horse. They take him to a local jail to await investigation and trial. Calverley maintains that he killed his children so they would not become beggars; he regrets that he was unable to kill the third one.

A succession of Jacobean horror plays followed, of which the most nightmarish were *The White Devil* (c. 1612) and *The Duchess of Malfi* (c. 1613), both by John Webster (c. 1580-c. 1635), both underscoring the macabre, the evil, and the shocking. The plot of *The White Devil* is complicated, focusing mainly on the lovers Bracciano and Vittoria, who are married to other spouses. They murder Bracciano's wife, the Duchess Isabella, by rubbing poison on the lips of a painting of Bracciano, aware that she habitually kisses the portrait before going to sleep. During a horse race, Bracciano breaks the neck of Camille, Vittoria's husband, and makes it look like an accident. Isabella's brother, Francisco, the Duke of Florence, takes note of the fact that Bracciano and Vittoria are getting married. He suspects foul play, vows vengeance, and engages two allies, Lodovico and Flamineo, to kill the bride and groom. The would-be assassins attend the wedding disguised as monks and sprinkle Bracciano's helmet with poison. Soon the groom tears off the helmet and gasps, "O, my brain's on fire." The two impostors enter Vittoria's chamber, take off their disguises, observe her shock with relish, and fatally stab her.

Webster's *The Duchess of Malfi* is a poetic tragedy infested by four stabbings, three strangulations, and a werewolf motif. The action unfolds in Malfi, Italy, at the dawn of the 16th century. The Duchess (who in the play has no name), does not hesitate to marry beneath her class and secretly weds Antonio Bologna, a much-admired steward of her household. Nine months later it becomes clear that the Duchess is pregnant. Count Ferdinand is enraged at the treachery of his "loose, strumpet" sister. Three years pass, and the Duchess has two more children, a son and a daughter. Concerned for Antonio's safety, the Duchess urges him to leave Malfi for Ancona, where she'll soon join him. He departs with their oldest child. Ferdinand orders the Duchess and the two remaining children to be locked in a wing of the palace. A morbid scene ensues under dim lights. The sadistic Ferdinand presents the Duchess with a dead man's hand, leading her to believe that it is Antonio's. The duke then exhibits, behind a sheer curtain, the figures of Antonio and the children, appearing as if they were dead. Soon executioners enter with a coffin and cords, strangle the Duchess, then leave to throttle the children in an adjacent room. The proceedings now speed up toward a final bloody denouement. A doctor diagnoses Duke Ferdinand as having lycanthropia, an ailment where one hallucinates being transformed into a wolf; he howls and digs up dead bodies at night. Meanwhile, the duke's henchman, Daniel De Bosola, tracks Antonio in Ancona and slays him with a dagger. He returns to Malfi, only to be confronted by the half-mad Ferdinand, who concludes that his man has outlived his usefulness and stabs him with his sword. With his last strength, Bosola plunges his dagger through Ferdinand.

The Witch of Edmonton (1621) is a cooperative venture by the English playwrights Thomas Decker (1572–1632), William Rowley (1585–1642), and John Ford (1586–1639). The title character is Mother Elizabeth Sawyer, an old citizen of the town of Edmonton, near London, who is avoided by her neighbors and harassed by her landlord. Hopeless and furious, Mother Sawyer calls on "some power good or bad" to help her get revenge.

Lucifer appears in the form of a black dog and strikes a bargain with Mother Sawyer; he will protect her "against thy foes" in exchange for "soul and body." The black dog commits a series of violent acts assigned by Mother Sawyer, including murder, but eventually she's arrested, tried, and executed. The topic reappeared in *The Late Lancashire Witches* (1634) by Thomas Heywood and Richard Brome, and again in *The Lancashire Witches* (1681) by Thomas Shadwell.[16]

The Changeling (1622), by Englishmen Thomas Middleton (1580–1627) and William Rowley (1585–1642), features a serpentine plot that contains lust, rape, blackmail, and murder, all taking place in Allicant, a town on the coast of Spain. The instigator of the dastardly events is the beautiful Beatrice Vermandero, who seems innocent on the outside but is corrupt within. Engaged to Lord Alonzo de Piracquo, who was chosen by her father but whom she detests, Beatrice coaxes an underling, De Flores, described as "ugly with pockmarked face," to kill her fiancé. The murder scene takes place in a shadowy, narrow hallway, where De Flores stabs Alonzo several times in the back. De Flores then notices a flash in the dark, a diamond ring sparkling on his victim's finger. He finds it hard to extract the ring, so he cuts off the finger and takes it with him. He reports his deed to Beatrice, shows her the dead man's severed finger, and comments wryly, "I was loath to leave it, and I am sure dead men have no use for jewels." Beatrice tells De Flores to keep the ring and gives him an additional 3,000 golden florins. De Flores explains that he did not commit murder for financial reward and attempts to kiss her, but Beatrice rejects him with disgust. De Flores insists that she must submit to him, as he can spread the word that she hired him to murder Alonzo; his life is worth nothing if he cannot have her. Beatrice points out the difference in their social class, but he claims that the foul deed has made them equal. Beatrice realizes that the act of murder triggered a vicious circle of sin and succumbs to the inevitable. But soon thereafter, Beatrice's fate is sealed. De Flores, under the impression that she intends to betray him, pushes her into a closet; soon screams are heard as Beatrice is stabbed repeatedly by De Flores with a knife.

The main character of Middleton's tragedy *Women Beware Women* (c. 1625) is Bianca Cappello, a historical figure—she was mistress, then wife, of Francesco de Medici (1541–1587) in Renaissance Florence. In the play, Bianca secretly marries a poor clerk, Leantio. The lecherous Duke of Florence spots Bianca in a window and decides to court her with the help of Livia, a widow. When Leantio is away, Livia plays a game of chess with his mother while the duke enters Bianca's bedroom and seduces her. The duke then solicits Livia's brother, Hippolito, to kill Leantio. The play's center scene takes place at a palace banquet. Liaisons and complications are revealed, ending in carnage. Characters are slain in multiple forms, such as contaminated alcohol, piercing arrows, and being pushed through a trapdoor to a sharp-edged death.

James Shirley's (1596–1666) *The Maid's Revenge* (1626) is a play of betrayal, kidnapping, murder, revenge, and suicide. It unfolds in Avero, Portugal. An elderly lord, Gaspar de Vilarezo, has a son, Sebastiano, and two daughters, Catalina and Berinthia. The aristocrat Antonio is in love with Berinthia, but Lord Gaspar insists that his elder daughter Catalina must be married first. Antonio pretends to be courting Catalina so that he can see Berinthia, and Catalina falls for her apparent suitor. When Catalina learns that she has been fooled, she locks up her sister and arranges for her to be kidnapped and poisoned. But Antonio discovers the plot and rescues Berinthia. The vengeful Catalina persuades her brother, Sebastiano, to duel with Antonio, and Antonio is slain. Berinthia, mourning her lost love, embarks on revenge of her own. She substitutes a love-potion with a lethal concoction, causing her "devil-sister" to die in agony, her "belly on fire." Berinthia then stabs herself.

Spanish Theater

Madrid-born Lope de Vega (1562–1635) was a key figure among Spain's poets and dramatists during the sixteenth and seventeenth centuries. He is reported to have written some 3,000 sonnets and 1,800 plays, making him the most productive playwright in the history of the theater. His most famous play, *Fuente Ovejuna* (c. 1614), relates how, following the brutal rape of the mayor's daughter, the villagers of a small town band together to kill a despotic military commander. The angry crowd surrounds him and tears him to shreds. A sergeant attempts to escape, but vengeful women toss him, scratch his face with their nails, and pierce him with the points of pitchforks.

Don Juan, the notorious lover, was invented by Spain's Tirso de Molina (1579–1648) in *The Trickster of Seville and the Stone Guest* (c. 1616). The playwright painted his bold character as witty, debonair, and irresistible to women. However, he added the traits of self-interest and contempt when brushing aside the feelings of his female victims, inflicting chaos on households, and resorting to spilling blood. In this play, Don Juan gets his just desserts. The proceedings depict Don Juan stabbing Don Gonzallo, the father of a betrayed girl, when he rushes to her defense. A while later, Don Juan passes by a churchyard and realizes that he faces the tomb of Don Gonzallo. He jokingly twists the concrete beard of the dead man's sculpture when the ghost of Don Gonzallo suddenly appears and grasps Don Juan by the arm. He cries in anguish, "Your hand burns," and falls dead. In the thick of thunder and lightning, a secret opening pulls down Don Juan and the specter.

The Mayor of Zalamea (c. 1643), perhaps the most celebrated play of Pedro Calderón's (1600–1681) 200 works for the stage, is a tale of rape and revenge, illustrating the concept that the *pandonor* (point of honor) affects not only aristocrats but also the common man. Set in the Spanish landscape, the play's unnerving moments include the seizing of the mayor's daughter, Isabel, by soldiers led by a lusty captain, who gang rape her. The suspenseful climax has the mayor, Pedro Crespo, disobey the military authorities and jail the captain. A back door is thrown open, and the captain is seen hunched over a chair, strangled by a metal neck band fastened around his throat.

English Theater

Nathaniel Lee's (c. 1649–1692) *Nero, Emperor of Rome* (1675) begins with Nero condemning his mother Agrippina for rebelling against the empire. When he decrees her death, she is given the choice of swallowing poison or piercing herself. She chooses both.

Aphra Behn (1640–1689), an Englishwoman of the 17th century, was among the first to earn a living by writing for the theater, paving the way for future female authors. Her most successful play (of 19) was the thrilling *Abdelazer or, The Moor's Revenge* (1676), an adaptation of the seventeenth century's *Lust's Dominion*, credited to Christopher Marlowe. The title character is a colorful Moorish villain who wins his way to the Spanish throne by romantic conquests, sly betrayals, and brazen assassinations. Among his victims are a royal prince and a chief cardinal. In order to cement his power, Abdelazer engages a henchman, Roderigo, "to have the Queen remov'd." Masquerading as a friar, Roderigo enters Queen Isabella's quarters, pulls out a dagger, and stabs her. Abdelazer enters, feigns shock at the bloodshed, and instantly knifes Roderigo to death. The expiring Isabella is mindful of the deceit and groans, "Thou art my murderer." Abdelazer chuckles, "Farewell, my greatest plague." He expresses joy for eliminating the queen, as he is now able to chase new targets of love. The last scene unfolds in a prison setting, where Abdelazer brags to a group of inmates that he'd "whor'd the Queen" and poisoned the late king. The convicts react by attacking Abdelazer and beating him to death.

Inspired by an Aphra Behn novella, *Oroonoko, or The Royal Slave*, Ireland's Thomas Southerne (1660–1746) wrote a five-act tragedy, *Oroonoko* (1695), the story of a noble African prince who in 1640 was seized by the British in Angola and dispatched as a slave to Surinam, South America. An uprising, a getaway, betrayal, and persecution trail each other to a suspenseful climax. Oroonoko leads a crowd of slaves in a rebellion against cruel plantation owners, but one of his men, hoping to gain favor, alerts the local army and the attempt fails. Imprisoned, Oroonoko and his wife Imoinda realize they are doomed. Imoinda suggests that to avoid torture and disgrace, they commit suicide. She takes up the dagger of a dead rebel, hands it to her husband, and says, "I'm ready." Oroonoko falters. Imoinda touches his hand and stabs herself. Oroonoko cries. When the lieutenant governor enters, Oroonoko leaps, kills the lieutenant governor, and pierces himself.

Sophocles' *Oedipus the King* (c. 429 BCE), considered the masterpiece of Ancient Greece, was adapted by Englishmen John Dryden (1631–1700) and Nathaniel Lee (c. 1653–1692) in 1678 with new angles and added subplots, a heightening of the play's whodunit concept, and a gory outcome in which all the principal characters are finished off onstage. Creon, Queen Jocasta's brother, is a sympathetic character in Sophocles' earlier version, attentive to the needs of Thebes. In the Dryden-Lee rendition, he is presented as a cunning, hunchbacked blackguard, plotting to take over the kingdom. The curtain rises on the carcasses of men, women, and children dead from a catastrophic contagion. Following a thorough investigation of the cause of the pestilence, Oedipus discovers that he inadvertently had killed Thebes's former king and married his own mother. Anguished, he gouges out his eyes, maintaining that they are not necessary anymore to see the truth. The climax of the play consists of rapid, bloody sequences: Creon stabs to death Eurydice, Jocasta's daughter by the late former King Lajus, for refusing to marry him; upon learning of her incestuous relationship with Oedipus, Jocasta kills their offspring, whose little bodies are scattered among red-stained pillows, then stabs herself; Oedipus, upon perceiving it all, hurls himself from a window.[17]

Tom Thumb (1730) by Henry Fielding (1707–1754) mixes terror and farce when a cow, "larger than the usual size," swallows the diminutive title character. The courtiers of King Arthur blame one another for the mishap and, in succession, stab one another. The king, surrounded by dead bodies, stabs himself, passing away with the notion that his only sense of grandeur is that he is the last to die.

Nineteenth Century Theater

The 19th century saw the genesis of several theatrical innovations: the introduction of the melodrama and the horror play, the presentation of the Native American as a sympathetic character, the creation of the American musical, the initiation of the psychological thriller, and the debut of the detective on stage. *A Tale of Mystery* (1802), which Englishman Thomas Holcroft (1744–1809) borrowed from the French, was the first play on the English stage described as a "melo-drame." Melodramas introduced unblushing, shocking cliffhangers with background music illustrative of the activity on stage, showing the battle between good and evil, featuring stock rather than fully developed characters, and providing a satisfying climax. The plot of *A Tale of Mystery*, punctuated by "music signaling terror, confusion, menace," involves the villainous Count Romaldi who plans to murder his brother Francisco in order to seize his estates.

Lord Byron (George Gordon, 1788–1824) described his incestuous relationship with his half-sister, Augusta, in the Faustian drama *Manfred* (written 1817; first performed 1852), dabbled in political intrigue in *Morino Faliero* (1821), and drew upon the Old Testament in *Cain* (1821), depicting the title character as a willing student of Lucifer who commits the world's first murder by striking his brother Abel.

In writing his verse tragedy, *The Cenci* (1819), Percy Bysshe Shelley (1792–1822) was influenced by the September 9, 1598, homicide of the Roman Count Francesco Cenci. Reports of the count's depravity and brutality spread across Rome, but Cenci's hefty donations to the church kept Pope Clement VIII from imposing penalties. Early in the play, Cenci confides to the audience that ever since he killed his first foe "and heard the groan," inflicting misery became his essential gratification. The count then vows to execute a crowning infamy—the ruin of his daughter—and rapes his daughter Beatrice. When her father keeps abusing her repeatedly, Beatrice decides to kill him. In collaboration with her stepmother Lucretia and her brother Giacomo, who were imprisoned

Lord Byron, England, 1788–1824, describes the world's first murder in his 1821 play *Cain* (n.d.; Billy Rose Theatre Division, The New York Public Library).

in the Cenci palace, they hire two hitmen to murder the count. The men enter Cenci's bedroom, strangle him, and throw the body out a window. Soon a pope's legate, Savella, arrives on the scene and emerges as an early detective, asking who had an interest in Cenci's death and checking marks of violence found on the victim's body. The assassins are discovered lurking among rocks nearby, each with a bag of coins. In the trial that follows, they admit that they committed the murder, implicating Giacomo and the women. The assassins die on the rack. Giacomo, Beatrice, and Lucretia are condemned to death. Beatrice walks calmly to the scaffold. Her final uttering is, "My lord, we are quite ready. Well, 'tis very well."[18]

On the night of June 19, 1816, four friends were confined by heavy snow at a cabin in the Swiss Alps: the host Lord Byron; Dr. John Polidori, Byron's physician; the poet Percy Bysshe Shelley; and Shelley's sweetheart, Mary Wollstonecraft Godwin. While waiting for the storm to pass, they made up ghost stories—a choice that resulted in two milestone literary creations. Mary would expand her yarn and pen the Gothic novel *Frankenstein, or The Modern Prometheus*, first printed in three volumes, on January 1, 1818; Polidori would enhance his mystic tale and publish *The Vampyre*, initially heralded in *The New Monthly Magazine*, London, on April 1, 1819, and in book publication later that year.

The French author Charles Nodier transferred Polidori's tale to the Parisian stage in 1820 under the title *Le Vampire*. The British dramatist James Robinson Planché (1796–1880) translated Nodier's play into English as *The Vampire, or The Bride of the Isles*, for a presentation at Lyceum's English Opera House, London, debuting on August 9, 1820. The first heart-pounding moment of the play occurs in a prologue that unfolds on a Scottish island during a storm. Lady Margaret escapes into a cave where she encounters a handsome young man who suddenly changes into a frightening specter. She flees, running into the rescue party. The last terrifying sequence takes place in a chapel, where Lord Ruthven guides a nervous Margaret to the altar. It is now the crack of dawn, and Ruthven, creature of the night,

Percy Bysshe Shelley, England, 1792–1822, writer of *The Cenci* (1819), a play in which the protagonist enjoys inflicting pain (artist: William Finden, 18th–19th century; Fine Arts Museums of San Francisco).

cries out, "I am lost!" Thunder rumbles. Ruthven is hit by lightning and disappears (through a trapdoor that became known as the "vampire trap").

In 1823, Planché's compatriot Richard Brinsley Peake (1792–1847) adapted Mary Shelley's novel for the stage, calling it *Presumption, or The Fate of Frankenstein*, the first theatrical rendering of the work. Peake shortened Mary Shelley's elaborate plot, eliminating Victor Frankenstein's and the creature's international travels and Captain Robert Walton's chronicle about his polar expedition. Conversely, Peake inserted a musical background and lots of broad comedy. Suspense is achieved early in the play when, behind the closed doors of Victor Frankenstein's laboratory, the scientist yells, "It lives! It lives!" Suddenly the door of the lab breaks to pieces with a loud crash. A gigantic creature advances forward, accompanied by menacing chords of music. The creature seizes Frankenstein, throws him violently to the floor, and disappears through a large window. The creature wanders through woods near Geneva; encounters a tribe of gypsies; kidnaps and kills Victor's young brother, William; and strangles Victor's beloved, Agatha. The last scene takes place at the foot of a snowy mountain. The creature begins to climb up, and Victor follows him with a loaded musket. A stage instruction explains: "The Demon and Frankenstein meet at the extremity of the stage—Frankenstein fires—the avalanche falls and annihilates the Demon and Frankenstein—loud thunder is heard, and all

MARY SHELLEY

Mary Shelley, England, 1797–1851, the creator of Frankenstein (Miniature by Reginald Eastman, by permission of the Bodleian Library, n.d.; Print Collection, The New York Public Library).

T. P. COOKE as the VAMPIRE.

Thomas Potter Cooke, England, 1786–1864, the first actor to portray a vampire on stage, Lord Ruthven in *The Vampire; or, The Bride of the Isles*, 1820 (painting dated 1822; The New York Public Library for the Performing Arts).

the characters form a picture as the curtain falls." (London theaters at the time were equipped to stage volcanic eruptions, storm effects, floods, battles, sailing boats, even side-by-side racing horses. The spectacular destruction of the creature at the resolution of the play became an essential part of the plot over the years.)

The play's success spawned more theatrical Frankensteins, notably H.M. Milner's *Frankenstein, or The Man and the Monster* (1826), in which the creature falls in love with Dr. Frankenstein's wife, kidnaps her, stabs his creator to death, and finally leaps into an active volcano.

Mr. T. P. COOKE,
Of the Theatre Royal Covent Garden
In the Character of the Monster, in the Dramatic Romance of Frankenstein.

Thomas Potter Cooke, of the Theatre Royal Covent Garden, as the Frankenstein Monster in *Presumption; or, The Fate of Frankenstein*, 1823 (painting issued 1823; The New York Public Library for the Performing Arts).

Jonathan Bradford, or The Murder at the Roadside Inn (1833), by Edward Fitzball (1792–1873), recreates a real-life crime committed at a roadside inn situated between London and Oxford. The guiltless landlord was charged with murder. Compelling proof faulted him. The jury declared "Guilty" without any deliberation! In staging the play, Fitzball created a ground-breaking set, considered the first of its form. He split the interior of the inn into four chambers, and the action transpires at the same instance in all four. As a clock strikes midnight, a flash of lightning shows one of the guests, Dan Macraisy, a seasoned racketeer, peering in the window of a room occupied by Adam Hayes, a wealthy merchant. Macraisy enters cautiously, notices a purse of money on a table, and picks it up. Hayes opens his eyes and asks, "Who is there?" He swiftly gets out of bed, snatches a knife from a tray, and blocks Macraisy from escaping. A struggle ensues. Macraisy drops the purse, gets possession of the knife and stabs Hayes. He hears noises and hurries out the window. The landlord, Jonathan Bradford, enters. Horrified, he picks up both the knife and the

Actor O. Smith, England, 1786–1855, gained fame as an early interpreter of the Frankenstein Monster (painting issued 1826; The New York Public Library for the Performing Arts).

purse. Several guests of the inn are at the door when Hayes whispers, "My purse—the knife in his hands—my assassin then," and dies. The guests believe that Bradford is the murderer. The dying man's last words, the money purse, and the blood-stained knife are brought as evidence against Bradford. He is convicted and sentenced to be hanged. The climax unfolds at the gallows, with a haunted Macraisy arriving in the last minute, confessing his guilt, asking Bradford's forgiveness, then stabbing himself and dying on the steps of the scaffold.

Among Edward Fitzball's 170 plays were *Giraldi: A Ruffian of Prague* (1820), a play about lycanthropy; *The Demon of the Wolf* (1824) in which demons wield authority over humans; *The Phantom of the Nile* (1826) wherein an Egyptian sorcerer plans to ravage the attractive heroine; and *The Devil's Elixir* (1829), a Faustian drama. Other plays with a supernatural motif include *The Flying Dutchman, or The Phantom Ship* (1827), in which the title character, armed with spectral powers, attempts to abduct a beautiful woman; and Mar*garet's Ghost, or The Libertine's Ship* (1833), about a murdered wife who comes back to punish her red-handed husband. Professor Larry Stephens Clinton provides a capsule description of many of Fitzball's plays in his 1993 study *The Terrible Fitzball*, and declares, "Over other melodramas of the time, Fitzballian plays had a unique flair to them: they were not only horror, only escapism, only musicals. They told a memorable story and gave a sultry philosophy of human values within the context of an exponential and extraterrestrial plot.... This was perhaps his unique flavor as a blood-and-thunder master of hallucination on stage."[19]

Maria Marten, or The Murder in the Red Barn (c. 1842), penned anonymously, tells the story of an attractive woman born in Polstead, Suffolk, England, who, at the age of 24, fell in love with William Corder, the son of a prominent family. Corder was two years younger than she was and had the reputation of a Don Juan. On Friday, May 18, 1827, Corder proposed that they abscond and get married in London. Maria went to meet him at the red barn, a local landmark, and disappeared. For a while, it was believed that Maria and Corder had moved abroad. Myth had it that Maria's stepmother began to have a repeated dream in which the girl had been killed and buried in the red barn. Maria's father, Thomas Marten, searched the barn and found the body of his daughter. Corder was arrested. On August 11, 1828, he was hanged outside Norwich Gaol with a large crowd attending.

The play follows the true-life events faithfully. Corder is a charming fellow. Maria is very much in love with him, and her family is happy with their union. But the audience becomes aware of Corder's true sentiments when he says in an aside, "Her very shadow moves a scorpion in my path" and resolves "to rid me of this hated plague." The scene in the red barn is harrowing. Maria enters happily. Corder steps out from a dark corner. Menacing music plays as he seizes Maria. She begs for mercy, clings to him for dear life, and is stabbed repeatedly. She gasps and falls to the ground. The curtain drops.

Act II unfolds four weeks later. Mrs. Marten relates to her husband a nightmare about their daughter: "Our child lies buried in the Red Barn." To appease her, he consents to go to the barn and verify. He finds his daughter "mangled and bleeding, pointing to her gory wounds." The last scene takes place in prison, where William Corder is in chains. An apparition of Maria Marten appears and declares that she forgives her murderer. Enter a hangman, with rope. Corder collapses. A bell chimes.

The String of Pearls, or The Fiend of Fleet Street (1847), by George Dibdin Pitt (1799–1855), is a horror play about Sweeney Todd, a character based on a real-life Parisian barber who slit his customers' throats and sent their bodies to a pastry shop below, where his partner, Margery Lovett, baked them into pies. The play depicts Todd shaving several customers, slicing their throats, then touching a spring, causing the chair to sink down to a basement where Lovett is waiting near a huge oven. An empty chair returns to its place. A quarrel between Todd and Lovett regarding the division of the spoils causes Lovett to pull a knife. Todd shoots her with a pistol, then hauls her body to the oven. Todd does not raise any suspicion until one of his victims, Mark Ingestrie, does not die; he survives his fall to the basement by landing on a corpse. Ingestrie's unexpected appearance unnerves Todd, and he confesses his guilt.[20]

The horror elements of *Jane Eyre* (1849), adapted by John Broughton (1814–1880) from Charlotte Brontë's novel, include the inhumane treatment of female orphans in an institution run by a cruel minister; the atmosphere of a haunted house where screams and wild laughter echo from the locked attic of Edward Rochester's manor; and the sudden appearance of maniacal Bertha, Rochester's wife, through a window with a torch in her hand. She sets the house on fire, climbs to the roof, and burns to death when it collapses.

The two most popular novels of the 19th century, each focusing on a hidden crime and earmarked by horrific incidents—Mary Elizabeth Braddon's *Lady Audley's Secret* and Wilkie Collins's *The Woman in White*—were adapted to the stage in 1863 and 1871.

Since its publication, Braddon's *Lady Audley's Secret* has never been out of print. The three-volume first edition of *Lady Audley's Secret* is one of the rarities of Victorian fiction. "Readers who devoured the book were thrilled and frightened by its inversion of the ideal Victorian heroine," wrote Susan Balee in her introduction to a 2005 printing of the book. "Lady Audley looks like the angel-in-the-house ideal of Victorian womanhood—she is blonde, fragile, childlike—but her behavior is distinctly villainous."[21] The novel inspired many dramatizations, of which the most woeful and most intense was written by Colin Henry Hazlewood (1823–1875) in 1863. A beautiful woman in her mid–20s, Lady Lucy Audley is married to Sir Michael Audley, 30 years her senior. They live in a sumptuous country manor. A former husband, George Talboys, unexpectedly appears and threatens to expose her. As they take a walk, she offers Talboys "every jewel, every penny" she has, but he rejects her proposal. Lady Audley suddenly groans and asks for water. She hands Talboys a white kerchief, and he walks to a well. As Talboys bends down to moisten the kerchief, Lady Audley slips behind him, pummels him with the well's metal crank, and shoves him in. She then exclaims, "Dead men tell no tales! I am free!" She has no inkling that a gamekeeper named Luke has observed the attack from behind a fence. Soon Luke begins to blackmail Lady Audley. Lady Audley, wearing a hooded cloak, goes at night to the nearby Castle Inn where Luke lives. She locks Luke's door, lights a candle, ignites a curtain, and sets the inn on fire. Luke wakes up and tries to open the door. He calls for help, stumbles, and suffocates. Toward the end of the proceedings, it turns out that George Talboys was not dead; he was saved by Luke. Talboys exposes Lady Audley as a bigamist and an arsonist. Overcome by stress and exhibiting signs of latent insanity, Lady Audley begins to talk incoherently, places her hands on her temple and says, "Let the cold grave close over Lady Audley and her secret." She falls, dying.

No Thoroughfare, "a drama in Five Acts and a Prologue" by Charles Dickens (1812–1870) and Wilkie Collins (1824–1889), heralded the lurid melodramas of the latter half of the 19th century. The play presents such repertory characters as the evil guardian who purloins his ward's wealth; the pretty ingenue who encounters a succession of hazards; the brawny hero who comes to her rescue; and the steward and maid who inject humorous interludes. *No Thoroughfare* was initially co-written by Dickens and Collins as a short story, and it appeared in the Christmas issue of Dickens' periodical *All the Year Round* on December 12, 1867.[22] Dickens planned to travel to America and suggested that Collins adapt the story for the stage. The theatrical version premiered on December 26, 1867, at London's Adelphi Theatre.

The villain of the piece is Jules Obenreizer, an agent of a Swiss wine company who poisons his partner in order to appropriate the firm's capital. In an aside to the audience, Obenreizer confides that he is low on money and hopes to turn a corner by marrying Marguerite Wilding, his victim's daughter and heiress. The suspenseful climax of

Charles Dickens, England, 1812–1870, the famous novelist who also dabbled in stage melodramas (photo by Jeremiah Gurney, 19th century; Fine Arts Museums of San Francisco).

Wilkie Collins, England, 1824–1889, a pioneering master of the macabre play and the mystery story (photo by Elliott & Fry Studio, late 19th century; Fine Arts Museums of San Francisco).

the play unfolds on a Swiss mountain trail, where Obenreizer assaults George Vendale, Marguerite's beau, with a knife but is circumvented by the arrival of Marguerite and two household servants. Obenreizer sips poison from a vial while Marguerite forgives him for foul acts perpetrated. By one of those coincidences that prevail in many of Dickens' and Collins' works, it is revealed that Vendale is the long-lost son and true heir to Wilding's possessions.[23]

The Woman in White, Wilkie Collins' celebrated novel, was serialized in Charles Dickens' magazine *All the Year Round* in 1860. It is the tale of young Laura Fairlie, who is expected to acquire riches but is hounded by her heavily-indebted husband, Sir Percival Glyde, and his stout, diabolic accomplice, Count Fosco. Dramatized by Collins, it opened at London's Olympic Theatre on December 9, 1871. It came to New York's Daily Theatre in 1874. While the proceedings focus on the dastardly schemes concocted by Glyde and Fosco to entrap and get rid of the heiress, the most jarring sequence of the play occurs before the final curtain, with Fosco sequestered at home, hiding from a band of gangsters he has betrayed. He is cooing to his caged birds, his "little feathered children," when a man opens the glass door, draws a dagger, and steals toward him. Closing in on the count, he bumps into a chair. Fosco instantly turns around. A second man, who has been out of sight, springs at Fosco from behind and throws an arm around his throat. The first man stabs Fosco in the heart. The count goes down with a gasp. The two men hurriedly exit. There is a momentary pause. Then the voice of Fosco's wife, Eleanor, is heard from the bedroom, "Count, may I come in?" The lights fade.

Wilkie Collins turned his lesser known novel *Armadale* into an intricate play of assorted personas, estranged siblings, and homicide, with a dash of mysticism. Titled *Miss Gwilt* and originally performed in 1875, the felon of the proceedings, Dr. Downward, and his aide, Lydia Gwilt, conspire to possess the assets of Allan Armadale. Much of the action takes place at Dr. Downward's clinic. Allan is thought to be asleep in room number 2 when a lethal haze is released in the air through a panel. Armadale will gradually perish, clarifies the doctor to Miss Gwilt, and when the medical examiner inspects him in the morning, all he'll uncover is that Allan died of blockage to the lungs. In the nick of time, Miss Gwilt catches the sound of a muted cry from inside the room and grasps that it is not Allan Armadale but her spouse, Ozias Midwinter, who is choking. She unlocks the door, and Midwinter collapses into his wife's arms.

Wilkie Collins' novel *The Moonstone* (1868) was inspired by the actual Constance Kent murder case of 1860. The crucial pieces of evidence in the novel are a smudged nightgown and a laundry checklist, both copied from the Kent trial. Sergeant Cuff, the investigator summoned to investigate the robbery of a priceless jewel, is the embodiment of the real-life Inspector Jonathan Whicher of Scotland Yard; Collins bestowed on him the hobby of growing roses. Collins dramatized his novel in 1877.

The proceedings unfold in the inner hall of Lady Rachel Veninder's country house in Kent, England. In a tense scene, Rachel, dressed in a nightgown, observes Franklin Blake, her beloved, descend the stairs, walk toward a cupboard, unlock a drawer, pull out a diamond, and go back up the stairs. Rachel is horror struck. In another electrifying moment, Sergeant Cuff orchestrates a reconstruction of the night's circumstances, and it turns out that Franklin is a somnambulist.

The Bells (1871), adapted by Leopold Lewis (1828–1890) from the French play *The Polish Jew*, was a pioneering psychological thriller. At its London premiere on November 25, 1871, the renowned Henry Irving played Mathias, an innkeeper who murdered a Jewish traveling salesman with an axe, and, overcome by the stress of conscience, succumbs to the constant ringing of bells in his mind. The nerve-wracking sound keeps reminding him of the bells that tinkled on his victim's sled.

The Irish author Bram Stoker (1847–1912) dramatized his own 1897 novel, *Dracula, or The Un-Dead*, for a one-time performance at London's Royal Lyceum Theatre on May 18, 1897, to copyright his work. A prologue describes the arrival of Jonathan Harker to the count's castle and his encounter with "a tall man, clean shaven save for a long white moustache, and clad in black from head to foot." The jarring moments include Harker's discovery of the count lying in a box filled with dug earth and the arrival of a schooner in an English port, where its captain is found tied to the helm, dead, and from which springs a gigantic dog, "disappearing into darkness." Lucy Westerna, a friend of Harker's fiancée, Mina Murray, is tackled by a new neighbor, Count Dracula, and she soon dies with a mark on her throat, two punctures over the jugular. A direct confrontation between Dracula and the vampire hunters ends with the mystifying disappearance of Dracula. The lunatic Renfield, a former ally of the count, is found dead on the floor with face damaged, neck crushed. In a graphic ending of the play, Harker cuts off Dracula's head, and the count's body melts away.

The Ghost of Jerry Bundler (1899), by W.W. Jacobs (1863–1943) and Charles Rock (1866–1919), unfolds in a small country hotel. Several bored patrons hear the rumor that the hotel is beset with a resident murderous ghost named Jerry Bundler. Two of the guests, Mr. Malcolm and Dr. Leek, pooh pooh the notion. Hirst, an amateur actor staying at the inn, bets a gold coin that the legend is true. The proceedings become tense as they are barely illuminated by the dim glow of the fireplace, accompanied by the ticking of a clock. The play offers two possible endings, tragic or comedic. In the first version, "The door slowly opens, a hand is seen, then a figure appears in dark pants, white stockings, buckled shoes, with a long handkerchief tied round the neck. It advances towards Malcolm. Dr. Leek fires his revolver. The figure, writhing, drops to the floor. Malcolm goes forward, kneels by the figure, and pulls a red wig off, discovering Hirst, the actor." The other ending has the "mortally wounded" Hirst suddenly sitting up, telling Dr. Leek, "You're a damned bad shot, Doctor," then, addressing Malcolm, "And I'll trouble you for that sovereign."

Bram Stoker, Ireland, 1847–1912, author of *Dracula*, 1897 (n.d.; Getty Images).

French Theater

Some great French masters inserted terrifying moments in their works: Pierre Corneille, Jean Racine, Voltaire, Victor Hugo, Émile Zola, and Honoré de Balzac. *Phaedra* (1677), by Jean Racine (1639–1699), blends passion, murder, and horror borrowed from Greek mythology. Famed actresses Rachel and Sarah Bernhardt

Playwright Jean Racine, France, 1639–1699, with coat of arms, signifying a Member of the French Academy, blends elements of passion, guilt, murder, and horror in his masterpiece *Phaedra*, 1677 (artist: Gerard Edelinck, 1700; Fine Arts Museums of San Francisco).

Jean Racine
de l'Academie Francoise.

both triumphed in the title role of a queen who becomes enamored with her stepson, provoking a series of deadly incidents. When Phaedra confesses her feelings to Hippolytus, her stepson reacts with shock and rejection. She then falsely accuses him of molesting her. Hippolytus flees the town in his horse-driven chariot. The palace tutor reveals to King Theseus the horrific circumstances of his son's death: Hippolytus was driving his chariot near the seashore when the god Neptune sent from beneath the waves a huge monster, half-bull and half-dragon. Hippolytus faced the creature and pierced him with his javelin. The dying monster spewed flames at the horses, and they ran wild, pulling

Bertram Ross and Matt Turney in a ballet of *Phaedra,* choreographed by Martha Graham, Joyce Theatre, New York City, 1969 (photo by Martha Swope, The New York Public Library for the Performing Arts).

the chariot toward the cliffs, and the vehicle came apart. The horses continued to tow Hippolytus, scattering fragments of his flesh. Phaedra, remorseful, tells Theseus that his son was innocent and kills herself by drinking poison.[24]

The tragedy *Herode et Miriamne* (*Herod and Miriamne*, 1724), by Voltaire (1694–1778), unfolds in biblical Jerusalem and centers on the poisoning of Miriamne by her envious husband, Herod the Great, King of Judea, who mistakenly blames her for betraying him with the Roman governor of Syria. Voltaire's *Zaire* (1732) also features a murder, by stabbing, instigated by the rumor that a bride is planning an assignation with her lover. In *Mérope* (1743), a young prince returns incognito from exile to avenge the murder of his father, King of Arcadia, and kills the usurper with an axe. *The Orphan of China* (1755) depicts the hordes of Genghis Khan who surround and capture the capital of China, muscle their way to the palace, and execute the king, queen, and their children.

In 1314, the three daughters-in-law of King Philip IV of France were convicted of infidelity, and their paramours were put to death. The scandalous orgies took place at the Tour de Nestle, a royal palace on the left bank of the River Seine, Paris. Alexandre Dumas, père (1802–1870), embraced the liaisons for an 1832 drama, *La Tour de Nesle*. In the play, veiled women deliver invitations to an orgy in the tower, and the next morning the dead bodies of "pretty young men" are found floating in the Seine. The homicidal hostesses are described as "beautiful, drunk on lust." When greeting their guests, they cover their faces with masks. A chilling moment occurs when one of the callers, Phillipe d'Audray, makes a fatal mistake: he plucks a pin from the hair of the hostess, Marguerite, and scratches her cheek. "Now I shall know you," he announces joyfully. She cuts his throat, and her sergeant carries the body to a boat. Later in the proceedings, she learns that she was guilty of incestuous love and had killed her own long-lost son. Diabolical music accompanies the events.

Lucretia Borgia (1833) by Victor Hugo (1802–1885) portrays the notorious Italian duchess who was rumored to have had incestuous affairs with her father and brother and murdered her husbands and lovers. At the beginning of the three-act drama, Lucretia encounters soldier of fortune Gennaro

The great storyteller Alexandre Dumas (père), France, 1802–1870, adapted a real-life event into the play *La Tour de Nesle* (1832), wherein the dead bodies of "pretty young men" are found floating in the Seine (ca. 1840–1899; Print Collection, The New York Public Library).

Victor Hugo, France, 1802–1885, features the notorious Italian duchess in *Lucretia Borgia* (1833), a chilling drama that climaxes in a blood-splattered banquet (ca. 1870–1885; Billy Rose Theatre Division, The New York Public Library).

and kisses him on the forehead; he falls in love with her. In a climactic scene that takes place during a banquet, Lucretia administers poisoned wine to a group of men who had slighted her. She is not aware that Gennaro is among them. A final startling moment between Gennaro and Lucretia exposes their blood relationship. In his last breath he fatally stabs her; dying at his side, she gasps, "Ah! You have killed me! Gennaro! I am your *mother!*"

The Mysteries of Paris (1843) by Eugène Sue (1804–1857) was the first serialized story in the French newspapers of the day (1842–1843). The outstretched melodrama—highlighting crime and adventure—became an immense success. In 1843, Sue adapted the novel to the stage, eliminating many of the characters and dispensing with most of the locales. The twisty plot focuses on a 16-year-old orphan, Fleur de Marie, who is tortured emotionally and physically by her adopters, La Chouette, a sadistic, one-eyed woman, and an arch-criminal nicknamed the School Master. An alarming moment occurs when one of the couple's conpatriots, the crooked lawyer Jacques Ferrand, attempts to kill Marie by pushing her into a riverboat, detaching a valve, and setting it afloat. The water soon seeps in, but luckily the boat collides with a pier, and several men jump into the river and moor it. Ferrand himself, after betraying his bosses and escaping with a bag filled with gold coins, comes to a sorry end. The School Master and members of his gang seize Ferrand in a forest clearing, haul him into a cave, and pull out his eyes. He exits the cave, crawling and weeping, "Blind! Blind! … No more gold! … Oh, my God! My God! My God!"

The Stepmother (1848), by Honoré de Balzac (1799–1850), takes place in a Normandy manor. General Grandchamp's daughter, Pauline, envious of her father's second wife, Gertrude, mixes her own tea with arsenic and stages the scene to seem as if Gertrude has poisoned her. The stepmother is charged with homicide. All seems lost, but Pauline, dying, confesses the truth to the authorities.

Émile Zola's (1840–1902) *Thérèse Raquin* (1873) also ends with remorse and the suicide of Thérèse and her lover Laurent, who had drowned Thérèse's husband. A shivering scene depicts the paralyzed mother of the victim managing painfully, slowly to move her hand and trace signs on the tablecloth with the tip of a finger, revealing the identity of the murderers.

Théodora, a Byzantine Empress, is the heroine of Victorien Sardou's (1831–1908) 1884 tragedy. Théodora comes to her husband's rescue when he is assailed by the schemer Marcellus; she pricks Marcellus to death with her hairpin. Before the final curtain, however, Théodora accidentally swaps toxic poison for medicine, drips it down her lover Andreas's mouth, and realizes in shock that he is dying in anguish. The fatal mistake led to her arrest and hanging. The part was one of Sarah Bernhardt's triumphs.

Sardou's tragedy *La Tosca* (1887) unfolds in 1800 Rome when the city is on the verge of a clash between the ruling Royalists and the emerging Republicans. Baron Scarpia, chief of the secret police, continually sends many Republicans to prison. On his

Émile Zola, France, 1840–1902, explored the darkest aspects of human experience in *Thérèse Raquin*, a sinister tale of adultery and murder, novel published in 1867, dramatized by the author in 1873 (photo by Étienne Carjat, ca. 1877; Fine Arts Museums of San Francisco).

A scene from Victorien Sardou's *La Tosca* (1887), with Sarah Bernhardt portraying the title role of a singer who gives refuge to a political refugee in Rome of 1800—and pays with her life. A melodramatic piece, it contains depictions of torture, murder, and suicide (n.d.; Billy Rose Theatre Division, The New York Public Library).

hunt for Cesare Angelotti, an escaped political convict, Scarpia tortures his friend Mario Cavaradossi, who stands firm despite his pain. But Mario's lover, the opera star Floria Tosca (another celebrated role by Bernhardt), cannot bear his screams, breaks down, and reveals Angelotti's hiding place. Angelotti commits suicide to avoid the rack and public hanging by taking poison hidden in his ring.

The Grand Guignol, a theater genre that started in 1898 in a seamy hall near the Place Pigalle in Paris, presented short, grisly, horror plays blending sex, sadism, and macabre humor, often ending with an ironic twist or physical atrocity.

German Theater

Miss Sara Sampson (1755) by Gotthold Ephraim Lessing (1729–1781) emerges as an early bourgeois tragedy, ignoring the classical theory that tragic protagonists must be men and women of noble rank. The proceedings take place in an English roadside inn, where Sara Sampson and her fiancé, Mellefont, stay in separate rooms before traveling to France to get married. Mellefont's former mistress, Marwood, tracks them to the inn. She introduces herself to Sara and relates that she had a ten-year relationship with Mellefont and bore his child, a girl, causing Sara to faint. Marwood mixes a potion of medicine with grains of poison and exits hurriedly to a coach, ordering the driver to rush to Dover. Mellefont now sits at the side of Sara's bed, asking for forgiveness. The last sight that Sara sees is that of Mellefont impaling himself with a dagger. He collapses and dies next to her.

Johann Wolfgang von Goethe (1749–1832) based his poetic, supernatural *Faust* (1808) on the German legend of a sixteenth-century charlatan, Georgius Faustus Helmstetensis—an arch-magician and perverse scholar infamous for his black arts. Alleged to have

made a pact with Lucifer, he died in 1540 of unexplained factors. Christopher Marlowe's *The Tragical History of Doctor Faustus* (c. 1588) was the first portrayal of the story on stage, defining Faust as a man desiring power and achieving it by submitting his soul to the devil.

English touring companies performing the Marlowe play reignited a fascination with the Faust myth in Germany, and for the next 150 years it had a regular niche in the repertory of many theaters. In his autobiography, Goethe relates that he saw a puppet show of the Faust story, and it "reverberated within me manifold times."[25] He struggled with the concept for many years and, progressively, a monumental poetic

Johann Wolfgang von Goethe, Germany, 1749–1832, introduced in his poetic, supernatural *Faust* (1808) a scholar who lusts for power and gains it by selling his soul to the Devil (artist: Joseph Karl Stieler, 1828; Print Collection, The New York Public Library).

drama emerged. Part I of *Faust* was published in 1808; part II, which he completed shortly before his 82nd birthday, came out after his death in late 1832.

Part I opens with a heavenly prologue, where Mephistopheles wagers with the Lord that he can lead Faust astray. In the next scene, at a city gate, a black poodle follows Faust and his friend Wagner. Soon the snarling dog swells to a monstrous size, revealing itself to be the devil's messenger, Mephistopheles. Mephistopheles proposes an agreement—Faust will surrender his soul to the devil, and in exchange, Mephistopheles will fulfill any wish that the doctor desires. They sign the agreement with the doctor's "wee drop of blood," and Mephistopheles guides Faust to lairs of degeneracy. His desires aroused, Faust seduces the attractive Margaret. When she is with child, her brother Valentine challenges Faust to a sword duel and is killed. Faust escapes. Margaret suffocates her newborn baby, is incarcerated, and found guilty of homicide. With a pang of remorse, Faust forces his way into the prison to rescue Margaret, but he does not make it on time. The distressed girl dies in his arms. Mephistopheles pulls Faust away, but Margaret's voice keeps repeating the doctor's name.

In Part II, Mephistopheles is a court clown. While the emperor is indulging in voluptuous engagements, the people are hungry and rebellious. The emperor, at a palace banquet, asks Faust to recreate the ideal model of glamour, Helen of Troy. Faust and Helen have a boy, Euphorion, an untamed, headstrong child who plunges from a rock while attempting to fly. Instead, he collapses fatally next to his parents. From the netherworld, his soul summons his mother and takes her down with him.

Time passes. Goethe, unlike previous authors who dealt with the topic, has the now experienced and rational Faust carrying out tasks that will benefit humanity. Upon Faust's death, demons and angels battle for his spirit; the angels win.

Russian Theater

Yevgeny Arbenin, the protagonist of *Masquerade* (written 1835, first performed 1852), a verse play by Russian dramatist Mikhail Lermontov (1814–1841), is a wealthy young man born into high society. Arbenin falsely believes that a masked lady who flirted with the royal prince during a costume party is his wife, Nina. Blinded by jealousy and pride, Arbenin mixes poison into Nina's ice cream. Later, realizing that he has murdered his beloved wife without cause, Arbenin goes insane.

Leo Tolstoy's (1828–1910) *The*

Leo Tolstoy, Russia, 1828–1910, who pictured the gruesome murder of an unwanted baby in *The Power of Darkness*, 1886 (1887; The New York Public Library of the Performing Arts).

Nikita, played by Lou Antonio, confessing his sins to his father Akim, played by Vladimir Sokoloff, in *The Power of Darkness*, York Playhouse, New York City, 1959 (photo by Friedman-Abelès, The New York Public Library of the Performing Arts).

Power of Darkness (written 1886; first produced 1888) is a fierce play of illusion and bloodshed among Russian farmers. It was initially considered too degenerate for public viewing. A terrifying scene depicts the protagonist of the play, the womanizer Nikita, digging a grave in the cellar, then getting rid of an unwanted newborn baby by forcing a wooden plank down on the infant's body until the bones splinter.

American Theater

America joined the scene with *Prince of Parthia* by Thomas Godfrey (1747–1825). It was the first American play to be seen on a professional stage—the Southwark Theatre, near Philadelphia, in 1767. Godfrey was influenced by real-life events that occurred at the kingdom of Parthia, east of the Caspian Sea, and added his own invention to a brew of incest, vengeance, and murder. The action is centered on the goal of Prince Vardanes to usurp his father's throne. He combines forces with Queen Thermusa, who hates her philandering husband, King Artabanus, for having sex with their daughter. They kill the king in his sleep and blame Vardanes' brother, Prince Arsaces, of the murder. Arsaces is arrested. Thermusa enters the jail with a dagger in hand to assassinate Arsaces, but just as she's ready to stab him, the bloody ghost of Artabanus appears. "All my brains[are] on fire," she says, and then commits suicide by hitting her head against a wall. The final scene pits Vardanes' men against Arsaces' followers. The latter win the encounter. Vardanes, mortally wounded, stutters, "Death is near—my breath goes short—my ebbing life is done—yet I die just as I wish, daring for a crown."

William Dunlap (1766–1839), who wrote more than 60 plays and has been called "Father of the American Theater," presented *The Fatal Deception* in 1794, a narrative of adultery, obsession, mistaken identity, murder, and revenge. The play's proceedings take place in Elizabethan England. Lord Leicester is returning home from the wars. Leicester's wife, Matilda, introduces him to her "brother," Henry Limmeric, who is actually Matilda's lover. Matilda convinces Limmeric to kill her husband. "If Leicester lives, we die," she says. Matilda produces a dagger from under her robe and hands it to Limmeric. He sneaks into a darkened room and does not realize that, mistakenly, he has stabbed his brother, Dudley. Matilda does not give up. During supper, she marks with a cross a dish containing poisonous meat and serves it to her husband. By now suspicious, Leicester manages to exchange dishes. Matilda dies.

In 1795, William Dunlap introduced Gothic elements to America in his play *The Fountainville Abbey* (1795). It is the story of a culprit who, hunted by the authorities, flees to an isolated convent. In a rundown cell he notices a rusty dagger, a skeleton, and a document concealed in an old trunk—items that will play an important role in the ensuing proceedings.

Early American plays were peppered with stereotypes. Today, minority stage characters of the 19th century may stir up controversy, as Jewish, Irish, and African American characters were often ridiculed. Native Americans were played by Caucasian actors in dark makeup and regularly portrayed as savages. However, the title character of *Metamora, or The Last of the Wampanoags* (1829), was depicted by John Augustus Stone (1801–1834) as a noble savage fighting to save his tribe from total annihilation by white settlers. The play, set in nineteenth-century New England, contains several unnerving moments. A strolling woman is attacked by a panther but saved by an arrow shot by Metamora which "felled the monster." Metamora kills a traitorous Indian with a hatchet in front of white council members. Metamora's wife, Nahmeokee, escapes from pursuing soldiers by jumping into a spring. Metamora fatally stab his wife so that she won't fall into the hands of the settlers, and soldiers shoot Metamora, whose last words are, "My curse on you, white men! ... Murderers! ... The last of the Wampanoags' curse be on you! ... I die! My wife! My queen! My Nahmeokee!" The celebrated actor Edwin Forrest played the role.

Harriet Beecher Stowe's 1852 novel, *Uncle Tom's Cabin*, paints the miserable existence of African Americans in the Old South—where flogging, degradation, and abuse were frequent. Stage adaptations of the book followed swiftly, the most popular being a version by George L. Aiken (1830–1876), which opened at Purdy's National Theatre,

New York, in 1853, to a lengthy run. Uncle Tom—a kind man of faith—keeps his humble demeanor while tormented for his viewpoints at the hands of Simon Legree, a cruel plantation master, a definitive rogue in world literature. A high level of suspense is achieved when the runaway slave Eliza, carrying her infant son, eludes her pursuers by escaping into an icy river, skipping across from one floating ice chunk to another. Another nail-biting moment occurs when Eliza's fugitive husband, George Harris, is tracked by two slave hunters and hides in a tavern cellar. In an ensuing struggle at the rocky border of Canada, George tosses the pursuers into the torrent below. Eliza, George, and their child, Harry, make it to Canada. Back at Simon Legree's plantation, Legree sexually abuses the enslaved Cassey. She escapes, and Legree demands that Uncle Tom tell him where she is. When Tom declines, Legree beats him with his whip, resulting in Uncle Tom's death. Soon, two officers arrive with a warrant to arrest Legree for past transgressions. Legree resists and is shot. He shrieks, "I am hit! The game's up!" and expires.[26]

Francesca da Rimini (1855) by George Henry Boker (1823–1890) depicts the real-life story of an attractive Italian noblewoman who was forced to marry a deformed lord, Lanciotto, to solidify peace between two warring families. Francesca grew to love her husband's younger brother, Paolo. They saw each other for nearly a decade, until Lanciotto startled them in Francesca's bedroom and impaled them both. In Boker's play, Francesca mistakenly believes that she is slated to marry the handsome Paolo but finds out to her chagrin that the bridegroom is Lanciotto, a "twisted monster" with a "huge dwarf arm" and "very hump." After her initial shock, she yields to her father's demand and marries Lanciotto but soon establishes a clandestine, romantic relationship with Paolo. A shady jester, Pepé, informs Lanciotto, who surprises the lovers kissing in the castle's garden. Lanciotto skewers Francesca first. Paolo lifts his sword, but ultimately lets his brother stab him. With deep sorrow, Lanciotto moves Paolo to slump next to Francesca. The lovers convey their understanding and empathy before they die. Lanciotto then stabs himself, sinks alongside his brother, and whispers, "I loved him more than honor—more than life."

Written by Dion Boucicault (1820–1890), *The Octoroon* (1859) was an admired play during the second half of the 19th century. The play's villain, Jacob McClosky, a whip-carrying plantation owner in southern Louisiana, covets the property of his neighbor Mrs. Peyton and has designs on her octoroon (one-eighth Black) slave, Zoe. Mrs. Peyton's plantation is mortgaged, and she expects a letter of credit from Liverpool, England, where a company owes her late husband $50,000. Mrs. Peyton sends her Black boy Paul and the Native American Wahnotee, devoted friends, to bring the mail from the post office, which is situated near a river wharf. They do so, and soon Paul enters, carrying two mailbags, followed by Wahnotee holding a tomahawk and a half-empty bottle of rum. They stop to watch a man inserting several plates into a camera on a stand, a new invention. The man leaves, and Paul throws down the bags and plays with the camera. Wahnotee drops the tomahawk and exits drinking. McClosky emerges from behind some rocks, snatches the tomahawk, and hits Paul in the face—taking his life. He then hurriedly shuffles through a mailbag and discovers a letter with a Liverpool postmark. He moves to a corner, opens it, and mutters, "You will find enclosed a draft to your order, on the Bank of Louisiana." Wahnotee returns and finds Paul dead. A crowd gathers. Wahnotee is accused of murdering Paul and is almost lynched, but Old Pete exhibits a photographic plate that caught McClosky's action. The crowd turns to McClosky, who tears himself away from his captors and escapes. Wahnotee follows him with his tomahawk in hand; screams soon are heard from outside.[27] *An Octoroon* was resuscitated by Soho Rep in New York City on May 4, 2014, directed by Sarah Benson, with original music by César Alvarez, and set design by Mimi Lien. It won an Obie Award for Best New American Play.

In 1852, Boucicault wrote *The Corsican Brothers*, based on the 1844 novella *Les Frères Corses* by Alexandre Dumas, and *The Vampire*, from an 1820 play, *Le Vampire*, by Charles Nodier. In *The Corsican Brothers,* Charles Kean played the twin Corsican brothers, Fabian and Louis Dei Franchi. Louis is killed by the philandering Charles Renaud over his beloved Madame de Lesparre. The ghost of Louis appears and discloses his death to Fabian. Fabian retaliates Louis' demise by piercing Renaud in a duel. The title character of *The Vampire* is Lord Ruthven, a debonaire undead. Influenced by an actual homicide, Boucicault penned a suspense play, *The Colleen Bawn* (1860). John Scanlan married Ellen Hanley, a 15-year-old girl, but when he found out that his family would reject her, he convinces his servant, Stephen Sullivan, to kill her. Sullivan guided Ellen to the bank of the River Shannon, shot her with a rifle, and threw the body in the water. Ellen's remains drifted ashore several weeks later. Scanlan and Sullivan made a run for it. Scanlan was soon captured, incarcerated, and hanged. Sullivan was detained not long afterward, pleaded guilty, and was executed. Boucicault renamed the characters of the dark drama and made extensive changes from the real-life events: the girl is pushed into a lake, is believed to be dead, but in court appears and refutes the allegations against her husband. *Arrah-na-Pogue* (1864) takes place during the Irish rebellion of 1798 and features larceny from a landlord, an escape from jail through a backway, and a humorous court scene. *After Dark* (1868), the story of a lord's son who weds a waitress in order to be eligible for an inheritance, is awash with lurid scenes that transpire in London's criminal underworld.

Boucicault's extensive output was produced continuously, and successfully, on both sides of the Atlantic.

Dion Boucicault, Ireland, 1820–1890, a prolific writer of blood-and-thunder melodramas (ca. 1874; The New York Public Library of the Performing Arts).

America's first accredited musical was 1866's *The Black Crook*, written by Charles M. Barras (1826–1873), in which a spectacular array of sets, costumes, and lighting focuses on a Faustian motif. The main character, Hertzog, an old, misshapen wizard, asks Zamiel, Hell's Lucifer, for extended life with "fresh charms and potencies." Zamiel is willing to grant it if Hertzog will deliver to him annually the soul of a young man. Surrounded by demons and skeletons, they sign the pact. Hertzog chooses for his first victim the poor artist Rodolphe Werner, who lost his bid for the lovely Amina when the powerful Count Wolfenstein came calling. Hertzog slyly suggests that Rodolphe can save Amina from Wolfenstein's unholy designs if he finds gold: "Gold can buy nobility." He directs Rodolphe to a small lake where he'll find a concealed boat. The boat will take him to the entrance of a cavern wherein his eyes will feast "on wealth far greater than the coffers of the world can boast." Hertzog believes that the lust for gold will affect Rodolphe's

soul. "He's mine, he's mine," he exults. Rodolphe goes on a wondrous and dangerous voyage accompanied by menacing musical chords. On the way, he manages to save the life of Salacta, Queen of the Golden Realm. Salacta returns the favor when Rodolphe is attacked by a sea creature. The queen guides Rodolphe to secret caverns where fairies dance a grand ballet, during which "gnomes and amphibea present Rodolphe with nuggets of gold and jewels." Salacta then gives Rodolphe a ring, saying, "Should danger threaten, press thy lips upon the gem and thou will find me by thy side." On his way back, the ring proves to be handy, for Rodolphe finds himself surrounded by Wolfenstein's guards in a forest; upon his kissing the ring, Salacta and her tribe leap from the thicket in glittering full armor and defeat the guards. Rodolphe wins back Amina, while at Zamiel's underworld headquarters, chords of demonic music play as Hertzog is grabbed by fiends and thrown into a blazing abyss.

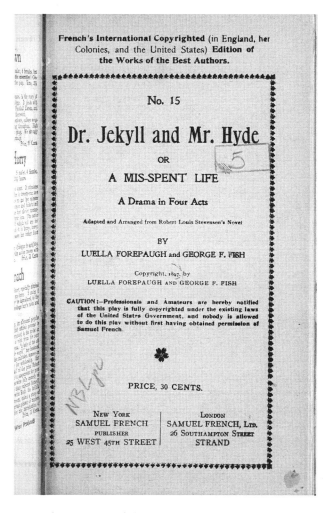

An early program of the play *Dr. Jekyll and Mr. Hyde: A Drama in Four Acts*, adapted and arranged from Robert Louis Stevenson's novel by Luella Forepaugh and George F. Fish (Samuel French, 1897; The New York Public Library for the Performing Arts).

Augustine Daly's (1838–1899) *Under the Gaslight* (1867) creates a terrifying image of the underbelly of metropolitan New York, where ruffians prowl in corners ready to attack gullible residents. The play was the first to feature the hero tied to a railway track with a highly suspenseful last-minute rescue.

One of the most harrowing plays written and produced towards the end of the 19th century was *Dr. Jekyll and Mr. Hyde* (1887), adapted by Thomas Russell Sullivan (1849–1916) from the 1866 novella by Robert Louis Stevenson. Richard Mansfield was the first to portray the role of a kind doctor who transforms, both physically and mentally, into an evil monster.

Twentieth Century Theater

American Theater

The 20th century began its theatrical offerings with blood-and-thunder melodramas—urban, Western, nautical, or war oriented—characterized by wild plots with little logic, black-and-white characters, broad comedy, and breathtaking cliffhangers at the end of each scene. Among the successful American melodramatic writers of the era were Theodore Kremer, Hal Reid, George Broadhurst, Owen Davis, Augustus Thomas, Langdon McCormick, Lincoln J. Carter, Charles E. Blaney, Willard Mack, and Max Marcin—prolific authors who were able to quickly create sensational five-act plays year in and year out.

Hal Reid's (1862–1920) melodramas are populated with white-collar schemers, dastardly foreigners, and savage Indians. His heroines are tied to a post near the East River and left to drown, thrown into an icy millpond, or almost run over by a trolley car. His heroes must duck a fusillade of bullets, the sling of arrows, or sticks of dynamite. The setting ranges from hidden caves in the Kentucky mountains to Colorado mining camps to opium dens in lower Manhattan's Chinatown. Reid's *The Prince of the World* (1901) is derived from the Old Testament. The emperor Caesar woos the Israelite Judith. When she rebuffs his overtures, Caesar commands that she be hurled into a lion's cage. Judith is encircled by live lions, who do not inflict any injury. The menacing moments of Reid's *Old Sleuth* (1902) include the damsel-in-distress, René, being shoved into a barrel and pushed over the edge of Niagara Falls, and, in the final scene that unfolds in a train underpass, two rail vehicles are advancing (moved by hidden stagehands on rollers) towards a potential collision, with lights shining and smoke swirling. The heroine is locked in a hermetic vault and saved from suffocating by the Secret Service in Reid's *Time Lock Number 776* (1915).

The title character of *Nellie, the Beautiful Cloak Model* (1906), by Owen Davis (1874–1956), is a model in the cloak department of a New York department store. She finds herself an heiress to great wealth but also the target of a series of attempts on her life by fortune-hunting relatives—bound to the tracks of an elevated train or threatened by an axe on a boat or by a bomb on a bridge—always with a last-minute rescue.

Davis's villains are often relatives or guardians who, with the help of an adventuress in red, will stop at nothing, including murder, in their pursuit of the property of wealthy young heiresses or wards. In *At the World's Mercy* (1906), they try to blast little Gracie off a viaduct with a booby trap. In *The Burglar's Daughter* (1906), they tie blind Ruth Holt in a runaway streetcar. In *$10,000 Reward* (1906), high society's Marian Grey is kidnapped by gangsters and shipped off to India for a transaction with a Hindu preacher. *Edna, the Pretty Typewriter* (1907) is sealed in a hermetic safe, while *Sal, the Circus Gal*, is padlocked in a Manhattan apartment building. Davis endeavored to enter the sphere of the undead in *Lola* (1911), the story of a scientist who has invented an apparatus to revive the deceased.

Superstition and bloodshed blend in *The Witching Hour* (1907) by Augustus Thomas (1857–1934). The climax of *The Girl and the Detective* (1908) by Charles E. Blaney (1868–1944) transpires in a New Jersey factory where Richard Tracy, the culprit of the piece, places two dazed persons on a gliding platform and activates it to move toward a flaming mallet.

Owen Davis, United States, 1874–1956, a popular American melodramatist (n.d.; The New York Public Library of the Performing Arts).

The Third Degree (1909) by Charles Klein contains a "third-degree" interrogation in which a murder suspect is grilled for seven hours at a New York police station, going through mental and physical abuse. A frightening scene unfolds in Paul Armstrong's *Alias Jimmy Valentine* (1910) when a little girl inadvertently locks herself in a bank vault. A blindfolded, retired cracksman unscrambles the combination.

It is presumed that a vengeful specter is the cause of mysterious murders in *The Ghost Breaker* (1913) by Charles W. Goddard and Paul Dickey. But a skeptical Yankee from Kentucky, Warren Jarvis, smitten with a beautiful Spanish princess, travels to Aragon and proves that a dastardly duke impersonated "the ghost" as a hideous form wielding a Damascus sword. Goddard and Dickey also parody the Frankenstein lore in *The Last Laugh* (1915), having its frenzied proceedings encircle a wooden coffin containing a wrapped body.

The Thirteenth Chair (1916) by Bayard Veiller (1869–1943) includes a breathtaking trick knife and atmospheric séance sequences before the criminal is unmasked by a clever medium.

The zenith of the macabre melodrama hit the stage in the 1920s. *The Green Goddess* (1920), by William Archer, was produced when anti–Asian "yellow peril" plays were in fashion. It is set in a Himalayan temple where a persecuted heroine is saved from the clutches of a lascivious raja by the last-minute arrival of the Royal Air Force. *The Bat* (1920) by Mary Roberts Rinehart and Avery Hopwood pits an elderly spinster against an arch-criminal and provides a wallop of a surprise ending. *The Cat and the Canary*

(1922) by John Willard is known for its imaginative use of trap doors and hidden passageways. Thomas Fallon's *The Last Warning* (1922) presents a play within a play in a decrepit theater that was closed for five years following the murder of a well-known actor. It is being restored by a former producer who is determined to unmask an obscure murderer. While rehearsing, the cast is harassed by a series of weird happenings—a huge spider creeps up the wall; the lights fade, and the murdered man's footsteps echo in pitch dark; the hanging portrait of the late actor unexpectedly tumbles down; a nauseating perfume and a repellent smog flood the stage; a black cat prowls around, its glittering eyes aflame in the dimness; a weighty sandbag falls from the beams; and a voice reverberates from a distance, "Dare ye not to reopen my theatre!"

ZaSu Pitts (left) and Lucille Watson in a revival of the classic melodrama *The Bat* (National Theatre, New York City, 1953).

The action of Owen Davis's *The Haunted House* (1924) unfolds in a shuttered country home abandoned for 20 years. There is a large pool of blood outside among the bushes. Was someone murdered? Following a series of suspenseful episodes, it is discovered that the blood belonged to a cow named Nellie who stumbled into the bushes and died there. George Broadhurst's *The Red Falcon* (1924) takes place in sixteenth-century Sicily. The leader of a ring of outlaws ransacks a convent and violates the Mother Superior. Two decades later, the man born from that union has become a kind priest possessed by homicidal tendencies—a split personality. The team of Paul Dickey and Bernard J. McOwen wrote the spirited *The Dust Heap* (1924), transpiring in the Canadian Yukon and featuring such varied characters as a devout Catholic priest, a wandering Jew, a mixed-race castaway girl, a young Eastern nobleman, a white slaver, and a vicious oriental innkeeper—many bearing weapons, all implicated in criminous affairs. John Willard's *The Green Beetle* (1924) unfoldss in San Francisco's Chinatown. Chang Hong, a merchant, hatches a ruthless payback on an American who years earlier sexually assaulted his dear Suey-Yen. Willard's *Fog* (1927) takes place on the deck of a yacht off the coast of Long Island, where three of the passengers are tossed to sea. An unaccountable vanishing, a ticking time bomb, and the literal swaying of the vessel on stage raised spectators' alarm. *Fog*, with a screenplay by Willard, was filmed in 1929 under the title *Black Waters* and was England's earliest "all-talkie."

Ralph Spence's *The Gorilla* (1925) is a mystery-burlesque that launched a trend of spilling frantic action into the auditorium. The Gorilla is the nickname of a wicked criminal as well as the real name of an ape named Poe, who escaped from a ship and prowls about. A serpentine plot unfolds in subterranean tunnels, dark staircases, and secret trapdoors. Jittery props include hanging skeletons and sharp battle axes.

The action of *Wooden Kimono* (1926) by John Floyd unwinds at The Red Owl Tavern, where three of the night boarders vanish under mysterious circumstances. From the opening curtain, the inn is filled with screams, revolver shots, and fresh homicides. Electricity turns off at crucial moments, unnatural figures peek from shadowy hallways, and escape hatches pivot nonstop. The audience eventually learns that a gang of dope smugglers, the Scarlet Scarabs, have been utilizing the Red Owl as their base.

John Colton's *The Shanghai Gesture* (1926) unfolds in a brothel in Shanghai, China, where Mother God Damn addresses a group of judges, politicians, business tycoons, and their wives and confides that she was once a Manchu princess who stole her father's gold and eloped with a young British man named Charteris. With her gold, Charteris established his trading firm but sold the princess to human traffickers. She became a prostitute and had a demeaning, tortured life. With the help of a Russian lover, she returned to Shanghai, where she set up a bordello. She has waited 20 years to get revenge, says Mother God Damn, and points at Sir Guy Charteris, a distinguished Englishman and

a pillar of the community. When Mother God Damn sends the stunned dinner guests away, they avoid the disgraced Charteris, who will now be shunned by their group. Mother God Damn discloses to Poppy Charteris that she's her birth mother. Poppy, intoxicated, yells that her mother was English and heaps insults on Mother God Damn, who soon explodes in rage and leaps at the girl. Poppy retreats and flees from one balcony to another with Mother God Damn running after her. At the highest balcony, Mother God Damn catches up with her. A confrontation ensues, the railing breaks, and Poppy's body drops three flights below. Mother God Damn rushes downstairs. She embraces the dead girl and starts to hum a quiet, gentle song.[28]

An asylum guard (Abe Vigoda) menaces the heiress Annabelle West (Adale O'Brien) in *The Cat and The Canary* (Stage 73, New York City, 1965).

The action of *The Call of the Banshee* (1927), by W.D. Hepenstall and Ralph Culliman, is set in Blackridge, New York, in the parlor of Peter Adair's house, where Mrs. Grimes, a superstitious Irish housekeeper, believes in the Banshee—a ghost that wanders the earth and whose cry predicts sudden demise. Mrs. Grimes assumes that the curse of the Banshee followed the Adair family from Ireland to America and is poised to strike again. At the end of Act I, the Banshee's roar vibrates, and Peter Adair dies abruptly. At the end of the second act, the family doctor trips and dies. In addition to the Banshee's signal, the play is filled with other noises that are meant to keep the audience on the edge of its seat: knocks on the door, footsteps on the staircase, and groans from the wings. Before the final curtain, it turns out that it was Yuru, an Indian servant, who killed Peter Adair and his doctor with darts dipped in curare shot from a blowgun looking for an inheritance gain.

The Clutching Claw (1928) by Ralph Thomas Kettering is set in the den of John Thornton's secluded house in Westchester County, New York. When the curtain comes up, Thornton, a man of 50, seems to be in mortal fear. Shaking, he tears open an envelope and finds a folded sheet of tissue paper with an imprint of a claw. He realizes that this is a caution sent by the underworld figurehead known as "The Clutching Claw," an extortioner, drug dealer, and ruthless killer. Later that evening, during a party celebrating the engagement of Thornton's daughter, Patricia, the lights go out. Hardly seen, a camouflaged form leaps up from behind the sofa and grips Thornton by the neck. When Patricia switches on the light, the mysterious form has disappeared, and her father is dead. (A production note suggests that the figure's face and head should be covered by black gauze so that his features are indistinguishable; his hands and arms should be covered with long, black cotton gloves, the bones of his hands and forearms painted in white on the gloves. Long claws can be cut for each finger from a celluloid collar and sewed on the glove fingers.) A moronic police chief gathers the mourning guests in the den. Who among them will emerge as the mystifying Clutching Claw?

The Skull (1928), a frenzied melodrama by Bernard J. McOwen and Harry E. Humphrey, introduces a band of gangsters headed by the mysterious Skull, "counterfeiter-forger-blackmailer-prince of burglars." The Skull conceals his identity under a hood and leaves the seal of a small skull at the site of each offense. The plot unfurls in an old chapel situated on a rural path. Spectral figures, bell tower bats, and screeching owls become visible and disappear into thin air during the proceedings, linked with an orchestration of explosions, thunder, strong winds, bell chimes, and intense musical notes. A large amount of money turns up in the basement. A casket filled with diamonds is discovered in the belfry. The arch-criminal turns out to be the investigative captain of Scotland Yard.

McOwen teamed with J.P. Piewerts on *The Blue Ghost* (1930), set in the California home of Dr. De Former. Characters enter and exit through a hidden bookcase, a gimmicky grandfather clock, and a window "eighty feet straight up from the sea." Dr. De Former is described as "the greatest chemist in the history of synthetic booze, master mind of the dope ring, forger and murderer." His adversary is The Blue Ghost, who "for months has committed crime after crime, yet the only clue they ever found is a card with his mark on it." The arch-criminal is seeking liquor worth millions, tucked away in the house. Ultimately, the butler Jasper, a diminutive African American, the cowardly, comic stock character of the time, is exposed as The Blue Ghost with a spin: the butler has put on the spooky attire, processed with phosphorous, for the purpose of catching the villains; he is "the Government's cleverest detective."

In Ralph Spence's *Sh! The Octopus* (1928), two inept detectives find themselves trapped with a pack of strangers in a deserted Long Island lighthouse. They are menaced

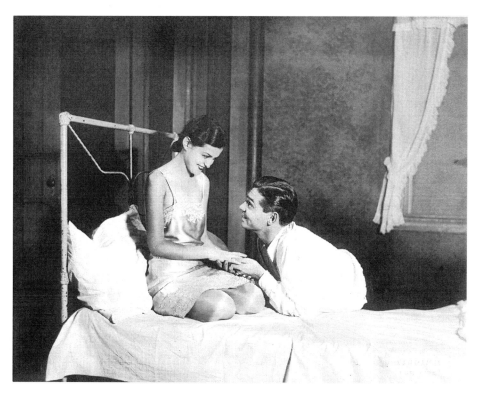

In the expressionistic play *Machinal* (1928), a despondent Young Woman (played by Zita Johann) falls in love with a Young Man (Clark Gable); kills her elderly husband; and is arrested, convicted and executed in the electric chair (photo by Vandamm Studio, The New York Public Library for the Performing Arts).

by the Octopus, an arch-criminal who has hatched a scheme to revolutionize submarine tactics. The ominous events progress with a free-handed percentage of moans, screams, and shots in the dark. An actual octopus arrives on the scene, its sharp tentacles stretching out for victims. The high point of suspense transpires when the water is rising, and the good guys are sealed in a subterranean tunnel.

In 1925, Elmer Rice's harsh play *The Adding Machine* presented a minor clerk who murders his employer when

Nobel Prize–winner Eugene O'Neill, United States, 1888–1953, was inspired by classical Greek drama when writing the dark *Mourning Becomes Electra*, 1931, and *Desire Under the Elms*, 1963 (printed 1982; International Museum of Photography at George Eastman House).

dismissed from his posi-
tion after 25 years of devoted
service and is consequently
hanged. Three years later,
playwright Sophie Treadwell
conceived *Machinal*, a play
about a stenographer named
Helen who marries and kills
her much older supervisor
and is punished for the crime.
The last scene unfolds in a
prison cell. A detached priest
goes through the ceremony
of prayer. Two guards collar Helen and steer her down
a hallway. Helen blurts out,
"Somebody! Somebod—" and
her plea breaks off. Curtain.

Eugene O'Neill's (1888–
1953) *Desire Under the Elms*
(1924) takes place around a
desolate New England dwelling. Seventy-five-year-old
Ephraim Cabot brings home
his third wife, Abbie, half his
age and "buxom, full of vital-
ity." Soon Abbie and Eben,
Ephraim's son, "25, tall and
sinewy," succumb to a mutual
attraction and fall in love.
Abbie becomes pregnant and

Colleen Dewhurst as Abbie and Alan Mixon as Eben in
Desire Under the Elms, the telling of a complex relation-
ship among father, son, and stepmother that culminates
in deadly results, Circle in the Square (Downtown), New
York City, 1963 (photo by Friedman-Abeles, The New
York Public Library for the Performing Arts).

tells Ephraim that he is the father. The old man is in rapture. A son is born. During a dispute with Eben, Ephraim says that Abbie wished a son only to swindle him from inher-
iting the farm. Eben is crushed. He confronts Abbie—"They must be a devil livin' in
ye!"—and wishes their son "never was born. I wish he'd die this minute!" In a desperate attempt to demonstrate to Eben that it was her love for him and not a craving for the
plantation that drove her, Abbie suffocates the child with a cushion. Eben, aghast and
outraged, departs to beckon the sheriff.[29]

Many of O'Neill's plays are steeped with violence. In *The Web*, a one-act play
penned in 1914, a friendly mobster offers a prostitute, Rose, cash to flee from her ruthless
pimp, Steve. But Steve shoots the sympathizer and incriminates Rose for the homicide.

Another early one-act play, *Recklessness* (1914), ends with a Grand Guignol touch.
An aged husband finds out that his young wife is having a liaison with the good-looking
chauffeur. He orders the chauffeur to go on an errand, arranging for the steering wheel
to break down.

Thirst, presented by Off-Broadway's Provincetown Players in 1915–1916, unfolds on
a life raft lost at sea. Three fugitives from a shipwreck include a showgirl, an aristocrat,

and a West Indian seaman. The woman pleads with the sailor for water and offers herself to him, but he refuses. She passes away. The sailor starts to grind his knife, saying to the gentleman, "We shall eat. We shall drink." The startled gentleman shoves the woman's body overboard. Furious, the sailor thrusts his knife into the gentleman's heart. The two men fall off the raft into the shark-infested ocean.

In *The Long Voyage Home* (1917), the crew of the *Glencairn* relaxes in a tavern on the Thames River. One of the sailors, Olson the Swede, does not drink. He has been saving his paychecks, intending to return home and put down roots on a farm. But Olson is persuaded by a cunning couple into sipping a drugged beverage. He is looted, dragged out, and placed on a boat sailing to Africa.

O'Neill's *The Emperor Jones* (1920) unfolds on a West Indian island. It is the tale of an Afro-Caribbean train baggage carrier, Brutus Jones, who knifes a man over a game of dice and escapes jail to a distant island. There, Jones declares himself an almighty sovereign. His jurisdiction is crooked and unscrupulous, and the islanders revolt, killing him with a silver bullet.

The Emperor Jones was the first American play to star a Black actor in a principal part. A year earlier, in 1919, O'Neill's one-act *The Dreamy Kid* was produced by Off-Broadway's Provincetown Players with a whole African American cast. The kid of the title is an escaped convict who goes back home to see his dying mother, though he is aware that as a result he will be captured by the authorities.

Gold (1921) commences on "a small, barren coral island on the southern fringe of the Malay Archipelago." Castaway Captain Isaiah Bartlett and his men discover a crate overflowing with gold coins and jewels. To avoid sharing the treasure, the captain instructs a dagger-carrying native, Jimmy Kanaka, to stab the ship's chef and deckhand.

In 1931, O'Neill updated Aeschylus's *Oresteia*, dividing the ancient Greek trilogy into a three-part drama—"The Homecoming," "The Hunted," and "The Haunted"—calling it *Mourning Becomes Electra*. The action takes place in a New England seaport town after the U.S. Civil War. Like the cursed lineage of Atreus, the Mannon family is defiled

Kathleen Harris and George Voskovek in *Agamemnon*, Vivian Beaumont Theater, New York City, 1977 (photo by Friedman-Abeles, The New York Public Library for the Performing Arts).

by Oedipal love, bloodshed, and vindictiveness. Brigadier General Ezra Mannon (Agamemnon's counterpart) returns home from the front only to be poisoned by his wife, Christine (Clytemnestra), so she can be with her lover, Captain Adam Brant (Aegisthus). Ezra's children, son Orin (Orestes) and daughter Lavinia (Electra), now plan to avenge their father's murder.

*   *   *

Plays that were highlighted by eerie moments include Mae West's *Diamond Lil* (1928), a nasty affair of dope smuggling and white slavery that takes place in a Chinatown saloon in the 1890s, and Elmer Rice's *Street Scene* (1929), a hard-knuckled slice of tenement life on the West Side of New York.

Preceding the publication of Agatha Christie's classic novel *And Then There Were None*, crime writers Gwen Bristow and Bruce Manning hatched the plot device of sending telegraphed invitations, signed "your host," to a group of men and women,

Colleen Dewhurst (left) and Pamela Payton-Wright in *Mourning Becomes Electra*, **an updated Greek tragedy that features adultery, incestuous love, murder, and revenge, Circle in the Square (Uptown), 1972 (photo by Friedman-Abeles, The New York Public Library for the Performing Arts).**

asking them to a party that begins cheerfully and ends with bloodshed. Bristow and Manning's 1930 novel, *The Invisible Host*, was dramatized by Owen Davis later that year under the title *The Ninth Guest*. Eight strangers are gathered in a plush Manhattan penthouse. They soon discover that the exit door is connected to a highly charged electric current, and they are locked in. A radio announcement warns that The Ninth Guest will be death. One by one the guests are killed—by poison, a gunshot, or plunging against the electrified door. Critic Robert Littell stated in the *New York World* of August 26, 1930, "*The 9th Guest* has the highest death rate among its characters of any play since *Hamlet*.... The guests die off like flies in a frost."

Paul Dickey's *The Sob Sister* (1931) takes place in a San Francisco souvenir shop, which is the center of operation for Chinatown's organized crime. A gang leader hatches an ambush to kidnap a female reporter designated to probe the clash among the Tong factions, but she manages to outwit him by donning a clever disguise.

Elizabeth McFadden, in *Double Door* (1933), created a ruthless dowager who lures her daughter-in-law into a secret, hermetically sealed safe.

The Two Mrs. Carrolls (1935) by Martin Vale provided a suspenseful climax. While a storm is raging outside, the murderous Geoffrey Carroll snips the telephone wire and breaks into his wife Sally's bedroom through a porch window. As Sally stares at him in horror, Geoffrey lunges at her throat with the bell rope. Sally cries out and attempts to fight back. A lamp falls and breaks. The lights go out. Suddenly the honk of a car blares, and headlights hit the window. Geoffrey remains paralyzed. Sally is rescued by her friends at the eleventh hour.

The merry-and-murder play *Arsenic and Old Lace* (1941) by Joseph Kesselring was first presented on January 10, 1941, at the Fulton Theatre in New York City and became a

Boris Karloff as the blood-thirsty Jonathan Brewster in the madcap comedy *Arsenic and Old Lace*, Fulton Theatre, New York City, 1941 (photo by Vandamm Studio, The New York Public Library for the Performing Arts).

triumphant hit, running for 1,444 performances and moving to London for 1,336 more. Kesselring came up with the topic of the play when trying to think of the most bizarre thing his grandmother would do. Murder, he imagined, and concocted the yarn of two mild sisters, Abby and Martha Brewster, who decide to solve the predicaments of forlorn old men by mixing their elderberry wine with a nip of arsenic.

The Brewster family also includes Teddy, who imagines himself to be Theodore Roosevelt and is in the habit of blasting his bugle and stampeding up the stairs as if they were San Juan Hill; Mortimer, a drama critic who despises theater; and Jonathan, an escaped psychopath altered into a Boris Karloff clone by an intoxicated plastic surgeon. The deranged happenings include a dead body carried across a pitch-black stage, a tormenting scene with alarming surgical appliances, and the entrance of Dr. Einstein—not Albert, but Herman. The curtain call includes 13 actors representing the cadavers buried in the cellar.

Boris Karloff appeared as Jonathan Brewster, the nephew who "likes to cut worms in two—with his teeth," and goes into convulsions when someone utters that he resembles Boris Karloff. "Mr. Karloff is overpoweringly sinister in a performance that would, I should think, scare other actors out of their makeup," quipped critic John Anderson in the *New York Journal-American* of January 11, 1941.[30]

Renowned mystery writer Lucille Fletcher penned a half dozen thrilling radio programs, most famously *The Hitch-Hiker* (1941) written for Orson Welles, a dark story about a Brooklynite undertaking a road trip, and *Sorry, Wrong Number* (1943), with Agnes Moorehead playing a highly strung woman who overhears a murder plot on the telephone, attempts to call the police, and pays with her life. Barbara Stanwyck played the part in a 1948 screen rendition; Shelley Winters in a 1954 television broadcast of *Climax!*; and Loni Anderson in a 1989 production for cable TV. Both *The Hitch-Hiker* and *Sorry, Wrong Number* have been dramatized by Fletcher and published by Dramatists Play Service.

A shifty murderer locks a newly married couple in a soundproof film vault in *The Four of Hearts Mystery* (1949), dramatized by Audrey and William Roos from Ellery Queen's Hollywood novel. Seven years later, in 1956, the Rooses again focused the action of their play *Speaking of Murder* around a soundproof, fireproof, airproof vault. A jealous governess imprisons her mistress in it.

Frederick Knott scored big with *Dial "M" for Murder* (1952) in which a greedy husband commissions the murder of his wife. In a nerve-wracking scene, the wife plunges a pair of scissors in the back of her attacker. Maxwell Anderson's *Bad Seed* (1954) introduces Rhoda Penmark, a beautiful eight-year-old girl who is also a triple murderess. *Compulsion* (1957), by Meyer Levin, dramatized the 1924 cause célèbre case of Nathan Leopold, age 19, and Richard Loeb, age 18, over-indulged sons of wealthy Chicago families, who teamed up to kill a 14-year-old boy for amusement.

Shirley Jackson's *The Haunting of Hill House* (1959), a supernatural tale about a concealed past exposed in an isolated mansion, was brought to the stage in 1964 by F. Andrew Leslie. "The Lottery," Jackson's 1948 short story, describes the annual ritual among the inhabitants of a New England village to choose a faultless prey who will be stoned to death. It was adapted for the stage by Brainerd Duffield in 1953. Duffield also dramatized, in 1970, Jackson's "The Summer People" (1950), in which New York tourists face a threatening welcome in pastoral New England. *We Have Always Lived in the Castle* (1966), adapted by Hugh Wheeler from Jackson's 1962 novel, is the story of two sisters who live in a remote Vermont home, surrounded by the ghosts of their dead father, mother, and aunt, who died after arsenic powder was spread on their blackberries.

The topic of good versus evil is at the heart of several allegories produced on Broadway in the 1950s. Herman Melville's *Billy Budd* (1951), dramatized by Louis O. Coxe and Robert Chapman, unfolds aboard a British war ship during the Napoleonic wars. The title character, a handsome and guileless sailor, inadvertently kills a sadistic master of arms and is condemned to hang. Arthur Miller's *The Crucible* (1953) turns the 1692 Salem witch trials into an allegory about the 1940s–1950s House Un-American Activities Committee, which pursued and prosecuted supposed Communists. In the play, the Rev. John Proctor of Salem, Massachusetts falls prey to the machinations of his niece, 17-year-old Abigail Williams. Abigail is enamored with the reverend, but he remains faithful to his wife, Elizabeth. Abigail, in the guise of a witch hunter, causes the destruction of both Proctors. Among the chilling moments are the frenzied dances executed by a band of girls, all seemingly possessed as they hysterically howl the names of townspeople they saw "with the devil"; the person they mention is clapped in jail and destined to be executed.

Racial animosities explode ferociously in *Blues for Mr. Charlie* (1964) by James Baldwin and *Dutchman* (1964) by LeRoi Jones.

The Spiral Staircase (1962), dramatized by F. Andrew Leslie from the 1933 novel *Some Must Watch* by Ethel Lina White, takes place in a shadowy residence during a gray winter day. A serial killer has been murdering girls afflicted with imperfections, and his next victim may be the deaf, live-in maid. In *The Playroom* (1965) by Mary

Arthur Kennedy (in the torn white shirt) as the persecuted Reverend John Proctor, surrounded by the villagers of Salem, Massachusetts, in *The Crucible*. Across the stage stands Beatrice Straight (holding a cane), in the role of his concerned wife, Elizabeth Proctor (Martin Beck Theatre, New York City, 1953).

Drayton, a ten-year-old girl is kidnapped by a group of pampered, vicious youngsters who plan to do away with her via an overdose of sleeping pills. Frederick Knott's *Wait Until Dark* (1966) depicts a terrifying cat-and-mouse encoun-
ter between a blind woman and
three ruthless gangsters in a
Greenwich Village cellar.

Child's Play (1970) by Robert Marasco is an enigmatic
play unfolding at the St. Charles
School for boys. Pupils hurt in
the chemistry lab, a free-for-all
in the dormitory, and an esca-
lating number of students
harmed between classes point
to the fact that many of the students have become unruly. The
upheaval mushrooms into fre-
netic malevolence, but the final
curtain descends without ever
explaining the esoteric puzzle at St. Charles. Ira Levin's
Veronica's Room (1973) features
a middle-aged couple, John and
Maureen Mackey, who bring a
young girl, Susan, to their suburban Boston home and treat
her as if she were their daughter
Veronica, who was murdered
40 years earlier. When Susan
stands by her identity, the
Mackeys lock her in Veronica's preserved room. Ultimately
broken, Susan acknowledges
that she is Veronica and confesses to Veronica's misdeeds,
including an incestuous rela-

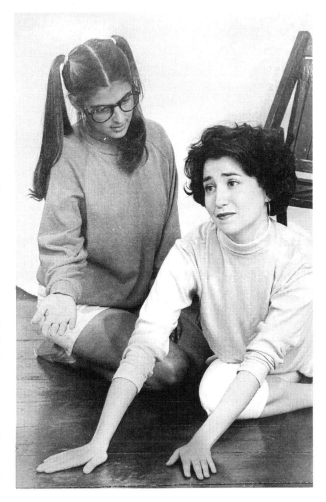

Little Gloria (Adi Kaye) comes to the rescue of blind Suzy Hendrix (Laura Stanczyk), who is menaced by hoo-
ligans in *Wait Until Dark* (New London Barn Playhouse, New London, New Hampshire, 1988).

tionship with her younger brother. The parents then kill Susan. It is revealed that this is not the first time that they have carried out such a murder, nor will it be the last.

Charles Ludlam's satire *The Mystery of Irma Vep* (1984) blends elements of the 1915 silent serial *Les Vampires* with fragments from *The Mummy* and *The Wolf Man*, while John Bishop's *The Musical Comedy Murders of 1940* (1987) is a bloodcurdling spoof that borrows from *The Cat and the Canary* and *The Mousetrap*.

In the 1980s, American playwright Tim Kelly dramatized two novels by the pop-
ular British writer Edgar Wallace: 1923's *The Green Archer* and 1926's *The Black Abbot*. Both adaptations get us back to the period of Gothic sensationalism; each is set in the 1920s in a medieval dwelling complete with underground cells, hidden corridors, and

wobbly stairways. Ghostly specters wander in dark galleries while a storm rages outside. In each play, the title character is revealed in the denouement as a masquerading murderer.

Some young, up-and-coming playwrights dabbled in graphic violence early in their careers. David Rabe became known for a trilogy of anti-war dramas, the last of which is 1976's *Streamers*. Taking place in a military camp in Virginia, the climax of *Streamers* is devastatingly bloody. Among Sam Shepard's 40-some plays is the Pulitzer Prize-winning *Buried Child* (1978), a drama centered on a maladjusted rural family with a terrible secret. In John Pielmeier's *Agnes of*

Ira Levin, author of *Veronica's Room* (1973), most famous for his horror novel *Rosemary's Baby*, 1967 (photo by Martha Swope, 1979; The New York Public Library for the Performing Arts).

Arthur Kennedy and Eileen Heckart as the villains of *Veronica's Room*, Music Box Theatre, New York City, 1973 (photo by Martha Swope, The New York Public Library for the Performing Arts).

Playwright William Mastrosimone and actress Farrah Fawcett in a publicity shot from the violent off-Broadway play *Extremities*, 1983 (photo by Martha Swope, The New York Public Library for the Performing Arts).

Tennessee Williams, 1911–1883, whose *Not About Nightingales* (written 1938, first produced 1998) is not for the squeamish (photo by Friedman-Abeles, n.d.; The New York Public Library for the Performing Arts).

God (1980), a psychiatrist examines the mental health of a young nun suspected of garroting her own baby. William Mastrosimone tackles the issue of sexual abuse in his tense, untamed *Extremities* (1980) and investigates teen turbulence in *Like Totally Weird* (1998), wherein Hollywood juveniles, inspired by violent movies, run amuck. Mastrosimone's *Bang Bang You're Dead* (1999), inspired by an actual case, is the story of a high school student who kills his parents and five classmates. Tracy Letts' *Killer Joe* (1993) is a taut drama about a dysfunctional provincial family and a murderer-for-hire. Romulus Linney's *True Crimes* (1995) paints a family seeped in greed, revenge, and murder in the Appalachian Mountains.

Tennessee Williams wrote *Not About Nightingales* in 1938, but the play, about a sadistic prison warden and the ill-fated inmates of Hall C, didn't make it to Broadway until 1998. The climax, taking place in a cell where the temperature reaches more than 125 degrees, is not for the squeamish.

Bram Stoker's Count reappeared in *Dracula* (1980), adapted by John Mattera, while Mary Shelley's *Frankenstein* was revamped by Victor Gialanella the following year. Both playwrights inserted a few touches of their own. Paranormal terror also prevails in Jack Sharkey's 1980 treatment of Oscar Wilde's *The Picture of Dorian Gray*, and Jeffrey Hatcher's 1996 adaptation of Henry James's novella *The Turn of the Screw*.

English Theater

In England, the protagonist of John Masefield's *The Tragedy of Nan* (1908) is Nan Hardwick, whose father, though innocent, was executed for poaching sheep. From that day on, Nan is enslaved by her uncle's shrewish wife and plain-looking daughter, Jenny. The two of them waste no time telling Richard Gurvil, Nan's beau, that Nan is a thief's daughter and penniless, while Jenny is guaranteed a bountiful endowment. Dick and Jenny become engaged, and Nan, outraged, gores Dick to death with a kitchen knife, then bolts out to dive into the river.

The stark action of *The Witch* (1910), modified by John Masefield from a Norwegian play, takes place in Bergen in the 16th century, when there was widespread belief in sorcerers, witches, and Satan. The lead character is Anne Pedersdotter, the 22-year-old second wife of Absolon Beyer, an elderly Lutheran minister. After five years of a loveless marriage, Anne challenges Absolon, blaming him for ruining her adolescence and relating that she has given herself to his son. Absolon clasps his heart and dies. Anne is taken to court for killing her husband by witchcraft. At first, she claims that she is blameless, but when the bishop decrees that she can verify her purity by laying a hand on Absolon's body, she kneels next to the corpse and declares, "Yes, I murdered you by witchcraft and I bewitched your son."

In John Galsworthy's *Justice* (1910), William Falder, a clerk in a solicitors' firm, is mistakenly accused of embezzlement and is sent to prison for three years. In a disturbing scene, Falder is shown confined in a narrow cell. Suddenly, a metallic banging is heard, initiated by his neighboring prisoners, growing stronger and stronger, reverberating to a crescendo. Shaking all over, he throws himself against the steel bars. When Winston Churchill, home secretary at the time, saw John Galsworthy's *Justice*, he was touched by the moment and lowered the length of solitary confinement in England's prisons from nine months to four weeks.

The Ghost Train (1925) by Arnold Ridley depicts dirty work in a haunted railway station. Ridley wrote a second railroad melodrama, *The Wrecker* (1927), the yarn of an unknown culprit who instigates a succession of train collisions that cause the death of many innocent commuters. At the climax, the wrecker, his identity revealed, jumps to his demise under an approaching locomotive.

Born in New Zealand in 1884 but raised in England, Hugh Walpole was tormented by nightmares his entire life. Walpole's bad dreams may have been the origin of his grisly works. None is more grotesque than *Portrait of a Man with Red Hair*, introducing a character with a deeply sadistic nature. Englishman Benn W. Levy adapted the

Nobel Prize–winner John Galsworthy, England, 1867–1933, whose harrowing prison scene in the drama *Justice* (1910) triggered a change in the British justice system (artist: William Strang, 1912; Fine Arts Museums of San Francisco).

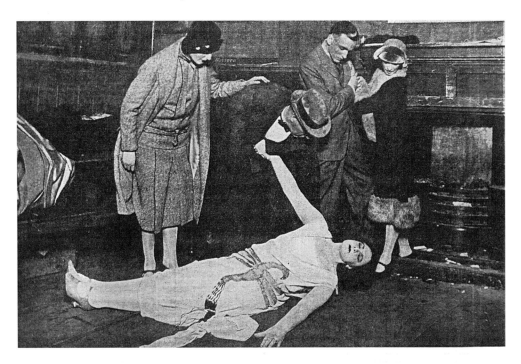

A scene from the nightmarish *The Ghost Train*, 1925. The play ran for more than a year in its original sold-out London theatrical run and is regarded as a minor classic.

novel in 1928 under the title *A Man with Red Hair*. The action unfolds in the living room of a vintage house outside Trellis in Cornwall, England, set on the edge of a cliff. The landlord is Mr. Crispin, a former surgeon, described as "fat, with powdered face and painted lips, and pudgy, soft white hands, and red hair." He believes that to comprehend survival, one must endure physical suffering; only through pain can one achieve ecstasy and dominance. With the help of three Japanese henchmen, Crispin imprisons the attractive Hester Tobin, her boyfriend David Dunbar, and an American art collector, Charles Perry Harkness. After experiencing a series of abuses and torture, including rape and whippings,

Born in poverty, Edgar Wallace, England, 1875–1932, became an internationally recognized author of macabre thrillers. His daughter, Penelope Wallace, 1923–1997, sent this undated photograph to the author in the early 1990s.

Dunbar manages to free himself and attacks Crispin. Both men plunge through a window, dropping to the cliffs below.

In addition to *A Man with Red Hair*, two other dark-edged works by Hugh Walpole were brought to the stage. *The Old Ladies* (1924), the tale of Agatha Payne, a dominant, hostile woman who exploits her neighbors, was adapted by Rodney Ackland in 1935. That same year, playwright Edward Chodorov adapted Walpole's most successful short story, "The Silver Mask," into the three-act *Kind Lady*, about a wealthy widow, Mary Herries, who is imprisoned in her London home by a band of brazen thieves who strip the house of rare paintings.

During the 1920s and early 1930s, Edgar Wallace (1875–1932) was the top-selling author in England. A fertile writer of more than 175 novels and multitude of short stories in the cloak-and-dagger genre, Wallace was the forefather of stage thrillers.

An early 1904 effort, *The African Millionaire*, was a typical melodrama of the era, filled with declamatory language, monologues addressed directly to the spectators, sweeping comedy, and one-dimensional characters: a heroine in constant life-and-death danger, a herculean hero, and a mustached villain. The action included homicides, face-to-face clashes in an underground tunnel, and the final blessing of a happy wedding.

After a number of failed attempts, Wallace's first theatrical success was his stage adaptation of his 1925 novel, *The Gaunt Stranger*, titled *The Ringer*. It is the saga of an avenger who kills evildoers who manage to outwit the authorities. *The Ringer* opened in the West End in 1926 and ran for 408 performances.

Wallace then continued to write plays with fluctuating levels of success. According to biographer Margaret Lane, *The Terror* (1927), adapted from his 1926 novel *The Black*

Abbot, included such familiar melodramatic ingredients as "the old mysterious house built over hidden dungeons, the master criminal disguised as the mildest character in the play, the super-detective masquerading as a drunken ne'er-do-well, the hidden treasure in the vault, hooded figure appearing on the moonlit nights and leaving a trail of murders in its wake."[31] *The Yellow Mask* (1928), book by Wallace, music by Vernon Duke, relates the theft of the crown jewels from the Tower of London by a foreigner and his escape by yacht with an abducted girl. The hero, her fiancé, arrives to save her aboard a plane. *The Man Who Changed His Name* (1928) is the tale of Nita Clive who finds out that her husband, an affluent entrepreneur, may be an infamous Canadian jail-breaker who assassinated his first wife, her mother, and her lover.

The Squeaker (1928) features two shadowy characters, one of which is the head of a violent racket organization, while the other is the Scotland Yard Inspector pursuing him. The proceedings of *The Flying Squad* (1928) unfold in a dark lair on the bank of the Thames, the headquarters of a thriving cocaine gang. *Persons Unknown* (1929) focuses on a reporter's pursuit of a thug who fatally slashed a "person unknown" on a crowded road.

Wallace's next successful play was *On the Spot* (1930), with Charles Laughton portraying Tony Perelli, an Al Capone alter-ego; Emlyn Williams, his cold-blooded bodyguard; and Gillian Lind his Chinese mistress. Fascinated with Sing Sing during an American tour and awed by its death chamber and electric chair, Wallace penned *Smoky Cell* (1930), delineating a collision between a police chief and a hazardous prisoner.

The Mouthpiece (1930) was flawed by a thin plot about an heiress ignorant of the riches soon to be granted to her and a band of fortune hunters plotting to marry her to one of their own. The actions of *The Old Man* (1931) unfold at the Coats of Arms Inn. A bearded old man cowers in the shadows, spying from corners. Rumor has it that the strange character is a fugitive from a nearby mental institution.

In *The Case of the Frightened Lady* (1931), the dignified Lord Lebanon pays a visit to Scotland Yard's headquarters to gripe about his tyrannical mother and the duo of armed henchmen she engaged to keep him under observation. After two murders—of Lebanon's driver and his doctor—an astonishing reversal divulges that in lieu of the autocratic mother, Lebanon himself, completely deranged, is the villain. The protagonists of *The Green Pack* (1932) are three gold prospectors who "have gone where the foot of a white man has never tread" before excavating a lavish mine in Angola, West Africa. They are betrayed by their English sponsor. When the man is found gunned down with his own revolver, the question arises: who among the miners shot their double-crosser?

Tenacious, Wallace also produced a show in London, brought from America. *Brothers* (1929), by Herbert Ashton, Jr., is a gritty thriller of the New York underworld. He wrote a number of screenplays, including 1931's *The Hound of the Baskervilles*.

In Hollywood, Wallace devised the plot of a horror film about ancient monsters and submitted a 110-page first draft of *King Kong*, but his effort was cut short when he passed away of double pneumonia on February 10, 1932, before the shooting of *King Kong* got underway.

End and Beginning (1933) by John Masefield describes a brutal execution of Mary Stuart, Queen of Scotland: "As one hangman gripped her hands, John Bull struck clumsily, and held the head aloft."

Night Must Fall (1935) by Emlyn Williams is an often-revived play about a baby-faced serial killer who carries a hatbox containing the gruesome relic of a horrible crime.

The Devil aka *The Devil Passes* (1930), by Benn Wolfe Levy, features Mephistopheles in the guise of a parson recruiting knaves and infidels. Levy's *Madame Conti* (1936) focuses on a prostitute who falls deeply in love with one of her clients, realizes that he plans to live off her earnings, and murders him. Levy's *The Tumbler* (1960) is a modernization of *Hamlet*. A farm girl has a liaison with a stableboy, learns that he married her widowed mother, and suspects that they killed her father. "Aeschylus, Euripides and Sophocles never had anything grimmer to deal with than Levy's tale of unintentional incest and equivocal death on a farm in England today," wrote Brooks Atkinson in the *New York Times* on February 25, 1960.[32]

In *Ladies in Retirement* (1940) by Edward Percy and Reginald Denham, the sixty-year-old Leonora Fiske, owner of a farmhouse next to the Thames River, allows her housekeeper, Ellen Creed, to invite her two senile sisters for the upcoming holiday. When the sisters outstay their welcome and Fiske orders them out, Creed throttles her with a coil and boards up the corpse in a brick fireplace.

Is it possible to bring a loved-one back from the dead? In Emlyn Williams's *Trespass* (1947), Countess Christine Henting certainly believes so and has already engaged various mediums in unsuccessful attempts to restore her recently dead second husband, Philip, to life. To the chagrin of her daughter, Gwan, Christine has now invited Saviello, an Italian medium, to fulfill the ghostly task. The ensuing séance, taking place at an eerie castle in a remote part of Wales, produces a frightening moment. Suddenly, in the half light, on the bottom step of the staircase, stands the slim figure of a man in black tails. "Philip," whispers Christine. Gwan switches on the lights, and all gasp in shock as they see a lifelike dummy of Philip. Despite the hoax, the play ends with unexpected results.

The homicidal Ellen Creed (Camille Mazurek) watches her fragile sisters, Emily (Carol Lambert, sitting at the table) and Louisa (Hanna Hayes), in *Ladies in Retirement*, Pulse Ensemble Theatre, New York City, 2010. A corpse is concealed in the upstage brick fireplace.

In James Hadley Chase's *No Orchids for Miss Blandish* (1978), a Kansas City heiress is kidnapped by ruthless gangsters and goes through a harrowing ordeal of rape and torture.

*   *   *

Stephen King said, "Clive Barker is so good that I am literally tongue-tied."[33] Barker's (1952–) main contributions to the horror genre on stage include *The History of the Devil* (1980) and *Frankenstein in Love, or The Life of Death* (1982). *The History of the Devil* was written for The Dog Company, a theater troupe he co-founded with friends in London. The plot centers on Lucifer denying involvement in the horrors of mankind and petitioning readmission into heaven. The play unfolds in the form of a courtroom drama set in Kenya. The prosecution contends that the Devil has had a disturbing influence on humankind; the defense maintains that the world's wickedness is solely humanity's fault. In the beginning of the proceedings, the devil is covered with blood, his mind hazy, and he unwittingly strangles his own daughter. As the trial progresses, however, he proves to have irresistible charm and a sense of humor. At the end he wins the case and strides to heaven.

Frankenstein in Love, or The Life of Death, is subtitled "*A Grand Guignol Romance.*" The unnerving tone of the proceedings registers immediately when the curtain rises on a set decorated with banners illustrating violent scenes from history and fiction. Loops of colored lights hang over the stage, mingled with bloody chains and butcher hooks. The head of a man impaled on a pole is seen upstage. Scattered about are surgical saws, drills, scalpels, hypodermics, and bloody sheets. It is the first horrific image to be followed by a succession of brutal murders, most taking place in a vault beneath the presidential palace that serves as the operating room of Dr. Joseph Frankenstein. "It's like a crazy-house in there, bodies on the floor, bodies in the sink. Two minutes and they're black with flies, another two and their eyes pop, maggots everywhere."

The action unfolds in a fictional Latin American country on the eve of a revolution. Explosions, gunfire, and screams can be heard nearby. We are told that it is the last night of the world, to expect an apocalypse. Because of a plague, "little coups and counter-coups are just lying in the streets." Almost the entire gallery of characters—human and robotic—ends up dying in gruesome treatment, some not once but twice: President Garcia Perez (stabbed by a knife); Cockatoo, a revolutionist (by a poisonous hypodermic injection); Cesar Guerrera, nicknamed El Coco, leader of the rebels (his skin stripped from head to foot); Maria Duran, a fan-dancer and palm reader (strangled); Cardinal Armitano (devoured by cannibals); Dr. Fook, a laboratory supervisor who always wears a bloody green apron and bloody gloves (strangled); Veronique Flocker, who has been a prisoner of Dr. Frankenstein for a year, the subject of rapes and experiments (buried alive under a heap of human debris); and Doctor Joseph Frankenstein, known as "The Angel of Auschwitz" (his heart dragged out by the clawed hand of an avenger and flung to the floor).[34]

Stephen Mallatratt's 1987 rendering of Susan Hill's novel *The Woman in Black* preserved the supernatural chills of the original and became a phenomenal success. Eleven years later, Phyllis Nagy's 1998 adaptation of *The Talented Mr. Ripley* faithfully follows Patricia Highsmith's novel, introducing Tom Ripley, one of the shiftyest scoundrels in modern literature. *The Collector* (1998), John Fowles's depiction of a schizophrenic who abducts a young girl, was adapted by Mark Healy with the action unfolding entirely in an isolated cellar, where a wrenching battle of wits develops between kidnapper and victim.

Irish Theater

The Gods of the Mountain (1911), by Edward John Moreton Drax Plunkett, Lord Dunsany (1878–1957), tells the fantasy story of seven vagabonds who wander to the city of Kongros, where they enter the Metropolitan Hall and seat themselves upon the floor in the pose of the seven gods of Marma. Their spokesman, Agmar, announces that a pestilence may fall upon this city as well as an earthquake. The city elders, frightened, "hasten to bring the 'gods' sacrificial lambs, orchard fruits, and Woldery wine."

Time goes by. Seven thrones have been built for the "gods," on which the beggars are sprawling comfortably, ridiculing the naive citizens. Unexpectedly, the sound of a heavy tread is heard, and amid flashes of ghostly lightning, a procession of seven huge stone gods enters in a single file: "Hands and faces are green; they wear greenstone sandals; they walk with knees extremely wide apart, as having sat cross-legged for centuries; they stoop grotesquely."

The primary god addresses the beggars, and, as he does, each beggar, panic-stricken, retreats to his throne. The beggars turn to stone as the gods walk out. Most theater critics

A scene from *The Queen's Enemies* by Lord Dunsany, with Alice Lewisohn as a vengeful, murderous Egyptian queen (here facing her foes), produced at the Neighborhood Playhouse, New York City, 1916 (The New York Public Library of the Performing Arts).

in London and New York found "poetic beauty" in the play and a climax that makes one feel "the presence of doom," but some believed that bringing the gods on stage was a mistake as one can imagine much-more-terrifying things than one can show, and when the gods entered, it was evident they were only actors in makeup, not gods at all.

In Dunsany's one-act *A Night at an Inn* (1912), four British Merchant Marines steal the ruby eye of an Indian icon and escape from country to country chased by the Priests of Klesh. The fearful sailors have taken cover in a forsaken tavern off the shoreline of East England. Three white-robed figures shuffle in, daggers in hand. The sailors leap forward and stab the intruders. The men are relieved. They intend to hide the bodies in the basement, depart at dawn for London, and sell the ruby. "We're millionaires now," they chuckle, when a bizarre jade figure enters, blindly gropes his way to the table, picks up the ruby, and screws it into a socket in his forehead. They all cower in horror at the idol. A voice with an outlandish accent is heard offstage, calling them by name to step outside. As if hypnotized, each of the men walks out, and moans are heard.

Dunsany's one-act *The Queen's Enemies* (1913) takes place in a subterranean temple on the bank osf the Nile. The Queen of Egypt and her maids put together a feast for eight perpetual foes from Ethiopia. The visitors, apprehensive, go down the stairs with swords drawn. They take their places around the table and order their lackeys to sample the wine and food. Soon the tension dissipates, and all make merry. The queen excuses herself, saying that she is going momentarily to honor "a very secret god." Abruptly, the torches blow out, and a stream of water floods the temple's basement. Death splashes are heard in the shadows. The queen, on the staircase, tells her maid, "Tonight I shall sleep sweetly."

Conor McPherson's (1971–) best-known play, *The Weir* (1997), takes place in a rural Irish pub, where four high-spirited men and an attractive woman, Valerie, tell stories with a supernatural slant, haunting yarns steeped in Irish folklore. Jake Mullon, a mechanic, relates that the house Valerie bought used to belong to Maura Nealon, a grand lady who, as a child, kept hearing knocks on the doors although nobody was ever there. Finbar Mack, a local businessman, recounts the story of the Walsh family who used to live nearby. A young daughter became hysterical one evening, saying that a woman was staring at her from the top of the stairs. No one else could see her, but the girl insisted. Finbar, a neighbor, came over to offer help and saw "the young one" lying down in the living room, covered with a blanket, and white as a sheet. When he returned home, continues Finbar, he was sitting at the fire having a last nip before hitting the sack. He had his back to the stairs and couldn't turn around because of a feeling that there was something on the stairs. He just sat there looking at an empty fireplace until the sun came up.

Jim Curran, a mechanic's assistant, remembers that 20 or more years ago he and his co-worker Declan Donnelly went to work digging a grave in the yard of a local cemetery. They saw a hearse arriving and the body of a covered man removed to the adjacent church. Declan went off to get a tarp to stretch over the grave, and he remained there by himself, says Jim. This was when he saw a man coming out of the church, walking through the gravestones. "That's the wrong grave," he says. "Come on, I'll show you.'" Jim tells that he followed the man just to get it over with, and they stopped at a grave, "a white one with the picture of a little girl on it." The man touched the gravestone and went back to the church. Jim continues his tale, relating that after a few days, he read the obituary column in the newspaper and noticed the picture of the man whose grave he had dug. At first, he thought that the man was a relative of the deceased, but Declan told him that the man whose grave they had dug had the reputation of being a pedophile. He shockingly realized, says Jim, that it was the man he had met and that he'd wanted to go in the grave… with the little girl.

Valerie plunges into her tale. She and her husband Daniel had a happy life, both working, but their bright, outgoing daughter Niamh, who started school at the age of five, had a problem sleeping at night. She was afraid of the dark, and she'd often come to sleep with them, saying that she saw people at the window, people in the attic, children knocking in the wall, and someone coming up the stairs. And there was always a man standing across the road.

In March of the previous year, continues Valerie, the school had a sponsored swim. Niamh hit her head in the pool and died. Then one morning, as Valerie lay in bed trying to sleep, the phone rang. "The line was very faint," relates Valerie. "I heard Niamh. She said, 'Mammy.' And I… just said 'yes.' And she said she was scared. There were children knocking in the walls and the man was standing across the road. Would I come and get her?"

Jack asks if it could have been a dream. Valerie answers curtly, "I heard her." Finbar suggests that she was in shock, but Valerie maintains, "It's something that happened…. I know I'm not crazy."[35]

McPherson's *Shining City* (2004) is a ghost story which recounts the visits of widower John to his therapist. John's wife died in a horrific car accident. He feels guilty for having become obsessed with a beauty called Vivien and claims to have seen his dead wife roaming his house.

The Seafarer (2006) is a Faustian play set on Christmas Eve in Baldoyle, a coastal suburb north of Dublin. The protagonist is James "Sharky" Harkin, an alcoholic who has recently been fired from his job as a chauffeur. A poker game among four men, ostensibly a harmless diversion, is in fact a game for the soul of Harkin, as the mysterious Mr. Lockhart gradually reveals himself to be a Mephistophelian figure.

In 2009, McPherson adapted Daphne du Maurier's 1952 horror story "The Birds" for the stage. The tale is set in a Cornish seaside town, where a farmhand, his family, and his community are attacked by flocks of vicious birds. *The Birds* was the inspiration for several radio and television series and for Alfred Hitchcock's 1963 movie of the same name. In McPherson's adaptation, colonies of birds begin a mass invasion, instigating Nat and Diane to escape into a deserted beach house. They make every effort to survive, hampered by meager resources. The unexpected entrance of a young, odd woman spoils the tranquility and imperils any potential to preserve their safety.

Spanish Theater

Jacinto Benavente's (1866–1954) *La Malquerida* (1913), translated into English as *The Passion Flower*, takes place in a small Spanish town. Raimunda, who was widowed at a very young age, learns that her second husband, Esteban, is enamored with her daughter, Acasia, and sent an underling to kill Acasia's fiancé. Raimunda then faces another shocking revelation when Acasia confesses that Esteban is "the only man I ever loved." Overcome, Raimunda calls for her neighbors to "come quick" and detain her husband—"The murderer! The murderer!" Esteban aims his rifle and fires. Acasia rushes to Raimunda, whose last words are, "This man cannot harm you now. You are saved."

Czech Theater

In Karel Čapek's (1890–1938) *R.U.R* (1921), the entire population of the universe is killed by Robots, artificial people created by an industrial plant called Rossum's Universal Robots. The Robots, having been marketed around the globe as low-cost employees, take possession of firearms, telegraphs, radio stations, railways, and ships. The last scene unfolds in the central office of the company on a remote island. Robots enter with daggers and guns, brutally killing the occupants. Their leader mounts the balcony railing

Nance O'Neil, playing the lead role of Raimunda, runs an emotional gamut in *The Passion Flower* (Greenwich Village Theatre, New York City, 1920).

A scene from Karel Čapek's *R.U.R.*, in which robots kill all humans, set designed by Lee Simonson, a Theatre Guild tour company, 1928–1929 (photo by Vandamm Studio, The New York Public Library of the Performing Arts).

and proclaims, "Robots of the world! The power of man has fallen! A new world has arisen, the rule of the robots! March!" The heavy footsteps of thousands of feet are heard as the unseen Robots tread in unity. *R.U.R.* is the Czech playwright's warning against the human obsession with advanced technology.[36]

Swiss Theater

Friedrich Dürrenmatt's (1921–1990) first success as a playwright came with *Die Ehe des Herrn Mississippi* (*The Marriage of Mr. Mississippi*, 1952), a dark pastiche in which a public prosecutor kills his wife and weds a woman who killed her first husband. The two are then appointed to take charge of the state's capital punishments. The drama

The climax of Friedrich Dürrenmatt's play *The Visit* depicts the lynching of Anton Schill (Alfred Lunt) by greedy townspeople, Morosco Theatre, New York City, 1958 (photo by Vandamm Studio, Billy Rose Theatre Division, The New York Public Library for the Performing Arts).

Der Besuch der alten Dame (*The Visit by the Old Woman*, 1956) introduces the wealthiest woman in the world, who comes back to the penniless Central European town of her early life to take revenge on the man who ravaged her when she was 17, impregnated her, then stranded her and ran her out of town. She will contribute 1,000,000 marks to the region only if the villagers will kill her seducer. In *Abendstunde im Spatherbst* (translated as *One Autumn Evening* and as *Incident at Twilight*, 1959), a private investigator verifies that the author of 22 detective novels hinged his storylines on real-life homicides that he had perpetrated. *Die Physiker* (*The Physicists*, 1962) is a thriller set in an insane asylum. A series of murders and cold war cloak-and-dagger plots are used by the dramatist to warn the world of a calamity in an era of advance technological discoveries. *Der Meteor* (*The Meteor*, 1966) is the story of a best-selling author who is pronounced medically dead but is restored to life. The author yearns to die like people everywhere, but to his horror, he learns that his wish to die will never be granted.

The era's spine-tingling plays include *The Deadly Game* (1960), adapted by James Yaffe from a radio play by Friedrich Dürrenmatt. It takes place in a remote Alpine manor, where three former men of law—a judge, a prosecutor, and a defense attorney—play legal skits with lost tourists. A fourth gentleman, who lingers in the background, has served as a government hangman.

Miscellaneous

Other mainstream playwrights who dabbled in theft, kidnapping, and murder, coloring the plots with terrifying elements, were Sidney Howard, Guy Bolton, Paul Green, Elmer Rice, Philip Barry, George S. Kaufman, Robert E. Sherwood, Maxwell Anderson, Sidney Kingsley, Irwin Shaw, and Lillian Hellman—the Who's Who of the era's American theater. In England, W. Somerset Maugham, A.A. Milne, John Galsworthy, Emlyn Williams, J.B. Priestley, Daphne du Maurier, and Terence Rattigan wrote plays of crime mingled with horrific touches. Betrayal, violence, and nail-biting scenes are key elements in the plays of the Hungarian Laszlo Fodor, the German Ernst Toller, the Spanish Federico Garcia Lorca, the Italian Ugo Betti, and the French Jean Genet. Nobel Prize-winners who wrote alarming plays include Eugene O'Neill, John Steinbeck, Ernest Hemingway, Albert Camus, and Jean-Paul Sartre.

The 20th century was splashed with nervy adaptations of Émile Zola's *Thérèse Raquin*, Fyodor Dostoevsky's *Crime and Punishment*, Theodore Dreiser's *An American Tragedy*, and H.G. Wells' *The Invisible Man*. Wilkie Collins' *The Moonstone* glittered on stage and kept spectators glued to their seats.

Several Gothic best-sellers from the Victorian era were adapted anew to the stage in the latter part of the century: *East Lynne*, based on the novel by Mrs. Henry Wood; *Jane Eyre*, influenced by Charlotte Brontë's famous work; and *Lady Audley's Secret*, from the story by Mary Elizabeth Braddon.

The last quarter of the 20th century boasted a series of plush, big-budget musicals sprinkled with chilling moments. *The Rocky Horror Picture Show* (1973) is a musical spoof of the science fiction and horror B movies of the 1930s-1960s. *The Mummy's Tomb* (1978) presents cliffhangers, physical altercations, and murders by strangulation. It liberally breaks the fourth wall, with the pianist of the show's band often mounting the stage and partaking in the action. *Sweeney Todd, the Demon Barber of Fleet Street* (1979) focuses on a barber who slits the necks of his clientele and pitches the corpses down a shaft to a meat-pie

A scene from the musical thriller *Lady Audley's Secret,* Off-Broadway's Eastside Playhouse, 1972 (photo by Friedman-Abeles, The New York Public Library for the Performing Arts).

Actors Howard McGillin (rear center) and Cleo Laine (right stage) with cast in an "opium den" scene from the New York Shakespeare Festival's production of the musical *The Mystery of Edwin Drood*, 1985 (photo by Martha Swope, The New York Public Library for the Performing Arts).

Victor Garber (left, as John Wilkes Booth) and Terrence Mann (as Leon Czolgosz) in a scene from the Playwrights Horizons' production of the musical *Assassins,* 1991, New York (photo by Martha Swope, The New York Public Library for the Performing Arts).

cook with whom he collaborates. *Little Shop of Horrors* (1982) is the story of a bloodthirsty plant that multiplies and initiates the conquest of the world. *The Mystery of Edwin Drood* (1985) proposes clues to the riddle embedded in Charles Dickens's final and incomplete novel: is young Edwin Drood dead, and if so, who killed him? *Sherlock Holmes—The Musical* aka *The Revenge of Sherlock Holmes* (1988) provides new angles to the canon of the Great Detective, particularly the arrival of young Bella Spellgrove, who is revealed as Professor Moriarty's vengeful daughter. In *The Phantom of the Opera* (1986) Erik, the murderous musician who resides in the catacombs under the Paris Opera House, menacingly tosses its chandelier toward the stage; *Phantom* is the most successful production ever presented on Broadway. *City of Angels* (1989) follows in the footsteps of Dashiell Hammett, Raymond Chandler, and Ross Macdonald in a parody about a scriptwriter and his character, a hard-boiled amateur detective. In *Jekyll & Hyde* (1990), graphic murders are depicted between songs and dances. *Assassins* (1990) sings the story of seven men and two women who have killed or attempted to kill the president of the United States. The lead character of *Zombie Prom* (1993) has returned from the dead and finds himself shunned by his fellow high-school students. *Dance of the Vampires* (1997) focuses on Professor Abronsius and Alfred, his bumbling sidekick, as they arrive in a small town somewhere in the Carpathians to investigate whether vampires exist. A huge hit in Germany and Austria, when mounted at New York's Minskoff Theatre in 2002 to the tune of $12,000,000, the show became one of the costliest flops in Broadway history.

Twenty-First Century

Several high-budgeted musicals that opened on Broadway during the first two decades of the 21st century with fanfare and high hopes ended up failures, both artistically and commercially. *The Woman in White*, a 2004 musical adaptation by Andrew Lloyd Webber of Wilkie Collins' 1859–60 novel, presents one of the most famous literary villains of Victorian literature, Count Fosco, as he hatches a nefarious plan to steal the estate of heiress Laura Fairlie.

Lestat (2006), with music by Elton John, is based on Anne Rice's popular series, *The Vampire Chronicles*. It tells the story of a young plantation owner in New Orleans who falls under the spell of the seductive vampire Lestat de Lioncourt and accepts his offer of immortality.

King Kong (2018), a musical that originated in Melbourne, Australia, was inspired by the classic 1933 film about a movie crew shooting a film on a tropical island and the snatching of its blond star, Ann Dvorak, by an enormous ape.

Night of the Living Dead, George A. Romero's milestone 1968 movie, was adapted for the stage by Group Rep at The Lonny Chapman Theatre, North Hollywood, California, October 4–November 10, 2019. Adapter Gus Krieger preserved the original time frame of autumn 1968, but added a few new touches, some questionable. The action takes place in an abandoned farmhouse located near a cemetery outside of Pittsburgh, Pennsylvania. Seven strangers hope to escape the flesh-eating zombies ravaging the countryside. A program note sums up the proceedings: "Beset by the walking dead outside, and ever-rising interpersonal tensions within, the group begins their desperate attempt to survive the night...."

The production, directed by Drina Durazo, incorporates video segments in which announcers describe the deteriorating situation on the East Coast. The zombies make their initial entrance from the back of the auditorium. However, the clever notion to scare the members of the audience as potential victims is not followed through and fizzles out. The reviewer of *Hollywood Gothique* felt that "this adaptation runs into the same hurdles that slowed down previous theatrical versions," but pointed out that this effort provides "a few new wrinkles to the withered walking corpse."[37]

Zombie's Joe Underground Theatre Group was established in August of 1992 in a garage in Northridge, California. It continues to push the limits of live theater in its present location in North Hollywood. Zombie Joe was born in June 1971 in Santa Monica, California, and prefers to keep his birth name a secret. He explained that his venture follows the dictates of Antonin Artaud, the French creator of the Theatre of Cruelty (*Théâtre de la Cruauté*), a theatrical form that assaults the senses of a passive audience through violent action.[38]

The macabre repertoire of the Underground Theatre includes the supernatural *Amber Sky* (aliens), *Deadwood Mansion* (zombies), and *Curse of Davy Jones* (ghost pirates). Gore and horror take center stage in *Blood Alley* and *Urban Death*. The company's last presentation of 2019, *Dark Dark Ride Ride* (for ages 18+) consisted of a 15-minute ride in a pitch-black maze. The audience is confronted by an energetic group of actors wearing bizarre makeup and exotic costumes, exhibiting, in a series of short vignettes, sodomy, oral sex, group sex, and sadistic variations on the theme, teasing the viewers to join the raunchy action.

In 2020, the world became the victim of a real-life invisible monster, the coronavirus. The theater of the future will no doubt be influenced by this pandemic, offering horrific new works.

1

Supernatural Monsters

The Vampire

"The Bible tells us, in Leviticus, that the life of the flesh is in the blood, and so has it been believed all through history," writes Drake Douglas in his study *Horror!* "From such beliefs, perhaps, came the terrible legend of the vampire. The vampire—who is a creature neither truly living nor really dead—must have blood in order to survive."[1]

There are chronicles of vampirism in the literature of Babylon, Assyria, Egypt, ancient Greece, Rome, and China. The word "vampire" was first noted in the English language in 1732. France's respected biblical scholar Dom Augustin Calmet published his famous *Treatise on the Vampire of Hungary and Surrounding Regions* in 1746. Voltaire, Diderot, Rousseau, Goethe, and the English Romantic poets Wordsworth, Coleridge, Byron, Shelley, and Keats penned various vampire works in the latter part of the 18th century and early 19th century.[2]

Then, on the night of June 19, 1816, Lord Byron hosted an impromptu party at his lodge in the Swiss Alps for three friends trapped by a storm: his personal physician, Dr. John William Polidori, and the poet Percy Bysshe Shelley with his lover, young Mary Wollstonecraft, daughter of author William Godwin.[3] To pass the time, they decided to make up ghost stories.

That night, two milestone works were created. Based on her tale, Mary Shelley would write the Gothic novel *Frankenstein, or, The Modern Prometheus* (first published, in three hardcover volumes, on January 1, 1818). John Polidori would expand his ghost story and pen the novella *The Vampyre*, introducing the undead Lord Ruthven (initially published in *The New Monthly Magazine*, London,

John Polidori, England, 1795–1821, whose *The Vampyre* (1819) is the first vampire novel (1820; Hulton Archive, Getty Images).

75

on April 1, 1819, and in book form—89 pages—later that year). Polidori's story spawned the genre of the undead featured in many stage adaptations over the centuries.

The Vampire, or, The Bride of the Isles (1820)
James Robinson Planché (England, 1796–1880)

The French author Charles Nodier adapted Polidori's story for the Parisian stage in 1820 under the title *Le Vampire*.[4] In turn, the English dramatist James Robinson Planché translated Nodier's play for a production at Lyceum's Opera House in London, opening on August 9, 1820. Although the myth of the vampire was tied to Eastern Europe, Planché moved the action to Scotland.

The first scene takes place on the Scottish Island of Staffa. Lady Margaret, the daughter of Baron Ronald, finds shelter in a cave during a storm while out hunting. A young, handsome man appears and approaches her. Suddenly, the features of the man grow frightfully distorted; his whole form assumes a terrifying appearance. Margaret flees in terror, running straight into the rescue party looking for her.

Scene two unfolds in Baron Ronald's castle. The baron tells Margaret that the man she is slated to marry will be arriving soon—Lord Ruthven, who had saved him from a band of highwaymen during his trip to Greece. When the lord arrives, Margaret, to her horror, recognizes "the phantom of last night."

Baron Ronald assures Ruthven that his daughter will marry him. Ruthven requests that the wedding ceremony take place that very night, for "business of utmost importance recalls me to London."

Later that day Ruthven grabs the maid Effie and attempts to carry her away. She screams, and the household servants rush in. Robert, an attendant, draws a pistol and shoots. Ruthven falls, mortally wounded.

Baron Ronald plans to tell his daughter of the death of her fiancé, when suddenly Ruthven enters. Ronald, shocked, exclaims, "Can the grave give up its dead?" Ruthven summons two servants and convinces them that their master is not well. The servants carry Ronald off. Margaret is shaken, but Ruthven begs her to "forget these idle terrors," and puts a ring on her finger.

At the chapel, Lord Ruthven is leading a reluctant Margaret to the altar when Baron Ronald arrives, followed by attendants, and stops the ceremony, to Margaret's relief. Ruthven draws his sword, but as the sun begins to rise, he cries out, "I am lost!" A loud crack of thunder reverberates through the chapel. Ruthven is hit by lightning and instantly vanishes through a trapdoor that became known as the "Vampire-trap."[5]

* * *

The 1820 premiere of *The Vampire* was well received. *The Times* of London stated: "It is one of those productions which, uniting dialogue and music with scenery of more than ordinary splendour, pass in the theatrical nomenclature under the title of Melodrama…. The performers engaged exerted themselves with considerable effect, and the whole drama met with a most encouraging reception."[6] The role of Lord Ruthven was played by Thomas Potter Cooke, who three years later would also play the first theatrical Frankenstein Monster. The cast included Mrs. W.H. Chatterley (Lady Margaret) and Mr. Bartley (Baron Ronald).

The Vampire had a long run. Nine years after its debut, in the summer of 1829,

Planché revived the play at London's Lyceum Theatre, placing the proceedings in Hungary. German composers Heinrich August Marschner and Peter Josef von Lindpaintner created operas on the topic, both called *Der Vampyr*, both in 1828. Alexandre Dumas, père mentioned Lord Ruthven in *The Count of Monte Cristo* (1845–46) and featured the character in his play *Le Vampire* (1851) wherein the lord "is a much more formidable night-stalker than Charles Nodier's somewhat effeminate creation," according to Frank J. Morlock, who adapted *Le Vampire* into English under the title *The Return of Lord Ruthven* (2004).[7]

"The legend of the vampire remains to this day a staunch favourite as a Gothic theme for plays, films and novels," wrote Michael Kilgarriff in *The Golden Age of Melodrama*. "The year 1820 also saw a version by W.T. Moncrieff; some of the others include *The Vampire Bride* by George Blink (1834), *The Vampire* by H. Young (1846), Dion Boucicault's *The Vampire* (1852), and Hamilton Deane's dramatization of Bram Stoker's novel *Dracula* which is still regularly revived."[8]

Vampire! or, The Spectre of Mount Snowden! by an anonymous author played at Liberty Hall, Lawrence, Kansas, in 1862. A program note stated, "This creature, living against the will of Heaven, eats not, drinks not, nor does it require the refreshment of sleep. This Phantom recruits his life by drawing the life blood from the veins of the living, but more specially it chooses victims from amongst maidens pure and spotless." *Ruddigore* (1887) by Gilbert and Sullivan lampooned vampire melodramas. A century later, in 1988, American playwright Tim Kelly wrote a two-act, one-set adaptation of John Polidori's *The Vampyre*, a version favored by community theaters and high school drama clubs.

Acting Edition: *The Vampyre* (from John Polidori's novella *The Vampyre*) by Tim Kelly, Dramatists Play Service.

Dracula, or The Un-Dead (1897)
Bram Stoker (Ireland, 1847–1912)

It is said that one night, in the 50th year of his life, Bram Stoker had a nightmare about a vampire rising from his tomb, and that was the genesis of his novel *Dracula*.[9] The novel, published in 1897, still stands as one of the most horrifying works in the English language and has rarely been out of print.

Born in Dublin, Ireland, in 1847, Abraham (Bram) Stoker joined the drama club at Trinity College and began reviewing theatrical productions in Dublin's *Evening Mail*. Stoker's rave review of Henry Irving's *Hamlet* brought the two men together, and in 1878, Stoker became the business manager of Irving's theater in London, The Lyceum, a position he held devotedly for 27 years, until the actor's death in 1905.

Simultaneously with running a theater company, Stoker wrote 18 books, fiction and nonfiction. He himself made the first adaptation of *Dracula* for a public reading at London's Royal Lyceum Theatre on May 18, 1897, to protect the copyright of his work. He rushed a stage version onto the Lyceum, cast it with young members of the Irving company, and presented *Dracula, or The Un-Dead*, for one showing that took four hours.[10] A program lists the actors only by their surnames. Count Dracula was enacted either by Whitworth Jones or by T. Arthur Jones (probably the latter), Professor Van Helsing by T(om) Reynolds, Jonathan Harker by H(erbert) Passmore, Doctor Seward by K(en) Rivington, Lucy Westenra by M(ary) Foster, and Mina Murray by E(dith) Craig.

Dracula, or The Un-Dead, is divided into 47 scenes. A prologue describes the arrival of Jonathan Harker at the Count's castle and his first meeting with his host, "a tall man, clean shaven save for a long white moustache, and clad in black from head to foot." Harker soon discovers vaulted coffins where "in one of the great boxes, of which there were fifty in all, on a pile of newly dug earth, lay the Count!"

The action moves to a dwelling in the village of Gillingham, England, where Lucy Westenra relates to her friend Mina Murray that she has just refused a marriage proposal by Dr. John Seward, director of a lunatic asylum, for she is in love with Lord Arthur Holmwood. In turn, Mina reveals that she is engaged to lawyer Jonathan Harker. A visiting coastguard officer tells the ladies of the unusual happenings when the boat *Demeter* was found between piers. Its captain was discovered dead, tied to the helm, and a huge dog jumped off the deck and "disappeared into darkness."

In the next scene, Lucy, sleepwalking, is attacked by a new neighbor, Count Dracula, who grips her, arching over her throat. Lucy's health soon deteriorates. Dr. Seward invites Professor Van Helsing of Amsterdam for consultation. He notices a mark on Lucy's throat, two punctures over the jugular. Van Helsing attempts to save her with a blood transfusion—to no avail. Lucy dies. A letter found next to her body tells of being awakened by the sound of a bat swinging against the window and being appalled when the head of "a great, gaunt, gray wolf" stared in.

Van Helsing suggests that they open Lucy's coffin, and when they find it empty, all are convinced that Lucy has become an undead. When she returns to her coffin, covered with the blood of a victimized child, Holmwood strikes her forcefully with a stake.

Count Dracula now becomes interested in Mina. One night, Van Helsing, Seward, and Harker come upon the vampire hugging Mina. The Count flings the girl aside and steps toward the men. They wave crucifixes, and Dracula retreats. When they light the gas lamp, there is nothing to see but a touch of ether. This is the first face-to-face encounter between the vampire and his pursuers—in Act IV, scene 8 of the play. There are five hunters in this original Stoker version, all borrowed from the novel: Van Helsing, Dr. Seward, Jonathan Harker, Lord Holmwood, and Quincy Morris, an American associate who is in love with Lucy. Later adaptations of *Dracula* eliminated the last two sleuths and concentrated on a trio of heroes.

Dracula escapes by sea. Time is short—Mina has begun to reveal the same symptoms that doomed Lucy. The action returns to Castle Dracula. Van Helsing, Mina, Morris, and Harker arrive and find a coffin; the Count is lying inside. As they sever his head, Mina's face shines. Says Morris, "See! The curse has passed away."[11]

With the theatrical copyright attained, the novel *Dracula* arrived at bookstores eight days later, on May 26, 1897. Bram Stoker never saw another production of *Dracula* in his lifetime. It took 27 years for the next adaptation to reach the stage.

Acting Edition: *Dracula, or The Un-Dead* by Bram Stoker, edited and annotated by Sylvia Starshine, Pumpkin Books, Nottingham, England.

Dracula (1924)
Hamilton Deane (Ireland, 1891–1958)

The suspenseful moments of this version of the play include the death of Mina Harker, who is found with two red-centered marks on the throat; the entrance of Count Dracula, who throws no reflection in the mirror over the mantelpiece; the disappearance of the Count courtesy of a trapdoor concealed behind the couch; the appearance of a bat flapping its wings against the window; the surrounding of Dracula by Harker, Dr. Seward, and Van Helsing, blocking his exit, which ends with the Count snarling, "Bah!" raising his right arm, sending out a flash of blinding white light—and vanishing. A distant church bell chimes as the vampire hunters encircle his coffin and stake Dracula through his heart. Harker finally confirms that Count Dracula is at rest. "*In Manus tuas Domine*," says Van Helsing and crosses himself as the curtain falls.

Following its lengthy tour on the road, *Dracula* opened at London's Little Theatre on February 14, 1927, and ran for 391 performances despite mixed reviews. Adapter Deane and his wife Dora continued in their roles of Van Helsing and Mina Harker; Raymond Huntley, at the age of 22, portrayed a young Count Dracula. A wire to the *New York Times* played up the production's nerve-wracking thrills: "Last night during the first act, a woman went into hysterics and four other women fainted during the performance. The management is so tired of calling for aid from a nearby hospital that it has engaged a trained nurse."[12]

Dracula (1927)
Hamilton Deane (Ireland, 1891–1958)
John L. Balderston (United States, 1889–1954)

Florence Stoker, perhaps displeased with the Hamilton Deane adaptation and openly unhappy with her share of royalties, authorized Charles Morrell to write a new rendition, more akin to the original work. "This 'authorized' version lays on the horror elements with a heavier hand," reports Roxana Stuart in *Stage Blood*. "Morrell's version includes the book's most powerful scenes: the breast feeding sequence between Dracula and Nina, and the branding of Mina with the Sacred Host."[13] Morrell's *Dracula* played at the Royal Court Theatre in Warrington, England, in September 1927, but did not move to London. It has never been revived.

The Deane replica, however, did cross the Atlantic, but prior to opening in the U.S., the play was doctored by dramatist John L. Balderston. The revised *Dracula*, now billed as co-authored by Deane and Balderston, and directed by Ira Hards (known for his staging of *The Cat and the Canary*, 1922), opened at the Schubert Theatre in New Haven, Connecticut, on September 19, 1927, then moved to New York's Fulton Theatre on October 5. The plotline remains the same, but the dialogue is simplified; the castle prologue is eliminated; the action shifts from the Harker home to Dr. Seward's sanatorium library; the characters of Lord Godalming and Quincy Morris are gone; the first entrance of Count Dracula (now a newly arrived neighbor, not a household guest) takes place later in the proceedings, with built-in expectations. In addition, Mina's name has been changed to Lucy (originally Mina's friend and a Dracula victim), who is now Dr. Seward's daughter, and Jonathan Harker's beloved, not his wife. Renfield does not die in this rendition; having escaped the sanatorium through a secret panel hidden in a bookcase, he unwittingly leads the vampire hunters to the whereabouts of Dracula's coffin.

During the curtain call, Van Helsing delivered a jocular speech: "Just a moment, Ladies and Gentlemen. Just a word before you go. We hope the memories of Dracula and Renfeld won't give you bad dreams, so just a word of assurance. When you get home tonight and the lights have been turned out and you are afraid to look behind the curtains and you dread to see a face appear at the window … why, just pull yourself together and remember that after all there are such things."[14]

* * *

J. Brooks Atkinson began his review of *Dracula* with a tongue-in-cheek statement: "In the first place, let every timid soul rest assured that the Evil Monster was slain last night, with a stake through his heart, in the last act of *Dracula*, played at the Fulton Theatre. He will no longer flutter through the dark night air, torturing his demented subjects while hungry wolves bay outside, or sucking fresh blood at the necks of fair young maidens."[15]

Other critics followed suit with a sly grin. "Though as foolish as the other theatrical creep machines, and often cumbersomely silly, *Dracula* should delight goose-flesh addicts and cause playgoers' teeth to chatter for a good long time," chuckled John Anderson.[16] Percy Hammond recounted with amusement, "Despite the fearful nature of the entertainment the audience shuddered happily and no hairs were turned white from shock."[17] There was general acclaim for Edward Van Sloan in the role of Professor Van Helsing and for the rest of the key players—Dorothy Peterson (Lucy) and Bernard Jukes (Renfield). But—unexpectedly—Bela Lugosi's performance in the title role was called stiff and declamatory.

Dracula ran on Broadway for 261 performances, then went on the road for several years. Lugosi, Van Sloan, and Jukes recreated their respective roles at the Biltmore Theatre in Los Angeles in 1928. Raymond Huntley came from England and headed an East Coast tour in 1929. Victor Jory played Dracula and a young Robert Young enacted Jonathan Harker at the Pasadena Playhouse, California, in 1930. On April 13, 1931, the vampire reappeared in New York's Royale Theatre for eight performances, with Courtney White as a Count Dracula "thickly coated with a greenish-yellow makeup."

Dracula proved to be undead when reincarnated Off-Broadway at the Cherry Lane Theatre (1944), Cubical Theatre (1971), and Theatre Studio (1972). A stylish production directed by Dennis Rosa, designed by master illustrator of the macabre Edward Gorey and starring Frank Langella, landed at New York's Martin Beck Theatre on October 20, 1977. The *New York Times* wrote, "Mr. Langella is a stunning figure as Dracula: tall, pale, Byronic…. He is a beautiful and sensual Dracula—his seduction of Lucy is very fine—but he

Bela Lugosi, Hungarian-American actor, 1882– 1956, the most famous interpreter of Count Dracula on stage and screen (photo by Vandamm Studio, 1947; The New York Public Library for the Performing Arts).

notably lacks terror. It is his lack of terror that makes the production hollow for all of its graces." Other reviewers, however, found Langella's performance elegant and acrobatic.

The show raised its curtain for a whopping run of 925 performances. During the long duration, Raul Julia and Jean LeClerc succeeded Langella, both continuing the assignment on the road. Jeremy Brett and Martin Landau starred in West Coast tours.

The Vampire (Frank Langella) attacks Lucy (Joanna Miles) in *Dracula*, Berkshire Theatre Festival, 1967 (photo by Friedman-Abeles, The New York Public Library of the Performing Arts).

Throughout the years, British audiences kept falling under Dracula's spell. In 1936, Hamilton Deane played Van Helsing in a revival of his adaptation and three years later switched roles, prowling the West End draped in Dracula's cape. Bela Lugosi traveled to England in 1951 and toured with "the vampire play" for eight months, playing over 200 performances in 22 cities. Terence Stamp personified the Count at London's Shaftsbury Theatre in 1978 but was savaged by reviewers. The Lord Mayor of Glasgow called for the closure of the City's Citizen's Theatre when it staged a partially nude version of *Dracula* in March 1977. On the other hand, London's Young Vic presented a sanitized *Dracula* in February 1981, attempting to attract youthful audiences to the theater.

The Deane–Balderston version of *Dracula* has become a fixture in little theaters. Among the American colleges that presented it were the University of Alabama (1937), Harvard (1942), Cornell (1966), Amherst (1970), Brown (1972), the University of Minnesota (1978), and Brooklyn College (1985).[18]

Acting Edition: Samuel French, Inc.

Dracula, Baby (1970)
Book by Bruce Ronald, lyrics by John Jakes (United States, 1932–), music by Claire Strauch

A 1970 musical comedy, *Dracula, Baby*, features the Count, Van Helsing, Seward, and madman Renfield singing and dancing in the plains of Transylvania, the pubs of London, and the catacombs of Carfax. The musical—book by Bruce Ronald, lyrics by John Jakes, and music by Claire Strauch—zips along energetically. The curtain rises on a chorus of Romanian peasants as they express a fear of the night. In this version, Dracula emerges from a pile of rocks, catches a girl, bites her arm, sucks her blood, and growls, "These local girls. Pfui! Anemic!" He decides then and there to leave for England, "the land of opportunity."

The matrons of Dr. Seward's establishment look for "patients" in the audience and sing cheerfully about their "little sanitarium, a safe little haven on the moors." But the snug atmosphere changes as Renfield escapes from his cell, searching for flies and spiders to consume. The Head Nurse greets a caped visitor, finds the Count handsome, and offers him a leg of mutton in the kitchen. "Alas, I am on a—liquid diet," he responds. When the nurse exits, Dracula mutters, "A woman like that could make me forget how much I hate Daylight Saving Time."

Among the humorous touches, there's an exchange between Dracula and Renfield in which the latter asks for sugar, and the vampire snaps, "Sugar in your blood is bad for my teeth." They launch into a duet in which they both agree, "It's good to be bad." In a nearby inn, escapee Renfield shares a beer with monster Frank and werewolf Harry. Van Helsing enters on a bicycle and immediately proves to be a klutz. He learns of Lucy's worrisome condition and rushes off to save the day, bumping, alas, into a tree.

In Lucy's bedroom, the young lady attempts to convince her bashful fiancé, Arthur, that it is time to hold and kiss her. Van Helsing arrives, checks Lucy's throat, and concludes that she is "in the evil grasp of a vampire." "Poppycock," declares Arthur, but the professor assures him that there are such things as vampires. They put Lucy to sleep with a strand of garlic around her neck. The nurse enters, sniffs, and detaches the garlic from the dozing Lucy to make sure that Arthur is not deterred by the smell. Dracula appears and wakes Lucy. He takes her in his arms, bends toward her neck as if to bite, but something stops him. He kisses her instead. Van Helsing enters, introduces himself as a "scourge of evil things that go bump in the night," and urges Dracula to repent, telling him that vampires can be redeemed if they perform a good deed.

Later, in the Carfax catacombs, Dracula orders the witch Sylvia to invite "some classy creatures" to his wedding ceremony with Lucy. But he is forlorn. He can't get the nurse out of his head. "I don't even know her name," he sighs.

The nuptial guests—ghosts, ghouls, warlocks, goblins, werewolves and mummies—enter from the back of the auditorium, come down aisles, and threaten the audience. They perform a lively ballet but stop when they realize that someone is approaching.

The nurse runs in, calling out, "Watch out, Dracula, baby! They're coming for you." Harry the Wolfman snarls, but Dracula says quietly, "No. We cannot fight them. They bring the garlic and the silver bullet. Go, my friends, go. I will meet them alone."

Slowly the creatures disperse. Van Helsing, Seward, and Arthur enter, armed with stakes, guns, and strings of garlic. The nurse steps in: "He's changed. He sent his friends away so no one would be hurt. He's done a good deed!" And so, in this musical pastiche, Dracula is reformed. When the rays of dawn begin to glow, the nurse produces big black Hollywood-style sunglasses: "Here, try these!"[19]

Acting Edition: The Dramatic Publishing Company.

Count Dracula (1971)
Ted Tiller (United States, 1913–1988)

In addition to the Deane–Balderston version, many other blood-drenched adaptations of the Bram Stoker novel were produced in the United States and abroad. *Count Dracula* (1971), by Ted Tiller, debuted at Stage West in West Springfield, Massachusetts, on December 10, 1971. The action unfolds at Dr. Seward's Asylum for the Insane, north of London. Here too the play was set in "the first half of the Twentieth Century," and here too the climax takes place at the Carfax crypt. The dramatis personae in *Count Dracula* correspond to those of Deane–Balderston's, but Tiller adds a buffoonish character, Sybil Seward, as the doctor's sister. She is painted as a fidgeting spinster with a lust for sherry and a roving eye for the Count.

The show incorporates such props and special effects as a lit cigarette materializing from thin air to be smoked by the Count; a tall chair manipulated to achieve the effect of the invisible Count swiveling in it; two moldable fangs, one for Dracula, the other for Mina; three bats constructed of wire; and a carton of sand erected to block a wooden stake as it is supposedly thrust into the Count's heart. A green spotlight and a fog machine also play their part in achieving edge-of-the-chair payoff. The mechanical sorcery is augmented by an usher standing at the back of the auditorium who screams to heaven when Count Dracula reveals his fangs and leans over Mina's neck. The usher penetrated the eardrums of the spectators at Stage West, and her associates did the same at the Cleveland Playhouse, Ohio, in 1974; at the Dallas Theatre Center, Texas, in 1975; at the Equity Library Theatre, in New York City, 1977; and at the Museum Theatre in Richmond, Virginia, in 1981.

Acting Edition: Samuel French, Inc.

Dracula (1973)
Crane Johnson (United States, 1921–)

An adaptation of *Dracula* by Crane Johnson premiered at the Royal Playhouse, Off-Broadway, New York City, in August 1973, and ran until June 1974. Johnson took liberties with some plot maneuvers and the cast of characters. Here, Dr. Seward and Lucy are lovers planning to get married. Mrs. Emily Harker, Lucy's aunt, is a house guest. Professor Van Helsing, summoned by Seward to look into his fiancé's deteriorating health, is a whip-carrying, cigar-smoking woman.[20]

Count Dracula appears only sporadically, while the role of the asylum inmate Renfield has been expanded, with more entrances and "moments" than any other character. A tantalizing scene depicts an encounter between Renfield and Van Helsing during which the professor declares, "We metaphysicians are interested in life both here and beyond life, of the transference of life." The madman responds, "Oh yes, the transference. I know…. I catch a fly and swallow it. That life—the life of the fly becomes part of me, part of my life, and the spider I swallow becomes part of me, part of my life, and the sparrow I swallow becomes part of me, part of my life, and I am no longer merely Renfield, but *am* the fly, the spider, and the sparrow."

New York Times' critic Howard Thompson lauded Johnson's "modest production" and its four interchanging casts: "Their unified dignity, the quaint, rustling Victorian garb and, above all, those lines make it eerily worthwhile. Leave the gore to all those flicks."[21]

Directed by Mario Lescot, the Johnson version was revived in 1995 by the Theatre District company of Costa Mesa, California. Reviewer Robert Koehler of the *Los Angeles Times* opined that in this replica, "Dracula [played by Victor Santana] becomes less a freak of nature than a tragic, flawed man without a country, which is how the historical Vlad still is viewed by many in Romania today. Though the cast isn't always up to the task of expressing it, nearly everyone in this *Dracula* is a kind of victim."[22]

Acting Edition: Dramatists Play Service.

The Passion of Dracula (1977)
Bob Hall (United States, 1944–) and
David Richmond (United States)

This adaptation preserves the unities of place and time by confining the continuous action to the study of Dr. Seward's home in the town of Whitby, near London. The Carfax crypt is eliminated, and there are fewer special effects—though a foghorn is active, bats fly around, and the lights go out at opportune moments.

Messrs. Hall and Richmond picked the autumn of 1911 for their setting, and there is some talk of a pending world war. The adapters chose to call Dr. Seward "Cedric" (instead of "John") and dispensed with Wilhelmina Murray's "Mina" in favor of "Willy." They recaptured the character of Lord Gordon Godalming from Stoker's novel and Deane's early version and added an Austrian doctor, Helga Van Zandt, as Seward's colleague, in their titanic struggle against the forces of evil. Helga misdiagnoses Willy's condition as "depression, lethargy, somnambulism, hyperactivity and euphoria," asserting that all this is not abnormal for an English woman of Willy's age. Helga, alas, becomes a victim of Count Dracula, and Lord Godalming shoots himself when he too is bitten and tainted.

In this version, Jonathan Harker is not a solicitor but a reporter for the *London Globe*. Instead of the Count's traditional missing image in a wall mirror, proof that he is a vampire is provided when he does not appear in a photograph taken by Harker for the *Globe*. While discussing the novels of Lytton Strachey and the plays of Oscar Wilde, Jonathan and Willy fall in love. Her frail condition does not deter Willy from kissing Jonathan on his mouth within a few minutes of their first meeting. Dr. Seward approves of this union when he learns that Harker is an Oxford man.

Count Dracula, a new arrival to the neighborhood, tells Seward that he is a descendant of Attila the Hun. One of his ancestors is Vlad Dracula, Vlad the Impaler, a warrior who was cruel but just and gained immortality by drinking the blood of his captives. When Willy offers their guest a glass of sherry, the Count declines but proceeds to hypnotize her. Soon Willy gives a throaty laugh, holds out a beckoning hand to Harker, pulls him down onto the chaise, and teeth exposed, bends toward his throat. Just in time, the howl of a wolf from the outside breaks the trance.

Dracula invites Van Helsing to join his fraternity: "Together we shall ride the dark winds past the edge of time." The professor declines. He'd rather serve heaven than hell. As the duel of wills progresses, Van Helsing takes a small vial from his pocket, scoops a suspicious-looking powder with his thumbnail, and snorts a healthy dose—shades of Sherlock Holmes's needle. The great detective's influence is also evident when Harker exclaims, "It's the dogs! We haven't heard them howling for some time now." Seward replies, "Damn! You're right! Something's afoot."[23]

The climax consists of a siege by "hundreds, thousands, millions of rats—with eyes blazing red." Dracula is heard on a voice-over track: "Come, my creatures of the night ... you shall gnaw English bones at my wedding." We hear the rats scrabbling closer and closer. Seward, Harker, and Van Helsing grab revolvers and commence firing on the terrace. When the battle is over, the sound of a heartbeat fills the stage. Dracula appears, tosses Harker aside, waves off Helsing's cross, and rushes to Willy with open arms. She stabs him with a stake, and he sinks to his knees. "My curse upon you for all eternity," he says as Van Helsing drives the stake deeper into his heart. The inmate Renfield, who rants throughout the proceedings, "The blood is the life," crouches near the dead Dracula and weeps, "What will become of poor Renfield?"

The Passion of Dracula, initially produced at George St. Playhouse in New Brunswick, New Jersey, was moved to Manhattan's Cherry Lane Theater, a prime Off-Broadway venue, on September 28, 1977. Eileen Hillary of the *Chelsea Clinton News* wrote, "It's all for fun and makes no attempt at being fiendish. When it's creepy, it is knowingly creepy (fang-in-cheek?). And when it is funny—and it is very often funny—it is with a wit and polish far more at home in the parlor-room than in darker chambers."[24] *The Passion of Dracula* ran for 714 performances.

Acting Edition: Samuel French, Inc.

Dracula (1978)
Tim Kelly (United States 1973–1988)

The prolific American playwright Tim Kelly dramatized Stoker's *Dracula* along the lines established by Deane and Balderston, confining the action to Dr. Quincy's sanatorium, an hour's drive from London. But the time is the present; cars and planes serve as modes of transportation offstage.

In this rendition, Dracula travels to England accompanied by three wives who emerge sporadically to menace the sanatorium's attendants. The trio is "beautiful—but their icy beauty inspires terror." However, the sensual element in Kelly's *Dracula* is anemic. Throughout the three acts of the play, there are no twosome scenes between the Count and Lucy. The closest he ever gets to Mina is to kiss her hand and promise that they shall meet again, a rendezvous that never materializes because the vampire hunters concoct a timely trap, coaxing Dracula to a confrontation at dawn, when the first rays of light melt his face into a "mask of flesh" and dissolve his body "to dust."

Reversing his sentiments, Tim Kelly created several additional stage treatments sympathetic to the vampire. *Young Dracula, or The Singing Bat* (1975) depicts a young nephew of the Count who is struggling to keep the mortgaged Castle Dracula afloat. The bank plans to tear down the edifice and in its place erect a pickle factory. The Count himself is now an ineffective "crazy old character in an opera cape" who will be stranded if the family loses its ancestral home. A group of touring American high school students, who arrive at the castle when lost in a storm, come to Dracula's aid by forming a plan to

The prolific American playwright Tim Kelly, United States, 1937–1998, resurrected on stage the characters of Count Dracula, the Frankenstein Monster, the Zombie, the Invisible Man, Dr. Jekyll and Mr. Hyde, the Phantom of the Opera, and other creatures of the night (n.d.; Amy Langton, Dramatic Publishing Company).

turn the abode into a tourists' attraction center like Disneyland or Sea World. The play was republished in 2010 under the title *Dracula: The Twilight Years.*

Lucy, the ingénue of Kelly's *Seven Brides for Dracula* (1983), complains that the Count has bad breath but falls under his spell when he croons the ballad, "Transylvania Trance." At the conclusion of *Seven Brides* (which is a musicalization by Kelly of his own *Seven Wives for Dracula*), Van Helsing and Seward discover to their chagrin that they have mistakenly impaled Renfield while the King of Vampires and his Countess embrace each other.

In Kelly's *The Dracula Kidds, or The House on Blood Pudding Lane* (1986), the Count and his bride show up at the Kidd Academy to demand a retraction from a teenage author who has written a book that debunks the legend of the undead.[25]

Acting Edition:
Dracula and *The Dracula Kidds* by Tim Kelly, I.E. Clark, Inc.
Young Dracula and *Seven Brides for Dracula* by Tim Kelly, Pioneer Drama Service.

Countess Dracula (1979)
Neal Du Brock (United States 1923–1994)

Countess Dracula by Neal Du Brock is sort of a sequel to the Stoker novel and the Deane–Balderston stage adaptation. Dr. John Seward, now in his 60s, has retired as head of the sanitarium at Purley. Dr. Robert Bartolomew, a man of 30, has taken over. R.M. Renfield does not appear in this version. Instead, a girl in a patient's gown stands up as the curtain rises, scurrying across the stage to a sink where she searches out a bottle and drinks from it. The girl hungrily takes a few swallows, spilling the remainder on her gown. It is blood.

The patient, Wandesa, is Lady Alucard's daughter. The lady, chic and elegantly groomed, is new to the area. Soon Lady Alucard seduces a fascinated Robert—loosening his tie, unbuttoning his shirt, baring his neck, and sinking her teeth into his jugular.

Another visitor arrives on the scene: Elisabeth Van Helsing, daughter of Abraham Van Helsing, the renowned vampirologist. She tells Dr. Seward and his good friend Jonathan Harker that her father died under suspicious circumstances. Little red dots in a circle of white were found on his neck—the kiss of the vampire! Seward finds it hard to believe that Count Dracula is still around, considering Van Helsing had defeated him, but Elisabeth reveals a surprise. Her father was not outwitted—but seduced. The vampire was a woman!

Harker deduces the identity of the vampire: "What is the cryptogram for 'Alucard'? A-L-U-C-A-R-D. Dracula! Countess Dracula!"[26]

Playwright Du Brock comes up with yet another twist: Elisabeth Van Helsing turns out to be Countess Alucard (indeed both parts are played by the same actress), a bloodthirsty figure modeled on the real-life Erzsébet Bathory, a medieval mass murderess. In a final battle, Dr. Seward's heart gives out, and he dies. Harker is dangerously enchanted by the countess but finds the gumption to drive a stake through her heart.

Countess Dracula had its world premiere at the Studio Arena Theatre in Buffalo, New York, on January 5, 1979, and ran for 34 performances. The play was directed by author Du Brock and starred Betsy Palmer in the roles of Lady Alucard and Elisabeth Van Helsing.

Acting Edition: Samuel French, Inc.

Dracula (1995)
Steven Dietz (United States, 1958–)

Dracula by Steven Dietz is debatably the most loyal stage adaptation of Stoker's novel. Unlike other theatrical renditions, Dietz establishes the action in 1897 but maneuvers the proceedings to travel back-and-forth through time. Dietz imitates the original book's format in which the tale of Dracula is told through letters and diary entries.

In Dietz's version, the setting is spread into several locales: Lucy's bedroom, Renfield's cell, a living room at Seward's asylum, and Dracula's mansion in Transylvania. Both Mina Murray and her friend Lucy Westenra turn up. Mina is Jonathan Harker's fiancé; Lucy is enamored with Dr. Seward. Images of a wooden casket and a run-down ship's wheel signify the Count's docking in England.

The action is tinted with blood. When Dracula sinks his teeth into Lucy's neck, Van Helsing brings on the appliances for a blood transfusion as he rubs Seward's arm with alcohol. Blood flows.

When Mina scrutinizes Harker's journal, a flashback visualizes Harker's arrival at Castle Dracula. The Count, an old man "with hair long, gray and wild, a pallid complexion to his face and long, yellowed fingernails," offers the lawyer a drink from an aged bottle—"A gift from Attila. The Huns were despicable, but they knew their wine."

That night Harker finds himself bound to his bed while two women glide towards his neck baring their long, sharp teeth. Dracula enters and claims Harker for himself. To appease them, he produces a crying baby from a bag. Harker watches mortified as the women devour the baby. Blood soon trickles onto Harker's chest.

More blood flows when the madman Renfield nicks Seward's arm with a sword. Renfield tastes the blood from the blade and mutters, "The blood is the life … the blood is the life." In his cell, Renfield is rewarded by Dracula with a fat rat. The Count cracks the rat's neck and forces a torrent of blood into Renfield's mouth.

Lucy yields to the Count's bites and joins his tribe of the undead. Soon she appears wearing a torn white gown smeared with the blood of bitten children. At dawn, Van Helsing, Harker, and Seward force Lucy into a coffin.

Mina is found in the morning with teeth marks on her neck. Van Helsing administers a blood transfusion during which Renfield flees from his cell. Dracula, too, suddenly appears and fractures Renfield's neck. The Count approaches Mina, opens his shirt and drags a fingernail across the chest, extracting blood—"Drink. And be mine." Mina stares into his eyes and slurps the wound.

In the climax of the play, as in Stoker's novel, the vampire hunters journey to the Count's dwelling in Transylvania. Mina has now joined the undead, but she is rescued when Harker plunges a wooden stake into Dracula's chest. The rite of blood prevails as Mina jabs a knife into the coffin and decapitates Dracula's (unseen) head, then backs away, her hand red.

Steven Dietz's *Dracula* was launched by the Arizona Theatre Company at the Temple of Music and Art in Tucson, Arizona, with previews beginning on March 25, 1995, and general admission from March 31 to April 15. The production was directed by David Goldstein and designed by Bill Forrester. Patrick Page played Dracula.

The Cleveland Playhouse in Ohio presented Dietz's *Dracula* from September 23 through November 8, 1997, celebrating the 100th anniversary of the publication of Stoker's novel. Peter Hackett directed; Seth Kanor portrayed the vampire. According to a notice by the management, "Dietz believes people love to be scared. That's why Dracula's fame has survived all these years. He says, 'We have a desire for the excitement of the dark, sensual and mysterious allure of the unknown.'"

Acting Edition: Dramatists Play Service.

Dance of the Vampires (2002)
Jim Steinman (United States 1947–) and
Michael Kunze (Czechoslovakia 1943–)

Dance of the Vampires, a camp musical loosely based on Roman Polanski's 1967 motion picture *The Fearless Vampire Killers*, was mounted at New York's Minskoff Theatre in 2002. Created by Jim Steinman and Michael Kunze (book, lyrics, and music), *Dance of the Vampires* revolves around the attempt by a diabolic yet melancholy Carpathian vampire, Count von Krolock, to seduce Sarah, a beautiful village girl. Among the characters are Sarah's protective parents; a young student who is enamored with her; the vampire's gay son, Herbert; his hunchbacked servant, Koukol; and the absent-minded Abronius, who provides comic relief.

Originally conceived as a Gothic rock opera, the production of *Dance of the Vampires* was reviled by most critics. Clive Barnes faulted the musical for going out, "not for the jugular but the giggular."[27] Ben Brantley asked cynically, "Where's a mask when you need one?" a dig at Michael Crawford (playing Count von Krolock), the Tony Award-winning star of 1988's *The Phantom of the Opera*. "With his swept-back lacquered hair and black-on-white contour makeup, he looks like a Goth version of Siegfried, Roy and Wayne Newton combined."[28]

Vampires opened on December 9, 2002, and closed after 61 previews and 56 performances. The play lost its entire investment of $12 million, taking its place alongside famous musical flops like *Carrie* and *The Capeman*.

However, *Dance of the Vampires* rose from its theatrical grave, and a newly mounted production ran successfully in Hamburg, Berlin, Vienna, Warsaw, Budapest, and Tokyo.

Lestat (2006)
Music by Elton John (England, 1947–),
book by Linda Woolverton (United States, 1952–),
lyrics by Bernie Taupin (England, 1950–)

Despite the dismal failure of *Dance of the Vampires* in New York, the following year Warner Brothers Entertainment commissioned Elton John to compose a Broadway musical based on Anne Rice's popular series, "The Vampire Chronicles." John recruited Bernie Taupin as lyricist, Linda Woolverton as librettist, director Robert Jess Roth, and choreographer Matt West. The creative team worked for several years on *Lestat*, streamlining the complicated Rice narratives into a two-and-a-half-hour show.

"This musical is the fulfillment of my deepest dreams," said author Anne Rice. "Elton's music and Bernie's lyrics have captured the pain and passion of the characters perfectly, and the entire adaptation has re-created the very essence of the books."[29]

Lestat tells the story of Louis de Pointe du Lac, a 25-year-old plantation owner in New Orleans who feels guilty about the death of his brother. Vulnerable, he falls under the spell of the seductive vampire Lestat de Lioncourt and accepts his offer of immortality. Louis joins a coven of vampires that includes Lestat's mother, Gabrielle, and his friend Nicolas. Also partaking in the proceedings of *Lestat* is their enemy Armand, a destructive vampire who heads his own "family" of the undead, teaching his followers satanic rituals and grooming them to make mortals suffer.

On its pre–Broadway trial, *Lestat* premiered at San Francisco's Curran Theatre on December 17, 2006, and was clobbered by the critics. "We have a lot of work to do," conceded Elton John. "We certainly ran into problems. But I think we can sort them out."[30]

Reshaping the show during a six-week run in San Francisco and 33 previews at the Palace Theatre in New York proved to be futile. *Lestat* opened on April 25, 2006, and was savaged again by the press. It closed a month later with a total loss of $12 million.

Vampire Fangs Off Broadway

The small theaters of Off-Broadway and Off-Off-Broadway in New York City have been meccas for additional vampire plays, all derived from Stoker's *Dracula*, but each with its own individual message and unique style.

The Vampire Show by Charles Pulaski, presented by the Stage

Vampire Lestat (Hugh Panaro) bites the neck of Beautiful Woman (Megan Reinking), Palace Theatre, New York City, 2006 (photo by Paul Kolnik, program brochure created by Design Management).

Lestat's Elton John, music (left); Bernie Taupin, lyrics; and Anne Rice, author (photo by Paul Kolnik, 2005; program brochure created by Design Management).

Lights Theatrical Club in 1969, is a playful one-act play about a conniving impresario who dupes two actors into impersonating a lady vampire and her victim and makes off with the night's receipts. A number of plot twists follow until the real Dracula, who happened to catch the act, comes forth from the auditorium. "The play is nonsense Grand Guignol without the macabre," wrote reviewer Jon Carlson. "The idea it exploits is slight, even obvious, but the writing is witty and the characters emerge as real and believable."[31]

Dracula Sabbath by Leon Katz, first performed at Purdue University in Lafayette, Indiana, on February 24, 1970, came to New York City's Judson Poets' Theatre seven months later. *Sabbath* is best described as a ritualistic pageant, structured with minimal dialogue and an emphasis on mime and tableaux. Critic George L. George was awed by the "majestically choreographed processionals, and Satanical Christian ceremonies in the Reinhardt tradition with Grand Guignol overtones."[32] Sam Coleman saluted "a fantastique display of beautifully staged erotica. It is a voyeur's delight."[33] However, Walter Kerr pouted, "For all its showman like expertise, *Dracula Sabbath* is a bit of a fake."[34] Duane Tucker in the role of Dracula and Crystal Field as his victim, Lucy, received kudos, as did John Herbert McDowell for his organ music. Director Larry Kornfeld won an Obie Award for his staging of the play.

Vampire Freako, proffered by the Ellen Klein Mime Troupe and Medicine Show at their École de Mime during Christmas 1970, exposed children to the myth of Dracula through mime art complete with sharp fangs and lots of blood.

Dracula, adapted and directed by Jerry Engelbach at Soho Rep, November 5, 1976, was a two-hour-plus production punctuated with a stream-of-consciousness soundtrack and peppered with images of Transylvanian castles projected onto the back wall. "The stage gimmicks reduce this version of *Dracula* to childish Halloween scariness," sniffed *The Villager*.[35]

With the author portraying his own title character, Norman Beim's *Dracula, A Modern Fable*, presented by the Troupe Theatre from February 3–26, 1978, was billed as "a satire on 1940's movies." A commercial artist arriving in Los Angeles for her brother's funeral discovers that the brother had become a vampire, his master is a descendant of Vlad the Impaler, and she herself is the master's reincarnated sweetheart, whom he has been seeking since she committed suicide in 1462. "The first act is ludicrous, the second is tedious," lamented John Bush Jones.[36]

An import from England, *Dracula, or A Pain in the Neck*, a spoof of the vampire legend by Phil Woods and Michael Bogdanov, arrived in Manhattan's Beacon Theatre on March 19, 1984. The romp, created at the New Vic of London, gathered a group of cheerful amateurs to present a rendition of *Dracula*, a sort of a play within a play, complete with eerie lighting, spooky music, and heavily made-up actors scurrying through the audience. A success abroad, New York audiences rejected the play, and critics concurred. The show had to close its doors after two performances.

In *The Vampires*, written and directed by Harry Kondoleon, "The playwright has assimilated gothic horror films, screwball comedy, TV family sit-coms, late night TV pop culture, and remixed it into his own brand of high camp," wrote Victor Gluck upon the opening of the play at Manhattan's Astor Place Theatre on April 11, 1984.[37] The main character is a drama critic named Ian who has gleefully panned his brother Ed's production and recently been fired because another of his caustic reviews drove an actor to suicide. Unemployed, Ian decides to "hate everything," declares himself a vampire, bites a chunk out of his wife's neck, and goes to sleep in the cellar. Ed complains bitterly that

Ian's newly acquired vampirism is "just another attention-getting-device, not unlike his fake colds, fake headaches, fake hives, fake depressions, and fake nervous breakdowns." Some confused reviewers concluded that *Vampires* "is yet another excursion into the dark heart of a crazy all-American family," and that the farce exhibited "Kondoleon's picture of selfish, blood-sucking, doomed America."

Vampire Lesbians of Sodom was the first presentation of Theatre-in-Limbo, a group headed by the notorious playwright-star Charles Busch. The 45-minute vaudevillian sketch, initially mounted in 1984 at the Limbo Lounge, was transferred to the Provincetown Playhouse in 1988. It is the story of two female vampires clashing fang to fang throughout the centuries. An early vignette takes us to biblical Sodom and Gomorrah where a young, trembling Virgin Sacrifice (played by Busch) is bitten by the vampirish Succubus (Meghan Robinson) and becomes a member of the undead. Both appear next in 1920s' Hollywood, competing for movie roles and luscious starlets. Their ensuing time travel takes us to present-day Las Vegas, where the vamp rivals continue to claw at each other. The press described the plot as "a twist on *Dracula* with a bit of H. Rider Haggard's *She* and something of *King Kong* thrown in." The production was dubbed "broad slapstick, outrageous satire and absolute silliness," and the event "a fruit cocktail of an evening—colorful, fresh and light." Not every critic agreed. John Simon declared, "Compared to Busch, Charles Ludlam (of the Ridiculous Theatre Company) is Eleonora Duse and Sarah Bernhardt rolled together."[38]

The Morse Mime Repertory Theatre presented *Dracula* in November 1984 and November 1985. The LaMama Experimental Theatre Club sponsored a contemporary version of *Nosferatu*, created by Ping Chong, as based on F.W. Murnau's 1922 film, in February 1985. The Bennington Marionettes Company resurrected the king of vampires in the form of a puppet in October 1992. Soho Repertory Theatre presented Mac Wellman's *Dracula* in April of 1994, generally following the Bram Stoker plot but placing the action in narrow alleys, low dives, backstreet booths, and peep shows. In November 1994, Soho Rep produced Wellman's comedy *Swoop* in which three vampires circle seven miles above the streets of Manhattan, "where the moon is bright and the night is fair," seeking prey and reminiscing about their long, long, long past. Both Soho productions were directed by Julian Webber and designed by Kyle Chepulis. A more traditional version of *Dracula* by Leonard Wolf was shown by the Drama Committee Repertory Theatre during July and August of 1999.

The HERE Arts Center included an adaptation of *Nosferatu*, written and directed by Rene Migliaccio, in its 1999–2000 festival. Migliaccio's rendition was highly stylized with the performers' faces painted with clown white and the settings projected by slides. David DeWitt appreciated the ideas that seemed "to be shouted from almost every nook and cranny of this production" but concluded, "The goals of *Nosferatu* remain out of reach. The show is ponderous; moments that could be laden with meaning are laden with earnest but empty silence."[39]

As part of New York's annual Spotlight on Halloween Festival, Alternative Theatre Machine (ATM) presented in 2003 a multimedia creation, *Dracularama*, written and directed by Jason St. Sauver. ATM announced, "With a cast of 10 actors, 5 cell phones, 3 laptops, 2 palm pilots, 1 hand held tape recorder and a huge video screen, the show is like a crazy music video to attack and attract you with sound, sight, fright and blissfully sleepless nights."

Ghost of Dracula (2010), written by Kenneth Molloy, directed by Daniel Johnsen, and produced by Wings Theatre, sinks its teeth into the blend of vampire horror and teenage angst. The show's publicists trumpeted it as "the bastard child of *Dracula* and *The Breakfast Club* with a lot more blood, and music."

On February 17, 2020, Classic Stage Company presented an adaptation of *Dracula* by Kate Hamill, exploring the themes of gender and sexuality. Hamill portrayed the insect-munching Renfield, with Matthew Amendt as Dracula and Kelley Curran as Mina. The play ran in repertory with *Frankenstein*, Tristan Bernays's adaptation of Mary Shelley's novel.

Acting Edition: *Vampire Lesbians of Sodom* by Charles Busch, Samuel French, Inc.

The Undead Invade the United States

Away from New York, the king of vampires flapped his wings in more stage adaptations derived from Bram Stoker.

Vampire Valley by Ralph Mead was produced at the Rockwood Outdoor Theatre in Green Bay, Ohio, in 1940. A natural pile of rock served as the setting—the ruins of an old castle, enhanced by the swish of waves 50 feet below the theater, the rustling of trees, and the cooing of night birds in the surrounding woods. *Dracula* by Kenneth Cavanaugh was presented in 1970 by the Yale Repertory Summer Theatre at the John Drew Theatre in Long Island, New York. Robert Drivas enacted the title role; Henry Winkler played Dr. Van Helsing. *Dracula*, subtitled *A New Environmental Ritual*, by Tom Thomas, was performed at the Pittsburgh Playhouse in Pittsburgh, Pennsylvania, 1970. *Dracula*, by Frederick Caines, was mounted at the Asolo Repertory Theatre in Sarasota, Florida, in 1972. *Dracula's Treasure*, by Dudley F. Saunders, was shown at the Children's Theatre in Louisville, Kentucky, in 1974. Have Nicky, age 11, and Nancy, 13, fallen under the spell of the vampire, or are the horrifying happenings just a bad dream? *Dracula* by Robert L. Odle was presented by the American Theatre Company in Tulsa, Oklahoma, in 1978, with program assurance: "This stage version of the Gothic horror is designed to thoroughly entertain in a very frightening way."

Dracula, by Donald Bangs and Robert Tolaro, was a sign language adaptation offered at Ohio's Cleveland Playhouse in 1981 by The Fairmount Theatre of the Deaf. *Bram Stoker's Dracula*, by and starring John Spitzer, was shown at the Northstar Theatre, Washington, D.C., in 1982, a production peppered with special effects and sound cues. When the curtain rises, "The moon casts its cold, blue shadow on the platform representing the Castle Dracula, Transylvania." The beating bat wings, the howling of wolves, and the shrieking of a baby can be heard. *Vampires in Kodachrome*, by Dick Beebe, was presented by the Yale Repertory Theatre in New Haven, Connecticut, in 1985. Here the bloodletting shenanigans take place off the coast of Maine at the end of World War II, an attempt to equate the Dracula legend with war atrocities. *Dracula* by Geoffrey Hitch was mounted at the Charlotte Repertory Theatre, North Carolina, in 1989. Playwright-director Hitch asserted in a program note, "If one of theatre's functions is to be the laboratory of the Human Condition, then with this production we attempt to break with as many needless restrictions as we can, and ignite the passionate spirit of Stoker's original work—bringing to light, as he did, the darkest aspects of our selves."

Jim Helsinger's *Dracula: The Journal of Jonathan Harker* (workshop production: Cape May Stage, Cape May, New Jersey, 1994; world premiere: Orlando Shakespeare

Theater, Orlando, Florida, 1995) depicts the journey of a real estate agent who finds himself held captive by the eerie Count. The playwright himself enacted all ten characters who partake in the proceedings. *Earl the Vampire* by Sean Michael Welch focuses on a group of vampires who share an apartment in a modern American city, attempting to blend into society and fighting against what they believe is discrimination against them. The two-act play was first performed in 1998 at the University of Michigan and directed by the author, who also helmed, the following year, its presentation at the Kennedy Center, Washington, D.C. *Nosferatu: Angel of the Final Hour* by Jon Kellman, Kaaren J. Luker, and Bernadette Sullivan was shown at Art Share in Los Angeles, 1999. That same year, Frank Semerano's *A Vampire Reflects* was presented at the Ventura Court Theatre in Studio City, California. It tells the story of Count Zescu, a vampire who takes up residence in an abandoned estate in the American southwest near a secret army base and stumbles upon a weapons experiment that involves turning living bats into flying bombs.

Vampire Cowboy Trilogy by Qui Nguyen and Robert Ross Parker (originally workshopped at Ohio University in 2000 and produced at the 2004 New York Fringe Festival) contains three irreverent comedies featuring hard-boiled detective Jake Misco (Dan Deming) in a triple bill that satirizes the horror genre. *Dracula* by Rick Rose was presented at the Barter Theatre in Abingdon, Virginia, in 2001. Here the undead descend upon a small Virginia community, buying all the real estate in sight. *Dracula*, an adaptation by William McNulty of the Hamilton Deane–John L. Balderston version, premiered at Actors Theatre of Louisville, Kentucky, in 2007 with the playwright directing and playing Abram Van Helsing. Misha Kuznetsov portrayed the Count, who is exceedingly resourceful, employing superhuman strength, psychic powers, and the ability to shapeshift to confound his antagonists. Also in 2007, Ellen Geer adapted and staged *Dracula* at the Will Geer Theatricum Botanicum, in Topanga, California, eliciting a mixed assessment by reviewer F. Kathleen Foley in the *Los Angeles Times*: "Rather than dramatically synthesizing Stoker's desultory yarn, Geer adheres to her source material with an acolyte's zeal. The overlong result may score as literary curiosity, but the horror sags under the weight of sheer conscientiousness."[40]

Drac's Back! written by Craig Sodaro and copyrighted in 2010, is a farcical treatment of the Dracula lore. The plot revolves around a group of high school students who, upon their return from the Regional Science Fair, find themselves lost when their school van runs out of gas in the middle of a rainstorm. The young scientists seek refuge in a spooky old house, where they are greeted by the very pale but suave Dexter Drackman. Buffy, a student leader, finds their host of special interest for he is a descendent of the great vampire hunter Dr. Van Helsing. Buffy recognizes the true identity of Drackman and his two sisters, Bella and Della, and leads the students' escape. *Drac's Back!* played at various high schools across the land.

The bottomless pit of United States *Dracula* adaptations also includes *I Was a Teen-Age Dracula* (1958) by Gene Donovan, where the dastardly proceedings take place in a small mid–American town. *Dracula* (1978), by Anthony Scull, presents Wilhelmina Murray as "a brilliant young actress on the edge of madness," a patient in Dr. Seward's sanatorium, and Van Helsing as a Catholic priest who locks horns with the Transylvanian Count over Willie's soul. *The Reluctant Vampire* (1979), by Teddy Keller, throws satirical darts at buffoonish lawmen, clumsy social agents, and overzealous reporters as they confront—ineptly—a young vampire who plunders the Bela Lugosi Memorial

Blood Bank. *Dracula, Darling* (1979), by Peg Kehret, is a whodunit variation highlighting a police investigation of "The Case of the Bitten Brides"—women found dead on their wedding nights with teeth marks in their necks—in Seattle, Portland, and Vancouver. In *The Count Will Rise Again* (1980), by Dennis Snee, the action swirls within the mists of the Deep South. Snee's one-act *Mid-Life Dracula* (2003) unfolds on the Count's celebration of his 400th birthday. He complains to his doctor that his age is showing ("Of late I find myself short of breath after climbing only one or two flights of the castle stairs"), and he has to cope with a nagging mother-in-law and a precocious teenage daughter. But all ends well as his beloved wife, Yvonne, coos, "I'm nuts about you" and places her arms around his neck. They begin to kiss as the lights fade to black. *Dracula* (1980), by Richard Sharp, incorporates into the traditional proceedings a silent "Nosferatu" chorus of three: "at times, part of the set, at other times, part of the action." *Dracula* (1984), by Tom Clapp, utilizes coffins, crypts, and tombstones as exteriors and interiors—"There is no conventional 'furniture.' Beds are coffins; sofas are coffins."

Dracula: The Death of Nosferatu (1991), by Christopher P. Nichols, is constructed along lines established by Deane–Balderston but adds a sequence in which Van Helsing hypnotizes Mina by swinging a prism in front of her. In this scenario, Renfield joins the vampire hunters as an ally, for which he pays with his life. The protagonist of Tom Jordan's *Dracula in Paradise* (1991) is Countess Dracula, who needs money badly, so she allows a movie to be filmed in her castle. Everybody is excited by the project, especially the kids, Doug and Donna Dracula. But when the loud movie director, the catty actresses, and the flirtatious dancers enter the scene, chaos ensues. Another high-society lady, Baroness Katarina Stephanowski of Rumania, is the title character of Billy St. John's *Dracula's Widow* (1993). The Baroness moves to England in search of fresh blood. The tense climax pits her against Lucy Seward, who has survived Dracula's bite herself and is willing to match wits with the monstrous fiend.

In 2006, *Dracula, Lord of the Undead,* penned by Mark Healy and directed by Michael D. Mitchell, played at the Fulton Theatre in Lancaster, Pennsylvania. A program note related several instances of reported vampire sightings: "All of which makes you wonder: doesn't that person who usually sits next to you at the Fulton look a little pale?"

The House of Besarab, by Terance Duddy and Theodore Ott, performing at the Hollywood American Legion, was greeted by a negative review in *LA Weekly* (December 11–17 2009): "A disappointing adaptation of *Dracula* ... a lackluster production design and stolid direction only compound the exposition-laden script's failure." That same year, *Courting Vampires,* by Laura Schellhardt, playing at The Theatre @ Boston Court, Pasadena, California, is the story of a young woman who falls victim to a fatal blood disease, and her protective older sister vows revenge on the vampire who infected her.

The Vampire in Europe

Europe, too, kept alive its fascination with the bloodsucking creature. Alfredo Rodrigues Arias, artistic director of the Argentinean group TSE, brought his variation of *Dracula* to Paris and Belgrade during the 1968–1969 season and to London a year later. "In *Dracula* this strange sense of hypnosis and paralysis on the part of the Arias' company was exploited with a unique power and effect," wrote Peter Ansorge in the journal *Plays and Players*. "Though we never saw the vampire, the point was made that all the characters were in the power of his mysterious sexuality—in a limbo they were being moved and stirred like pieces on a chess board."[41]

David Compton based his drama *Carmilla* on a story by Sheridan Le Fanu, setting the action in and around a continental castle in the early 19th century. It is the story of a young woman, Laura, who falls into the clutches of Carmilla, a female vampire. Alan Ayckbourn staged Compton's adaptation at the Library Theatre, Scarborough, England, in 1972. Laura was played by Philippa Urquhart and Carmilla by Jennifer Piercy.

A Dracula look-alike steals across the stage in the first act of Snoo Wilson's *Vampire*, but the standard fixtures of howling wolves, flying bats, swirling capes, and gleaming teeth are missing. It was given its first London production by Paradise Foundry at the Oval House in 1973. According to the playwright, "Every age has its vampires.... Political as well as spiritual vampires.... Totally predatory and enormously attractive—who suck the people dry." In 1979, Wilson's *Vampire* came to New York, sponsored by AMDA Studio One, garnering kudos from the fringe press.

Eight authors had a hand in a scrapbook *Dracula*, examining the myth of the undead by placing the vampire in varied guises and periods: Dracula as Ulysses, Dracula as witch-hunter, Dracula as the butt of Sigmund Freud, etc. Reports indicate that despite "some swishing of cloaks, baring of fangs, and dripping of blood," the whole affair, unveiled at the Bush Theatre of London in 1973, was rather tame.

In 1974–1975, Londoners crowded the Theatre Workshop for 59 performances of *Dracula* by Ken Hill, who served as director and set the sinister proceedings in genteel surroundings, a Victorian school for young ladies, sacrificing macabre elements in favor of broad comedy.

In 1978, Constance Cox, noted for stage adaptations of Oscar Wilde's *Lord Arthur Savile's Crime* (1963) and M.E. Braddon's *Lady Audley's Secret* (1976), penned *The Vampire, or The Bride of Death*, where she pictured the immortal creature, masquerading as Sir Edward Clevedon, tortured by pangs of conscience but unable to overcome his bloodlust.

Dracula, adapted by Anne Pearson for the Torch Theatre Company of Milford Haven, England, in 1978, begins with a slide of a shipwreck accompanied by a sinister voice-over warning that a large wolf seen leaping ashore the moment the ship grounded is "the embodiment of a malignant being more feared than any other in the legions of the damned—Count Dracula." The ensuing action replicates the plotline established by Deane–Balderston with the participation of the usual suspects—Jonathen Harker, Mina Murray, Lucy Westenra, Renfield, Van Helsing, and Dr. Seward (who is here named not John but Robert).

In November 1984, a new version of *Dracula* appeared at London's Half Moon Theatre—this one by Christopher Bond (whose *Sweeney Todd* served as a base for the celebrated Sondheim–Wheeler musical), featuring Daniel Day-Lewis who, according to sardonic reviewers, "hobbles, crouches and snarls like a bleach-blond bloodless Richard III" and "goes monstrously over the top in black knee-breeches, wolf teeth, white hair, George Robey eyebrows and a hobble like Quasimodo."

A three-and-a-half hour rendition of *Dracula* by the Scottish poet Liz Lochhead played at the Royal Lyceum, Edinburgh, from March 14 through April 6, 1985. "It delves deep beneath the psycho-sexual surface of Stoker's story in an attempt to marry his imagery with modern ideas about women's sexuality," stated reviewer Joyce McMillan.[42]

Irish playwright Frank McGuinness penned a new *Dracula* for the Druid Theatre Company in Galway that opened on April 10, 1986. "*Dracula* belongs to a diseased universe, full of blood loss and bloodletting and madness," wrote McGuinness in the play's program. "He is not the source, but a symptom of that universe, longing for its death."

In the 1940s, Universal Pictures collected recognized monsters and set them loose in *The House of Frankenstein* (1944) and *The House of Dracula* (1945). An enterprising Englishman, Martin Downing, gleefully adopted the scheme for the stage in two "comedy-horrors." Downing's *The House of Frankenstein*, presented in London in March 1989, unfolds at a Carpathian castle where Baron Victor Frankenstein, a scientist, hosts Count Vlad Dracula (who is allotted the Crypt suite) and Countess Ilona Bathory (the Lugosi suite), a pair of vampires who keep begging the baron to help them escape their "hellish existence." The baron's repulsive servants include Ygor, a hunchback who "speaks and shambles like Charles Laughton's Quasimodo," and The Monster, who "resembles the 'Creature' as played by Boris Karloff," both providing comic relief. The Phantom of the Opera, his face concealed by a mask, arrives on the scene unexpectedly, followed by Harry Talbot, who on a night of the full moon turns into a werewolf, sprouting fur, fangs, and a tail. The phantom and Talbot are also unhappy with their lot. Just when it seems that Baron Frankenstein will be unable to rescue the group from their bitter fate, everyone's spirits lighten as they swallow an antidote fetched from the castle's cellar: lager. Gradually their faces brighten, and a celebration ensues. A strange voice cuts across the noise: "Excuse me—is anyone invited? I'm The Invisible Man and I just adore parties."

The House of Dracula, originally performed by The Screaming Blue Murder Company at the Civic Theatre in Leeds on Halloween 1991, is a wild sequel populated by most of the *Frankenstein* characters, but playwright Downing adds the Mummy Ka-Seet, the zombie Groat, and the schizophrenic Doctor Jekyll/Mr. Hyde. All hell breaks loose at a ramshackle Transylvanian fortress.

A Czech musical entitled *Dracula*, created by composer Karel Svoboda, premiered in Prague in 1995 with Daniel Hůlka in the title role. The first act focuses on the death of Dracula's wife, Countess Adriana, in childbirth. Dracula blames God for her demise, attempts to commit suicide, and learns that he is immortal. The story moves forward to the 19th century. Dracula is now living in a castle with three "nymphs," but he is still mourning the death of Adriana. A young orphan girl, Lorraine, comes to the castle seeking refuge and falls hopelessly in love with her host. When she learns that the Count is a vampire, she begs him to transform her too. He reluctantly complies but cannot forget his true love. He is finally allowed to die, and Lorraine decides to join him in death. They both descend to hell.

Two award-winning British playwrights, Jane Thornton and John Godber, collaborated on yet another adaptation of Stoker's novel, first presented by the Hull Trunk Theatre Company in Hull, England, on October 25, 1995. Thornton and Godber judiciously follow the original novel, delivering the elaborate plot on an essentially bare stage. A few chairs and a plethora of coffins are scattered around to serve a cast of six actors, some of whom play double roles. This is a dark, heavy, static affair embedded with long monologues and frequent asides. Thornton and Godber send Harker, Van Helsing, and Seward on a lengthy pursuit, by sea and land, until they arrive at Castle Dracula. The three men surround Dracula, and a battle ensues. At the inconclusive end, the trio remain bloodied and desperate, gasping for breath, while the vampire calmly walks away.

Dracula the Musical, a Swedish endeavor produced in 2010, follows the Stoker novel closely, even including Lucy Westenra's mother, a character omitted from most adaptations. The first act begins with Jonathan Harker arriving in Transylvania for a real estate transaction and prompts Count Dracula's interest in Carfax Abbey. Dracula warns Jonathan about the dangers hovering around his castle in the song "Children of the Night." A few months later, in London, a strong storm hits the mainland, carrying with it a boat ("The Ship on the Thames"). A strange wolf-creature is seen leaving the deck. Mina Murray marries Jonathan ("Wedding in the Abbey") as her best friend, Lucy, falls prey to a deadly bite by Dracula. Following "The Funeral," Abraham van Helsing arrives from Amsterdam and convinces the Harkers that vampires are real ("The Man Who Once Was"). While van Helsing and Jonathan go looking for the Count, Dracula visits Mina and forces her to drink his blood ("The Princes and the River"). The last number ("The Final Battle") begins as van Helsing and associates challenge Dracula. Mina finishes off the vampire by driving a stake through his heart. But appearing ever more demonic, Mina laughs as the curtain closes.

Acting Edition:

The Vampire, or, The Bride of Death by Constance Cox, Samuel French, Inc.

The House of Frankenstein and *The House of Dracula* by Martin Downing, Samuel French, Inc.

Dracula by Jane Thornton and John Godber, Warner/Chapell Plays, London.

Frankenstein

Presumption; or, The Fate of Frankenstein (1823)
Richard Brinsley Peake (England, 1792–1847)

Mary Shelley's Gothic novel *Frankenstein; or, The Modern Prometheus* was first published, in three hardcover volumes, on January 1, 1818. In 1823, Englishman Richard Brinsley Peake converted the novel to the stage under the title *Presumption; or, The Fate of Frankenstein*. Peake tightened Mary Shelley's elaborate plot and eliminated Victor Frankenstein's continental voyages as well as the prologue and epilogue of Captain Robert Walton's chronicle. The clash between Frankenstein and the monster is confined to one scene.

Peake has created a comic couple in *Presumption*: Fritz, Frankenstein's Swiss attendant, and his wife, Madame Ninon. Fritz and Ninon are a lower-class pair, contributing amusing interludes within the gloomy environment. The goofy Fritz has a vital role created especially for Robert Keeley, the admired comedian of the era.[43]

The action of *Presumption* take place in and around Geneva. The lights fade up on the Gothic house of Doctor Frankenstein. Music signals an emerging storm. Attendant Fritz stands on a footstool to peep through the small window of the laboratory. A sudden vibration is heard from within, accompanied by Frankenstein yelling, "It lives! It lives!"

Fritz, alarmed, jumps down hastily and stumbles. He stammers, "There's a hob-goblin 20 feet high," and drags himself off. Frankenstein bolts from the laboratory, locks the door, and sprints down the stairs.

Suddenly the door of the laboratory shatters. The gigantic Creature emerges. Thunder roars as the Creature grabs Frankenstein, hurls him aside, and vanishes through a large window.

In the woods, a cluster of gypsies sits and eats around a fire. The Creature appears nearby. They scream and disperse. The Creature advances toward the fire and puts his hand into the blaze. He swiftly pulls his hand out. The sound of a flute echoes from afar. The Creature listens in rapture and grasps the empty air, attempting to catch the music with his hands.

The Creature next encounters William, Victor's young brother, snatches him, and rushes away. Fritz yells in panic, "Help! Help! Murder!—Oh, my nerves!"

After slaying the boy William in the woods, the Creature now seeks Frankenstein's fiancé, Agatha. He mounts the balcony of the Belrive villa and sneaks into Agatha's room. Just then, Frankenstein enters and is startled to observe in a mirror the image of the Creature tightening his hand on Agatha's throat, suffocating her, and exiting through a window. Frankenstein kneels mournfully by Agatha's body.

The last scene unfolds on a "wild border of the lake. At the extremity of the stage, a lofty over-hanging mountain of snow." The Creature hurries in and begins to climb the mountain. Frankenstein enters with a loaded musket and dashes after the Creature. Stage instructions inform us that The Creature and Frankenstein met face to face. Frankenstein fired. An avalanche erupted and buried both the Creature and Frankenstein while heavy snow kept falling—"and all the characters form a picture as the curtain falls."[44]

* * *

Presumption; or, The Fate of Frankenstein debuted at London's English Opera House (1,500 seats) on July 28, 1823, and ran for 37 performances. The cast included James Wallack (Frankenstein), Robert Keeley (Fritz), Master Boden (William), Elizabeth Austin (Elizabeth), and Mrs. T. Weippert (Madame Ninon). In the original playbill, the actor Thomas Potter Cooke, who played the Creature, is not credited by name but instead is earmarked by a line of dashes (—).[45]

Professor Jeffrey N. Cox, editor of *Seven Gothic Dramas, 1789–1825*, reports, "The play was thought by some to be impious, and it was picketed with leaflets opposing it, but the *Morning Chronicle* (26 July 1823) found a 'striking moral, an attempt to penetrate, beyond prescribed depths, into the mysteries of nature.'"[46]

Mary Shelley attended a performance on August 29, 1823, denoted her approval, and related to a friend, "I found myself famous!"

Presumption continued to be performed until 1850. The triumph of the play endangered mimicries, satires, and spoofs. Peake concocted a parody titled *Another Piece of Presumption*, which was shown at the Adelphi Theatre, London, on October 20, 1823. It features a servant named Frizzy who helps a tailor, Mr. Frankinstitch, sew together body parts, devising a giant named Hobgoblin. The last scene takes place in Mrs. Frankinstitch's garden, with Hobgoblin accidently activating a spring gun, causing an "avalanche of cabbages and cauliflowers."

Within several years, 14 other adaptations of *Frankenstein* were produced in France and England, of which the exceptional ones are *The Monster and the Magician* by John Atkinson Kerr and *The Man and the Monster* by Henry M. Milner. Both were presented in 1826, the first in Paris, the latter in London, each taking liberties with Mary Shelley's story.[47] The peak of *The Monster and the Magician* occurs in a boat on the Adriatic Sea during a violent storm. The Monster pounces at Dr. Frankenstein while the vessel sinks, and the two of them are "engulfed in the waves." The climax of *The Man and the Monster* takes place on top of Mount Etna, where the Monster pierces his creator fatally then tries to flee a mob of armed peasants. He reaches the peak of the mountain, is surrounded by burning lava, and the curtain descends.

A third play inspired by the Frankenstein motif, *The Devil Among the Players*, was also performed in 1826 at London's Opera Glass. It featured three characters of horror: the Frankenstein Monster, the vampire, and Faust. A burlesque adaptation of Mary Shelley's novel, penned by "Richard-Henry" (Richard Butler and H. Chane Newton) and titled *The Model Man*, premiered at London's Gaiety Theatre in 1887, with Dr. Frankenstein now played by a woman, the company's top star Nellie Farren. The Gaiety's second renowned actor, Fred Leslie, enacted the Monster. Donald F. Glut relates in his study *The Frankenstein Legend*, "Leslie's interpretation of the Monster was hardly terrifying. Leslie combed his hair straight down and wore an outfit including high boots, a large coat with an enormous flower in the lapel, a hat, and a monocle in his eye. In some scenes the Monster paraded about in the costume of a ballerina."[48]

Original Complete Edition:

Richard Brinsley Peake, *Presumption; or, the Fate of Frankenstein*, London, England: John Dicks.

H.M. Milner, *Frankenstein; or, The Man and The Monster*, is included in the anthology, *The Hour of One, Six Gothic Melodramas*, London, England: Gordon Fraser.

Frankenstein: An Adventure in the Macabre (1927)
Peggy Webling (England, 1871–1947) and John L. Balderston (United States, 1889–1954)

In the 20th century, the first play to offer a Frankenstein chronicle was *The Last Laugh* (1915) by the American playwrights Charles W. Goddard (1879–1951) and Paul Dickey (1885–1933). *The Last Laugh* satirizes the Frankenstein tale by having its action occur around a wooden crypt where a body wrapped in bandages is hidden—the core piece in the laboratory of a doctor bent on constructing a new human form.

Peggy Webling's *Frankenstein: An Adventure in the Macabre* arrived in 1927. Actor-manager Hamilton Deane, following the success of his production of Bram Stoker's *Dracula*, coupled Webling's *Frankenstein* and *Dracula* to run by turns in the English countryside, with himself starring as the two monsters. *Dracula* then ran successfully in London (391 performances) and was later taken to New York (261 performances).[49]

Deane brought *Frankenstein* to London's Little Theatre on February 10, 1930. The show was savaged by the critics. *The Graphic* of February 22, 1930, said, "There are times when we wish that the authoress would cut the cackle and come to the monster."[50] *Frankenstein* ran for 72 performances. Producer Horace Liveright planned to take the play to New York in 1931 and hired John L. Balderston to doctor it. But Liveright lost his entire fortune in the stock market crash and sold his rights to Universal Studios. The rest is cinema history. The Webling-Balderston version served as the basis for Universal's two classic horror films—*Frankenstein* (1931) and *Bride of Frankenstein* (1935), both directed by James Whale, both starring Boris Karloff as the Monster and Colin Clive as Dr. Frankenstein.[51]

The Webling–Balderston version exchanged the first names of Victor Frankenstein and his friend, Henry Moritz. Webling and Balderston also eliminated some of the novel's characters, including Robert Walton, the arctic seaman who found the frozen Victor Frankenstein near the North Pole; William Frankenstein, Victor's younger brother, who is slayed by the Monster; and Justine Moritz, the young girl incarcerated and hanged for William's murder.

The curtain rises on Henry Frankenstein's home in Ingolstadt, Bavaria. It is a gusty evening. The dim light of an oil lamp reveals a door locked with an iron bar leading to a laboratory. Henry dashes in from the laboratory and excitedly asks his professor, Dr. Waldman, and his boyhood friend, Victor Moritz, to join him.

They approach a long table covered with sheets, set under a galvanic battery. Henry connects wires to the arm of a corpse. He crosses to the cupboard, fetches a small bottle, and pours its contents down the dead man's throat.

Thunder cracks and lightning flashes as the cadaver's hand slowly moves. Rasping sounds echo from under the sheet. Henry roars, "I have made life!" Dr. Waldman falls to his knees in a prayer.

A few weeks later, a distraught Henry tells Victor that he has to keep his creation in the cellar, chained. During a visit from Henry's fiancée, Amelia (in the novel, Elizabeth) Lavenza, the iron bar cracks, and the Monster staggers in. He gets a glimpse of Amelia and hobbles towards the girl, who scurries out. The Creature says haltingly, "Fran-ken-stein want—woman." Henry grips a whip, but the giant clutches him by the throat and croaks, "I am—your master—now."

A series of murders have occurred in the area. Corpses of peasants have been found brutally mutilated. Among the Creature's victims was Katrina (in the novel, Justine), an adopted daughter of the Frankensteins, whom he unintentionally drowned. He stutters that he wanted the beau-ti-ful girl to float on the shin-ing wa-ter.

In desperation, Henry shreds his creation formula and crushes the machine. The Creature pounces at him, and with one powerful blow flings Henry to the floor—dead. The Creature then moans, "Not want—kill—more"—and is struck by lightning. He drops down dead, his face expressing, say the playwrights, "a look of peace." Dr. Waldman places a cross on the Creature's breast as the curtain comes down.

*　*　*

It has taken more than 70 years for the Webling–Balderston adaptation of *Frankenstein* to be performed. *Frankenstein* was offered at Chandler Hall in Newtown, Pennsylvania, from October 31 to November 3, 2002, by permit from Jack Balderston, the author's son. Directed by Eric Stedman, the cast featured Blaise Guld as Henry Frankenstein, Antonio Mastrantonio as Dr. Waldman, and Brian Albert as the Creature.

"For a production mounted on a miniscule budget," opined scholar David J. Skal, "the stage effects were frequently impressive…. The Creature's demise in an electrical crucifixion was Stedman's original contribution, but perfectly in keeping with the script."[52]

Acting Edition:

Peggy Webling's *Frankenstein*, as doctored by John L. Balderston, is included in *Hideous Progenies* by Steven Earl Forry (Philadelphia, Pennsylvania: University of Pennsylvania Press, 1990, pp. 251–286).

Frankenstein: The Gift of Fire (1959)
David Campton (England, 1924–2006)

David Campton's 1959 *Frankenstein: The Gift of Fire*, A Gothic Thriller in Two Acts, is split into three areas: Victor Frankenstein's laboratory, Henri Clerval's home, and a neutral space in between. "This arrangement," relates a production note, "made it possible for the scenes to flow into each other almost cinematically."[53] The first scene depicts Victor confining himself in his laboratory. At the home of Henri Clerval, Victor's friend, there is conversation during supper about a grave robbery; a body was plucked right after the funeral. Elizabeth shares with Henri her worry about her fiancé, Victor, who keeps vanishing, and each time he returns, she feels more and more ignored.

During a thunderstorm, a huge creature surfaces from under a blanket. Henri begs Victor to slay the monster. Instead, Victor sends the Creature to hide in the mountains.

Soon, Master William, Victor's young brother, is found dead in his bedroom. The maid Justine, who was discovered in the child's room, is blamed for his murder. The proof against her is that the snow beneath the window had no tracks. Despite Victor's dissent, Justine is adjudged guilty. Before Henri Clerval can verify Victor's testimony, he is found lifeless on the outskirts of town, his spine crushed.

In the last scene, the Monster enters Clerval's house and accosts Elizabeth. In a diversion from Shelley's original novel and from all stage versions, Elizabeth shoots the Creature herself. The Creature topples. Victor promises Elizabeth that from now on he will avoid unholy experiments.

David Campton's dramatization was first shown at the Library Theatre in Scarborough, England, on July 16, 1959. Campton himself portrayed Mr. Clerval, Henri's father. Alan Ayckbourn, destined to become a significant playwright, played Henri. William Elmhirst appeared as Victor. The Creature was played by Stephen Joseph, who also directed.

Acting Edition:

J. Garnet Miller Ltd.

Frankenstein: The Gift of Fire is part of David Campton's *Three Gothic Plays*, accompanied by *Usher*, based on the horror story by Edgar Allan Poe, and *Carmilla*, derived from Sheridan Le Fanu's vampire tale (J. Garnet Miller Ltd, London, 1973).

Frankenstein (1965)
by The Living Theatre Ensemble

In the mid–1950s, the experimental Living Theatre Company, established in New York City by Julian Beck and Judith Malina and famous for its avant-garde productions, began to rehearse its conception of *Frankenstein* while touring Europe. The play evolved through actors' improvisations. The curtain opens as a girl is flung into a coffin. The girl's executioners carry the coffin down the aisle alongside the audience. Destined to be buried alive, the girl's wailing is heard from inside. The executioners re-enter, mount the stage, and turn into victims themselves. One by one they too are slayed by assorted methods: crucifixion, beheading, guillotine, electric chair, firing squad. Dr. Frankenstein (played by Julian Beck) is concerned. "How can we end human suffering?" he asks and begins to dissect the corpses. He devises a plan to create a New Person, free from society's injustice.

In Dr. Frankenstein's laboratory, an executioner's dead body lies on an operating table. The doctor and his assistants attach elastic tubes to the corpse. After pumping blood, they insert a third eye into the center of the Creature's abdomen. "Slowly, with a sort of whistling of lungs," states Pierre Biner in his book *The Living Theatre*, "the dead begin to detach themselves from the lit ground, and create in Chinese shadow silhouette the effect of a three-storied monster with red eyes. The curtain slowly descends."[54]

In the second act we are introduced to Fritz, a convict who survived a hanging because the rope broke. Dr. Frankenstein engages Fritz as his personal assistant. His main duty is to equip his boss with vital intestines.

The Creature blinks his eyes and slowly comes to life. Through earphones, Frankenstein imparts to the Creature the history of the ages, highlighting the dictates of Buddha.

The doctor does not anticipate the extreme shift of his illustrious intentions. Soon the Creature throttles a policeman who attempted to arrest him and squashes Fritz with his foot when he provoked him with a scorching rod. More acts of brutality prevail.

Act III unfolds in a prison. The executioners search for prey in the auditorium, lead several planted viewers to the stage, and dispatch them to isolated cells. Dr. Frankenstein is detained and imprisoned. He guides the convicts to an uprising, but once again, he causes upheaval and demise. To hinder the guards, he lights a fire in his cell, but—alas—it mushrooms and grows out of control. Behind a cluster of fumes, the grunts of choking prisoners are heard. The smoke evaporates to disclose a pile of bodies.

The "dead" crawl toward the center of the stage and gradually shape into the form of The Creature. The Creature blames Frankenstein for causing the death of innocent people, but the altercation results in reciprocal understanding, hugs, and kisses. So, in this singular, abstract, chilling adaptation, the legend of Dr. Frankenstein and his Monster climaxes on a positive, upbeat assertion, with the characters engaging in acts of love.

*   *   *

When The Living Theatre's *Frankenstein* debuted at the Teatro La Perla in Venice, Italy, on September 26, 1965, the performance was six hours long. A second rendition, five hours long, opened at the Festival of Cassis, Provence, France, in the summer of 1966. A much shorter third depiction of *Frankenstein* played at Dublin's Olympic Theatre in October 1967.

On September 9, 1968, the Living Theatre troupe came back to New York, and soon thereafter *Frankenstein* opened at the Brooklyn Academy of Music. *New York Times* critic Clive Barnes found, "The evening is at times repetitious, at times banal, here and there (and only here and there) a little boring. But the overwhelming impression is of a new physical style of theatre, raw, gutsy and vital."[55] *Frankenstein* won an Obie Award.

During 1968 and 1969, The Living Theatre hit the road. A performance of *Frankenstein* at the University of Chicago on January 9, 1969, evoked a warm review from Glenna Syse of the *Chicago Sun-Times*: "It is completely unique, often totally theatrical, funny, devastating and notably ingenious."[56] Conversely, when *Frankenstein* played at the University of Southern California, Los Angeles, on February 25, 1969, reviewer Dan Sullivan sniffed, "The Living Theatre's tendency to do its own thing no matter what makes *Frankenstein* a much deader show than it should be…. Too many scenes go on long, long after you have got the point…. I am afraid that more than one nap was taken in USC's Bovard Auditorium Tuesday night as *Frankenstein* lumbered along to midnight."[57]

The Living Theatre continued to haul the three-ton scenery of *Frankenstein* to the Yale School of Drama in New Haven, Connecticut, and to other learning institutions, including MIT, Detroit Institute of Art, Lawrence University, and the University of Colorado.

Columnist Renfreu Neff describes *Frankenstein* in her book *The Living Theatre:*

USA, as "a collage of pop art, mytho-science-fiction, and the Late Late Show, all of it buttressed by political dogma and moral polemic. It is essentially naïve and corny in plot concept, yet it is so theatrically spectacular, so brilliantly mounted and performed that a kinetic tension is produced, an existing force that is truly electrical."[58]

Frankenstein (1974)
Tim Kelly (United States, 1931–1998)

The American playwright Tim Kelly combined elements from Mary Shelley's original novel with bits and pieces from several movie releases and added angles of his own when adapting *Frankenstein* in 1974 into a two-act play that unfolds in a villa on the banks of Lake Geneva, Switzerland.

Kelly's *Frankenstein* begins with an introduction of a Swiss police inspector, Ernst Hessler, who is investigating the murder of a child, William Frankenstein, the brother of scientist Victor Frankenstein. Hessler interrogates Frau Frankenstein, her son Victor, and housekeeper Sophie. The inspector confides that William's dead body was discovered near a camp of gypsies. A girl named Justine was apprehended trying to sell William's cross. Justine insists that a man gave it to her, "a man large and stitched together like a rag doll," but she continues to be the prime suspect.

Victor reveals to his friend Henry Clerval that he has discovered how to create life and has committed himself to the creation of a human being. He has stolen into the city morgue and area hospitals, spirited away human parts, and manufactured a live Creature. His monster is probably responsible for William's death: "There is blood on my hands for having created him." Neither he nor Henry intervenes to save Justine from the gallows.

However, belated pangs of conscience instigate Victor to destroy his lab's power-driven machinery. In his rage, the Creature strangles Henry and warns Victor, "I shall be with you on your wedding night."

The last scene takes place on the day of Victor and Elizabeth's wedding. The happy couple comes back home after the nuptials. Inspector Hessler encircles their villa with guards carrying rifles.

Victor enters the laboratory to burn files. The Creature descends from the attic, where he has been lurking, approaches Elizabeth, and grabs her by the throat. However, Tim Kelly's version ends happily. At the critical moment, Victor emerges from the laboratory with a pistol in hand and shoots the Creature. Wounded, the Creature topples out the window. From the garden we hear bursts of gunshots.

Inspector Hessler returns to announce that the Creature, fatally injured, managed to dive into the lake; his unit will search for the body. Elizabeth is soothed: "It's ended, Victor. Forever." Victor Frankenstein goes to the window and glares at the lake. "I wonder," he mutters.

Called *The Rage of Frankenstein*, the play was offered by Off-Broadway's Carter Theatre on October 31, 1979. Ted Bank assessed in *Show Business*, "Playwright Tim Kelly has given us an unusually articulate and intelligent Monster who speaks at length about his feelings and desires."[59] In addition to *Frankenstein/The Rage of Frankenstein*, Kelly also wrote *Bride of Frankenstein Goes Malibu* (1976), *The Frankensteins are Back in Town* (1980) and *Frankenstein Slept Here* (1984).

Acting Edition: Samuel French, Inc.

Frankenstein (1981)
Victor Gialanella (United States, 1949–)

The Monster shuffled to Broadway's Palace Theatre on January 4, 1981. *Frankenstein* by Victor Gialanella featured David Dukes (Victor Frankenstein), Keith Jochim (the Creature), Dianne West (Elizabeth Lavenza), and John Carradine (hermit DeLacey). Tom Moore directed.

The action occurs in and around the Frankenstein Chateau, Geneva, Switzerland, in the mid–1800s. An introductory scene takes place in a gloomy graveyard, where two brawny men, Hans Metz and Peter Schmidt, lift a corpse from a open grave. Victor Frankenstein enters and instructs the men to drop the body "in the usual place." Schmidt informs him that the remains are those of a hanged man. The two grave robbers cover the body with cloth as the lights fade.

In the waiting room of the chateau, Victor confides to his friend Henry Clerval that he's able of reinstate life; thus disease and death will at last be eliminated forever.

Victor leads Henry to the laboratory, a large room filled with electrical devices. In the center there is a long plank on which lies a body. A storm rages outside as Henry fastens a band across the dead man's chest, and Victor maneuvers switches. Machinery vibrates. The plank rises toward the ceiling, along with a crack of thunder and a flash of lightning. The plank descends, and the machinery winds down. Victor checks the figure and yells, "It's alive!"

Victor and Henry are elated by the enormous achievement but soon discover that they have no influence over the Creature, who climbs out of the window and vanishes.

The following scene, appropriated from the motion picture *The Bride of Frankenstein*, recounts the Creature's arrival in the insulated hut of a blind hermit, DeLacey, who then coaches the odd stranger how to speak. While the Creature is out collecting logs, the grave robbers, Metz and Schmidt, enter and begin to shove items into their sacks. Delacey tries to stop them. Metz squeezes a sash around the blind

Keith Jochim as the Monster in *Frankenstein* by Victor Gialanella, Palace Theatre, New York City, 1981 (photo by Martha Swope, The New York Public Library for the Performing Arts).

man's neck and smothers him—the first of several cruel murders committed throughout the play.

The Creature enters carrying a pile of logs, stares at the body, and steps toward Metz, who draws a knife and stabs the Creature. He pulls out the knife and rams a pitchfork into Metz, who topples with a shriek. The Creature sits by DeLacey, rocks him soothingly, and mutters a word he has lately learned, "Friend!"

Act Two describes the endeavors of the Creature as he returns to the Frankenstein Chateau, plays with William, Victor's eight-year-old brother, and unintentionally suffocates the boy. A clash in the laboratory ends with the Creature propelling Henry fatally towards the high-voltage electrical machine. A year later, on Elizabeth's wedding day, the Creature, not aware of his own strength, inadvertently strangles Elizabeth in the bedroom. Victor shoots the Creature who, mortally wounded, breaks Victor's back. The Creature then staggers to the electrical knobs and breaks them one by one. The machinery rattles. A blaze sparks, fumes glow, and the lab crumbles, eradicating the Creature and his creator.

In the published Acting Edition of *Frankenstein*, playwright Victor Gialanella states that the destruction of the laboratory "can be accomplished by the use of flash-pots, smoke, flickering colored lights and the appropriate accompanying sound. At the very end, almost simultaneously with the curtain, a few chunks of painted Styrofoam thrown from the wings or dropped from the flies add greatly to the illusion."[60]

Frankenstein premiered at New York's Palace Theatre on January 4, 1981, and was hit by harsh reviews. Frank Rich wrote, "This playwright has merged the most memorable scenes from James Whale's 1931 Hollywood version with random scraps from the 1816 Shelley novel only to end up with a talky-stilted mishmash."[61] Christopher Sharp concluded, "Victor Gialanella's new play at the Palace is not scary, not funny, not dramatic, not melodramatic, not even entertaining."[62]

Frankenstein raised its curtain for only one performance; it opened and closed on the same night, forfeiting the total financial backing of $2,000,000.

Acting Edition: Dramatists Play Service.

Other Adaptations of Frankenstein

Many other dramatizations of *Frankenstein* were produced during the 20th century. Gladys Hastings-Walton's adaptation was seen in Glasgow in 1936. Donald F. Glut writes that this version was loyal to the original story and adds, "Miss Hastings-Walton tried to show the very real horror of man's being replaced by the machines that he created."[63]

In the early 1940s, the drama department at Fairmont High School in Manion, Indiana, offered a parody, *Goon with the Wind*, in which a young student, who would later become a household name, played the Frankenstein Monster: James Dean.

Written by Sheldon Allman and Bob Pickett, *I'm Sorry, the Bridge Is Out, You'll Have to Spend the Night* is a musical satire of horror films of the 1930s and 1940s. The play opened at Hollywood's Coronet Theatre on April 28, 1970. The quirky action focuses on Dr. Frankenstein's mission to acquire a brain for his Monster. A storm destroys a nearby bridge and propels John David Walgood and his fiancée, Mary Ellen Harriman, to take cover in a neighboring castle. The couple is unaware of danger when confronted by the

Mummy, the Wolf Man, and other ghostly creatures. A musical sequel to *I'm Sorry, the Bridge Is Out*, called *Frankenstein Unbound*, was created by Allman and Pickett in 1995.

The Frankenstein Affair, by Ken Eulo, was presented at Off-Broadway's Courtyard Playhouse in 1979, interweaving the action between Mary Shelley's bedroom and Dr. Frankenstein's laboratory in an attempt to depict a similarity between Shelley's troubled marriage with the predicaments of the Monster.

In Brighton, England, a version of *Frankenstein* by Geoff Parker was performed at the Gardner Centre in 1984 and drew an assessment by the *London Theatre Record*: "Geoff Parker has unwisely spread his net wide, following the Mary Shelley novel from childhood to death. The result is a broad unfocused evening that could do with a fair degree of pruning."[64]

Back in the States, Manhattan's City Stage Company displayed an alteration of *Frankenstein* by Laurence Maslon in 1985. Here the Monster is a sympathetic creation. In 1986, Second Avenue Theatre offered the musical *Have I Got a Girl for You!* This "wildly campy spoof of *The Bride of Frankenstein*"[65] unravels east of Hollywood and is cast with a blended chorus of peasants and movie actors.

In the late 1980s the Monster came into existence on the stages of Cincinnati's Playhouse in the Park (by David Richmond and Bob Hall) and the Tyrone Guthrie Theatre in Minneapolis (by Barbara Field). George Abbott wrote the book for *Frankie*, a 1989 musical comedy produced Off-Broadway by the York Theatre Company. The endeavor was described as "a woeful modernization of *Frankenstein*" in *The Best Plays of 1989–1990*.[66]

During the 1990s the Monster continued to shock audiences on both sides of the Atlantic. *The Bride of Frankenstein*, adapted by David Yeakle from the original screenplay by William Hurlbut and John L. Balderston, was produced by the Hip Theater, Fort Worth, Texas, in 1991, staged by Yeakle, with Bob Allen as the Monster. A rendition written and directed by Julia Bardsley raised its curtain at the Haymarket Studio, Leicester, England, in 1992. "It's a dazzling demonstration of the use of imagistic theatre techniques to grab the audience by its imagination," complimented the *Royal Exchange*, Manchester.[67] A year later, New York's Off-Broadway's Triangle Theatre Company mounted Barbara Field's *Playing with Fire (After Frankenstein)*, in which the final clash between Dr. Frankenstein and the Monster takes place at the North Pole. In 1999, the Sandbach Players of Cheshire, England, presented *The House of Frankenstein* by Martin Downing, highlighting a gaggle of monsters—Frankenstein, vampires, werewolves, zombies, and the phantom of the opera—assembling under a full moon in an ancient castle. A year later, the creatures got together at Off-Broadway's Triad Theatre in *Miami Beach Monsters*, advertised as "a vaudeville with a bite."[68]

The Creature continued his ruckus in the 21st century. Off-Broadway's La Mama presented *Frankenstein: The Rock Musical*, with book, music, and lyrics by William Electric Black, in 2000. For Halloween 2001, Tim Kelly's *Frankenstein* was staged by Stewart F. Lane at the Powerhouse Performing Arts Center, New Canaan, Connecticut. Howard Brenton's drama, *Blood Poetry*, transpiring in a Lake Geneva lodge in 1816 with Mary Shelley, Percy Bysshe Shelley, Lord Byron, and Dr. Polidori discussing ghost stories, was reincarnated in 2001 at the Connelly Theatre, East Village, New York City.

Adapted and directed by William Gilmore for Off-Broadway's Looking Glass Theatre, *The Tragedy of Frankenstein* was mounted in 2001 in the manner of classic Greek drama. A chorus master (Tod Butera) and his chorus of imps recount the tragic events surrounding Victor Frankenstein (Matthew Bray) and his quest to create life. Online reviewer John Chatterton related, "This show was not about monsters and mad scientists; it was a thoughtful and faithful, if sometimes blunt and muddy, adaptation of an important book."[69]

The year 2002 was a popular year for Frankenstein productions. In January, Manhattan's Classic Stage Company showed *Monster*, a risqué version of Shelley's novel by Neil Bell. Directed by Michael Greif, the Monster walks around naked, Frankenstein's fiancée bares herself, and the doctor fondles a male patient. Critic Donald Lyons found it "a preposterous and unintentionally funny vulgarization of the tale."[70] In February, the Scottish Opera of Glasgow proffered *Monster* by Sally Beamish. Her libretto centers on the 1816 house party attended by Lord Byron, Mary Wollstonecraft, and Percy Bysshe Shelley. In October, H.K. Gruber's mischievous oratorio *Frankenstein!* was played by the Cleveland Orchestra. Bernard Holland stated in the *New York Times*, "The wild-eyed Mr. Gruber recites, rants, mugs, sings and plays toy instruments."[71]

In mid–October, Off-Broadway's Looking Glass Theatre brought back its 2001 production of *The Tragedy of Frankenstein*, a reworking by William Gilmore, which activated the chorus to interact with the audience. Later in October, Off-Off-Broadway's The McGinn/Cazale Theatre put on Scott Blumenthal's *So Frightful an Event is Single in the History of Man*. The action unfolds at Dr. Frankenstein's home where we are introduced to his parents, his fiancée Elizabeth, and his friend Henry (both later murdered by a raging Creature). In the last scene, the Creature flees to a remote haven by racing through the audience.

In early November, The Company Chandler Hall Stage mounted the world premiere of a new adaptation of *Frankenstein* by Eric Stedman, who also directed. Blaise Guild appeared as a young Victor Frankenstein, and Brian Albert was the Creature.

Robert George Asselstine is the composer, librettist, and lyricist of *Frankenstein.... Do you Dream?* The piece, promoted as an "epic musical experience, a faithful telling of Mary Shelley's original story," was launched in Toronto, Canada, in 2003 and moved the following year to New York City's fringe Belt Theatre.

Catherine Bush's *The Frankenstein Summer*, another fictitious exploration of the actual get-together of Mary Shelley, Percy Bysshe Shelley, Lord Byron, and Dr. Polidori, was brought to Manhattan's Theatre at the Clements in October 2004. It concentrates on the topics of love and desire.

The Flying Machine, a mime company, brought its *Frankenstein* to Off-Broadway's Soho Theatre in December 2004. The stage setting was a curved maze. "All of mankind appears monstrous in this production," reported *New York Times'* reviewer Jason Zinoman. "Every actor wears pointy ears and fake protruding teeth, making them look vaguely animalistic, an effect emphasized by the cast's bustling, sweaty energy."[72]

Frankenstein, the Musical, by Robert Mitchell, was produced at Off-Broadway's Wing Theatre in 2006. The show had 40 musical numbers—none catchy—and hardly any dialogue. Some excitement was reached during the last scene when Victor Frankenstein challenges his creation. Andrea Stevens of the *New York Times* rebuked director John Henry Davis for "mistaking melodrama for drama by increasing the violence."[73] The *New York Post*'s Frank Scheck found the "new Creature more cheesy than scary."[74]

In 2007, two more musicals based on the Frankenstein myth reached New York. *Frankenstein*, with music by Mark Baron, book and lyrics by Jeffrey Jackson, was trumpeted as "extraordinarily faithful to Mary Shelley's original novel while offering a bold, new experience for modern theatre audiences." The spectacle, shown at Off-Broadway's

37 Arts, was negatively reviewed by the *New York Times'* Charles Isherwood, who describes the Creature prowling the stage "in something between a swagger and a stagger" as if he "was fighting through a fearsome case of constipation."[75]

Opening at Broadway's Hilton Theatre on November 8, 2007, the musical *Young Frankenstein*, for which Mel Brooks composed the music, wrote the lyrics, and collaborated with Thomas Meehan on the book. Directed by Susan Stroman, the original Broadway cast came with the show to Los Angeles's Pantages Theatre for a two-week run, July 27 to August 8, 2010.

Frankenstein (Mortal Toys), a puppet show created by Erik Ehn, debuted at the Velaslavasay Panorama of Los Angeles in December 2007, and wandered east to New York's HERE Arts Center, where it opened in January 2008. The *New York Times'* Rachel Saltz praised directors-designers Janie Geiser and Susan Simpson: "They have deftly recreated the atmosphere of Shelley's novel in poetic, visual terms … we are treated to the spectacle of artists, fully engaged, transforming and illuminating material they obviously love."[76]

Man-Made, written and directed by Susan Mosakowski, went through two workshops and eventually was presented by the Creation Production Company at Off-Broadway's Ohio Theatre from February 29 to March 22, 2008. The characters include the originators of the evolution theory: Charles Darwin and Alfred Russel Wallace. Mary Shelley implores them to locate a suitable mate for her Creature.

Chicago's company 500 Clown presented its comedy *Frankenstein* at the Orange County Performing Arts Center in Costa Mesa, California. In February 2011, the National Theater in London offered a two-hour, intermission-free production of *Frankenstein*, faithfully adapted by Nick Dear and grittily directed by Danny Boyle. Benedict Cumberbatch and Jonny Lee Miller alternated in the portrayals of Victor Frankenstein and the Creature, both actors garnering praise. "Unfortunately," wrote critic Ben Brantley in the *New York Times*, "the Creature is more compelling than his creator here. Though this play (like the novel) presents its man and superman as different sides of the same personality, only the Monster persuasively grabs our empathy."[77]

In July 2012, Off-Broadway's Atlantic Stage 2 revived Neal Bell's *Frankenstein* reboot *Monster*, directed by Jim Petosa, calling it "a taut and chilling stage adaptation of Mary Shelley's Frankenstein," but earning a negative assessment by Helen Shaw in *Time Out New York*: "Here it's all yelling and shambling and passionate clutching at one another, every actor's worst instincts are on display. And for my part, reviewing it seems more than a little … monstrous."[78] In January 2013, Radiohole, a Brooklyn-based experimental theater company, mounted *Inflatable Frankenstein*, in which most of the hour-long drama was dedicated to a sort of symposium, with six actors passing a microphone, talking about the Frankenstein myth.

Frankenstein—A New Musical opened in October 2016 at The Complex Hollywood, Hollywood, California. In December 2017 the Ensemble for the Romantic Century presented *Frankenstein* at Off-Broadway's Pershing Square Signature Center, directed by Donald Sanders and featuring former ballet dancer Robert Fairchild in the role of the Monster. The production, fusing classical music, dance, and storytelling with three musicians accompanying the action on stage, was deemed a failure by *New York Times* critic Laura Collins-Hughes: "For all of the show's flashes of beauty, it remains a collection of disparate parts, not a whole charged with lightning and brought to animated life."[79] That same month, *Glass Guignol: The Brother and Sister Play* opened at Manhattan's Mabou Mines theater. It was a puppet presentation of scenes from several

Tennessee Williams dramas, utilizing Lord Byron, Mary Shelley, and Frankenstein as a framing device. The Zombie Joe's Underground Theatre Group, North Hollywood, California, presented a horrific *Frankenstein* in 2018.

In January 2019, a modern makeover of Mary Shelley's novel was offered by the arts collective Manual Cinema at Off-Broadway's Public Theater. A team of actors, musicians, and technicians presented, as described by Ben Brantley of the *New York Times*, "on screen images summoned into being by overhead projections, shadow and stick puppets."[80]

Matt Sweeney created, composed, and staged the world premiere of a musical *Frankenstein* ("After Mary Shelley") that opened on February 12, 2020, at the Wallis Annenberg Center for the Performing Arts in Beverly Hills, California, for a three-week run. Sebastian Peters-Lazaro designed and choreographed the show. The venture was advertised as "an exuberant amalgamation of dynamic physical theatre, live music and experimental design that brings Mary Shelley's *Frankenstein* to life in today's world of unregulated technology, and questions the moral responsibility for each generation."

The following week, on February 17, Off-Broadway's Classic Stage Company presented its own *Frankenstein*, a metaphysical adaptation by Tristan Bernays, directed by Timothy Douglas. Stephanie Berry played both Victor Frankenstein and his misshapen creature. The show ran in repertory with *Dracula*, Kate Hamill's adaptation of the Bram Stoker novel

Horror buffs should look forward to new stage adaptations of Mary Shelley's novel that currently are being developed for future presentations.

One-Act Plays

Two one-act plays about Frankenstein's Monster were published in 1981 and 1998. Murder and mayhem are at the core of John Mattera and Stephen Barrows' *Frankenstein* (1981). The action takes place at the London home of Henry Clerval, a friend of Victor Frankenstein. Inspector Erickson of Scotland Yard investigates a series of brutal murders. The gigantic Creature is the main suspect, but the denouement comes up with a surprising solution.

Larry Hillhouse's *Doctor Frank's Styne*, subtitled *A Parody of the Frankenstein Myth* (1998), unfolds in a manor inherited by Franklin Kenneth Styne, a budding poet. Upon arrival, he introduces himself to the Styne Castle staff: Egor, a hunchbacked attendant, and Hilda, a strict housekeeper. A local constable and his beautiful niece drop by to welcome Styne and become immersed in the age-old secrets of the manor. Three singing specters contribute comic relief.

Acting Edition:

Frankenstein by John Mattera and Stephen Barrows, The Dramatic Publishing Company.

Doctor Frank'n Styne by Larry Hillhouse, Eldridge Publishing.

The Werewolf

While the vampire and Frankenstein's Monster are creatures of the imagination, conjured by creative writers and filmmakers, scientists claim that the idea of a human being morphing into a wolf is within the realm of feasibility.

Dr. Franklin Ruehl, in his Forward to Brad Steiger's *The Werewolf Book*, chronicles real-life instances of such transformations: "Intriguingly, the first depiction of a man-wolf was apparently inscribed on a cave wall, suggesting that even prehistoric *Homo sapiens* may have been cognizant of this incredible duality." Ruehl describes early accounts of lycanthropy in the Scriptures' Book of Daniel, where King Nebuchadnezzar exhibited symptoms of werewolfism, and in the Greek legend of King Lycaon of Arcadia being transformed into a wolf by Zeus after offending the god by serving him a meal of human flesh. This legend gave birth to the scientific term for werewolf, "Lycanthrope."

Professor Ruehl continues his survey on werewolves: "Later in the fifth century BC, the celebrated historian Herodotus reported on the Neuri, a strange people who became wolves once a year. In the first century AD, noted Roman poet Virgil described a sorcerer who transmogrified himself into a wolf by the use of secret herbs."[81]

In the Middle Ages, accounts of lycanthropy mushroomed. In France alone, 30,000 individuals were charged with werewolfism between 1520 and 1630.

Lycanthropy is mentioned in the plays *The Duchess of Malfi* (c. 1613) by John Webster; *Giraldi, or A Ruffian of Prague* (1820), and *The Demon of the Wolf* (1824), both by Edward Fitzball. A werewolf is imprisoned in a dungeon in the 1824 horror novel *The Albigenses* by Charles Robert Maturin, a pioneer of Gothic literature.

In modern times, several motion pictures spread the notion that a person may become a werewolf by being bitten by one—notably *The Werewolf of London* (1935), starring Henry Hull, and *The Wolf Man* (1941), featuring Lon Chaney, Jr. Curses can also lead to transformation, as presented in the Gothic television soap opera *Dark Shadows* (1966–1971). Heredity, too, may trigger the condition, as suggested in the films *The Undying Monster* (1941), with John Howard as the lycanthropic heir, and in *Cry of the Werewolf* (1944), with Nina Foch as a female descendant of a gypsy werewolf.

In most cases, the werewolf is to be pitied. While the vampire is evil, with no human feelings or emotions, the werewolf goes through inner anguish and despair, fully aware of what he has done. During the cycle of a full moon, his blood undergoes a chemical change, and he cannot help becoming a ferocious beast, attacking all within his reach, killing and feeding on the flesh of his victim. The taint can come to anyone—even to honest, upright persons.

The only security measure against the werewolf is the covering of windowsills and doorsteps with garlic blossoms or garlic oil. An ordinary bullet will not harm a werewolf, but a silver bullet will bring instant death.

The werewolf, like the vampire, has been the subject of many literary treatments.

Margie and the Wolf Man (1950)
Robert St. Clair (United States, 1898–1967)

Subtitled "A Comedy Mystery Drama in Three Acts," the action of *Margie and the Wolf Man* unfolds continuously on one summer evening in the living room of the Wilson home on a quiet residential street in a Midwestern city.

The household consists of Ursula Wilson, a gentle, middle-aged woman; Joan Wilson, Ursula's pretty daughter, a budding writer seeking an innovative topic for a new television program; and Joan's bright and feisty teenage sister, Margie. When leaving a visiting carnival, Margie happens to catch a glimpse of the escaped robber of a local canning factory—a redheaded woman with a big brown mole on her chin, wearing a hat with a yellow ribbon. Ursula intimates that the incident may be suitable for a TV topic, but Joan rejects it because it isn't strange enough.

Margie relates that she saw a wolfman at the carnival, a creature who was kept in a wooden box—"like a coffin"—exhibiting a wolf's head, a man's body, long talons for fingernails, and dressed in an old suit. Margie believes the creature "was just a fake." Ursula suggests that Joan should use this idea in her play: have a man turn into a werewolf during a full moon and "go around biting people." Joan is intrigued but skeptical, assuming that everyone would "scoff at such ridiculous superstitions."

The doorbell chimes. Madame Leo, one of the ladies from the carnival, enters, asking to use the phone. Buxom, heavily made-up, her hair bleached blond, Madame Leo speaks loudly and jovially, relating that her truck broke down in the street right outside, and she has to call a garage. She introduces herself as "Madame Leo, Leo the Lioness," and rattles that her "real, honest-to-gosh name's Arabella Henrietta Johnson McCormick MacGillicudy," explaining she has been married three times but was never divorced because all her husbands passed away: "Johnson had a sudden heart attack. McCormick jumped off a bridge and drowned himself, and I guess I just naturally talked poor old MacGillicudy to death! Ha! Ha! Ha!"

Madame Leo picks up the phone to call a garage and asks permission to bring in a box containing a werewolf, promising, "He wouldn't be no trouble at all." Ursula explodes, "You certainly may not!" but Margie intercedes, and Ursula gives in.

A series of scary-yet-funny incidents occur as the gruesome-looking creature emerges from the box and scares the wits out of a nosy neighbor and Joan's two competing beaux. But at the end, when the wolfman takes off the gloves and mask, "he" is in reality a very redheaded "she"—a beautiful woman, the daughter of Madame Leo. Mother and daughter used the gambit to rob the payroll at the canning factory in the morning and were on the way out of town when their truck broke down.

A police siren sounds. Madame Leo and her daughter are hustled into a car. Margie exclaims that the proceedings are "a perfectly terrific plot for a television show." Joan agrees.

Acting Edition: Eldridge Publishing Company.

The Curse of The Werewolf (1976)
Ken Hill (England, 1937–1995)

Unlike the broad, farcical acting style recommended by the authors of most werewolf plays, Ken Hill warns that his play, *The Curse of the Werewolf,* "only works on a very truthful level. It must be played in deadly earnest—one must believe in werewolves—one must believe in the people—and one must *care* what happens to them."[82]

When the lights come up, it is 1922, and the proceedings unfold at Walpurgis-dorf Castle, located in a small German village. Enter the formidable Eunice Bancroft, her meek husband, Dr. Hugo Bancroft, and their pretty daughter, Kitty. Mrs. Bancroft rebukes her husband for suggesting that they travel to this "pig sty" to visit with his friend Professor Konrad Steiner, an old medical school chum.

The lighthearted beginning changes abruptly when the Bancrofts become aware that their host has been studying lycanthropy—a mental condition in which the patient thinks he is an animal—and has a werewolf locked in his basement. In a tense scene, Kitty is strapped to what looks like a dentist's chair. Accompanied by heavy musical chords, Steiner has donned a green operating gown, complete with big rubber gloves, rubber boots, and a little light in the center of his forehead. He tells Kitty she has "the privilege of participating in a unique historic moment, the creation of an entirely new species…. Lupus Steinerii!" Kitty is destined to be the mother of his new species.

Steiner approaches Kitty with the syringe but suddenly freezes. The moon grows brighter. He pulls off his rubber gloves and stares in horror at his hairy hands. "No!" he cries. "Not me!" He stumbles out but returns immediately, face hideous and hairy—a different actor.

Steiner crosses to Kitty, puts his hands around her neck and—snarling horribly—bends to bite her. Loud growling is heard from the hallway. Another werewolf, the neighbor Martin von Hellman, springs in and faces Steiner. The two werewolves circle one another, then fight. Bancroft rushes in and releases his daughter. Steiner snatches a lantern and hurls it at Martin. Martin dodges, and the lantern starts a fire.

All stumble out, leaving the two werewolves to battle it out. The smoke fills the stage. The effects projector bathes the entire stage in leaping flames. The piano plays thunderous music. The werewolves howl in terror, and the lights fade to black.

* * *

The Curse of the Werewolf was first produced by the Contact Theatre Company, Manchester, England, on October 6, 1976. The play was directed by Kenneth Alan Taylor and designed by Marty Flood. The cast included Christopher Ravenscroft (Professor Konrad Steiner) and Nicholas Geake (Baron Martin von Hellman). Hugo, Eunice, and Kitty Bancroft were played, respectively, by Peter Dudley, Judith Barker, and Joanna Mackie.

A 1994 revival of the play at the Theatre Royal, Stratford East, London, garnered a mixed online review by Paul Taylor in *The Independent*: "The songs are, frankly, no great shakes and there are patches where you may feel that an evening of harmless fun imposes its own kind of strain. An engaging cast stops your smile from getting too glassy, though."[83]

London's Union Theatre mounted *The Curse of the Werewolf* in 2007 and received a glowing online assessment by Marcela Olivares, in *Indie London*: "This was a very enjoyable play that expertly combined horror with comedy and even some singing!"[84]

Acting Edition: Samuel French, Ltd.

The Werewolf's Curse
or Hair Today, Gone Tomorrow (2002)
Billy St. John (United States, 1942–2017)

The published version of *The Werewolf's Curse* includes the subtitle, "A Totally Outrageous Supernatural Comedy," and the following production note to the actors: "*Werewolf's Curse* is a spoof of Universal Studio's classic horror films of the 1930s, *The Wolf Man*, *Frankenstein*, and *Dracula* in particular. The style of acting in these movies is very different than today's more naturalistic approach … camp it up and have fun!"[85]

The proceedings unfold in 1930s Romania. Act I, Scene 1 takes place in a forest. Lightning and thunder signify an approaching storm. A few standing cutouts of trees are downstage right, while downstage left encompasses a heavy wooden door with a huge metal knocker, representing the entrance to Castle Einstein.

Harry Cate and Etta Greenleaf, good-looking American students in their 20s, brave the storm and knock at the castle door. They tell a butler that Dr. Einstein is expecting them and are ushered in.

Dr. Frank Einstein is described as "30's or older, a mad scientist, though he seems 'normal' at the moment." Harry says he's majoring in veterinary science at the University of Lipsync, where he met and fell in love with Etta, and in the break between semesters, they took a trip to the Wacherstepinder Forest and got lost in the woods. As night fell, they heard a whimpering sound that was obviously made by a creature in distress. They followed the sound and came upon a wolf cub whose leg was caught in a steel trap. "I sprang the trap and set its leg free," continues Harry. He reached to pet it, and the cub bit his finger. At the next full moon, he felt a tingling sensation all over his body, suddenly grew hair, and had a ravenous craving for very rare beef.

"That doesn't sound so bad," Dr. Einstein says, but Etta explains that she is a dedicated vegetarian, and the thought of eating meat repulses her. Harry is willing to convert to vegetarianism, but as long as this lycanthropic curse is on him, he cannot control himself. Harry laments, "You see, doctor! Etta and I will never find happiness together unless you can lift this curse!"

Dr. Einstein believes he can help Harry. He will solicit the assistance of a gypsy fortune teller, Madam Clara Voyant.

At the top of Act II, the villagers, aware of "unholy experiments," set the castle on fire. In the laboratory, Harry lies on the gurney, roped at the wrists and ankles. Dr. Einstein, not aware of the approaching flames, flips switches and turns dials. "In just a few minutes, I am going to perform a little surgery on you, Harry," he says. "Before the night is over, you will be a hairy, snarling beast of a man—a werewolf!"

There is a loud banging on a side door, shades of the 1932 movie *The Bride of Frankenstein*, and the guttural sounds of a Monster are heard: "Mate ... want mate ... now!" Dr. Einstein crosses to the door, opens it a crack, and says, "Good Grief! Stop acting like a baby! You'll have to be patient."

Dr. Einstein picks up a scalpel and apologizes for being out of anesthetic. "I am afraid this is going to hurt a little." The doctor flips a switch and a strobe light flickers. Approaching Harry, he lifts the scalpel when the villagers burst in, untie Harry, and turn off the strobe light. Dr. Einstein grabs Etta and holds the scalpel to her neck. "Move aside!" he orders. The Monster's hand appears behind him, seizes him, and pulls him out of sight.

All escape to a clearing in the nearby forest. Harry, now hairy and deformed, grudgingly tells Etta that he cannot join her and suggests that she complete her studies "and make a happy life for yourself." But then Madam Clara, the fortune teller, thrusts her hand into her pockets and brings out a piece of raw spinach leaf.

Harry puts the leaf into his mouth and chews it. He starts to choke. The villagers make a semicircle around Harry, who removes the wig and beard and hands them to an unseen stagehand. The troupe ad libs astonishment, then parts to reveal Harry, who says, "Food! I want turnip greens! Lima beans! Squash!"

Everyone cheers. Etta rushes to Harry, and they kiss. Lively music comes in and the cast takes their bow.

Acting Edition: Samuel French, Inc.

More Werewolves on Stage

Werewolf? (1972), a one-act by William K. Gleason, is the story of Harold Worley, a timid man smothered by a possessive mother and defenseless against a shrewish wife. He meets with a psychiatrist, whose first question is, "What seems to be the trouble, Mr. Worley?" Harold answers, "I'm a werewolf." Coaxed by the doctor, Harold relates in detail his problems with the two women in his life. The doctor treats him with professional tolerance until he observes that his patient's hands and face begin to grow thick hair. Harold growls horribly and moves in for the kill. He backs the doctor into a corner, throws him to the floor, and howls with delight. He then looks menacingly at the audience and stalks off. The playlet could have ended then and there, but the doctor gets up, brushes himself off, walks over to his desk, and picks up the phone. He instructs his secretary, Miss Stanley, to call Mrs. Worley and set another appointment for her husband on the 15th at the usual time.

The title character of Eugene Jackson's *Coffey Pott Meets the Wolf Man* (1982) is the world's youngest and prettiest detective, sometimes assisted by her younger sister, Sugar. When the girls decide to visit the long-abandoned, old family home, they find that it's not abandoned after all. In fact, it's buzzing with activity. Teen Films, Inc. is shooting a wolfman movie in the spooky Victorian mansion. The plot thickens when the wolfman comes in and carries off the movie's beautiful heroine. Apparently, he is not an actor but a real wolfman. Coffey suspects there is more here than meets the eye and begins to examine the clues.

In *Cinderella Meets the Wolfman!* (1987), Tim Kelly and Jack Sharkey have taken the famous Cinderella story and given it a twist. In this version, the tiny kingdom of Vestigia is bankrupt, so the prince must marry for money. The prince, by the way, is a werewolf. The court is adamant that the bride not discover the truth about her husband until after the wedding—or until her check clears. When Cinderella and her nasty sisters arrive on the scene, a full moon is on the rise, with all its repercussions. Not to worry. Everything turns out well at the madcap finale.

The stylistic approach to Tim Kelly's *Curse of the Werewolf* (1990) is earmarked by the play's subtitle: "A Hair-raising Comedy Spoof in Two Acts." The action of the play unfolds in the sitting room of Gargoyle House, a spooky castle on a lonely New England island. Buzz Halliburton, an entertainer fallen on hard times, is summoned by his uncle to the reading of a will. He encounters a bizarre assortment of family and household members. Little Messalina, the resident child terror, keeps baby piranhas for pets. The menacing housekeeper often appears without her head. The gardener is probably insane. And due to a family curse, there is a wolfman in the house.

Mystery of the Blood Beast Horror of Wolfbane Manner Mystery (2007) by Julian Harries is a horror farce about an army veteran who attempts to find work in the wrong place, a pretty girl who may not be who she seems, and a housekeeper who turns into a witch during a full moon and bites necks.

The Golem

Traditionalists believe that Kabbalistic Rabbi Judah Loew of Prague (1512–1609), known as The Maharal,[86] molded a mammoth human being from clay, the Golem (the

Hebrew word for simpleton), to defend Jews from genocide. The Catholic priest Tadeus protested to King Rudolph II, "The Jews kill our sons and with their Christian blood they bake matzoh for Passover." The Gentile community was enraged, and the Jewish ghetto feared repercussions.

The saga's most celebrated theatrical version is Halper Leivick's (Russia-born American, 1888–1962) *The Golem*, "a dramatic poem in eight scenes." It starts at sunrise on the shoreline of the Vltava river on the outskirts of Prague. Reb Levi Bar-Bezalel, the Maharal, a man of 70, is forming a body out of clay. A jet-black silhouette floats over the river, and a specter surfaces near the Maharal, warning him that his creation will cause utter destruction. The Maharal counters that the Golem is destined to fulfill "great things, mysterious and hidden" and continues with his task.

In the subterranean tunnels of the Fifth Tower, the priest Tadeus and a monk devise their vile enterprise. The monk relates how he seized a child and slit his throat; he then filled bottles with the infant's blood. The Golem, described as "a powerful giant," enters with an axe.

Strong winds whirl. The Golem swings his axe wildly. Cave ghosts appear from all corners, surround him, then vanish.

The last scene transpires in the foyer of the synagogue. It is dusk on Friday, before the Sabbath worship. The Golem is reclining on a bench, forlorn and disheveled. Villagers peep in and mock him. They are not aware of the fact that the Golem saved the ghetto from genocide.

The Golem gets up, grasps his axe, breaks the window, and surges through it. The people take off in all directions screaming, "The servant! The Golem! With an axe! Hits people over their heads! He wrecks houses! He devastates Prague!"

The Maharal steps out for a moment and comes back ushering the Golem, who is carrying a bloodstained axe. A mob attempts to attack the Golem, but the Maharal directs them to the synagogue.

The Maharal now comprehends that the entity of might he has invented to save his people is dangerously unstoppable. He instructs the Golem to stretch out on the floor and shut his eyes. The Golem asks anxiously, "What are you going to do with me? You will not leave me, Rebbe?" The Maharal says, "I command…. Return to your place of rest. Exhale your last breath. Amen."

The Golem is still. The Maharal leaves. The Sabbath prayer trickles in.

* * *

H. Leivick's *The Golem* was first published (in Yiddish) in New York in 1921 and was first performed (in Hebrew) by the Habimah Company in Moscow on March 15, 1925. When they emigrated to Palestine in 1931, the Habimah ensemble kept *The Golem* in their repertoire.[87] The Habimah imported *The Golem* to Boston, Chicago, and New York in 1927 and 1948. In 1989, Israel's Chamber Theatre presented its own version of Leivick's drama.

Throughout the 20th century, Leivick's *The Golem* was adapted by multiple authors for production in assorted venues. A production in Yiddish took place at the Civic Repertory Theatre, New York, on November 5, 1931, with Alexander Granach lauded in the title role. Versions in English were shown at the Kenneth Sawyer Goodman Memorial Theatre in Chicago, Illinois, in 1929; at the El Capitan Theatre, in San Francisco,

California, during the 1932–1933 season; and at Town Hall in New York City in 1939. Twenty years later, in February 1959, an adaptation by Ruth Rehrer Wolff was seen Off-Broadway at the St. Marks Playhouse, running for two months. Also Off-Broadway, The Jean Cocteau Repertory reincarnated *The Golem* in March 1982, translated by Joseph C. Landis. Critic Richard F. Shepard labeled the play, "A powerful and poetic inquiry into man and the use of violence, even in a good cause…. The central mes-

Randy Quaid as the Golem, Delacorte Theatre in Central Park, New York City, 1984 (photo by Friedman-Abeles, The New York Public Library for the Performing Arts).

sage seems to be that even a strong arm, a needed deterrent, can become uncontrolled and can destroy even those it was meant to protect."[88]

On August 3, 1984, the New York Shakespeare Festival presented—for 30 days—a colorful production of Leivick's *The Golem* in a translation by J.C. Augenlight. It was directed and designed by Richard Foreman and featured F. Murray Abraham (a rabbi), Randy Quaid (Golem), and Joseph Wiseman (Tadeus).

The Yale School of Drama in New Haven, Connecticut, put up *The Golem* on March 7–13, 1999, adapted and directed by Eyal Goldberg. The Manhattan Ensemble Theatre made use of a translation by Joseph C. Landis and an adaptation by David Fishelson for an April 1, 2002, premiere, directed by Lawrence Sacharow, with Robert Prosky (Maharal) and Joseph McKenna (Golem). Reviewer Bruce Weber stated, "Among the play's themes is that faith and rage can be dangerously difficult to tell apart. As Israelis and Palestinians persist in their agonizing war, the contemporary pertinence of *The Golem* is painfully apparent."[89]

An opera based on Leivick's play, commissioned by the Ford Foundation and composed by Abraham Ellstein, debuted in 1962 at the New York City Opera.

*   *   *

Other playwrights who dramatized the Golem saga include Stephen Lackner (*Golem*, 1961); Moni Ovadia and Daniele Abbado (*The Golem*, 1992); Vit Horejs (*The Golem*, 1997); Ernest Joselovitz (*Vilna Got a Golem*, 1997); Gary Winter (*Golem*, 2000); Alix Sobler (*The Golem*, 2001). Off-Broadway's La Mama Theatre presented differing Golem interpretations in 1974, 1982, 1992, 1997, and 1998, the last being a dance recital with music by Frank London.

The Golem fable may have influenced Goethe when writing *Faust II*. Other authors who may have been influenced by the Golem legend are Mary Shelley (*Frankenstein*) and

Karel Čapek (*R.U.R.* and *Adam the Creator*). Gustav Meyrink's novel, *Der Golem*, was published in serialized form in Germany in 1913–1914, adapted as a silent feature in 1915,[90] and translated into English in 1928. More recently, Isaac Bashevis Singer, Elie Wiesel, and Pete Hamill have written stories about the Golem. Alice Hoffman transported the legend to 1940s' Germany and France in her novel *The World That We Knew* (2019).

Acting Edition:

H. Leivick's *The Golem*, translated by Joseph C. Landis, is included in *Three Great Jewish Plays* (Applause Books).

Adapted by David Fishelson (Dramatists Play Service).Adapted by Ruth Rehrer Wolff (Samuel French, Inc., in manuscript form).

The Mummy

The early Egyptians believed in life after death, that each person had a soul or spirit that would live on and be capable of eating, drinking, and moving about, so they filled their graves with food, water, ornaments, and weapons. The wealthy earned better gravesites and more protection from the depredations of weather and animals. For those who could afford it, rooms were created in the ground, roofed with wood. The richness of the goods that accompanied the king and his nobles became a temptation for grave robbers.

The first step in the process of mummification, relates Drake Douglas in his study *Horror!,* "was the removal of all parts of the body which might be subject to decay and cause general desiccation.… The mummifier covered the body from head to foot with ten perfumes, giving special care to the head itself."[91] The pharaoh was placed in the tomb lying on his back, his arms crossed at his breast, the body tightly wrapped in white linen, and the tomb was sealed.

There is also the matter of the curse. Generally, this curse takes the form of an invocation to the great Osiris, god of resurrection, or to the great Amon-Ra, king of the gods of Egypt, to bring violent death and destruction to anyone who enters and defiles the tomb of a pharaoh. When the sponsor of the 1922 Tutankhamun digging, Lord George Herbert Carnarvon, died under mysterious circumstances on April 5, 1923, rumors soon began to circulate that the earl was the victim of a curse that had been placed on the young pharaoh's tomb.

Brian J. Frost, an authority on bizarre fiction, states in his *The Essential Guide to Mummy Literature*, "This view was strengthened when several other people who had been present at the official opening of the tomb also sickened and died. The press, which from the outset had been hungry for a sensational story, was quick to cite these mysterious deaths as further evidence that a curse had indeed been activated."[92]

The curse has been the topic of several plays, the first of which was written by artist-archeologist Joseph Lindon Smith in collaboration with Arthur Weigall, an inspector of antiquities for Upper Egypt. The plot dealt with the curse of Amon-Ra, placed on the pharaoh Akhnaton, who overthrew the worship of Amon-Ra and other gods for his own god, Aton. When Akhnaton died, likely by murder, Amon-Ra was restored, and the heretic pharaoh was placed under the god's curse, his body and soul condemned to wander forever. The short play by Smith-Weigall is about removing the curse and allowing Akhnaton to find eternal rest after three millennia.

In January of 1909, the playlet was rehearsing in the Valley of the Kings. Hortense Weigall, Arthur's wife, portrayed Akhnaton; Corinna Smith, Joseph's wife, was Queen Tiyi, the mother of the pharaoh; and Joseph Smith appeared as Horus, a hawk god. The plan was to present the piece on three successive days, at nightfall, for the leading Egyptologists of the day. As described by Drake Douglas, the dress rehearsal proceeded smoothly "until the moment when Mrs. Weigall, as Akhnaton, made her first appearance. With the first utterance of Akhnaton's lines, there was suddenly a tremendous burst of thunder, brilliant flashes of lightning, and a fierce, howling gale swept down the valley. The rehearsal was stopped and, in few moments, the sudden storm passed, after which Smith and his party resumed acting. The climax approached with Mrs. Smith, as Tiyi, beginning the beautiful Hymn to the god Aton. At the opening line, a second storm of tremendous fury swept the area, dropping hailstones on the cast, together with heavy clouds of dust from the desert." Douglas relates that Mrs. Smith was undaunted and continued with the blasphemous hymn.[93]

That evening, Mrs. Weigall complained of cramps in her stomach, while Mrs. Smith suffered pain in her eyes. Later that night, both women were visited by peculiar dreams. Weigall found herself in the temple of Rameses II, a devotee of Amon-Ra, standing before a giant statue of the pharaoh. The statue seemed to come suddenly alive and struck her in the stomach. To the shock of the entire party, Smith related that she had experienced an identical dream, save for the fact that Rameses struck her in the eyes.

The following morning, both women were seriously ill. Weigall suffered extreme abdominal pain, and one of Smith's eyes was nearly closed. They were rushed to a Cairo hospital. Misfortune continued to haunt the party, with Arthur Weigall suffering a nervous breakdown, and Joseph Smith falling victim to an exceptionally severe attack of jaundice.

The play has never been performed.[94]

The Mummy's Tomb (1978)
Ken Hill (England, 1937–1995)

The Mummy's Tomb by Ken Hill is peppered with cliffhangers, physical altercations, murders by strangulation, and contrasting moments of song, romance, and humor. It liberally breaks the fourth wall, with the pianist of the show's band often mounting the stage and joining the action. The set is composed of two levels, and there is a much-used trap in the center.

A prologue unfolds in Thebes, Egypt, in 1380 BCE under dim light, "greenish and mysterious." Paul Conway, the pianist, dressed in a white tuxedo, introduces the audience to Inmutef-Amun, a high priest, and his lover, Ashayet, the pharaoh's wife.

The Pharaoh Amenhotep suddenly enters, scoffs at Ashayet for betraying him, and motions to his guards to bandage Inmutef. The pharaoh orders them to carry the doomed priest to a tomb "so deep and distant that none shall ever discover his whereabouts." As to Ashayet, the pharaoh orders her banished "into the Great Desert in the East."

A guard returns to report that everyone in Inmutef's burial party has died. "In that case," says Mahu, a pharaoh's attendant, and stabs the guard, who dies with a scream. "Are the slaves dead?" asks Amenhotep. Mahu bows, "As you commanded, great lord." The pharaoh mumbles, "In that case," and stabs Mahu, eliminating the last witness to Inmutef's burial.

The prologue over, the action jumps to 1922 CE. Professor Niven embarks on an expedition up the Nile to unearth the ancient tomb of Inmutef-Amun. He is joined by his pretty daughter, Nancy; her present beau, Paul Conway, who leaves the piano and climbs onto the stage; and Lord Rodney Soper, who will pay for the trip. Their guide is Kenal, a local explorer.

Aboard the *Alexandria*, the actors sway to indicate a raging sea. When the party lands at Karnak, the site of an ancient Egyptian city, a sandstorm is their next hazard. They cower for protection in desert ruins until the storm subsides. A giant cobra crawls into Nancy's makeshift tent, and she's saved by Kenal, who kills the snake with a knife.

Eventually the explorers find the tomb of Inmutef-Amun. They open the tomb, and the figure of the mummy is revealed. The band's music rises to a climax as the mummy comes to life. The mummy lumbers toward Nancy; she faints in his arms. The mummy carries her away. Paul, Niven, and Lord Soper dash after them.

At Ashayet's palace, a statue of the Pharaoh-God is up center. The lighting is dim, eerie, greenish. Suddenly Ashayet crawls out from behind an altar, her face withered and gray. She calls out for Kenal and tells him that she desperately needs "the blood of a virgin."

The mummy appears, carrying Nancy. He places the girl on the altar and advances toward Kenal, who draws his knife and plunges it into the mummy's chest. Undaunted, the mummy strangles Kenal. Paul, Niven, and Lord Soper rush in. Paul moves slowly around and above a trap, which now functions as a well. The mummy follows him and steps on the edge of the well. For a minute, it teeters on the edge, then falls in.

The last scene takes place in a rocky grotto, set above the trap. The sound of running water is heard. Nancy is bound. Mist fills the stage. Ashayet cuts Nancy's wrist. The water turns red; the mist turns pink. Nancy is saved, however, by Paul masquerading as a mummy and Niven assuming the voice of the Pharaoh-God, commanding Ashayet to release the girl. Ashayet backs away from Paul's "mummy" and is lost in the mist. There is a loud bubbling noise, and the disintegrating figure of Ashayet (a dummy) rises up out of the mist, then disappears.

The entire cast, including the dead, sings "Sailing Away," vowing to launch other adventures and explore other places, other times.

*   *   *

The Mummy's Tomb was originally commissioned and produced by the Phoenix Theatre, Leicester, England, in 1978, under the direction of Ian Giles. The play was fully revised when presented by the Theatre Royal, Stratford East, on September 8, 1980. The playwright, Ken Hill, directed, with set design by Sarah-Jane McClelland.

The cast included Michael Poole (Professor Niven), Adrienne Posta (Nancy), Francis Thomson (Paul), Tony Scannell (Lord Soper), Anna Sharkey (Ashayet), Maynard Williams (Kenal), and Michael G. Jones as Inmutef-Amun (the mummy).

Acting Edition: Samuel French Ltd.

The Mummy's Claw (1992)
Mark Chandler, pseudonym of Jack Sharkey
(United States, 1931–1992)

In 1903, a party at the home of archeologist Sir Nevil Blore, in Egypt's Nile Valley, about two hundred miles south of Cairo, turns into a struggle for survival when the translation of several stone tablets resurrects an ancient evil.

The action unfolds in Sir Nevil's trophy room on a sultry tropical night. The furnishings include a cabinet cluttered with Egyptian curiosities and a closed mummy case against an upstage wall. A few crumbling stone tablets are scattered on a central table. Sir Nevil, in formal evening wear, is seated at that table, intently studying one of the tablets. He learns from one of the hieroglyphic symbols that his house stands on the site of an ancient temple!

Sir Nevil's wife, Eliza, enters and rebukes him for neglecting their guests: Catharyn Ashley, a neighboring Englishwoman; Poppy Lachoy, an Egyptian described as "a lady of considerable mystery"; Fern Hansen, Nevil's secretary; Idris Glennoch, Nevil's feminist solicitor; Lucy Ross, his bubble-headed niece, an aspiring poet and an heiress; Brick Brock, Lucy's fiancé, a famous football fullback; and Rula Palazzo, a visiting operatic soprano.

The Egyptian Poppy draws attention to the fact, "The pieces of these tablets all fit together, not unlike a jigsaw." Suddenly the lights flicker, a heavy rumbling is heard, the mummy's case opens, and a bandaged hand-and-arm reaches out. The entire room starts to shake. Sliding panels outside the French windows begin a slow, upward movement, giving the illusion that the house is sinking.

A sacrificial altar pivots into view. Azuris Baka, the priest of Khopsis, steps into the room, wearing an ancient Egyptian toga—cloak, ornaments, headdress. He announces, "It is *death* for non-believers to intrude." Rumbling begins. Everybody passes out. Azuris laughs menacingly as the curtain closes on Act I.

Act 2 begins as the characters awaken. The scary situation elicits several confessions. Fern Hansen reveals that she's a special agent of Scotland Yard assigned to keep an eye on Nevil and his wife, who are not Lucy's uncle and aunt. The impostors sent for Lucy so they could have her *murdered* in this far-off land and then falsify the circumstances of her death. Claiming to be Lucy's only living relatives, they would inherit her fortune.

Fern draws a pistol and covers Sir Nevil, his wife Eliza, lawyer Idris, singer Rula, neighbor Catharyn, and the exotic Poppy, who are all members of the gang that planned to defraud heiress Lucy. Brick says, "Let me help," and produces a revolver from inside his jacket, leveling it at the sextet. He explains to Lucy, "the fullback thing" was his *cover*; he's actually an agent with the United States Treasury Department. Lucy's mother is an American, and they would like some of her inheritance taxes.

Now Poppy produces a pistol and pivots so that she is now with the "good guys" keeping the "bad guys" covered. "I am an agent of the French Sûreté," she says. "Lucy's late father was half–French! We became suspicious when Sir Nevil advertised for somebody who could read hieroglyphics! Obviously, that means that *he* could *not*!"

Azuris appears and picks up the sacrificial dagger from the fireplace mantel. Eliza remarks with satisfaction, "Well, we want Lucy dead, don't we? If we can't kill her, we may as well let Azuris do it!" The high priest orders Lucy to climb onto the altar. She does, complains that the stone is cold, and asks for a pillow. Azuris becomes impatient: "If Khopsis doesn't come back to life again, he won't be able to guard the Pharaoh's jewels!" All become alert: "Pharaoh's jewels?" Rula asks, "Where are these jewels?" Azuris answers, "Oh, if you must know, right there at the end of the grotto—just beyond the end of the house."

The scoundrels are itching to find the gems and rush off through the French windows. Poppy attempts to stop them, to no avail. Offstage dialogue informs the audience that the group is facing a massive stone door, finds a rusty handle, and pulls on it in unison. A loud crack is followed by a crash, the gurgling of water, a series of snapping noises, terrified screams—and then silence.

Poppy says, "Well, it's not as if I didn't try to warn them. 'Pharaoh's jewels' is ancient Egyptian slang. That was the Pharaoh's pet name for his favorite *crocodiles!*"

All cringe, then Brick helps Lucy down from the altar and declares happily, "And now, my darling, we can be married at last."

*   *   *

The Mummy's Claw played at the Dallas Children's Theatre on Halloween 2008. The *Observer* reviewer Elaine Liner compared the show to "a 1930s RKO mystery-comedy, gathering a dozen characters to the reading of a spooky will outside Cairo.... Aimed at kids, but full of sly jokes for the grown-ups, *The Mummy's Claw* is mirth on the Nile."[95]

Tahlequah Community Playhouse, Tahlequah, Oklahoma, presented the play in November 2017, directed by Mike Phillips and Steve Ball. The producers urged to public to "join the dizzying gallop through Egyptian temples, fiendish curses, evil spells, ancient incantations, terrifying sorcery and hideous plots by the crazed author of *I Shot My Rich Aunt* and *Doctor Death*.... This evening of non-stop hilarity has so many surprises and twists you'll lose count."

*   *   *

Mark Chandler is a pen name for Jack Sharkey, a prolific American playwright who penned dozens of melodramas and thrillers under his own name and several pseudonyms: Rick Abbot, Mark Ferris, Mike Johnson, and Mark Chandler. The plays are performed around the world.

Chandler's *Doctor Death* unfolds on a yacht in the French Riviera. The happy guests of a mysterious host discover that they are all marked for a madman's murderous vengeance. Soon thereafter comes the horrifying realization that one of them is a cruel and calculating killer. But which one? They'd better find out soon; the yacht is slowly sinking—and none of them can swim.

Published under Sharkey's pseudonym Mike Johnson, *Return of the Maniac* is a rip-roaring thriller set in London. When Emma Lorrison is called away from her boardinghouse by a fake telegram, her daughter, Ann, is left to rent out the garret, where a horrible hatchet murder took place three years earlier. Suspense mounts as a picture hidden in the garret proves to be painted over—quite possibly holding the identity of a mad killer who may still be residing in the house. Ann realizes that she'd been the intended victim of the earlier murder and is still being stalked by a relentless killer.

The Creature Creeps! was published using the name Jack Sharkey and involves an ancient castle in the Carpathian Mountains, creaking doors, a secret laboratory, shrieks from the depths of the cellar, a mad scientist, his misshapen assistant, his dopey daughter, a grim housekeeper, a stalwart but stupid hero, and disappearing villagers. Sharkey's

The Murder Room is a zany spoof of British whodunits. When Edgar Hollister, the master of Bynewood Cottage in Yorkshire, asks his radiant wife Mavis to put "a little something extra" in his cup of cocoa, she readily complies. Mavis stands smiling behind him as Edgar drinks his last cup.

Jack Sharkey wrote the book, and Dave Reiser composed the score of *The Pinchpenny Phantom of the Opera*, a mélange of crazed desire, gruesome death, and bone-headed ambition. Gaston, proprietor of a shabby opera house, can only afford to hire one soprano lead per opera. Airwick (Phantom of the Opera) wants his beloved Christine to star—and gets rid of her rivals with falling chandeliers.

Acting Edition: Samuel French, Inc.

The Zombie

"The horror of the zombie has its origin in a different world, a different time," writes Drake Douglas in *Horror!* "Two and a half centuries ago, Africa was still the Dark Continent. The vast, mysterious interiors were still untrodden by white men, and there were strange tales of impenetrable forests, mist-enshrouded jungle, tremendous mountains and mysterious plateaus, of strange tribes and horrifying customs." Douglas continues to relate that invading Caucasians found in the African inhabitants a source of wealth, "and so began one of the most shameful and horrible stories in the long and violent history of man—the African slave trade."[96]

Bewildered, confused, and frightened, African natives were herded onto huge ships, where they were chained in pairs for weeks under closed hatches. Many died, and their bodies were tossed unceremoniously over the side into the sea. "Once the slaves were landed in the Indies and placed on the market," says Douglas, "a new kind of horror began. Often they lived in chains, working all through the long day in the fields or the mills, poorly fed, subject always to the whip and scourge."[97] Slaves living under such brutal conditions had but one relief, one solace, and that was their religion, brought with them from the forests of their distant lands: voodoo.

According to voodoo belief, the zombie is a dead man restored to life as a mindless automaton, an empty shell of a human being, yielding to the will of his master. In the dark of night, following a funeral, assistants of the voodoo priest bring the corpse to the hut of the holy man. The priest injects a serum into the corpse, "Slowly, the body begins to rise as the dead man sits up in his coffin," voodooists maintain. "With quiet, effortless grace, the corpse rises from the coffin and stands…. He is a silent, dark statue of horror, his arms at his sides, his face a mask, his eyes staring sightlessly ahead. So a zombie has been created."[98]

Jamie Russell, in his brilliant film study *Book of the Dead*, approaches the origins of the zombie from a different angle. He writes:

It was in 1899 in the pages of *Harper's Magazine* that the zombie made his debut appearance in the English-speaking world, in a short article by journalist and amateur anthropologist Lafcadio Hearn entitled "The Country of the Comers-back." Although the term "zombie" was first recorded in *The Oxford English Dictionary* in 1819, and was frequently heard mentioned by slaves in America's Deep South in the latter part of the 18th century, it was Hearn's article that became the first widely circulated report of the existence of the living dead.[99]

Russell reports that in 1928 the American adventurer William Seabrook (1886–1945) arrived in Haiti, the so-called "Voodoo capital" of the Caribbean. He threw himself into researching the occult phenomenon and took part in voodoo rites. Interviewing many islanders, Seabrook learned, "The Zombie was supposed to be a soulless human corpse, still dead, but taken from the grave and endowed by sorcery with a mechanical semblance of life—it is a dead body which is made to walk and act as if it were alive."[100]

However, as Seabrook continued his research, he changed his mind. In *The Magic Island* (1929), he notes that he came to the realization that the staring blank eyes of the zombies did not belong to the dead brought back to life, but to "members of Haiti's underclass—mentally challenged unfortunates who were being exploited under the guise of some ancient superstition. They were nothing more than poor, ordinary human beings, idiots, forced to toil in the fields…. These living dead corpses might be nothing more than drugged sleepwalkers whose appearance of 'death' had been manufactured through the use of some kind of toxic substance."[101]

The success of Seabrook's *The Magic Island* turned the zombie into a popular horror monster. Among the first to tackle the subject, in the short story format, were Henry S. Whitehead with *Jumbee* (1930), an undead saga unfolding on St. Croix, another island in the Caribbean Sea, and August Derleth with *The House in the Magnolias* (1932), a zombie tale set in New Orleans.

On February 10, 1932, *Zombie*, "a drama in three acts by Kenneth Webb," premiered at Broadway's Biltmore Theatre. The action unfolds at the bungalow of Jack and Sylvia Clayton, the owners of a Haitian plantation, where the natives believe that it is possible to bring the dead to life. Sylvia is unsure whether she loves her husband or her friend, Dr. Paul Thurlow. Jack drinks a prescription prepared by the doctor and seemingly dies. Several nights later he is roused from the dead, as a zombie, and—as described in *The Best Plays of 1931–32*—"goes stalking about the place scaring the daylights out of everybody."[102] It takes quite a bit of voodoo influence to bring Jack back to life and to the arms of Sylvia, who finally realizes that he is her true mate.[103]

Directed by George Sherwood, *Zombie* featured Pauline Starke (Sylvia Clayton), Robert J. Stanley (Jack Clayton), and Hunter Gardner (Dr. Paul Thurlow). A pair of Haitian laborers were played by white actors (Peter Clarke and Lackaye Grant) in black face. The reception by the press was scathing, and the show could not replicate the enormous success of 1927's *Dracula*, lasting just 21 performances. Webb relocated his play to Chicago's Adelphi Theatre, where it opened on March 13, 1932, running for two months. Jamie Russell reports that it "moved to a couple of smaller theatres in the city, then suddenly closed for good. However disastrous the production was," continues Russell, "*Zombie* secured a place in the history books by helping pave the way for the film that would make the living dead truly famous, Victor and Edward Halperin's *White Zombie* (1932). Intrigued by Webb's stage-play, the Halperins decided that there might be money to be made from bringing the dead back to life."[104]

The zombie was soon added to cinema's cadre of thriving monsters: Dracula, Frankenstein's creature, the werewolf, and the mummy. But it has taken many decades for the zombie to appear again on the boards of the legitimate theater.

Zombie Prom (1993)
Book and Lyrics by John Dempsey (United States)
Music by Dana P. Rowe (United States)

Zombie Prom takes place in the nuclear 1950s. The musical is set in the hallways and classrooms of the Enrico Fermi High School, the newsroom of *Exposé Magazine*, and Toffee's bedroom.

The principal of the high school is Miss Delilah Strict who, true to her name, is an autocratic, by-the-book administrator. She is no friend of the transfer student Jonny, who insists on spelling his name without the usual "h" and is an independent sort. Miss Delilah warns the sweet teenager Toffee about establishing a relationship with a "motor-cycle" and "leather jacket" fellow. In the school hallway, Toffee tells Jonny that she can't see him anymore. Crushed, he commits suicide by hurling himself into the waste treat-ment silo of a nearby nuclear plant.

Mourning, Toffee decides to skip the senior prom. Jonny unexpectedly returns from the dead. He tells Toffee that she's the one who brought him back. They sing about their "forbidden love" and vow to remain together "now and forever." Her classmates hang posters in the hallway: "Zombie Rights" and "Even the Dead Have Feelings," but Miss Strict takes them down, pointing to the school's "Rule Number 7, Subsection 9, on the handbook of student life—No Zombies!"

Miss Strict softens, however, when Eddie Flagrante, the editor of *Exposé Mag-azine*, arrives in the school and reminds her of their long-ago relationship. He warns Miss Strict that expelling Jonny would be a huge mistake—because he's her son, the one her parents sent away after she gave birth to him in home for unwed mothers. In a sharp turnabout, Miss Strict asks Jonny to give her another chance. Being dead is a mere detail, she asserts. She'll throw a "big fancy funeral," and Jonny can have any flavor ice cream he wants. They embrace.

The kids celebrate the prom dressed in macabre zombie-ish clothes. Eddie and Delilah enter in wedding attire that resembles Frankenstein's Monster and the Bride of Frankenstein. All sing "Zombie Prom." Balloons drop from the flies as the curtain descends.

*   *   *

Zombie Prom was first produced at The Red Barn Theatre in Key West, Florida, in February 1993. The show was directed by Joy Hawkins, and its composer, Dana P. Rowe, served as the musical director. In August that same year, *Zombie Prom* was offered by The New River Repertory Theatre in Ft. Lauderdale, Florida, under the direction of Hugh M. Murphy. It subsequently came to New York City, first as a workshop in 1995, then as a full-scale production at Off-Broadway's Variety Arts Theatre, opening on April 9, 1996. Philip Wm. McKinley directed, Tony Stevens was the choreographer, and Dar-ren R. Cohen the musical director. The cast included Karen Murphy (Delilah Strict), Jessica-Snow Wilson (Toffee), Richard Roland (Jonny Warner), and Richard Muenz (Eddie Flagrante).

The reviewers were not kind. Greg Evans asserted in *Variety*, "Comparisons to *Grease* and *Little Shop of Horrors* are as unavoidable as they are unfortunate. Lacking the spark of the former or bite of the latter, *Zombie Prom* is like any old human prom, a lot of fuss for a very little fun."[105] The show ran for twelve performances.

Zombie Prom crossed the Atlantic and in October 2009 opened at the Landor, a pub theater in Clapham, Southwest London. Critic Gail Haslam wrote in the *Londonist*, "Musical numbers proved to be the highlights of the night…. Overall, though, it's the thinness of the writing that lets down the considerable talent."[106]

The following year, Saint Monica Players of North London produced the musical at The Intimate Theatre under the direction of Chris O'Shea. In 2015, The Elkhart Civil Theatre presented *Zombie Prom* at the Bristol Opera House, Bristol, England, receiving a positive online assessment in *Marcia*: "It is two hours (including intermission) of great fun for all ages, zombie-lovers or not."[107]

In 2017, the TILT Performance Group mounted *Zombie Prom* at the Balance Dance Studios, Austin, Texas, directed by Adam Roberts, and garnered praise from reviewer Shannon Weaver in the *Austin Chronicle*: "As with any good zombie yarn, but especially here, *Zombie Prom* becomes a poignant parable about discrimination and acceptance of those who are 'different.'"[108]

2018 was a banner year for *Zombie Prom*, with performances of the musical at Ole Miss Theatre at the University of Mississippi, Oxford, Mississippi; Theatre in the Park, Overland Park, Kansas; and The Kalamazoo Civic Theatre, Kalamazoo, Michigan.

Writer-director Vince Marcello adapted the musical to a short movie, filmed in Los Angeles, California, in 2006, for a budget of $1,000,000. Drag queen RuPaul portrayed Miss Strict, supported by Candice Nicole (Toffee), Darren Robertson (Jonny), and David Engel (Eddie Flagrante). Marcello dropped a great deal of dialogue and music (although the plot is still roughly the same), giving the film a runtime of slightly more than thirty minutes.

Acting Edition: Samuel French, Inc.

Attack of the Pom-Pom Zombies (2000)
Stephen Murray (United States, 1963–)

The setting is an outdoor eating area at Barnacle Betty's Surf Club, a pirate-themed hot dog stand located next door to a nuclear power plant.

It's the 1960s. School is out for summer and the teenagers of Ocean View High are ready to surf, sun, and have some fun. Cindy Sue Murdock, the most popular senior, leads the cheerleaders into the restaurant, where she exhibits a ring given to her by boyfriend Roger Spaulding, the star running back of the football team. Soon Roger and his friends join the all-girl group. They all poke fun at the student nerds who clean tables and take orders.

Ivana Ratnik, described in the cast list as the "evil and greedy owner of the power plant," enters with two of her atomic energy technicians. Ivana tells Betty Barnacle, the restaurant's owner, that she needs more storage space and offers $500,000 for her establishment. Betty rejects the proposition but agrees to help out by letting Ivana store a few things in the backroom. No, no pay is required. Ivana thanks Betty and sends her two men to bring some items for storage. Ivana then says that she would like to try some American food and orders French fries, English muffins, Canadian bacon, and salad with Italian dressing.

The men return with containers of green radioactive goo. Betty directs them to a storage shelf in the back.

Cindy Sue orders a hot dog with extra relish. Myron, one of the nerdish waiters, informs Betty that they're out of relish. She sends him to refill the relish dispenser; it's in one of those green containers from the back room.

Myron arrives with a jar of nuclear waste and pours it on the hot dog. Cindy Sue takes a bite, says, "This is the best hot dog I've ever tasted," then adds, "kind of strange," and dies.

Betty says, "I hope the health inspector doesn't come today," then orders the nerds to cover the body and take it to the back room. A green-faced Cindy Sue returns and goes on a rampage, biting her fellow cheerleaders, who fall to their death only to rise moments later in a zombie trance. We soon learn that Cindy Sue has managed to turn every cheerleader on Santa Muerto Beach into a flesh-eating monster.

Just when everything seems hopeless, the nerds come up with a solution, creating a radioactive wave device to reverse the effects of the mutagenic relish—a bizarre contraption with flashing lights "that looks something like a large ray gun from a science fiction film, except it is made from common items and held together with duct tape."

The nerds fire the Zombie Zapper, and the zombies fall to the ground. Everything is still for a moment. Then the zombies arise and behave as humans again.

Acting Edition: Eldridge Publishing Company.

Swamp Pirate Zombies (2011)
Andrew Ross (Australia)

Swamp Pirate Zombies is a farce. Much of the action is set in Brenda's Bistro and Bait Shop in the tiny town of Key Wurst, near the Florida's Everglades. Upstage is a wall with signs such as "Good Food and Good Bait," "Gator Sushi," "Hungry? Try our Gator Omelet." Three café tables are Up Right, Up Center, and Up Left.

The play begins with a spotlight illuminating the Up Right table, which represents a Hollywood office. Rachel Reeks, a movie producer, assigns Zane Gray, a director, and Mandy Mulch, a writer, to "make a pirate movie for the least amount of money in the history of pirate movies." It is to be shot in South Florida's Key Wurst. No, not Key West. Key Wurst. She wants it to be wrapped up in two weeks: no artsy stuff, just a pirate story with some epic battles and a love interest.

Lights go up full on Brenda's Bistro and Bait Shop. Steven Kingston, a horror writer, makes notes in the margins of his latest novel. Brenda, the owner of the restaurant, asks Steven if this is the one about the crazy man in the empty hotel who chases his family around with an axe, turns into a vampire, howls at the moon, travels in time, and then turns into a giant insect. Steven relates that he has finished that one last week; this one is about flesh-eating zombies who crawl out of their graves and chase people around.

Zane and Mandy enter Brenda's joint. Mandy takes out a pad and pen from her briefcase and starts writing, but it's a struggle. She jots down a word, tears off the page, and tosses it over her shoulder. The floor is soon littered with crumpled sheets of paper.

Steven tells Mandy that he is a writer too, with thirty novels to his credit, though none have yet been published. Mandy opens one of Steven's binders and reads, "Swamp Zombies—The Living Dead of Key Wurst." She peruses the manuscript, mumbles, "This is awful," and thinks aloud, "Hmm. Maybe this is the angle we've been looking for. A horror movie. Pirates meet zombies." She tries out some titles—"Pirate Zombies of Key Wurst," "Pirate Zombies of the Swamp"—and settles on "Swamp Pirate Zombies." She begins to write furiously.

Zane enters the Bistro and Mandy hands him her pad. She says, "Let's have the pirates stumble upon the living dead." She got the idea from a local guy, Steve Kingston, who writes novels. Zane thinks it's risky but agrees to give it a shot.

Lights shift Down Stage, where a group of actors enter wearing zombie makeup. Locals follow, wearing pirate shirts, hats, and eye patches. Director Zane sets the scene—pirates attack the zombies with swords; zombies go after the pirates and turn them into zombies. "When I yell action," he says, "I want to see some carnage. Action!"

Zombies slowly move towards the pirates. Pirates charge the zombies. Zombies swat at the pirates, and several fall to the ground. The remaining pirates run off screaming, and the zombies exit after them. Zane calls, "Cut!" and expresses satisfaction: "Not bad. Not good, but not bad."

Brenda asks Steven if he's working on a new novel. He says no; he's collaborating on a project with the movie company and has just finished *Snow White and the Seven Zombies*.

In Hollywood, Rachel welcomes Zane and Mandy with a dubious compliment: "*Swamp Pirate Zombies* is great. Well, not great. Actually it's pretty bad. But people love it." She has a new project for them—*Romeo and Juliet* with zombies.[109]

Acting Edition: Pioneer Drama Service.

2

Real-Life Monsters

Jack the Ripper

At least five women, all prostitutes, most middle-aged, were murdered in the Whitechapel district of London's East End between August and November 1888. Mary Ann Nichols was found dead on August 3, Annie Chapman on September 8, Elizabeth Stride and Catherine Eddowes on September 30, and Mary Jane Kelly on November 9. In each instance, the cause of death was either a slashed throat or strangulation, and the victim's body was severely mutilated. Certain incisions suggested that the killer had some knowledge of anatomy. The authorities received taunting notes from a person calling himself Jack the Ripper and claiming to be the murderer, but the cases remain unsolved.[1]

In spite of public uproar, the murders remained unsolved, forcing the home secretary and the London police commissioner to resign. Many theories regarding the Ripper's identity have been floated, but none could be verified. Adding to the puzzlement was the notion that "he didn't kill for money, to eliminate an enemy, or punish a spouse," wrote historian Josh Clark. "The killings seem random, and he caught the London force completely off guard."[2]

Among the more controversial suspects were the painter Walter Sickert; author Lewis Carroll; actor Richard Mansfield (who at the time was on the London stage portraying the double role of Dr. Jekyll and Mr. Hyde); and Prince Albert Victor, heir to the throne. One scenario claimed Jack was really "Jill the Ripper," a woman.

From the first murder to the last and well beyond, Jack the Ripper remained in the public's consciousness. The case spawned more than a hundred books, many of which offer theories that claim to unmask his or her identity, as well as movies, television shows, and video games.

As early as 1889, an English actor, Mariande Clark, appeared on stage as Jack the Ripper in Brooklyn, New York. "After devious meanderings," wrote the *Brooklyn Daily Eagle*, "the plot leads up to the hanging of the Ripper and everybody is contented."[3] The play obviously strayed from the facts.

The following year, an American actor, Jack Cone, played the title role in *Jack the Ripper* on tour. The *Galveston Daily News* wrote in January 1890 that "Jack Cone, who recently arrived in Dallas, personated the Whitechapel fiend, going through a few scenes with a description of which the public are familiar, and then appearing in others, such as his capture, trial, and execution, which have no foundation in fact, but which throw the crowds into ecstasy." The nameless reporter then described a mishap that could have cost the actor his life: "Last Monday night about midnight, Jack the Ripper stood on the scaffold gazing wistfully into the jaws of death, then started down for a 5 foot fall, but the rope broke and Cone fell with violence, the head striking the trapdoor…. As he lay limp and bleeding on stage, the curtain fell and the music ceased and doctors were sent for, and after working some time with the patient, succeeded in restoring him to consciousness."[4] More than a year later, in October 1891, the *Brooklyn Daily Eagle* related, "Jack the Ripper was played so realistically in St. Louis a few nights ago by Jack Cone that it took half an hour to restore him to consciousness after his execution. He was nearly strangled to death."[5] One wonders if Cone's brush with death was actually a publicity stunt.

The Degollado Theatre of Guadalajara, Mexico, presented *Jack the Ripper* in August 1896, "with a penchant for the morbid," according to *The Two Republics*.[6]

The Ripper next reached the stage in Frank Wedekind's play *DieBuchse der Pandora* (1904), the story of an attractive dancer, Lulu, who rises in German society through her relationship with wealthy men but eventually falls into poverty and prostitution. Her final client, the shadowy Jack the Ripper, murders her at the end of the play. A restricted performance due to difficulties with the censor took place in Nuremberg on February 1, 1904, followed by another restricted showing in 1905 Vienna. Wedekind portrayed the role of the Ripper while Lulu was enacted by Tilly Newes, who later became the playwright's wife.

A widely hailed opera, *Lulu*, by the Austrian composer Alban Berg (1935, premiered posthumously in Zurich, Switzerland, 1937), was mounted in 1979 in France, in 1985 in Switzerland, and was shown on Swiss TV in 2002.

Adapted by the British dramatist Peter Barnes, *Lulu* premiered in 1970 at the Nottingham Playhouse. A revival of Barnes' play was produced by the Pacific Resident Theatre of Venice, California, in 1999, featuring Valerie Dillman as the doomed heroine and Scott Conte as Jack. Reviewer Amy Karpinski wrote in *Variety*, "Wedekind makes Lulu the victim, the comedy outlet of a repressed society, and we are given no choice but to feel sorry for her as we wait for her untimely end. Unfortunately, it is too long a wait."[7]

Marie Belloc Lowndes' 1911 novel, *The Lodger*, was adapted for the stage by Englishman Horace Annesley Vachell under the title *Who Is He?*, opening at Haymarket Theatre, London, on December 9, 1915. It is the story of a landlady and her stepson who suspect that the strange tenant upstairs is The Avenger, a Jack-the-Ripper clone who scatters corpses of mutilated women throughout Bloomsbury. The suspect was played by Henry Ainley, the leading man of several Vachell plays, and the drama ran for 157 performances. When it crossed the Atlantic, *Who Is He?* reverted to the title of Lowndes' novel, *The Lodger*, anchoring at New York's Maxine Elliott Theatre on January 8, 1917—for 56 performances—with Lionel Atwill directing and playing the title role. The *New York Times* asserted that the proceedings "entertainingly unfolded," and that Beryl Mercer "is enormously laughable as the tender-hearted but suspicious landlady." However, the critic scoffed at Atwill who "drives his every point as if he were bound that no defective in the last row of the gallery should miss one of them."[8]

Though a cast had been selected, the rehearsals started, and scenery painted, a week before its scheduled opening in April 1930, the proprietor of the Grand Theatre, Brighton, England, was refused a license to present a play titled *Jack the Ripper*. The Lord Chamberlain considered "the theme and title extremely undesirable." The Grand Guignol of Paris offered *Jack l'Eventreur* by André de Lorde on September 30, 1934. Claude Pirkis' drama *Murder Most Foul* (1948) unfolds in 1894 and proffers a solution to the identity of the Ripper, an eminent London surgeon, here called "Dr. Stanley." Pirkis borrowed the character from Leonard Matters' *The Mystery of Jack the Ripper* (1929), the first full-length book about the elusive murderer. The motive? The doctor's son died from syphilis caught from a prostitute. After the murders, "Dr. Stanley" escapes to Buenos Aires, where he dies.[9]

England's Phyllis Tate composed the opera *The Lodger*, with a libretto by David Franklin, which had its world premiere at the Royal Academy of Music, London, on July 16, 1960. David Bowman, high baritone, appeared as the sinister suspect who is revealed as Jack the Ripper. In 1964, the opera was broadcast on the BBC Third Programme, with Joseph Ward as The Lodger.

Two British musicals, *Ripper!* by Terence Greer and *The Jack the Ripper Show and How They Wrote It* by Frank Hatherley, were staged in 1973. *Ripper!* was performed at the Half Moon Theatre, not far from the location of one of the real-life murders in 1888. *The Jack the Ripper Show* was mounted by The London Bubble Theatre Company in a pub. Tim Kelly's *Bloody Jack* (1981), a winner of several playwriting awards, played across the U.S., including Northern Michigan University at Marquette and Wayne State University in Detroit. The play offers a guessing game for the audience to determine "who-dun-it?": Red-painted cans with pictures of the cast members identified by character name were placed on a table in the lobby. The program contained a "ballot" that the audience member could sign and drop in the can of his or her choice during intermission. The winner, drawn from the proper can, received a copy of the play autographed by the cast.

In 1986, London's Young Vic Theatre produced *Force and Hypocrisy* by Doug Lucie, who based his solution on the royal conspiracy theory expressed in Stephen Knight's non-fiction book *Jack the Ripper: The Final Solution* of ten years earlier.

In 1996, a rock opera entitled *Yours Truly, Jack the Ripper* was created by composer Frogg Moody and lyricist Dave Taylor portraying the Ripper as an ordinary man. It was performed at the National Jack the Ripper Conference on April 18, 1998, in Norwich, England by The Midnight Theatre Company. The one-act *Miller's Court* (2005) by James Jeffrey Paul is a fictional story of Jack the Ripper and his last victim, Mary Jane Kelly, with the entire play unfolding in Mary's small, bare room at 13 Miller's Court in the East End of London. Máire Martello's *The Lodger*, billed as "a new play about Jack the Ripper," was performed January 8 through February 1, 2009, at Off-Broadway's Workshop Theatre.

Alias Jack the Ripper (1984)
Gene Traylor (United States)

Gene Traylor's *Alias Jack the Ripper* captures the atmosphere of a city shrouded in fog, with danger lurking in dark corners.

The first harrowing moment occurs on a gloomy Whitechapel street. Polly Wilson, a barmaid, is on her way home. She hears the sound of a cane tapping the cobblestones and becomes frightened. Out of the shadows emerges a blind man, who taps his way past Polly and exits. Polly heaves a relieved sigh when a dark figure steps silently behind her, his face half concealed by a long woolen scarf. He grabs Polly and draws a large knife across her throat. Polly utters a muffled cry and, as rivulets of blood flow, the lights slowly fade to black. In the darkness, the voice of a newsboy is heard from the back of the auditorium: "Murder! Ripper strikes again! Another girl found dead in Whitechapel!" The newsboy moves briskly down the aisle, offers a paper to an audience member, mounts the stage, repeats one of his headlines, and disappears into the wings.

The next scene is composed of several quick vignettes, all taking place on a foggy street. A uniformed policeman stands under a dim streetlight. A young woman enters, studying a scrap of paper. She mutters, "Fifty-two Hadley Street," and asks the policeman for directions. He turns suddenly toward the girl, his face hidden by a long woolen scarf. With a yellow-gloved hand he grabs her and swiftly cuts her throat. Blackout.

The lights come up. A beggar, with a wooden leg and crutch, limps past the streetlight. A young woman enters and goes to help as he stumbles. The beggar drops the crutch, straightens up, slits the woman's throat. Blackout.

The lights come up on an old beggar woman, her face obscured by rags, sitting on a small stool with a box of violets on her lap. A girl enters. The old woman holds out a bunch of flowers. The girl stops and says, "Oh, violets! What a lovely idea." As she reaches out for the flowers, the beggar woman's upstage hand, wearing a yellow glove, comes up above the girl's head. We see the gleaming blade of a knife. Blackout.

The next murder takes place in the dingy dressing room of the Swan Music Hall, where the body of Taffy O'Reilly, a budding actress-singer, is found in a blood-soaked petticoat, hanging lifelessly on a hook. Her throat has been slashed from ear to ear.

The last scene is set in a shabbily furnished room in Limehouse. A storm is raging outside when Rose Hanshaw, a friend of Taffy's, is attacked by a dimly seen figure. Rose stumbles and falls. The figure hovers above her, knife poised for the kill, when a Scotland Yard Inspector appears at the door and fires. The figure drops the knife and falls through the window to the street below.

Acting Edition: The Dramatic Publishing Company.

Jack's Holiday (1995)
Book by Mark St. Germain (United States, 1954–),
Music by Randy Courts (United States),
Lyrics by Mark St. Germain & Randy Courts

Jack's Holiday, a two-act musical, begins as a play-within-a-play, performed by a small touring company. The curtain rises on Spencer (Actor Manager), Sarah (his wife), Edward (Leading Man), Elizabeth (Leading Lady), John (juvenile), Jennie (Ingénue), and Jack (a character's name) singing "Who Am I Tonight," introducing themselves as actors "changing faces," "dress to fit the part," losing their own identity under mascara, rouge, and various postures.

It is 1891. A budding reporter, Will Bolger, makes the acquaintance of the *New York Herald* crime editor, Max Pierce, and accompanies him to a central police station, where Inspector Thomas Byrnes brags that he could catch Jack the Ripper if he killed anyone in New York. Says Byrnes, "Thirty-six hours! Thirty-six hours after any murder, we have our suspect behind bars!"

Lights come up on Jack disguised as an Old Man. He is holding a copy of the *New York Herald*. He takes off his crushed hat, his putty nose, and his white wig as he sings "Letter #1," in which he places a bet against Inspector Byrnes.

In Slobbery Jim's Saloon, the prostitutes Mary Healey and Shakespeare look for customers. A Drunk in a worn-looking coat approaches them. Shakespeare takes the drunkard's arm, and they exit upstairs. The action shifts to a squalid second floor bedroom. The Drunk, now sober, takes off his coat, revealing an expensive suit of clothes.

Music wafts from the bar downstairs They sway to the song "Never Time to Dance." Shakespeare's last words are, "My name is Carrie Brown."

Max shouts headlines: "Jack crosses the ocean!" "Bloodbath on Water Street!" "Whitechapel horrors in New York City!" He and Will rush to the bedroom and inspect Shakespeare's corpse. They find marks about her throat; she was choked or strangled. After cutting her neck, the killer slashed the body up and down. He pushed aside the intestines. Stunned, they notice a bloody-smeared statement on the wall: "2 A.M. 36 Hours. Jack."

Several more murders are committed by Jack in a variety of disguises. The Company sings "Stage Blood."

Jack approaches Mary Healey on a street corner and says that such a beautiful woman should not spend "an unprofitable evening." She offers to take him to her room, but he suggests "a better idea." He leads Mary to the East River pier, where he points at the stars and invites her to dance to distant band music. They go through several steps, and Jack's hand brushes Mary's neck. At that moment, Will runs in, followed by Inspector Byrnes and Sergean Clubber with guns trained.

Jack threatens to kill Mary unless the officers toss their weapons into the river. They reluctantly comply. Jack pushes Mary away from him, says, "I keep my promises, Inspector," and turns to bolt away. Will pulls a pearl handled pistol from his belt and shoots. Jack is hit. He tumbles off the dock and disappears in the water. Byrnes orders Clubber to drag the river—"I want the body."

Lights go up on the touring Acting Company. As they pack for a voyage, they sing a reprise of "Changing Faces."

∗   ∗   ∗

Produced by Off-Broadway's Playwrights Horizons, *Jack's Holiday* began previews on February 10, 1995, had its world premiere performance on March 5, and ran through March 26. The play was directed by Susan H. Schulman with musical direction by Steve Tyler, choreography by Michael Lichtefeld, sets and projection effects by Jerome Sirlin.

The main roles were played by Greg Naughton (Will Bolger), Judy Blazer (Mary Healey), Dennis Parlato (Inspector Thomas Byrnes), Alix Korey (Shakespeare), and Allen Fitzpatrick (Jack).

The producers touted their show thus: "Based on the premise that Jack the Ripper made a deadly 1891 visit to New York City—actually chronicled in the newspapers of the day—*Jack's Holiday* delves into the nature of evil and holds a mirror up to our own time." *Jack's Holiday* was nominated for three Outer Critics Circle Awards, including Best Musical.[10]

Acting Edition: Samuel French, Inc.

Lizzie Borden

Andrew Jackson Borden and his wife Abby were gruesomely killed by someone wielding a hatchet at their home in Fall River, Massachusetts, on the morning of August 4, 1892. Andrew's daughter, Lizzie Andrews Borden, was accused of the crime; following a sensational trial, she was acquitted. No one else was ever arrested, and Lizzie has remained the main suspect in American lore.

The Borden case has spawned studies, novels, songs, operas, ballets, comic strips, television shows—and plays.

Nine Pine Street (1933)
John Colton (United States, England-born, 1886–1946)
and Carlton Miles (United States, 1884–1954)

Among the plays dealing with the case of Lizzie Borden, *Nine Pine Street* (1933) stands out. The authors have altered the names of the real-life characters, but the happenings are based on Borden's 1892 hatchet-whacking.

The Holden residence is located at Nine Pine Street. The family members include an uptight father, Edward; a delicate mother, Nell; and two daughters—the younger, good-looking Clara, and Effie, pleasant yet strong-willed.

Effie relates to her parents that her fiancé, minister Warren Pitt, intends to emigrate to China. She wants to go along with him, but her puritanical father prohibits her from leaving home.

A new neighbor, the attractive Mrs. Carrie Riggs, rents a place nearby and soon begins to toy with Edward Holden. When Nell becomes severely ill with heart trouble, Mrs. Riggs lets a critical medicine bottle slip, and it breaks.[11] Nell dies.

A month later, on Effie and Pitt's wedding day, her father escorts home a wife himself—Carrie Riggs. Effie revokes her nuptials and, to spite her stepmother, continues to remain at the Holden dwelling.

When Mr. Holden refuses to release money that Effie inherited from Grandma Tate and requests a warrant to incarcerate Pitt, accusing him of stealing church funds, Effie bashes her stepmother with a steam iron and strikes her father with a walking stick, killing them both.

Effie is detained. After a lengthy trial, she is found "not guilty." The jury felt that such a brutal homicide could not have been carried out by a woman. Effie is released from prison to find that her friends reject her, the maid departs, and Pitt ends their relationship. Her sister Clara informs Effie that the family doctor advocated that she move out to avert a meltdown.

An epilogue unfolds twenty years later. Effie is still an outsider, trapped in her own lodging. She is encircled by a pack of dogs, her only companions. A New York columnist, Martin Lodge, arrives on the scene and requests an interview: "You're part of—history—Miss Holden—you're Americana." Effie refuses: "I have nothing new to say."

* * *

Following a numbers of previews, from Providence to Philadelphia, *Nine Pine Street* opened at New York's Longacre Theatre on April 27, 1933, with Lillian Gish cast as Effie Holden. The reviewers unanimously praised Gish's "sincere" and "lovely" performance, but several of them had misgivings about the play itself. "It grows tedious," sniffed the *New York Times*.[12] "Most of its characters are as lifeless as those old-fashioned mantelpiece figures that used to be covered with glass," ridiculed John Mason Brown.[13]

Nevertheless, Burns Mantle described *Nine Pine Street* as "a robust drama,"[14] and Robert Garland applauded the playwrights who "have gone about their business artfully, lending credibility to an incredible happening by means of understatement, implication and general playing down."[15]

The Holden/Borden play failed to draw audiences and went dark after 28 performances.[16]

Acting Edition: Samuel French, Inc.

* * *

Opening on February 9, 1959, at New York's 54th Street Theatre, *The Legend of Lizzie,* by Reginald Lawrence, earned forty whacks from the press. *The Legend of Lizzie* captures the Borden calamity from the perspective of District Attorney Sewell, enacted by Douglass Montgomery. Sewell goes back to Fall River, Massachusetts, and rehashes what happened during the gruesome events of 30 years ago. A succession of short segments spins the action from home, to court, to the lawyer's firm, to alleys—"a kind of subway-shuttle technique that takes us a very short distance at a time, doubles back in its tracks, and leaves us with a stronger sense of vertigo than of psychological discovery," wrote Walter Kerr.[17]

"*The Legend of Lizzie* succeeds only in further confusing the facts in the case and revealing the principals as a group of dreary and excessively unattractive people," denounced John McClain.[18]

The only kind review came from John Chapman: "The Lizzie Borden affair is even now our most notable murder case, because it is so tantalizing … of all the Lizzie Borden stories I have read and seen, *The Legend of Lizzie* is the best."[19]

Starring Anne Meacham, *The Legend of Lizzie* endured for only two performances. Elizabeth Montgomery played the title role in 1975 on ABC-TV. The axe murders of Lizzie's father and stepmother—by a nude murderess—were explicitly pictured. Some ABC stations (in Boston, Philadelphia, and Birmingham) declined to broadcast it because of the carnage.

* * *

Goodbye, Miss Lizzie Borden, subtitled "A Sinister Play in One Act" (1948), by Lillian de la Torre, depicts a clash between the Borden sisters, Emma and Lizzie. A newspaper reporter, Nellie Cutts, turns up to question the shunned siblings. Cutts' interrogation brings up painful memories and exposes that it wasn't Lizzie who swung the axe but her sister, Emma.

In a climactic scene, the deranged Emma threatens her sister with an axe, but reporter Cutts enters in the nick of time and saves Lizzie's life.

Goodbye, Miss Lizzie Borden was presented in Colorado Springs, Colorado, in 1948.[20]

* * *

The main character of *Murder Takes the Stage* (1957) by James Reach is Mitzie Bond, an aspiring actress who joins a New England summer theater and finds herself immersed in back-stage shenanigans and on-stage murder. An unknown member of the troupe exchanged the blank shells of a prop pistol with live pellets and caused the death of the company's abhorred leading lady, Hazel Laverne.

Mitzie, an avid reader of true crime, believes she knows who's the culprit. She identifies Liz Truesdale, the seventy-year-old owner of the barn theater, as the accused in a years-ago axe murder case of her aunt and uncle. The jury had declared Liz innocent.

Mid play, Truesdale, a proxy of Lizzie Borden, walks upon the stage with an axe, but the perilous moment turns out to be a skillful ruse. Mitzie collaborates with Sheriff

Wiley to set a trap for the murderer, exposing the culprit as Bob Rayfield, the actor who shot Laverne on stage with presumed harmless bullets.[21]

* * *

The playwright Tim Kelly incorporated some ideas of his own in *Lizzie Borden of Fall River* (1976). Kelly begins his two-act play by setting-up the gloomy household of the Borden family and the deep ill will between Lizzie and Emma and their father Andrew and stepmother Abby. During a torrid August morning, a few angry people skirmish with Andrew and Abby: Bridget, the family maid, who is being abused; Sousa, the handyman, who is defrauded out of his earnings; and Aunt Vinnie, who is divested of her lawful inheritance. They all turn into suspects when Andrew and Abby are dispatched by axe blows.

The murders are committed off stage and in this treatment of the Borden affair, doubt remains as to the identity of the culprit until the final scene, during which Lizzie admits her guilt to her sister Emma.

* * *

Blood Relations (1980), by Canadian playwright Sharon Pollock, unrolls in 1902, ten years after the axe murders in Fall River. A visiting actress from Boston, with whom Lizzie has a close personal relationship,[22] tries to wheedle from Lizzie a confession—"Did you, Lizzie, did you?" The present action merges with a cycle of flashbacks.

The atmosphere at the Borden home is strained. Events that lead to the bloody climax include daily clashes between Lizzie and her stepmother, Abigail; Father Andrew's demand that Lizzie marry a widower with three children; Andrew's plan to disinherit his two daughters and give the family's farm to Abigail; and the massacre of Lizzie's pet pigeons by her father.

At the end, the dismembering of Abigail takes place in the bedroom off-stage, and the curtain falls before the killing of Andrew. The intriguing query remains unanswered: "Did you, Lizzie, did you?"

Blood Relations was first performed by Theatre 3 in Edmonton, Alberta, Canada, in March 1980, winning the Governor-General Award for best Canadian play. Ensuing productions performed at the National Arts Centre, Ottawa, Ontario (1981); Manitoba Theatre Centre, Winnipeg, Manitoba (1982); and the Hudson Guild Theatre, New York City (1983). There the press assessment ranged from "absorbing, provocative theatre" to "an absolutely bloodless drama." At the Young Vic Studio, London (1985), the play received reviews that ran the gamut from "remarkable," "fascinating" and "intriguing" to "evasive," "lackluster" and "needlessly complicated." At the Alice B. Theatre in Seattle, Washington (1990), most reviewers scoffed at the "rather slight piece of work" providing "one-dimensional characters." At the Shaw Festival in Niagara-on-the-Lake, Ontario (2003), critic Lynn Slotkin believed that the "psychological thriller-mystery" was endowed with "conclusions that are startling."[23]

Playwright Sharon Pollock offered the television rights of *Blood Relations* to the Calgary TV station, CFCN, and received $13,500 for submitting the initial draft. When her script was rewritten, Pollock filed suit for the "mutilation" of her play. An out-of-court settlement was rendered a few days before the hearing was to begin.

* * *

Slaughter on Second Street (independently published by the author, David Kent, in 1991) unfolds in two locations, The first act is set in the Fall River police headquarters, where we learn of a double murder committed on Second Street through local residents who arrive in the office of City Marshal Rufus Hilliard with observations about the bloody incident.

Facing the outrage of an aroused public, Hilliard and his men rush to gather odds and ends of circumstantial evidence and charge Lizzie Borden with the murder of her parents. She was alone in the house at the time; she threw her stained blue dress in the fireplace the day after the murders; she is the inheritor of the family's estate.

The happenings transfer to the Superior Court in New Bedford. Various witnesses are summoned by the prosecution and the defense: the household maid, the family physician, an old neighbor, police investigators, the medical examiner, and Emma Borden, Lizzie's older sister.

As the witnesses are grilled with queries, the prosecution's case lapses. The verdict is "not guilty."

* * *

In 1993, Lazarus Press of Providence, Rhode Island, published *Lizzie!*, an amusing play by Owen Haskell. Here every member of the Borden household—father Andrew, Mother Abby, daughters Lizzie and Emma, and maid Bridget—is obsessed with food. Most of the action unfolds around the dining table during breakfast, lunch, or dinner, with the piggish family feasting on bread, butter, mutton, eggs, cookies, milk, tea, and coffee.

The key subjects of discussion within the Borden family are castor oil and the maid's kitchen duties. The quarrels between Lizzie and her stepmother consist of such important issues as whether to call the maid "Bridget" or "Maggie." And the only recognizable change in Lizzie following the horrible morning of August 4, 1892, is that now she welcomes mutton as a tasty dinner.

Lizzie! has one memorable scene in which the accused woman is grilled by her lawyer, Andrew Jennings, in a warm-up before the trial. Jennings focuses on motive (Lizzie's unmistakable animosity for her stepmother and a potential inheritance of $250,000), opportunity (Lizzie was in the house when the double murders were executed), character (her hysterical temper), and detrimental clues (the next morning, she was seen burning a stained dress). The verdict is "Not Guilty," but when Lizzie returns home, the neighborhood kids recite:

> "Lizzie Borden took an axe,
> And gave her mother forty whacks.
> When she saw what she had done,
> She gave her father forty-one."[24]

* * *

The action of George C. Koch's *The Axe* (copyrighted in 2006, still unpublished and unproduced) occurs in Provincetown, Massachusetts, in 1893. The play is based on the morbid incidents that took place in Fall River the year before.

The setting is the home of John Bingham, a bank president who has recently been murdered. The curtain rises on the jubilant return of Bingham's daughter, Elspeth, who was cleared in court of the hacking death of her father.

Ezra, a handyman who disappeared during the Bingham investigation, has surfaced in the neighborhood. A visiting uncle, Martin Phelps, is also under suspicion, as is neighbor Thaddeus Clegg, a former inmate of a mental asylum. Sheriff Mitch Middleton and his deputy Bill Evans do not rule out the victim's daughter, Elspeth, for she is the sole heir to her father's fortune. Elspeth's fiancé, Tom Barrett, who may have had designs on the money, is under suspicion as well.

But then, the unknown murderer strikes again, chopping Barrett with an axe and strangling the household maid, Bridey Monaghan.

In a surprising plot maneuver, it is revealed that John Bingham was not killed at all; it was his brother Martin Phelps who was mutilated to the point of being unrecognizable. Bingham formed his fiendish plan, in collaboration with daughter Elspeth, in order to leave behind his failed bank, collect a large amount of insurance money, and live in Ohio as Phelps. Bridey and Barrett were eliminated for fear that they would recognize Bingham when he masqueraded as Phelps.

In a violent climax, Elspeth shoots both her father and deputy sheriff Middleton, then stages it to seem as if they killed one another. Not unlike Lizzie Borden, Elspeth Bingham gets off scot-free.

* * *

Other plays about the Fall River events include *Lizzie Borden in the Late Afternoon* by Cather MacCallum (1982); *Lizzie Borden* by Amy Powers and Christopher McGovern (1998); *The Fall River Axe Murders*, a dramatization of Angela Carter's short story (2003); and the one-woman shows *Miss Lizzie A. Borden Invites You to Tea* by Marjorie Conn, and *Lizzie Borden and Lesbian Theatre: Axes to Grind* by Carolyn Gage.

The big hit from the Broadway revue *New Faces of 1952* was the song *You Can't Chop*

(From left) Nora Kaye, Lucia Chase, and Dimitri Romanoff in Agnes de Mille's ballet *Fall River Legend*, Metropolitan Opera House, New York City, 1948 (George Arents Collection, The New York Public Library).

Your Papa Up in Massachusetts. Musicals derived from this infamous murder include *Lizzie Borden* (1994); *Lizzie Borden* (1995); *Lizzie Borden: The Musical* (2004; revised version 2009; final version 2013).

Jack Beeson composed the music and Kenward Elmslie wrote the libretto for a chamber opera, *Lizzie Borden*, which premiered at the New York City Opera on March 25, 1965. Brenda Lewis appeared as Lizzie. Since then, The City Opera has revived *Lizzie Borden* twice, a recording was issued, and a televised rendering was presented by NET Opera in 1967. A CD with a recording of the opera was re-released in 1995. Phyllis Pancella sang the part of Lizzie in a production broadcast by PBS-TV's *Live from Lincoln Center* on March 24, 1999.

Agnes de Mille choreographed *Fall River Legend*, a ballet that begins and ends with a hanging scene, first performed at the Met, New York, on April 22, 1948. Morton Gould composed the music and Nora Kaye was the ballerina most associated with the role of Lizzie Borden. Kaye danced the part in the London premiere at Covent Garden, August 29, 1950.

Acting Edition:
Goodbye, Miss Lizzie Borden—Baker's Plays
Murder Takes the Stage—Samuel French, Inc.
Lizzie Borden of Fall River—Pioneer Drama Service
Blood Relations—Canadian Theatre Review, Winter 1981, 46–107.
Slaughter on Second Street—David Kent
Lizzie!—Lazarus Press

3

Harrowing Adaptations

Dr. Jekyll and Mr. Hyde

"The germ of *Dr. Jekyll and Mr. Hyde* came to [the Scottish author] Robert Louis Stevenson in a cocaine-induced nightmare in their Bournemouth home," wrote *The Guardian*. "His screams aroused [his wife] Fanny, who indignantly woke him. 'Why did you wake me?' he said. 'I was dreaming a fine bogey tale.'"[1]

Stevenson hurriedly penned the story within a few days, then embellished it during the next six weeks.[2] First published in 1886, "the novella's impact is such that it has become a part of the language with the venecular phrase 'Jekyll and Hyde' referring to people with an unpredictably dual nature, outwordly good but sometimes shockingly evil."[3]

Drake Douglas in his reference book *Horror!,* writes:

> In the best tradition of the Victorian mystery story, *Dr. Jekyll and Mr. Hyde* opens on a peaceful note, with mystery added to mystery until the shattering climax of the story, when Jekyll's friend, Dr. Utterson, bursts into the laboratory and finds the body of the detestable Edward Hyde, but no trace whatsoever of Dr. Jekyll. It is only after this sequence of apparently inexplicable events and after the discovery of Hyde's body that the solution of the mystery is provided ... we of today have, unfortunately, lost one of the prime pleasures of this exciting tale—the element of suspense and surprise—for we are fully aware from the opening pages that Henry Jekyll and Edward Hyde are, in fact, one and the same man.[4]

The famous American actor Richard Mansfield became fascinated with the notion of adapting the novel to the stage. "He secured the right for theatrical production in the United States and the United Kingdom," relate editors Martin A. Danabay and Alex Chisholm in *Jekyll and Hyde Dramatized*, "and turned to a friend, Boston writer Thomas Russell Sullivan, to create a script; Mansfield would undertake the dual title roles himself. The changes Sullivan and Mansfield made to the original story—introducing the addition of female characters, a more sympathetic Dr. Jekyll, and a more significant role to Inspector Newcomen—would become standard for subsequent stage and screen adaptations."[5]

Sullivan's adaptation, called *Dr. Jekyll and Mr. Hyde*, was produced at the Boston Museum on May 9, 1887. The reviews were kind. The *Boston Post* confided, "'The applause throughout was long and loud" and "The climax is very striking and vivid."[6] The *Boston Globe* praised Richard Mansfield for "a great piece of character acting."[7]

After some rewrites, the show moved to New York in September and London the following year. The period's audiences were not yet familiar with the resolution of the play. The viewers were amazed to learn before the final curtain that the generous Dr. Jekyll and the wicked Mr. Hyde personified the dual nature of the same individual.

The play follows, more or less, the action of the novel. In the first scene, set in the tea-room of Sir Danvers Carew, a dignified Member of Parliament (M.P.), we are introduced to some of the play's main characters: the host, Sir Danvers; his daughter Agnes; his friends Dr. Hastie Lanyon, attorney Gabriel Utterson, and Dr. Henry Jekyll, Agnes's fiancé.

As they drink tea, Lanyon relates "a strange story" he heard from his acquaintance Enfield. Enfield was on his way home about three in the morning, when he saw a man run into a little girl and casually step over her. Enfield confronted him. The man proposed to give a tidy sum of money to the girl's family, unlocked the rear door of an adjacent house, and came back with a check for a hundred pounds. His name was Edward Hyde. Utterson is taken aback because the door opened by Hyde leads to Jekyll's laboratory.

Sir Danvers and Lanyon exit the living room. Utterson corners Jekyll and confides that he's troubled about the new will that the doctor has advocated, bequeathing much of his property to "friend and benefactor Edward Hyde." There was also a stipulation that in case he vanishes,

Robert Louis Stevenson, Scotland, 1850–1894, famous author of *Dr. Jekyll and Mr. Hyde* (portrait by Henry Walter Barnett, 1893; Billy Rose Theatre Division, The New York Public Library for the Performing Arts).

Hyde shall promptly receive his assets. Jekyll attests that he can dispose of the man whenever he wishes.

His guests departed, Sir Danvers reclines in an armchair by the fireplace. Agnes informs her father that Henry has been summoned to a patient. Edward Hyde turns up at the window. Both father and daughter are aghast at the sight of Hyde. Sir Danvers sends Agnes out of the room and orders the "scoundrel" to depart. Hyde laughs and says that "the girl" will be his if he so desires. Sir Danvers lunges at Hyde. They scuffle and Hyde strangles him.[8] Agnes comes in. The curtain descends as she hovers over her father's body while Hyde is at the window chuckling.

The action now focuses on the investigation of the murder by Inspector Newcomen of Scotland Yard and the hunt for Mr. Hyde. Utterson commits himself to finding Hyde and uncovering the rationale behind his curious friendship with the doctor—"let him be Mr. Hyde, I'll be Mr. Seek." A dispute occurs at Dr. Jekyll's laboratory, where the

lawyer watches Hyde's shocking changeover into Jekyll. The moment is spiked by booming thunders and flickering lightning.

The last scene takes place at Jekyll's laboratory in the early evening. Jekyll, out of the essential tablets that can help him negate the alteration to Hyde, waits for his butler Poole, who has gone to every pharmacy in London.

Poole returns with bad news—the tablets are not to be found anywhere. "I am a dead man, Poole," Jekyll says. "The evil power within me has the mastery. It is Hyde now that controls Jekyll—not Jekyll, Hyde."

Jekyll asks his butler to fetch Agnes and place her below at the courtyard's window, so that he can observe her face one more time.

Poole exits. Jekyll gradually turns to Hyde, sees himself in the mirror, and shrieks. He hears loud thumping on the door. Heavy blows ensue, and it breaks. Utterson enters, followed by Poole, Lanyon, Agnes, and Inspector Newcomen. Hyde sips from a phial of poison. Newcomen demands, "Murderer! What have you done with Jekyll?" Hyde snickers, says "Gone, gone," and falls. Curtain.

* * *

Richard Mansfield rehearsed for just two weeks before the opening of *Dr. Jekyll and Mr. Hyde* at the Boston Museum on May 9, 1887. Martin A. Danahay and Alex Chisholm report:

> Mansfield approached the experiment with grave foreboding. Could he in the presence of a vast audience effect the transformation from Hyde to Jekyll in such manner as to strike absolute conviction? He afterwards confessed: "That night in the third act where as Hyde I grasped the potion, swallowed it, writhed in the awful agony of transformation and rose pale and erect, the visualized embodiment of Jekyll—an ague of apprehension seized me and I suffered a lifetime in the silence in which the curtain fell. In another instant I realized that silence was the tribute of the awe and terror inspired by the reality of the scene, for through the canvas screen came a muffled roar which was the sweetest sound I ever heard in my life, and I breathed again."[9]

Danahay and Chisholm recount:

> One of Mansfield's purely theatric devices for horror was to convey the suggestion that Hyde was coming. This was effected with an empty stage, a gray, green-shot gloom, and oppressive silence.... Then with a wolfish howl, a panther's leap, and the leer of a fiend Hyde was miraculously in view. It was at such a time as that that strong men shuddered and women fainted and were carried out of the theatre. People went away from *Dr. Jekyll and Mr. Hyde* afraid to enter their houses alone. They feared to sleep in darkened rooms. They were awakened by nightmares. Yet it had fascination of crime and mystery, and they came again and again.[10]

The show came to New York's Madison Square Theatre on September 12, 1887. The *New York Herald* said, "The two changes made in view of the audience were really wonderful, and the whole impersonation was, on the whole, so powerful and consistent that the actor had most numerous and hearty curtain calls, mingled on one occasion by many shouts of 'Bravo,' both during and at the close of the play."[11]

On July 11, 1888, Mansfield and his cast left for England, and on August 4, *Dr. Jekyll and Mr. Hyde* opened at London's Lyceum Theatre. Three days later, the corpse of Martha Tabram was found with 39 stab wounds on a staircase in Whitechapel. On August 31, September 8, September 30, and November 9, the mangled bodies of four more prostitutes were found. The cycle of Whitechapel murders was soon attributed to the enigmatic

"Jack the Ripper." It was assumed that the heinous assassin was a sailor, butcher, police-man, journalist, the Royal Surgeon to Queen Victoria, even the Queen's grandson Prince Albert. As a result of Richard Mansfield's credible characterization of Dr. Jekyll's alteration into Mr. Hyde, the actor was included in the lineup of suspects![12] The bleak cover-age of the play convinced Man-sfield to discontinue the run. The *Daily Telegraph* supported the "wisely withdrawal of the creepy drama" on October 20, 1888.[13]

Upon their return to New York, Richard Mansfield and his ensemble played *Dr. Jekyll and Mr. Hyde* in the Garden Theatre (November 20, 1899– January 13, 1900) and contin-uously in 1904, 1905, 1906, and 1907 at the New Amsterdam Theatre.

* * *

Beginning with the 1887 adaptation by Thomas Russell Sullivan, more than 120 Jekyll/ Hyde plays have been pro-duced in the United States and Europe. H.B. Irving (Henry Irving's son) portrayed the duo role at Queen's Theatre, Lon-don, in 1910. A 1915 version, by Anna Burt Stewart, made both

Richard Mansfield, England, 1857–1907, playing the title roles of *Doctor Jekyll and Mr. Hyde* (1885; Billy Rose Theatre Division, The New York Public Library for the Performing Arts)

protagonists female, while a 1932 rendition by Betty Rolands begins with Christmas scenes from Jekyll's childhood. A 1941 version by Richard Abbott utilizes two actors in the leading role(s).

Several stage adaptations of Stevenson's novella saw light in the mid-20th cen-tury. In 1954, Frédéric Dard wrote and Robert Hossein directed *Docteur Jekyll et Mister Hyde* for the famed Théâtre du Grand-Guignol in Paris. In 1961, Italian actor Carmelo Bene scripted, staged, and starred in *Lo stranocaso del dottor Jekyll e del signor Hyde* in Genova. Seven years later, a musical version named *After You, Mr. Hyde*, helmed by Howard Da Silva and featuring Alfred Drake, disbanded before coming to Broadway. A musical spoof, *I Was a Teenage Jekyll and Hyde*, with book and lyrics by Randall Lewton, music by Peter Miller, was first presented at Alsop Comprehensive School, Liverpool, England, on July 14, 1981. Also in 1981, Kurt Vonnegut penned a story line for a musical play based on Stevenson's novella; the manuscript is housed at the Indiana University library. Orson Bean portrayed Jekyll, and Eric Booth was Hyde in *Problem Potion*, a melodramatic version by Colston Corris that premiered at the Apple Corps Theater, New York, in 1983.

Two American playwrights approached Stevenson's tale with a humorous vein, both in 1984: Jack Sharkey's *Jekyll Hydes Again!* and Tim Kelly's *Under Jekyll's Hyde*. Off-Broadway's Ridiculous Theater Company poked fun at the topic in *Dr. Jekyll and Mr. Hyde* (1989), written by Georg Osterman and starring Everett Quinton. Also in 1989, the Natural Theatre Company produced its own humorous version, *Jekyll and Hyde Follies*, winning the London Fringe Award for Best Comedy. Florida's Asolo Touring Theatre commissioned Eberle Thomas and Barbara Redmond to adapt *The Strange Case of Dr. Jekyll and Mr. Hyde* for performance during its 1989–1990 season. The play, framed within a coroner's inquest, was directed by John Gulley.

In 1991, David Edgar adapted a variant faithful to the novel's scenario for the Royal Shakespeare Company, London. Peter Wood directed. Two years later, California State University, San Bernardino, offered *The Trial of Dr. Jekyll*, written and directed by William L. Slout, who set the action in an imaginary court room, where Jekyll fantasizes that he is on trial. In James W. Nichol's *Dr. Jekyll and Mr. Hyde: A Love Story* (1996), first performed by the Canadian Stage Company, Toronto, Canada, central to Dr. Jekyll's transformation is his disturbingly intimate affection for his teenage daughter. A musical treatment of *Dr. Jekyll and Mr. Hyde* was written and directed by Graham Devlin (book) and Felix Cross (music and lyrics) for a 1996 tour by Major Road Theatre Company. Another musical, *Jekyll & Hyde*, with a score by Frank Wildhorn, book and lyrics by Leslie Bricusse, debuted in 1990 at the Alley Theatre, Houston, Texas, and after extensive changes it eventually opened at Broadway's Plymouth Theatre on April 28, 1997. Even though the show received poor reviews, *Jekyll & Hyde* ran for 1543 performances, closing its doors on January 7, 2001. Robert Cuccioll portrayed the title roles.

Two interesting adaptations of the story premiered in 1997: Frederic Fort's *L'etrange cas du Dr. Jekyll et de Mr. Hyde*, first performed by the Compagnie Annibal et ses Éléphants at the Avignon Festival, France, had a cast of five actors wearing masks. The production, directed by Mario Gonzales, was influenced by the Commedia dell'arte tradition. In Mark Ryan's *The Strange Case of Dr. Jekyll and Mr. Hyde as told to Carl Jung by an Inmate of Broadmoor Asylum* (also titled *Prime Evil*), which premiered at the Equinox Theatre, Edinburgh Fringe Festival, Hyde has been committed to Broadmoor (institute for the criminally insane) to be treated by Dr. Jung but gradually the tables turn, and doctor becomes patient. Noah Smith's *The Strange Case of Dr. Jekyll and Mr. Hyde,* presented by the Summer Theatre at Mount Holyoke College, August 10 to 14, 1999, featured a maid and a butler who maneuver the furniture between scenes to indicate changes of locale while serving as a Greek Chorus to introduce characters. A unique ending has lawyer Utterson contemplating whether to throw Dr. Jekyll's serum formula into the fireplace or keep it for a time when it might "come in handy."

Sleep in Chains: Jekyll's Nightmare (2005), by Jules Tasca, is an innovative retelling of the story, spreading the duality of good and evil to other characters—Jekyll's wife, Grace, who after the death of her husband does not remain in mourning long; her sister, Pamela, the "black sheep" of the family and Hyde's mistress; and their father, the Reverend Danvers, who has a shadowy past. A rendering by Jeffrey Hatcher, with four actors playing the role of Mr. Hyde, premiered at the Cincinnati Playhouse in the Park in 2009 and continued to run at a few urban theaters. Dramatists Play Service issued the Hatcher interpretation in 2008, calling it "a new and shocking version of Robert Louis Stevenson's classic tale of depravity, lust, love and horror."

New variations of *Dr. Jekyll and Mr. Hyde* have been produced in the second decade of the 21st century. In 2010, the Holden Kemble Theatre Company showcased *The Scandalous Case of Dr. Jekyll and Mr. Hyde* at the Edinburgh Fringe Festival, then continued to perform it for three weeks at the Tabard Theatre in Cheswick, London. In 2012, Synetic Theater of Arlington, Virginia, staged a highly regarded *Jekyll & Hyde*, headlining Alex Mills in the lead. The following year, Flipping the Bird, an Oxford theater ensemble, mounted an adaptation of the story in which Jekyll is a woman. Doctor Tajemnica Jekyll arrives in London from an unidentified country and asserts that she is Edward Hyde's aunt. Gabriel Utterson is her lawyer and suitor.

In 2013, the Four of Swords company performed an adaptation at Poltimore House, a decaying home near Exeter, Devon County. The critics greeted the location as an ideal spot for Stevenson's eerie narrative. Audiences were guided through several rooms of the house while the story evolved. Across the ocean, also in 2013, Mix Studio Theatre of Ypsilanti, Michigan, presented *Hollywood and Hyde* by Timothy Henning, in which Jekyll is an out-of-work actor who starts to exhibit strange behavior. And that same year, back in England, James Hyland unveiled a one-man show, *Strange Case of Dr. Jekyll and Mr. Hyde*, himself playing the title roles, first at the Harrogate Theatre Studio, then on a UK tour.

In 2015, Lung Ha Theatre Company of Edinburgh, Scotland, a troupe of and for young people with learning disabilities, set the story at Edinburgh's New and Old Towns. Also in 2015, Sell a Door Theatre Company went on a U.K. tour with a three-actor *Jekyll & Hyde* by Jo Clifford, wherein the action takes place in the future, and Doctor Jekyll is a star medical researcher who, through his experimentation with various drugs, produces the murderous and uncontrollable Hyde. In this version, Jekyll is gay and makes love with his lawyer Utterson, who was part of a movement that ensured homosexuality was re-criminalized.[14] In 2016, the Bangor, Wales, English Dramatic Society produced *A New Case of Jekyll and Hyde* at the Edinburgh Fringe Festival, shifting the plot to the present day. Elizabeth Jekyll aids her husband to rehabilitate from PTSD. In 2018, writer-performers Burt Grinstead and Anna Stromberg redefined Robert Louis Stevenson's Victorian horror tale at the Los Angeles LGBT Center's Davidson/Valentini Theatre.

Dr. Jekyll and Mr. Hyde (1989)
Georg Osterman (United States, 1953–1995)

In 1989, Off-Broadway's notorious Ridiculous Theatrical Company presented a raunchy stage adaptation of *Dr. Jekyll and Mr. Hyde* by Georg Osterman, who also played a key role in the production. With the exception of Dr. Henry Jekyll/Mr. Edward Hyde, none of the play's characters appeared in the original Robert Louis Stevenson novella. In fact, Stevenson was not given any credit in the playbill nor in the Samuel French acting edition.

The proceedings take place in the fictional town of Coxsakie. Act I, Scene 1 unfolds at Dr. Jekyll's home. The household maid, Minerva (described as "a tough cookie"), serves Mary Jekyll, Henry's wife ("a little on the dizzy side"), her breakfast and hands her the *Coxsakie Tatler*. Mary reads aloud that the town's mild-mannered librarian,

Basil Hickock, "was caught late last night in the act of dismembering the dead body of his 68-year-old mother. Further investigation revealed a horrifying collection of other human remains. Hickock's refrigerator was filled with human organs, and a large freezer in the cellar was packed with butchered parts."

The action shifts to the laboratory. Dr. Jekyll ("A brilliant scientist and devoted husband") is muttering mathematical equations and begins pouring liquids from various vessels into a test tube, which begins to smoke. Jekyll drinks the formula and is seized with racking pains. A stage instructions states: "Henry gasps wildly for breath as everything spins around him. Suddenly the pains cease and the spinning stops. He is transformed from Henry Jekyll to a smaller, hideous Edward Hyde." He uses a luncheon tray as a looking glass and exclaims cheerfully that even though he's ugly, he feels young, happy, reckless, with sensual images running through his mind.

The next scene takes place in "The Fruit Bowl" nightclub, where Hyde meets Lily Gay, the club's pretty singer, shoves a twenty-dollar bill down her bra, and escorts Lily to her apartment. They enter joking and laughing, and she turns on a lamp. A stage instructions states: "He pulls out his tiny, dog-like penis." Lily screams and says, "Do I know how to pick 'em. Again I get a raw deal." He begins playing with himself as he slowly approaches her, slaps her face, and pushes her to the bed. He handcuffs her to the bedpost, tears off one of her nails, and punches her in the jaw, knocking her out cold. He then begins to remove her clothes and tickles her foot, which brings her around. She desperately tries to free herself, in vain. He unzips his pants, croaks, "Mr. Hyde's gone wilding," and lasciviously rubs himself against Lily while strangling her. "Was this the face that launched a thousand ships?" Hyde exclaims cheerfully as Lily goes limp.

The final scene of Act I takes place in a dimly lit street. An elderly Jehovah Witness stands on a corner with a sandwich-board that reads, "Repent! Faith Heals All!" Hyde enters, mocks the old man, pulls off his sandwich-board, and uses it to beat him to death. Police sirens are heard approaching. Hyde runs away as the lights fade.

Act 2 begins at the laboratory. Hyde puts on Jekyll's lab coat and quickly prepares the formula that will restore him. He finishes mixing the ingredients and toasts, "Here's looking at you, kid!" Dr. Bernice Braintwain, Jekyll's associate, enters the room, and a surprised Hyde drops the formula. Bernice aims a gun at him and orders, "All right, Hyde! Hold it right there!" He grabs his crotch, says, "I'm holding," and lunges at her. They struggle, and the gun goes off. Hyde is shot and turns into Jekyll. Bernice is seized with fright and a stage instruction says that "her hair turns white."

Jekyll coughs and says weakly, "I'm dying." He asks Bernice to destroy the formula and all records of his experiments and to vow that the secret of Edward Hyde "will never leave this place." Bernice promises.

Mary and Minerva enter. "Henry, what are you doing on the floor?" asks Mary, then lets out a blood-curdling scream: "I see blood!" Henry says, "I've been shot, Mary my love…. Mr. Hyde shot me, then escaped." Everyone weeps when suddenly the tragic tableau is broken by a flash of lightning, a clap of thunder, and a puff of smoke. Mr. Hyde appears with a sickle in hand and says, "Home is where the *horror* is!" Everyone screams and the curtain falls.

* * *

Dr. Jekyll and Mr. Hyde was originally produced in New York City by The Ridiculous Theatrical Company, opening on November 10, 1989, running for 103 performances.

The play was directed by Kate Stafford, with scenery designed by Mark Beard. The cast consisted of Everett Quinton (Henry Jekyll/Edward Hyde), Eureka (Mary Jekyll), Mary Neufeld (Bernice Braintwain), Terence Mintern (Minerva), and the playwright, Georg Osterman (Lily Gay).

Reviewer Laurie Winer of the *New York Times* welcomed a play "full of gloriously goofy performances and raunchy sight gags…. Everett Quinton, as an anxious, nearly bald Jekyll, makes his hilarious transformation into the foul Hyde lurking within…. The brassy Lily Gay is deliciously played by Mr. Osterman in a beehive hairdo and becoming eyelashes."[15]

Edgar Allan Poe

Edgar Allan Poe (1809–1849), guru of the macabre and father of the detective story, penned only one play, *Politian* (1835), which is unfinished and has never been produced. Poe composed it in blank verse and based it on events that transpired in Kentucky. Anne Cooke of Frankfort, Kentucky, had a child with the state solicitor general, Solomon P. Sharp. She married Jereboam O. Beauchamp in 1824 with the demand that he murder Sharp. Beauchamp kept his obligation, killing Sharp on November 5, 1825. In court Beauchamp maintained his innocence but was ordered to be hanged. Cooke tried to overdose on laudanum on the eve of her husband's execution on July 7, 1826.[16]

The case became a national sensation and was fictionalized by many authors. Poe chose to set the plot in sixteenth-century Rome. Castiglione, a Duke's son, plans to marry his cousin, Alessandra, triggering the jealousy of his father's ward, the orphan Lalage. Lalage meets Politian, an earl, and after some flirtation convinces him to murder Castiglione.

The first installment of *Politian* was published in the December 1835 issue of *Southern Literary Magazine* and the second in January 1836. The play received scorching reviews, and the failure convinced Poe to drop playwriting and focus on narrative prose.

Poe would later pen a short story about another factual murder case, *The Mystery of Marie Roget* (1842). It was left for other hands to transfer his suspenseful and horrific yarns to the stage.

Edgar Allan Poe, originator of the modern horror story, United States, 1809–1849 (artist: Douglas Crane, 1937; Fine Arts Museums of San Francisco).

An Evening with Edgar Allan Poe (2007)
Robert Mason (United States, 1949–)

Robert Mason stepped into the creepy world of Edgar Allan Poe with six one-act adaptations, notably *The Cask of Amontillado* and *The Fall of the House of Usher*.

THE CASK OF AMONTILLADO

The Cask of Amontillado takes place in the early 19th century. The action commences at midnight under a lamppost on a Paris street corner (the locale was changed by the adapter from the nameless Italian city of the original story to the French capital). Montresor, a middle-aged aristocrat and a renowned wine expert, relates to the audience that he bears deep animosity toward Fortunato, a wealthy, overbearing man who fancies himself a wine connoisseur. Montresor confides that he has hidden his grudge and has always been "most ingratiating" to Fortunato.[17]

Enter Fortunato, inebriated, wearing the party clothes of a jester, on his head "a comical hat with bells." Montresor tells Fortunato that he has purchased a cask of what he believes is a rare vintage of Amontillado and invites him to come to his vaults to verify the authenticity of the rare nectar.

The lights come up on a cellar vault. Fortunato stumbles into it and leans against the back wall. Montresor quickly shackles him to it with chains and pockets the key. He then gathers bricks and mortar from a dark corner and walls Fortunato in.

As Fortunato's intoxication wears off, he realizes what is happening. He screams, only to have Montresor cheerfully inform him that no one can hear him as they're too far underground.[18]

THE FALL OF THE HOUSE OF USHER

Edgar Allan Poe's "The Fall of the House of Usher" is a Gothic short story, first published in September 1839 in *Burton's Gentlemen's Magazine* and subsequently included in the collection *Tales of the Grotesque and Arabesque* in 1840.

Much of the action in Robert Mason's adaptation is set in Roderick Usher's studio in the family mansion. It is dimly lit. Dark draperies cover the walls. Antique furniture, books, and musical instruments are scattered about.

The curtain rises in late afternoon. Roderick Usher, a middle-aged, tall, pale man, gloomily tells Rhodes, his long-time friend, that he's beginning to feel the symptoms of a mental disorder—part of the curse of the Ushers.

Usher explains that he can only stand the faintest of sounds, the lightest of scents, the dimmest of light. He bemoans the sickly condition of his twin sister, Madeline, who is cataleptic and falls into trances that have the appearance of death. In fact, says Usher, "Over the centuries that we've been in this house, some of the Ushers who had been thought dead awakened out of their stupor to find themselves buried prematurely." He adds with a shudder that the exhumed bodies were discovered with their fingernails ripped out from clawing at the casket lid.

Next morning, Rhodes and Usher are in the studio, the former painting at an easel, the latter playing a guitar and declaiming Poe's poem "The Haunted House," which pointedly foreshadows the Usher doom.[19]

Usher then shocks his friend by revealing that Madeline seems to have died during the night. But in view of her flushed appearance, he is not sure. He will entomb her body in a vault beneath the mansion for a fortnight, then bury her in the family cemetery.

The proceedings shift to night inside the vault. Rhodes and a doctor are carrying a coffin. Usher says that he must have "one last look," opens the top half of the coffin to reveal Madeline, then replaces the lid as the lights fade out.

Four days later, Usher is pacing back-and-forth in his studio while Rhodes observes him with concern. There is a faint sound of scratching in the background. "It's Madeline," Usher groans. Rhodes insists that it's merely the wind blowing the tree branches against the house.

Seven days pass. The storm builds, but the sound of the scratching is heard more forcefully. Suddenly the door opens revealing a trembling and bloody Madeline. She falls on the floor as Usher collapses into the chair. Rhodes crosses to Madeline, then turns to Usher: "I think she is dead, Roderick…. Usher? Usher?" Fade out.[20]

*   *   *

"The Fall of the House of Usher" is considered among Poe's most profound works of prose. G.R. Thomson writes in his introduction to *Great Short Works of Edgar Allan Poe*: "The tale has long been hailed as a masterpiece of Gothic horror; it is also a masterpiece of dramatic irony and structural symbolism."[21]

Twentieth Century Interpretations of The Fall of the House of Usher (1969), edited by Thomas Woodson, contains a collection of essays about Poe's story, including a whimsical theory by Lyle H. Kendall, Jr. that Madeline Usher is a vampire and "the terrified and ineffectual Roderick, ostensibly suffering from pernicious anemia, is her final victim."[22]

In addition to Robert Mason's adaptation of the Gothic tale, other plays about the doomed Ushers include *Usher* (1962) by David Campton, *The Fall of the House of Usher* (1979) by Tim Kelly, and *The Fall of the House of Usher* (1991) by Gip Hoppe.

Richard McElvain's *Poe's Midnight Dreary* (1991) includes a short vignette about the Ushers while *Night Chills* (1992) by Billy St. John features a three-scene treatment of the topic. In *Murder by Poe* (2004), Jeffrey Hatcher re-imagines the Usher story and other yarns of terror by Poe, such as "The Black Cat," "The Tell-Tale Heart," and "The Murders in the Rue Morgue." Eric Coble's *Nightfall with Edgar Allan Poe* (2004) collects four stage adaptations of Poe's chilling tales while Lance Tait's *The Fall of the House of Usher and Other Plays* (2005) contains ten adaptations.

The story gets turned upside down in two spoofs: *Usher: A Totally Teen Comedy* (2007) by Flip Kobler and Cindy Marcus, and *The Rise of the House of Usher* (2009) by Sean Abley.

The entire *An Evening with Edgar Allan Poe*, including "The Fall of the House of Usher," was presented by Wilkes Playmakers of Wilkesboro, North Carolina, on October 11–14, 2018, each show helmed by a different director.

Acting Edition: Playscripts, Inc.

Night Chills (1992)
Billy St. John (United States, 1942–2017)

THE TELL-TALE HEART

In *Night Chills*, playwright Billy St. John collects several adaptations of Edgar Allan Poe's nerve-wracking short stories, including "The Tell-Tale Heart" and "The Murders in the Rue Morgue." The playlets are introduced by Poe himself as he addresses the audience directly.

"Perhaps the best known of my tales involves murder, guilt and greed," says Poe. "I call it *The Tell-Tale Heart*. Imagine, if you will, that you are in a decaying house on the edge of a small Eastern village. It is a rainy summer evening."

The lights come up on the parlor of a dilapidated home. The table is covered with a dirty tablecloth. The sofa is draped with a tattered blanket. Ragged curtains hang on an upstage window. The sound of rain continues through the play, and there are occasional flashes of lightning.

Jess Stark, a young man in a wet jacket, appears at an entrance Down Right, a lantern in his hand. He moves up stage furtively, shows his wife Lorna a gold coin and whispers enthusiastically that he can put his hand "on hundreds of other little gold mates just like it!" He discovered where the old fool hides his treasure—in the cellar.

Lorna objects to stealing from the elderly man who gave them shelter from the storm. Jess insists that they can be safe hundreds of miles away with all that plunder; he does not wish to peddle hardware the rest of his life. He picks up a knife. Lorna is horrified by her husband's decision to kill their host, but the more she attempts to stop him, the more aggressive Jess becomes. He assures Lorna that "it will be peaceful—painless and quick," and exits to Zolka's bedroom. Lorna, frozen, hears the old man asking, "What do you mean—taking my pillow?" He then calls for help until his voice is muffled, then—silence.

Jess enters and wipes his knife with a handkerchief. "The man had smothered," he explains to his shocked wife, "but his wicked old heart beat on—and on—and on—and on! There was no other way to halt that hideous heart than impale it!" Lorna says that they must leave immediately. Jess insists that first they get the gold, when two women enter, carrying old-fashioned umbrellas. Jess and Lorna explain that they were caught in the heavy rain, and Mr. Zolka kindly offered them shelter and food. The newcomers introduce themselves as sisters Kristin and Metti Holub, nieces of Nathan Zolka; they came to inquire about their dear uncle's deteriorating health.

Jess says that the old man is asleep and should not be disturbed. When Kristin insists on entering the bedroom, he locks the door. Kristin, brass-voiced and fearless, sends her sister to fetch Master Branneman, whom she says is "a friend of our uncle," but he turns out to be the local constable.[23]

Constable Branneman enters the bedroom and initially does not discern any foul play. But Jess, pacing back-and-forth in the living room, begins to hear the sound of heartbeats emanating through the open door. Lorna frantically tugs on his arm, urging him to escape, but louder and louder come the heartbeats until Jess shouts over their volume, "I suffocated the old man! I killed him! But his heart beats on! I stabbed it through with my knife-blade! But the hideous heart beats on! And on and on!"

He sinks to his knees, sobbing, "Stop the beating, or I go mad!" Branneman, Kristin, and Metti stare at Jess, as his frantic cries are drowned by the now-thundering sound of a beating heart.[24]

* * *

Based on a very short story, the National Theatre, London, mounted a 2 hour and 20 minute production of *The Tell-Tale Heart*, written and directed by Anthony Neilson, running December 2018–January 2019. The show was touted as "a twisted, graphic and darkly-comic treat," with a warning: "This production contains strobe lighting, provocative language, some violent scenes, and moments and themes that some people may find distressing." In September of 2019, The Roads Theatre of Studio City, California, presented a spoof of "The Tell-Tale Heart," written and directed by Ari Stidham, as part of *The Edgar Allan Show*, a reenactment and recitals of several Poe stories, all done with great silliness.

Other adapters of "The Tell-Tale Heart" include Robert Brome (1966), Luella E. McMahon (1967), Richard McElvain (1991), L. Don Swartz (1998), Eric Cole (in his collection *Nightfall with Edgar Allan Poe*, 2004), and Robert Mason (in his collection *An Evening with Edgar Allan Poe*, 2007).

THE MURDERS IN THE RUE MORGUE

Edgar Allan Poe's short tale, "The Murders in the Rue Morgue," published in *Graham's Magazine* in 1841, has been described as the first modern detective story. Poe referred to it as a yarn of "ratiocination." C. Auguste Dupin, the first fictional detective, became the prototype for many future literary sleuths, notably Arthur Conan Doyle's Sherlock Holmes and Agatha Christie's Hercule Poirot. And, like Dupin, they too are served by a personal friend who tells the story and, like him, they outwit the bumbling police. Dupin reappears in Poe's "The Mystery of Marie Rogêt" (1842) and "The Purloined Letter" (1844). Poe's role in the creation of the detective story is reflected in the Edgar Awards, given annually by the Mystery Writers of America.[25]

Poe's story begins with Dupin and his roommate, the nameless narrator, reading a newspaper account of a baffling double murder. Madame L'Espanaye and her daughter have been found dead at their home in the Rue Morgue, a fictional street in Paris. The mother was found in the yard behind the house, with several broken bones, her throat so deeply sliced that her head fell off when the body was removed. The daughter was discovered strangled to death and stuffed upside down into a chimney. Oddly, the murders occurred in a fourth-floor room that was locked from the inside.[26]

Billy St. John's adaptation is set at the living room of a flat in Paris. At curtain rise, Madam Jeanne L'Espanaye, a fortune teller, is seated at a desk, with gold francs scattered before her. As she counts the coins, Madame pushes them, one-by-one, into a leather pouch. Camille, her sixteen-year-old daughter, dressed in a flannel nightgown, enters from the bedroom and angrily accuses her mother of rattling around "half a night," disturbing her sleep. Madame explains that she must finish packing before they can leave for their trip to Bordeaux.

Camille says that she changed her mind. She is not going because she expects Adolphe Le Bon to propose marriage. Her mother scoffs at the wedding plans of a sixteen-year-old to a bank clerk who may have designs on the 4000 francs he delivered yesterday. Besides, Paris is not safe nowadays; within a single week three young women were murdered, their cases not yet solved. The Chief of Detectives, Monsieur Dupin, has voiced alarm.[27]

Madame tells her daughter that she recently read their fortune in the cards and only drew black cards from the deck. Camille bursts into laugher. Madame shuffles a deck of card and insists that her daughter draw the top cards. Camille, grudgingly, picks three cards: the Queen of Spades, the Queen of Clubs, and the Ace of Clubs.

Madame says gravely, "Three black cards, *death*." Camille accuses her mother of cheating in order to make her leave Paris. Madame slaps her face. Camille stalks into the bedroom. The stage is quiet when Camille's scream is heard—a cry of terror. Madame rushes to find the cause and emits a blood-curdling howl. The shrieks of the women grow in intensity as the lights fade out.

Scene 2 takes place in the afternoon, two days later. C. Auguste Dupin, 39, Chief of the Sûreté, wearing a light coat and chewing on an unlit cigar, is gazing out the window. His assistant Robert Roche reports that he has narrowed down the suspects to the bank clerk, the house manager, and the woman in the next flat. The evident strength in the execution of the murders, says Roche, points to Adolphe Le Bon, the bank clerk, who had been there the same day. Dupin comments that the 4000 francs Le Bon had delivered were found intact, so theft was not the motive.

Dupin concentrates on the fact that the door to the corridor was locked; the authorities had to force it open. The window too was fastened. The one in the bedroom was open, but the only means of getting from the alley below to that open fourth-floor window would be the cable of the lightning rod, which is five feet from the window at the nearest point. Roche leans out the window and notes that a three-inch ledge runs across the building.

Dupin allows Roche to interrogate the suspects. A gendarme sends in the neighbor, Mademoiselle Duval, and the manager, Madame Aubourge. Duval mentions acidly that Aubourge was the last to see the victims alive while Aubourge introduces a new element. She heard the voice of a man crying, "Mon Dieu! Sacré Diable!"

The ladies are dismissed, quarreling. Roche is excited, "The voice of a man!" He greets the third witness, Le Bon, with suspicion. The bank clerk, squeamish during the interrogation, admits to his delivery of the 4000 francs. He argues that he hoped to marry young Camille, but not for material gain; and, yes, he loathed her mother. He explains that when on the night of the murders he was discovered in the street two blocks from the building, he was suffering from insomnia and had gone for a walk.

Roche declares that Le Bon's service in the navy of the Republic of France proves that his duties in the rigging of ships might have enabled him to climb four stories of cables and balance on a three-inch ledge. He announces, "I am placing you under arrest," and orders the gendarme to take Le Bon to Headquarters.

Roche believes that the case is closed, but Dupin disagrees. He removes a small paper bag from his pocket and shows Roche a lock of hair he had found clutched in Madame L'Espanaye's hand. "This is the hair of an animal," asserts Dupin, "one known for agility, superhuman strength, brutal ferocity." He has consulted experts at the Paris Zoo. That is the hair from the orangutan of the East Indian Islands.

Dupin then exhibits a new clue. At the base of the lightning rod, he found a ribbon peculiar to the cap of a merchant seaman. He placed a notice in yesterday's *La Monte*: "Found in the Bois de Boulogne a very large, tawny Orangutan of the Bornese species. Owner may claim animal upon identification at 37 Rue Delaine." It is a ruse to trap the owner of the ape.

Dupin places two pistols on the desk. Soon a gendarme knocks on the door and ushers in Pierre De Monte, a large, powerful man who wears dirty trousers, a soiled sweater, and a merchant seaman's cap—sans ribbon. He waves a folded newspaper and barks, "What does this all mean?" He came to 37 Rue Delaine for a lost property, was seized by two gendarmes, and brought here against his will.

Dupin calms Pierre and asks about the lost orangutan mentioned in the ad. Pierre admits to the ownership of the animal, which he brought from Borneo in a wooden cage, intending to sell it to a zoo. It has been kept in temporary quarters and somehow managed to escape. He pursued it to the Rue Morgue. The only lights burning were in this flat. The ape seemed mag-netized by the lights. It quickly climbed the wire of the light-ning rod and swung itself into the bedchamber through the open window. He followed, relates Pierre, but by the time he reached the window, the young woman had been stran-gled. As he stood there helpless and cursing aloud, the older woman suffered the same fate. "The sight was horrible—hor-rible," Pierre says. "It had seen blood—it was wild, enraged—I dared not get in its path."

The animal crawled out the window, continues Pierre, went along the narrow ledge, and down another cable. It then disappeared. He was fearful of being linked to the crime and sent to the guillotine, so he fled. "I cannot say that I blame you," says Dupin, and promises that no charges will be filed.

Dupin issues an alert to find the still-at-large orangutan and sends Roche to Headquar-ters to release Le Bon. The cur-tain descends.

A scene depicting the murderous gorilla and one of its victims in *Murders in the Rue Morgue*, 1897 (Billy Rose Theatre Division, The New York Public Library for the Performing Arts).

*   *   *

Billy St. John, a native of Clarksville, Tennessee, wrote more than forty plays—comedies, mysteries, thrillers, melodramas, horrors, musicals—that have been pro-duced in all fifty U.S. states, Canada, Australia, New Zealand, and the United Arab Republic.

In St. John's *Mystery Weekend*, several guests assemble in a remote ski lodge, where the host is murdered, the cable car is sabotaged, and the phone lines are cut, stranding everyone with a ruthless killer. In *Fantastical Friends*, young Fred goes to the library to write a report. He meets the Book Master, a magical character who intro-duces him to some of the most popular fictional characters ever created. Before Fred's eyes, sections from several great books are acted out, including *Jane Eyre* (Gothic), and *Dracula* and "The Monkey's Paw" (horror). A similar idea is at the center of St. John's *Hooray for Hollywood*, where a group of high school students compete for a scholarship by acting out scenes from well-known movies that include *Frankenstein*, *Psycho*, and *The Terminator*.

The title character in *Ghost Detective* is a young private eye, Jeff Burke, who is investigating the murder of an international film star found dead in the swimming pool of his remote island estate. Before Jeff gets very far, he himself is shot and killed. As a spirit, Jeff is physically helpless, but he can communicate with one person, his girlfriend Jennifer, and together they pursue the identity of the murderer.

Spook House is the home of ten nice but misunderstood monsters. Tax assessor Abraham Van Helsing tries to wrest the property from its ghoulish, but lovable, tenants. However, Vickie Stein, a descendent of Frankenstein, and her boyfriend Roger, throw a "monster mash" to raise the money to pay the taxes. Subtly wrapped in this comedy is the message that it's all right to be different.

St. John set *Evil Doings at Queen Toot's Tomb* in the 1920s, focusing on an expedition to unseal the burial chamber of Queen Tootsiwootsi. Professor Artie Facts and his men get a taste of the curses threatened in ancient scrolls to any who dare disturb the queen's rest. The publishers tout the play as a "comic thriller full of memorable characters, a whacky chase scene, a touch of romance, plus a mummifying surprise ending."

Murder in the House of Horrors unfolds in a museum, where Professor Dirk Carlton, a renowned Egyptologist, lectures on "Monsters, Murderers and Madmen" and tells of discovering Pharaoh Menkaura's tomb. Suddenly, while showing a slide of the ruler's sarcophagus, the projector turns off, plunging the auditorium into darkness. When the lights come on, the professor is dead, and the priceless jewel he was holding has vanished. Lt. Dan Morrow arrives and attempts to find the killer.

*   *   *

Edgar Allan Poe appeared as a fictionalized character in the play *Poe! Poe! Poe!* (1981) by Kathryn Schultz Miller and in several theatrical adaptations from his stories, including *Tales of Mystery & Imagination: The Edgar Allan Poe Show* (1991) by L. Don Swartz; *Poe's Midnight Dreary* (1991) by Richard McElvain; *Night Chills* (1992) by Billy St. John; *Nightfall with Edgar Allan Poe* (2004) by Eric Coble; *Nevermore* (2006) by Dominic Orlando; *Poe-Dunked* (2007) by Burton Bumgarner; and *Rise of the House of Usher* (2009) by Sean Ably.

Oscar Wilde

The Picture of Dorian Gray (1975)
John Osborne (England, 1929–1994)

In 1889, while having dinner at a London restaurant, the American publisher Joseph M. Stoddart invited Arthur Conan Doyle and Oscar Wilde to submit an off-beat story for his *Lippincott's Monthly Magazine*. Doyle proffered his second Sherlock Holmes novel, *The Sign of Four*, and Wilde hatched *The Picture of Dorian Gray*.

The Picture of Dorian Gray was printed in the June 20, 1890, issue of *Lippincott's*. With a few revisions, the book was published by Ward, Lock and Co. in April 1891.[28]

The Picture of Dorian Gray has since been transformed for the stage, screen, and television. British playwright John Osborne adapted the novel in 1972. Osborne wrote:

"The fact remains that *The Picture of Dorian Gray* is not only a remarkable achievement of its time, given all its faults, but the germinal story is an inspired one like, say, that of Jekyll and Hyde. It is a variation on the Mephistophelian bargain with the devil.... One of the things that has struck me about the original book is the feeling of willful courage and despair, the two qualities only too clearly embodied in the spirit of Wilde himself."[29]

Osborne thought that the role of Dorian Gray should be enacted by a woman and that the set needed to be "an all-purpose hole-in-the-ground world."[30] The lights come up on Basil Hallward's studio. Basil, a celebrated artist, is painting at a vertical easel. His friend, Lord Henry Wotton, is fascinated by the contents of Basil's portrait, young Dorian Gray, with whom the artist became acquainted at a high-society party.

Dorian Gray enters. Upon scrutinizing his portrait, the aristocrat groans, "This picture will always remain young. It will never be older than, than this particular day in June. If only it were the other way around." Dorian remarks that he would sacrifice his soul to preserve his youth.

Oscar Wilde, Ireland, 1854–1900, as an undergraduate, 1876 (The New York Public Library for the Performing Arts).

The naive Dorian and sardonic Lord Henry form an instant bond and go out together—the beginning of an alliance between a handsome Faustian man and his mentor.

Dorian confides to Lord Henry that he is enamored with an actress, Sybil Vane, whom he had noticed in a fringe theater portraying Juliet. He has frequently gone to see her backstage. He intends to marry Sybil and remove her from this second-rate company to a West Side theater where she should be. Dubious, Sir Henry consents to join Dorian for a performance of *Romeo and Juliet*.

After the performance, Dorian Gray, Lord Henry, and Basil Hallward walk into Sybil's dressing room. An uproar of catcalls echoes from the auditorium. Dorian is perturbed: "Last night I thought she was a great artist. This evening she's merely commonplace and mediocre." Lord Henry says, "What does it matter if she played Juliet like a wooden doll? ... She's beautiful. What more can you want?"

Dorian asks the two men to depart. Sybil enters exalted. She declares that prior to meeting Dorian, she had deemed acting on stage her only goal. Now, she gushes,

Dorian's love has demonstrated what real-life actually is, and now she finds it impossible to perform. Dorian flatly says that Sybil, who used to pique his imagination, now doesn't stimulate any interest. As a matter of fact, he states, she manifests no impact on him at all; he will never see her again, never think of her, will even forget her name. He strides out.

At his studio, Dorian detects a minor modification in his portrait. There is a new, indistinct wrinkle of harshness about the mouth. He drapes the picture with a screen.

Lord Henry notifies Dorian that Sybil Vane has committed suicide. Her body was found on the floor of her dressing room. Dorian condemns himself, certain that he murdered Sybil as if he "had cut her throat with a knife." But Lord Henry emphasizes that if he had wed the girl, "the whole thing would have been an absolute failure." Dorian's mood brightens, and he readily consents to accompany Sir Henry to the opera that night.

Basil Hallward arrives to console Dorian and is surprised at Dorian's indifference regarding Sybil's death. Basil wants to display his picture in Paris, but Dorian vehemently objects, even prohibits the artist to raise the screen and look at it. "There is something fateful about the portrait," he says. "It has a life of its own." Basil exits, puzzled. Dorian takes the portrait, climbs several steps, and puts it in a shadowy attic. He covers the picture, lowers the window curtains and departs, bolting the door.

During the first two acts, the action unfolds slowly and rationally. In the third act, the rhythm speeds up, and a supernatural motif enters the proceedings. The curtain rises on Dorian's dim rooms; flying about are spectral, grotesque images of Sybil, Basil, and Lord Henry. Conversely, Dorian Gray appears dressed in evening clothes, youthful and good looking.

Dorian beckons Basil to look at his portrait in the attic. He takes off the screen. Basil yelps and buckles to his knees. "Kneel with me, Dorian. Kneel," he says in distress. Dorian hoists a knife. Basil groans and collapses dying. Dorian exits, locks the door, and goes down the steps. He catches sight of Basil's bag and coat and throws them into a cupboard. He puts on his coat and hat and exits. He presses the doorbell. His valet, Francis, appears, half-asleep. Dorian clarifies that he had left behind his latchkey and asks what time it is, thus validating an alibi.

The plot accelerates. In order to demolish all evidence, Dorian threatens a young chemist, Alan Campbell, to publicize an incriminating secret unless Alan puts to use his skills to pulverize Basil Hallward's dead body and turn it into "a handful of ashes that I may scatter in the air."

An older James Vane, Sybil's brother, arrives from Australia aiming to retaliate for his sister's death. He tracks Dorian and in an isolated alley sets to attack him. Dorian points at his face. Sybil committed suicide eighteen years earlier, yet he looks to be no more than twenty years old. Persuaded now that Dorian could not have known his sister, James is dismayed by his error. "My God!" he hollers, "I would have murdered you!"

Dorian contemplates tearing down the picture that has logged his accumulation of crimes. He walks up to the attic and, using the knife with which he had killed Basil, he maniacally tears the canvas into shreds. The lights fade out, and a woeful cry is heard.

Aftermath, the door opens, and Francis ushers in two uniformed policemen. Shocked, they see the scattered fragments of the portrait and the body of a skeletal old man in evening dress, a knife in his hand. It is the now-dilapidated corpse of Dorian Gray.

*   *   *

Directed by Clive Donner, John Osborne's adaptation opened at the Greenwich Theatre, London, on February 13, 1975. The cast included Michael Kitchen (Dorian Gray), Anton Rodgers (Lord Henry Wotton), John McEnery (Basil Hallward), and Angharad Rees (Sybil Vane). In his tepid review, playwright-critic Frank Marcus stated in the *Sunday Telegraph* that he believed it to be "a respectful rendering of the original, amounting in theatrical terms to no more than a hollow piece of Grand Guignol."[31]

The Picture of Dorian Gray ran for 32 performances. Osborne transposed his play to a 100-minute television rendition that was broadcast by BBC *Play of the Month* on September 19, 1976, featuring Peter Firth (Dorian), John Gielgud (Lord Henry), Jeremy Brett (Basil Hallward), and Judi Bowker (Sybil). Critic Martin Amis asserted in *New Statesman*, "Faced with the challenge of telescoping Dorian Gray, Osborne hit upon a novel and ingenious procedure: he took a bit from the beginning and he took a bit from the end.... The heart of the story—which is the story of Dorian's corruption—is the section Osborne omits."[32]

*   *   *

London audiences saw an adaptation of *The Picture of Dorian Gray*, by G. Constant Lounsbery, at the Vaudeville Theatre, on August 28, 1913, directed by and starring Lou-Tellegen, playing for 36 performances. New Yorkers attended the Broadway productions of *The Picture of Dorian Gray* in May 1928, adapted by David Thorne (Biltmore Theatre, 16 performances); in July 1936, adapted by Jeron Criswell (Comedy Theatre, 16 performances); and in August 1936, adapted by Cecil Clarke (Comedy Theatre, 32 performances), all dismissed by the press. The same outcome sank the Off-Broadway productions at the Bleecker Street Playhouse, in August 1956, of a rendering by Justin Foster labeled by the *New York Times* "superficial and amorphous,"[33] and at the Showboat Theatre, in August 1963, of a version adapted and directed by Andy Milligan. As stated in the *Times*, "Nothing that Wilde might have done in this extravagant search for experience could have been as horrifying as what the company associated with *The Picture of Dorian Gray* did to his memory last night."[34]

"A working script for the stage from the novel by Oscar Wilde," written by Jim Dine, was published by London's P. Petersburg in 1968. Also that year, a one-character version, *Dorian*, written and performed by John Stuart Anderson at London's New Arts Theatre, was scorned by playwright David Hare, who believed, "Anderson isn't capable of feeling each character anew when he's just whipped away from the last."[35] In 1982, a musical version by the team of Jack Sharkey and Dave Reiser was published by Samuel French, Inc. Other musicalizations of *The Picture of Dorian Gray* were composed by the Hungarian Matyas Varkonyi (1990); the Americans Lowell Liebermann (1996), Allan Reiser and Don Price (1996), Richard Gleaves (1997); and the Canadians Ted Dykstra and Steven Mayoff (2002).

A triumphant dramatization of *The Picture of Dorian Gray* was produced by Off-Broadway's Irish Repertory Theatre in 2001. Recognizing that the story is too renowned to convey any surprise or impact, adapter-director Joe O'Bryne was dead set, as reported by the *New York Times*, to "rediscover Wilde's wit and language. The Lord Henry character gets most of the Wilde-icisms, many of them still ringing with relevance."[36]

The Wilde tale compelled Robert Hill to concoct a dance-drama for the American Ballet Theatre, which opened at Manhattan's City Center in 2003, and spawned a rock opera written and produced by Barry Gordon, displayed at Off-Broadway's Barrow Group Theatre in 2005. A Czech musical influenced by the novel premiered in Prague a year later.

The year 2008 was rife with Dorian Gray showings: an adaptation by the Australian playwrights Greg Eldridge and Liam Suckling; a dance interpretation of the story by choreographer Matthew Bourne, debuting at the Edinburgh International Festival; a Grand Guignol modus operandi production by Canadian Ian Case performed on Halloween at Craigdarroch Castle in Victoria, British Columbia; a Robert Kauzlaric version at the Lifeline Theatre in Chicago, Illinois, exploring the themes of fate, obsession, and retribution; and a musical with book, music, and lyrics by Randy Bowser premiering at Pentacle Theatre in Salem, Oregon.

In 2009, *The Picture of Dorian Gray*, adapted by Linnie Reedman, with music by Joe Evans, played to capacity at London's Leicester Square Theatre. Glory Bowen directed a new two-hour revision for Off-Broadway's 440 Studios, running from June 5 to June 21, 2010.

On April 4, 2017, the Habimah National Theatre of Israel produced *The Picture of Dorian Gray* in a Hebrew adaptation by Yehezkel Lazarov, who also directed, choreographed, designed the show, and played the title role. It was a one hour 45 minutes rendition, with no intermission.

Driving Wilde, a modern-day update of *The Picture of Dorian Gray* by Jacqueline Wright, was presented by Theatre of Note, Hollywood, California, in August–September 2019, under the direction of Bart DeLorenzo. Michael Kodi Farrow portrayed Dorian, supported by David Wilcox (Henry), Carl J. Johnson (Basil), and Raven Moran, who played two of Dorian's ill-fated lovers. Oscar Wilde himself appeared in the play (enacted by Stephen Simon)—"a meta-theatrical presence whose own sad decline mirrors that of his literary creation," according to the *Los Angeles Times*.[37]

The supernatural elements of *The Picture of Dorian Gray* have attracted filmmakers since the early days of the cinema. Six silent pictures based on the novel were made in 1910–1918. Most notable is MGM's 1945 talkie version, scripted and directed by Albert Lewin, starring Hurd Hatfield as Dorian Gray, George Sanders as Lord Henry Wotton, and Angela Lansbury as Sybil Vane. *Dorian*, from 2001, aka *Pact with the Devil*, is a modernization derived from the Wilde story, depicting a New York model (played by Ethan Erickson) selling his soul to a manager-devil (Malcolm McDowell). Portrayed by Stuart Townsend, Dorian Gray is one of the Victorian hero/villains assembled in the 2003 adventure movie *The League of Extraordinary Gentlemen*.

Acting Edition: Faber and Faber.

The Picture of Dorian Gray (1980)
Jack Sharkey (United States, 1931–1992)

In 1980, the American playwright Jack Sharkey and composer/lyricist Dave Reiser teamed on "a musical drama" based on Oscar Wilde's novel *The Picture of Dorian Gray*. In a Forward to the published manuscript, Sharkey and Reiser reveal that they "read the book thoroughly, noticed several scenes that would play eminently well on stage, and several moments that could be rendered in song quite easily—but we also noticed something else, something that began pervading our minds with its downright creepy possibilities: Oscar Wilde had not only written a novel—he had written what amounted to a mystery story—a mystery story without a solution! Or—and this is when we started getting goosebumps—was there a solution—an implied solution—all clues given—just waiting for the reader to ferret them out and realize the enthralling truth?!"[38]

Sherkey and Reiser found the answers to such perplexing questions as: why does Alan Campbell consent to assist Dorian get rid of a murdered body? Why does Dorian visit an opium den? Who was the mesmerizing Hetty Duval whom Dorian fell in love with? And what factor influences Dorian to demolish his portrait?

Unfolding across London in the mid–1800s, the Sharkey-Reiser musical raises its curtain on the studio of Basil Hallward, where the celebrated artist is finalizing the portrait of aristocrat Dorian Gray. Hallward sings "The Best I've Ever Done," during which he turns the easel towards the audience, and we view Dorian as "a truly magnificent picture of youth, against a brilliant background of flowers and blossom-laden boughs and brilliant blue sky."

Hallward offers the portrait to Dorian. "This picture will always show you at the height of your youth," he says. The young man sighs, "How I wish it could be otherwise, that the picture could change and grow old, and I could remain this way forever."

Dorian begins to lead a life of depravity. He gets embroiled with a few ill-fated love affairs, courting and rejecting a young actress, Sybil Vane, who commits suicide, and a high-society matron, Gwendolyn Langdon, who ends up as a prostitute in an opium den. As the years come and go, Dorian stays young and handsome while his portrait progressively alters, first developing a harsh smile, and later turning into a deformed demon.

Basil Hallward visits Dorian and denounces him for his ill-reputed behavior. Basil sings "Prayer," pleading with Dorian to ask God to be his guide. Dorian clutches a small fruit-knife and stabs it into Basil numerous times. Basil staggers, and as the curtain descends, the hands in the picture trickle with blood.

Dorian acknowledges to his latest ladylove, Hetty Duval, that he is depraved. Hetty says that she wishes to marry him and relates that she is "the bastard child of an unfortunate woman," Gwendolyn Langdon. Dorian realizes shockingly that Hetty is his daughter. He hurries to the attic and exposes the portrait, now displaying young Dorian in the full vigor of youth. Dorian grasps the knife with which he killed Basil Hallward and is ready to stab the portrait when he hears footsteps drawing near. He conceals himself behind a curtain. Hetty enters. Dorian emerges, looking like the Monster from the canvas in all his odious abomination.[39] Hetty squeals. The Monster steps toward her, hands extended. She retreats and falls through the window to her demise.

The Monster yells, "Oh, no," snatches a hand-mirror, scrutinizes his face, collapses, and sinks lifeless on the floor next to the portrait. The lights fade, with a spotlight lingering momentarily on the painting, seen in all its glory, as the curtain falls.

*　*　*

Jack Michael Sharkey and David Reiser are part of a clique of creative American playwrights whose works are often presented by little theaters throughout the U.S. but rarely in New York City.

In addition to *The Picture of Dorian Gray*, Sharkey and Reiser collaborated on many musicals, including *Not the Count of Monte Cristo?* (1977), a play-within-a-play about three novice actors staging a musical adaptation of the Dumas classic; *And on the Sixth Day* (1982), a humorous prank peppered with oral disputes between God and Satan; and *The Saloonkeeper's Daughter* (1982), a musical melodrama featuring a damsel-in-distress, a mustached villain, and a cowardly hero. In *Jekyll Hydes Again* (1984), Junior Jekyll, a graduate of a medical school, uncovers the toxic sedative that transformed his father into Mr. Hyde. Junior sips the libation and changes to a monster. *The Pinchpenny Phantom of the Opera* (1988) borrows the Gaston Leroux story with a chorus of two and one lead soprano. The soprano's life is menaced by garroting, electrocution, and a tumbling chandelier, for the theater director wishes his beloved chorus girl to replace her and star in the show.

By himself, Sharkey wrote the criminous comedies *The Creature Creeps* (1977), interweaving suspense and humor high in the Carpathian Mountains of Transylvania; *The Murder Room* (1977), a parody of thrillers highlighted by underground chambers, secret panels, and trapdoors; and *Par for a Corpse* (1980), in which patrons of a Catskills hotel are murdered one-by-one. *While the Lights Were Out* (1988) opens on a blonde dressed in black clutching a bloody knife while hovering over a dead man.

David Reiser has written music and lyrics for nearly 50 musicals since 1970. In addition to his collaborations with Sharkey, Reiser worked with others on *Robin Hood* (1971), enacting the adventures of the Sherwood Forest rebel and his merry men; *Alas! Alack! Zorro's Back!* (1995), an updated yarn about the masked swashbuckler; and *I Want My Mummy!* (1995), in which Baroness Frankenstein invites to her castle the monsters of the world who cannot conform to modern society. The guests include the Mummy, a Werewolf, a Vampire, The Invisible Man, and a grandson of Dr. Jekyll.

Acting Edition: Samuel French, Inc.

Lord Arthur Savile's Crime (1952)
Constance Cox (England, 1912–1998)

Based on an 1891 short story by Oscar Wilde, Constance Cox's three-act *Lord Arthur Savile's Crime* keeps the original's wisecracking but adds heart-pounding moments.

Lord Arthur Savile, a "young and pleasant but not overburdened with brains," learns from fortune-teller Podgers that at some time in the future he will commit a murder. Savile relates to his butler, Baines, that he finds himself compelled to slay someone before his wedding date to "beautiful, sweet, gifted" Sybil Merton, for he thinks that it would be improper to kill somebody after they were married. Baines advises that they dispatch Lady Clementina, an aunt who always complains of pains, constantly announcing that she wouldn't object to sleeping forever. The aunt has a sweet tooth—poisoned candy will do it.

They place a poisonous capsule in the center of a *bonbonière*. A humorous scene follows, with visiting relatives reaching for bits of candy. Baines stealthily takes the capsule from the box, submerges it in a glass of wine, and brings it to Lady Clementina. There is a moment of suspense—will the aunt drink the toxic concoction? Aunt Clementina offers the wine to Arthur, and he gulps it.

Arthur becomes severely sick but revives after a nasty procedure with a stomach pump. Seeking out the next victim, Arthur and Baines choose an uncle, the Dean of Paddington. They then engage the services of an international anarchist, Herr Winkelhopf. The Dean comes for a visit, and Winkelhopf places a bomb in his black umbrella set to go off when it opens. However, the Dean makes a mistake and departs with the anarchist's similar umbrella. They anticipate an explosion that never happens. Flustered,

Arthur opens and closes the Dean's umbrella a few times and throws it through the window. An immense explosion is heard, and Arthur passes out.

The anarchist Winkelhopf comes with more deadly recommendations—slashing the Dean's throat, suffocating him with a pillow, and stringing a thread across the stairs—but Arthur, by now frustrated, plans to cancel his engagement and travel abroad. The psychic Podgers appears and requests a thousand pounds for keeping mum about Arthur's attempts to carry out a murder. He will wait for the Lord at midnight to hand over the money on the Embankment by Cleopatra's Needle.

The next morning, Arthur tells Baines that he could only come up with 150 pounds. When showing up for the appointment, he notices the blackmailer bending over the railing, glaring at the water. He recollects that it was Podgers who has caused so much anguish, so if he is destined to murder someone, why not Podgers? He grabs Podgers' legs and casts him into the Thames. A ripple is heard—a gurgle—then all is still. The only thing seen is Podgers' silk hat gliding on the waves.

*   *   *

Lord Arthur Savile's Crime previewed at the Theatre Royal in Aldershot on July 28, 1952, and, directed by Jack Hulbert, moved to London's Court Theatre on October 7, running for 21 performances. The main roles were played by Claude Hulbert, the director's younger brother (Lord Arthur), Peter Haddon (butler Baines), John Garley (blackmailer Podgers), and Jean Lodge (Sybil Merton). On October 23, another adaptation of Oscar Wilde's story, by Basil Dawson and St. John Clowes, directed by Alec Clunes, debuted at the Arts Theatre in London's West End and ran for 30 performances. Nearly half a century later, in November 2000, the Constance Cox dramatization was reincarnated by the Boundary Players at the Newbury Theatre, UK.

Oscar Wilde's story was adapted to the screen in Hungary (1920) and Sweden (1922) as silent features and as a fragment in the three-part film *Flesh and Fantasy* (1943), directed by Julien Duvivier, with Edward G. Robinson obsessed by the murder foretelling of medium Thomas Mitchell.

Lord Arthur was the comedic lead of television versions in Norway (1955); the Netherlands (1957); the United States (1958); England (1960); France (1968); Spain (1969); and Russia (1991).

*   *   *

Constance Shaw Cox had several plays presented in the West End during the 1940s, including *The Picture of Dorian Gray* (1947), based on the Oscar Wilde novel.

Cox was affiliated with the Brighton Little Theatre from the early 1950s and staged many of her plays there, including variations of such classics as Alexandre Dumas' *The Count of Monte Cristo*, Charles Dickens' *A Christmas Carol* and *A Tale of Two Cities*, Wilkie Collins' *The Woman in White*, Charlotte Brontë's *Jane Eyre*, Emily Brontë's *Wuthering Heights*, Mary Elizabeth Braddon's *Lady Audley's Secret*, and Jane Austen's *Northanger Abbey, Pride and Prejudice,* and *Mansfield Park*.

Some of Cox's original plays hinged on crime, suspense, and terror: *Maria Marten, or Murder in the Red Barn* (1969), was inspired by an 1827 actual murder in Suffolk, England. A young woman, Maria Marten, was killed by her fiancé, William Corder, in the Red Barn, a known hometown spot. Her remains were found buried there, and Corder was executed after a tantalizing trial.[40]

In *The Murder Game* (1976), a husband hires a friend to murder his wealthy wife and finds himself in the hold of a blackmailer, who takes over the husband's riches, moves into his home, and controls his way of life.[41] *Vampire, or the Bride of Death* (1978) is about a nobleman who asks the attractive daughter of an English lord for her hand in marriage, but is exposed as an undead mutation.

Acting Edition: Samuel French, Inc.

Awards and honors: Constance Cox's BBC serial of Charlotte Brontë's *Jane Eyre* garnered the News Chronicle Award for Best Television Play in 1956. Her dramatization of Charles Dickens' *Martin Chuzzlewit* received the Television and Screenwriters Award in 1964. Cox's play *Maria Marten, or Murder in the Red Barn* won the Advanced Cup and the Highest Marks in the 1969 Drama Festival of the Sussex Federation of Towns-Women's Guilds.

* * *

Oscar Fingal O'Flahertie Wills Wilde (1854–1900) was born in Dublin, Ireland, into an Anglo-Irish family. He moved to London and in 1880 wrote his first play, *Vera*, or *The Nihilists*, a melodrama set in Russia. The main character is a barmaid who joins the Nihilists, a terrorist group, and becomes the organization's top assassin. She is in love with a fellow anarchist, Alexis Ivanacievitch, but he has vowed never to marry. Czar Ivan is assassinated, and Alexis takes over as King. Vera's new mission is to secretly enter the palace, stab Alexis, and fling the dagger out the window as proof to the Nihilist agents below. But Vera is loath to kill the man she loves. Instead, she stabs herself, throws the dagger, and the agents leave satisfied. The play's initial performance took place at the Union Square Theatre, New York, in 1883. Wilde took a boat to America to inspect the production, but the reviews were unfavorable, and the show closed after only one week. *Vera* is seldom revived.

Wilde wrote a second melodrama, *The Duchess of Padua*, in 1883. The yarn revolves around a young man, Guido Ferranti, who intends to revenge the slaying of his father by executing Simone Gesso, the Duke of Padua. In time, Guido falls in love with Beatrice, the Duke's wife. He decides not to kill the duke; instead, he plans to leave his father's dagger at the duke's bedside to let him know that his life was in jeopardy. However, Beatrice herself stabs her husband so that she might marry Guido. Guido is incarcerated and put on trial. In order to protect Beatrice, he confesses to the murder. On the day of his hanging, Beatrice visits Guido in his cell and explains to him that even though she confessed to the murder, the judges did not believe her. Beatrice drinks poison, Guido stabs himself, and they die next to one another. *The Duchess of Padua* opened in 1891 in New York, featuring Lawrence Barrett as Guido Ferranti and Mina K. Gale in the title role. It ran for 21 performances and was mostly forgotten. The play reemerged in England in 1907; it was not performed there again until 2010.

In the 1890s, Wilde's novel *The Picture of Dorian Gray,* two volumes of fairy tales, and the collection *Lord Arthur Savile's Crime and Other Stories* established his literary reputation. On stage, he offered a series of popular comedies, notably *Lady Windermere's Fan* (1892), *A Woman of No Importance* (1893), *An Ideal Husband* (1895), and *The Importance of Being Earnest* (1895).

Wilde penned the biblical tragedy *Salomé* in 1891 in French. The proceedings take place in King Herod's palace and portray a clash between the prophet Jokanaan and King Herod, who is increasingly distracted by his beautiful daughter, Salomé. When Jokanaan rejects the erotic overtures of the princess, she alluringly dances for the king, asking for the head of the prophet. In a hideous climax, the executioner presents Joka-naan's head on a metal salver. Salomé snatches it and kisses it on the mouth. Herod pro-claims Salomé barbaric and commands the palace guards to crush his daughter to death with their shields.[42]

Madame Sarah Bernhardt planned to proffer *Salomé* at the Palace Theatre, London, in 1892, but the censor refused a performance license on the basis that it was illegal to reproduce biblical characters on stage. When published a year later, the manuscript was received with harsh assessments. *Salomé* was first performed by the Théâtre de L'Oeu-vre, Paris, in 1896. The famous opera *Salomé*, by Richard Strauss, debuted in Dresden, Germany, in 1905. *Salomé* was the first movie made by horror master Clive Barker in 1973. It is an 18-minute short that was produced on a small budget with Barker writing, directing, and producing.

A Florentine Tragedy is a little-known, blank-verse play, written by Wilde in 1893 but never completed. The action, unfolding in sixteen-century Florence, Italy, surveys an amorous triangle—a woman, her husband, and her lover—that flares into ferocity, murder, and a horrific reversal at the end.

Wilde's homosexual relationships, notoriously with Lord Alfred Douglas, trig-gered three successive *cause célèbre* trials, at the end of which he was convicted of "gross indecency" and sentenced to two years' hard labor.[43] Plays about the case include *Oscar Wilde* (1936, filmed 1960) by Leslie and Sewell Stokes; *The Trials of Oscar Wilde* (1974) by Gyles Brandreth, *Gross Indecency* (1997) by Moises Kaufman, and *The Judas Kiss* (1998) by David Hare.

A mischievous stage pastiche by Graham Greene, *The Return of A.J. Raffles* (1975), spotlights Oscar Wilde's lover, Lord Alfred Douglas, who asks gentleman-burglar

A scene from an all-male stage production of *Salomé*, Theater Enceinhle, New York City, 1976, with Lindsay Kemp (center) playing the title role (photo by Kenn Duncan, The New York Pub-lic Library for the Performing Arts).

Raffles to break into the safe of his father to get even for terminating his allowance after the affair with Wilde became public.

An offbeat couple of the Victorian era, Sherlock Holmes and Oscar Wilde, encountered one another on three occasions. While researching a double murder in Nicholas Meyer's novel *The West End Horror* (1976), the Great Detective makes the acquaintance of some literary suspects, including Bram Stoker, George Bernard Shaw, Gilbert & Sullivan—and Oscar Wilde. In the play *The Incredible Murder of Cardinal Tosca* (1980), by Alden Nowlan and Walter Learning, Dr. Watson learns from his roommate that his latest case focused on a stack of compromising letters written by Wilde. In Russell A. Brown's novel, *Sherlock Holmes and the Mysterious Friend of Oscar Wilde* (1988), Wilde turns up at 221B Baker Street to ask the Great Detective for aid in a case of blackmail.

Vincent Price scored a theatrical triumph playing Oscar Wilde in a one-man show. It opened at the Marines' Memorial Theatre, San Francisco, on July 11, 1977, and ran in various venues during 1977–1980 (photo by Martha Swope, The New York Public Library for the Performing Arts).

H.G. Wells

The English author Herbert George Wells (1866–1946) was prolific in many genres, writing dozens of novels, social commentary, satire, and biography, but he is best remembered as the torchbearer of science fiction with his classic novels *The Time Machine* (1895), *The Island of Doctor Moreau* (1896), *The Invisible Man* (1897), *The War of the Worlds* (1898), and *The First Men in the Moon* (1901). Wells' works foresaw the advent of aircraft, space travel, nuclear weapons, and satellite television. Containing horrific elements, the novels have been adapted for radio, television, and film. Some were adapted to the stage.

The Invisible Man (1991)
Ken Hill (England, 1937–1995)

THE INVISIBLE MAN

Wells' novella *The Invisible Man* was originally serialized in *Pearson's* magazine in 1897 and published in book form the same year. Wells treated the theme with menacing overtones. The novel has engendered a number of motion pictures, beginning with *The*

Invisible Thief, made in 1909 by Charles Pathé, the French film pioneer, and culminating with a 2020 version, written and directed by Leigh Whannel, which uses invisibility as part of a revenge scheme by a sadistic scientist against the lover who ditched him. Notable are *Hollow Man* (2000) and *Hollow Man 2* (2006), directed by Paul Verhoeven, and the most highly regarded is the classic 1933 Universal version, *The Invisible Man*, directed by James Whale and starring Claude Rains. However, *The Invisible Man* was only converted to the stage a few times, with Ken Hill's 1991 adaptation ahead of the rest.

The lights come up on the Saloon Bar in the village of Iping. Among the main characters are Mrs. Hall, the innkeeper; Millie, a young maid; Burdock, the town's squire; and Miss Statchell, the new Scottish schoolmistress. The door opens with a flurry of wind as Jack Griffin enters, holding a doctor's bag. His face is fully bandaged, and there are jet black glasses over his eyes.

Griffin turns to Mrs. Hall, asking about a room. Millie is nervous about showing the newcomer to his quarters. Mrs. Hall carefully takes his bag and guides him upstairs.

Fingers dangle from the upper part of the door. Millie observes them and instantly starts whimpering. All swivel to look and move toward the door. They slowly open it and find a naked man hanging. Millie yells, "It's Dr. Cuss! And not a stitch on him!"

A few days pass. In the vicarage, the Reverend Bunting is counting a cash box containing church funds. Suddenly the window crashes, and scraps of glass scatter on the floor. A chair is pushed aside, papers are scattered, desk drawers fly open, and books are tossed about. Bunting, pushed to a corner, stares in shock as the cash box travels in the air. The window shades are thrust aside, and Bunting hears the stomping of running feet grinding the driveway.

In the Village Green, constable Jaffers, squire Burdock, and Mrs. Hall chatter about the robbery. Jaffers confides that bare footprints were discovered outside the windows. From the pub echoes a frenzied howl. They all dash in. Millie is frozen stiff by the staircase, clasping her broom. She says that when she was wiping the railing, she saw Mr. Griffin's door was open, assumed it was vacant, and entered to clean. Suddenly the window blew open and in floated a bundle of money "hanging in the air right in front of my eyes!"

Jaffers and Burdock crash through Griffin's door. To the accompaniment of sinister music, Griffin throws his glasses at them, takes the bandages off the top of his head, pulls off his gloves, and tosses them at the constable who, horrified, stares at the empty sleeves. Jaffers aims a mighty blow with his truncheon, and there is a squeal from Griffin. A moment later, Jaffers drops his truncheon, and invisible hands squeeze his neck. Jaffers manages to seize a knife from the table. His hand is apparently seized, the knife begins to point towards him, and after a vigorous effort, the knife is forced into his neck. Jaffers falls dead.

Act II begins with a confrontation between Griffin and Dr Gerald Kemp, his former associate. Griffin reminds the doctor that he caught him copying his notes and that during an ensuing scuffle, the laboratory caught fire. He had to restore the experiment. When he used it on himself, the results were disastrous: after a sleepless night, he faced the mirror and saw himself "turn milky, then glassy, then became a mist and fade until all that was left was—space." He hasn't yet figured out how to restore his body to visibility.

Increasingly excited, Griffin informs Kemp that he has decided to utilize his invisibility to initiate an atmosphere of fear, and together they can achieve world domination!

Griffin, delighted, does not notice Kemp stepping toward the windows, opening them to let in Colonel Adye and three police officers. "Invisible man, you're under arrest," declares Adye, after which he is kicked in the groin and squirms. Kemp is flung aside, and the door opens. A commotion is clamoring outside.

At the Village Hall of Iping, the Reverend Bunting informs the citizens that the Invisible Man has cut all the telephone wires, burned down the police station, spilled numerous trash cans, booted a cat into a haystack, pushed Mrs. Moffatt into the lake, and bullied Miss Batchett in her bath.

Bunting swings a bat and assures everybody that "the viper shall be destroyed!" Behind the Reverend, a cane flies through the air and swats him intensely. Steps are heard coming down into the theater auditorium. The men hurry into the house, seeking the Invisible Man in the side booths, the rear boxes, and the balcony. They return to the stage despondant.

Spotlights focus on six newsboys as they trumpet headlines while gunfire, blasts, roars, and sizzling fires can be heard. Newsboy One declares, "Massive Train Crash! Hundreds Killed!" Newsboy Two hoists a sign, "Huge Explosion Rocks Capital!" Newsboy Three announces, "State of Emergency Declared! All Police Leave Cancelled!" Newsboy Four bellows, "Acid Poured into House of Lords' Bath-Water!" Newsboy Five: "Lions Released from London Zoo Eat War Cabinet!" Newsboy Six: "All Troops Mobilized! House of Parliament Razed! Buckingham Palace Destroyed!"

The last scene takes place in the Village Green, where Kemp threatens Griffin with a hammer. The hammer is yanked from the doctor's hand, and he is tossed to the ground. His arms and legs are pulled back. He groans, powerless. The villagers appear from all sides, Burdock with a shovel, Bunting lifting his cane, Hall flaunting a broom, and Millie wielding a vacuum. They surround Kemp and pound the area in the vicinity of the beleaguered doctor. The shovel appears to strike the mark. Griffin emits a dreadful scream.

Miss Statchell reaches down and holds Griffin's hand. The Invisible Man moans and passes away. Gradually, the dead man appears. Miss Satchell is astounded by the transformation, and Mrs. Hall states, "Funny. He looks the same as anybody else."

* * *

Written and directed by, Ken Hill, *The Invisible Man* debuted at the Theatre Royal, Stratford East, on October 18, 1991. Jon Finch played Jack Griffin. The set was designed by Robin Don, using whirling platforms, silk draperies, and descending backdrops to maintain continuity when the action changed venues. The effects were constructed under the watchful eye of Paul Kieve.[44]

The reviews were laudable. Andrew St. George applauded "a vastly enjoyable and rollicking version of the original spine-tingler."[45] Jane Edwards praised the "mind-boggling effects" and noted that "the audience, ranging from babes in arms to asthmatic grans, reveled in the gruesome events."[46]

* * *

Several other playwrights have adapted for the stage the H.G. Wells novel, each with their own inserts. Tim Kelly, the American dramatist, dealt with *The Invisible Man* (1977) as a parody. In his version, the maid Millie has the last laugh. When at the end the villagers identify Griffin by his footsteps in the snow, wrestle him to the ground, and are relieved "to see the last of such a creature," they hear giggling from Griffin's room and pivot. They see Millie draped in Griffin's coat, with hat, gloves, glasses, and bandages covering her face. Holding a mug, she declares, "I drank what Griffin drank. I'm going to make you pay for the bad time you gave me! I'm going to take over the village! Ha, ha, ha!"

Playwright Eddie Cope, who is the author of 1975's parody *Agatha Christie Made Me Do It*, wrote in 1980 "a comedy thriller" influenced by H.G. Wells' *The Invisible Man*. Cope's play unfolds in the foyer of Rainbow Lodge, a secluded hotel in the Colorado Rockies. Six female college students from Denver arrive on a cold winter day and take possession of the hotel as a Christmas assignment. Soon the girls find out that a former landlord hid a bag of gold somewhere in the hotel, and they find themselves pitted against a ruthless gang searching for the treasure. In this version, Jack Griffin, the Invisible Man, is an English actor who came to New York in a reincarnation of a Bernard Shaw comedy, and at the end of the run settled in the U.S. He got a job at the Three Mile Island nuclear power plant, was transferred to an unprotected branch, and his body's makeup reacted: he mutated into an invisible man. Three murders are committed before Griffin comes to the rescue of the students, ties the hands of the gang's leader, and calls the police.

The bar and a bedroom at Iping's Coach and Horses Inn are the set of *The Invisible Man* (1990) by Craig Sodaro. Jack Griffin, the strange boarder whose face is concealed by bandages, introduces himself as a scientist, and true enough, soon his tests are disturbing the peace of the other guests.

In this adaptation, Millie is not a maid but the Halls' eighteen-year-old daughter, who is engaged to the elegant Dr. Kemp. A new character, Jenny Jeffries, is a *London Times* reporter.

The cozy atmosphere of Iping is ruined. Customers of the grocery store report to have seen a shirt and a pair of trousers wandering about. A bag, a pear, and a loaf of bread are seen drifting in mid-air. And someone stole from the church its weekly donations. On a more somber note, one of the inn's lodgers, Mr. Wickem, is found strangled.

At night, on his way out, Griffin collides with an elderly boarder, Mrs. Henfrey. We see her struggling as if someone has her by the throat until she falls next to the bar lifeless. Mr. and Mrs. Hall enter in nightshirts, followed by several lodgers. The Invisible Man smacks Mrs. Hall, drags Jenny by the hair, and kicks Millie. Dr. Kemp storms in with gun in hand and fires several rounds into the air next to Millie. We hear a yelp behind a screen. When they move it, the actor playing Griffin is revealed. "Look! He's … he's becoming visible," says Jenny. Kemp kneels at his side. "Take my journals," Griffin whispers his final words, "It's all in there…. Try again. Try…."

Jenny informs Kemp that her editor would be willing to pay a large amount of money for Griffin's papers, but the doctor throws them into the fireplace.

*   *   *

The Aquila Theatre, a Professional Company in Residence at New York University, brought a movement-dance interpretation of *The Invisible Man* to Manhattan's Baruch Performing Arts Center for a limited run, October 21–November 6, 2005. With the collaboration of choreographer Doug Verone, silent movement conveyed the narrative with limited dialogue from the original novella. The action unrolls on a vacant stage depicting a doctor's office and a patient's wing. The nurses are in hysterics as the insane doctor appears wearing a long coat and dark glasses and convulses on the floor.

Early in 2006, Anglo-Canadian dramatist Michael O'Brien incorporated a few notions of his own when adapting *The Invisible Man*. A flashback exposes that when he was in medical school, Griffin was rejected by a girl who preferred his more affluent friend; that disappointment made him perpetually bitter. Canada's Shaw Festival offered the O'Brien version in October 2006.

Acting Edition:
The Invisible Man by Ken Hill—Samuel French, LTD
The Invisible Man by Tim Kelly—Pioneer Drama Service
The Invisible Man by Eddie Cope—I.E. Clark, Inc.
The Invisible Man by Craig Sodaro—Eldridge Publishing Company

Horrors of Doctor Moreau (1972)
Joel Stone (United States)

DOCTOR MOREAU

Joel Stone's adaptation of H.G. Wells' *The Island of Doctor Moreau* skips the early part of the novel in which Edward Prendick, an English lepidopterist and the narrator of the proceedings, is returning home by ship from an expedition in Peru when it wrecks in the Southern Pacific Ocean. Prendick is saved by the crew of a passing trading vessel bringing a cargo of animals to a secluded island. The sadistic captain of the boat, Davies, insists that Prendick is cast out at the island, and Prendick finds himself at the mercy of Doctor Moreau, a mad scientist who creates human beings from animals by dismemberment and operation. Prendick remembers that he has heard of Moreau, formerly an eminent London physiologist, who fled England after his gruesome experiments in vivisection had been exposed.

The Stone adaptation eliminates several key characters of the novel, including Dr. Moreau's alcoholic assistant Montgomery and his strange servant M'ling. Of the many beasts that take part in the original story, only four are featured in *Horrors of Doctor Moreau*—The Ape Man, The Pig Woman, The Tiger Woman, and The Sayer of the Law. Doctor Moreau himself never appears. His voice is heard through a sound speaker. (A production note suggests that the sound speakers be placed behind the audience, facing the stage, shooting sound directly over the heads of the viewers).

The first scene takes place in the evening. The stage is totally dark. The four Beast Folk are situated on the edge of a jungle, listening to the tortured cries of a panther. The Ape Man relates that he saw the panther on the beach when it came in a boat with other caged animals, and a Man, a Man who walked upright, not on all fours.

Soon they hear the distant barking of dogs. The New Man from the Sea enters exhausted, sickly, deathly pale. He holds a broken branch in his hand as a weapon. Two gunshots are fired at close range, and the Beast Folk drop to the ground, quivering. The rich voice of Moreau is heard on tape, played from speakers. He admonishes Edward Prendick for escaping: "I mean you no harm." He then orders the Beast Folk to leave and explains to Prendick that the creatures he has seen in the House of Pain have never been human; they were animals, triumphs of surgery. His aim is to eventually create graceful and rational human beings.

Prendick goes back to the House of Pain. The Beast Folk stealthily return, and a production note states, "more animal-like than in the previous scene." The Tiger Woman enters on all fours, with a bloody rabbit in her mouth. She drops the rabbit on the ground. The others slowly approach the dead animal.

Moreau's stern, angry voice booms loudly, accusing them of breaking the Law—not to eat flesh—not to spill or taste blood!

Suddenly the sound of fire is heard from the direction of the House of Pain. Moreau gasps audibly. His voice fades into the distance as he runs toward the House, gasping, "God, no! It can't be!"

The Beast Folk watch the rising smoke and decide to go and see what happened. They scurry into the auditorium, pass through the aisle, and disappear in the back of the theater. They return carrying Prendick, who is stained with soot and coughing. The Ape Man returns last and relates that the House of Pain is in flames. Out of the fire bursts a screaming Man, naked, scarred, his body wrapped in bloody bandages. This New Man attacked his tormentor then rushed back and plunged into the roaring flames.

Time passes. The Beast Folk are now almost all-animal in their movements. The Ape Man and the Sayer of the Law fight over a flute. After a brief struggle, the Sayer bites the Ape Man, killing him. In semi-darkness, during Prendick's final speech, the Sayer is devouring the Ape Man. Prendick tells the audience how he found a small boat hidden on the other side of the island, gathered "some fruit, some vegetables, some water," and set out to sea. He drifted for days until he was picked up by a ship. No one believed his story, thinking him insane.

"And," says Prendick, "strange as it might seem, with my return to England came a strange enhancement of the uncertainty and dread I felt on that island…. I could not persuade myself that men and women I met were not also part-beast…. I walked the streets in fear. I'd look around me at my fellow-men and shake with terror…. I felt as though animals were always surging up in them."

*   *   *

Horrors of Doctor Moreau was presented by the Theatre Asylum company at Off-Broadway's Jean Cocteau Theatre on November 16, 1972, directed by adapter Joel Stone. The cast consisted of Joseph Zwerling (Edward Prendick), Marc Kaplan (Ape Man), Eleanor Schulusselberg (Pig Woman), Deborah Nadel (Tiger Woman), David Sternberg (Sayer of the Law), and Lowell Kirschner (Voice of Doctor Moreau). More than a quarter of a century later, in 1998, the play was revived as a script-in-hand reading by the New Jersey Repertory Company.

Acting Edition: Samuel French, Inc.

The Island of Dr. Moreau (2007)
Robert Kauzlaric (United States, 1974–)

While Joel Stone's *Horrors of Doctor Moreau* unfolds with a cast of five and a voice over, Robert Kauzlaric's adaptation, *The Island of Dr. Moreau*, utilizes twenty speaking roles plus assorted sailors, shipwreck survivors, and Londoners. Also, in contrast to the former play, the latter shifts the action to numerous locales.

The Island of Dr. Moreau begins with a thunder-and-lightning storm, the sound of a ship crashing, and sailors streaming down from the ceiling of the theater as the ocean claims the *Lady Vain*. In a succession of quick scenes, passenger Edward Prendick is pulled from the sea into a dinghy by two survivors; the men pass a cask of water until it's empty; one survivor attacks the other and both tumble overboard; Prendick remains alone, starved and barely conscious; he is later lifted from the dinghy by a shadowy form and finds himself on Dr. Moreau's isolated island.

Prendick relates to his saviors, Montgomery, Moreau's assistant, and his servant M'ling, who sports glow-in-the-dark eyes and furry ears, that he studied rare butterflies in Peru, and on his way back to England, his ship sank.

Dr. Moreau is "an intense man in his fifties." The captive that he dissects is a puma, described as looking hellish, not human, not animal, but a mass of blood, bandages, flesh, and scars. She is still bound to the rack, moaning pitifully, when Moreau draws out her tail to demonstrate his point that the vivisected woman was a puma. But why not alleviate the suffering with anesthesia, asks Prendick. Moreau believes that one cannot incite the development of anything—a greater society, the improvement of mankind—in a world devoid of suffering. Real progress can only be achieved by those who are as remorseless as God Himself.

The puma tears the rack to pieces and charges at Moreau. He shoots her in the leg. She charges again, and Moreau shoots her in the other leg. Gasping in pain, she crawls on. Moreau says, "Don't let me kill you," and shoots her in the shoulder. The puma collapses. Moreau stands over her as she writhes in agony. Then, without warning, with her last ounce of strength, the puma rips open Moreau's gut with her claws. Moreau sinks to his knees, and the puma tears his throat with her teeth. Finally, falling atop one another, they die.

Montgomery says, "I don't think it ever occurred to me that Moreau could die." He pulls out his flask for comfort and begins to drink. Soon inebriated, he gets a bottle of brandy from the compound, passes it among the Beast Folk, and leads them into a primal dance. By now feverish, he grabs a lantern and throws it onto the bonfire.

Realizing that the bottle of brandy has been drained, the Sayer of the Law and the Satyr demand more liquor. Eventually the Satyr charges Montgomery. M'ling roars in fury and pulls the Satyr to the ground, instigating a mighty struggle. Montgomery fires, intending to shoot the Satyr, but the bullet hits M'ling. Montgomery, furious, now aims at the Satyr and pulls the trigger. Nothing happens. The gun is out of bullets. "You are weak," the Satyr says to Montgomery and knocks the whip out of his hand.

Montgomery grabs a burning brand from the pyre and crushes the Satyr's skull. The Sayer of the Law leaps on Montgomery and opens his gut with his claws. Prendick, by now as savage as the other inhabitants of the island, strikes the Sayer fatally with a rock.

The Dog Woman approaches him. "I love the Law," she whimpers. "I will keep it." He flogs her savagely until she dies. Prendick screams at the sky as the stage goes to black.

A single light rises on Prendick as he addresses the audience. He put out to sea and was saved by a French brig bound for Marseille. Eventually he made his way to London but met a strange world: "A hideously deformed elephant person was the favorite pet of high society. Terror in Whitechapel. Headless corpses found in police headquarters. Everywhere poverty. Disease. Filth. And death...." He withdrew "from the confusion of cities and multitudes," kept no household, devoted his days to reading and his nights to the study of astronomy. "There is to me a sense of infinite solace in the vast, eternal heavens," says Prendick, "that perfect emptiness devoid of human life, human arrogance, the human capacity for destruction…. Perhaps there, if nowhere in this world, there can be found peace."

Pendrick's spotlight fades, leaving only the stars in the darkness.

*   *   *

Robert Kauzlaric's *The Island of Dr. Moreau* received its world premiere at Lifeline Theatre in Chicago, Illinois, on October 22, 2007. The play was directed by Paul S. Holmquist, with scenic design by Tom Burch, costumes and mask design by Kimberly G. Morris. The leading roles were performed by Phil Timberlake (Prendick), Yosh Hayashi (Montgomery), Nigel Patterson (Moreau), Sean Sullivan (M'ling), Tony Bozzuto (Sayer of the Law), and Jonathan Stutzman (Puma).

The show received five Non-Equity Joseph Jefferson Awards, including Best Production-Play and Best New Adaptation.

Acting Edition: Playscripts, Inc.

The Crazy, Mixed-Up Island of Dr. Moreau (1977)
Tim Kelly (United States, 1931–1998)

Tim Kelly's *The Crazy, Mixed-Up Island of Dr. Moreau* is a one-act farce. The action unfolds in a spooky hotel on the island of Dr. Moreau, somewhere in the South Pacific. A group of show people are shipwrecked on the island, and the mad doctor decides to test their reactions to his experiments. With the help of his assistants Hedda and Montgomery, he turns his compound into a makeshift "resort hotel" and introduces his creations—Seal-Lady, Snake-Lady, Bird-Lady, Ape-Man, Cat-Girl, and Sayer-of-the-Law—as guests of the establishment. The encounter between the creatures and the show people results in all manner of hilarity.

The newcomers consist of a comedian, Eddie Prendick; a singer, Kitty; a dancer, Shirley; and a society matron, Mrs. Van Dazzle, who has taken the performers under her wing as their producer. They are puzzled by a registration clerk, M'ling, who holds his hands like paws and pants a great deal, and by a cook, Hedda, who cracks a whip and serves them a meal of bananas, birdseed, and orange peels.

The Beast People enter and grab bowls of food. They eat like animals. The visitors are aghast. "What shocking table manners," say Mrs. Van Dazzle. The Ape-Man picks some of the imitation fruit from her hat and eats it.

The behavior of the Beast People becomes ever more menacing, so Eddie steps to center and, like a night club Master of Ceremonies, announces, "We've a little show ready to go for your entertainment and pleasure." Kitty and Shirley sing, "Give My Regards to Broadway," and the Beast People, delighted, form a chorus line behind the two girls and repeat the verse. Shirley does a simple tap dance routine, which the Beast People immediately copy.

Montgomery says, "You ain't seen nothing yet." He leads the Beast People to the back of the house, where, he promises, "some of them can do wonderful things on the trapeze."

The Beast Folk return, followed by Kitty, Shirley, and Mrs. Van Dazzle. The three ladies are overwhelmed. "One of them can climb a tree like a monkey and swing from branch to branch," exclaims Kitty. "Another one can wiggle on the ground like a snake," declares Shirley. Mrs. Van Dazzle points to the Cat-Girl: "You ought to see her imitate a kitten with a ball of string and swallow a goldfish. It's unbelievable. Edward, we must engage them. Our show will be a sensation."

The sound of a whistle is heard, and Montgomery explains that a mail boat has docked. A Man enters and states that there is no mail to deliver, but he has arrived to see if anyone wants a ride to the mainland. Montgomery calls, "We are going to be in show business, ain't we?" Moreau objects, but Eddie says, "Follow me to fame and fortune," and leads an exodus to the boat.

Moreau thrashes about, mumbling incoherently. Montgomery tells Hedda, "I'll give him the adult dose," and picks up a medicine bottle from the registration desk. "Come on, open your trap," Montgomery orders, and the doctor swallows the liquid. He immediately gasps, "You fool! You gave me the Secret Potion." Hedda is shocked, "It reverses the formula. The doctor's going to turn into a beast." Montgomery chuckles, "Who'll know the difference?" and leaves for the boat.

Moreau drops to his knees, eyes wild, hands held like paws. He utters, "Woof," then recites, "Not to go on fours. That is the Law. Not to bite people. That is the Law. Not to claw bark of trees. That is the Law." Hedda moves to the kitchen, saying, "I'll get you a dog biscuit." Moreau babbles on, "Not to scratch the furniture. That is the Law. Not to scare mailmen. That is the Law." Curtain.

Acting Edition: Baker's Plays.

The Time Machine (1977)
Tim Kelly (United States, 1931–1998)
Inspired by H.G. Wells' 1895 novel

THE TIME MACHINE

The Time Machine's narrator and protagonist is a nameless inventor called The Time Traveler. After dinner one evening, he leads a discussion about time and space. He expresses the theory that time is a fourth dimension. To the astonishment of his guests, he exhibits a model of his Time Machine, which, he declares, can travel backward or forward in time. His guests—a Scientist, a Psychologist, a Physician, a Provincial Mayor, and an argumentative gentleman named Filby—pooh-pooh the notion.

Tim Kelly adheres to the basic plot of the novel but takes some liberties. He gave the Time Traveler the name of Filby, and had his rather comical housekeeper, Mrs. Watchett, join him on the trip.

The first scene concludes with Filby seated in his Machine, saying, "Don't forget, Thursday at seven," then pressing a lever. Sound effects build, the lighting begins to flicker—faster and faster. The effects are deafening, blinding.[47]

Filby and Mrs. Watchett check the Machine's dials and find that they are in the year 802,701! They hear laughter, and a race of people known as the Eloi enter. Short in stature, their garments resemble Grecian robes, and they carry garlands of flowers. Without a common language, Filby and Mrs. Watchett communicate with their new acquaintances using gestures and signs.

The strangers are led to "the palace of the Eloi." Filby learns that everyone is a vegetarian, animals having become extinct. He also finds that the Eloi are not able to concentrate, tire quickly, and seem interested in nothing. When a drowning girl named Weena calls for help, they ignore the pleas, and it is Filby who rescues her.

Expressing her thanks, Weena detaches a flower from her wet costume and hands it to Filby.

Enter Grunt, a character invented by Tim Kelly. A unique creature, dressed in animal pelts, Grunt is a cross between an Eloi and a Morlock, a race that the newcomers are still to meet. Grunt has none of the Eloi grace or beauty. Weena says that the Eloi are afraid of the Morlocks because they are cannibals.

That night, Filby, Weena, and Mrs. Watchett join the sleeping Eloi. Several Morlocks creep into view from right and left. Their clothes are a mixture of rags and pelts. They are almost blind, their eyes hypersensitive to light. Their leader is King Morlock, who carries a large club.

Filby pulls out a flashlight from his knapsack. Its beam hurts the Morlocks' eyes. They groan, cover their eyes, and retreat, but they manage to surround the Time Machine. King Morlock points to the Machine with his club. "Show!" he commands. "What machine do!" Filby directs Mrs. Watchett to enter The Time Machine and push away the front lever. He gets behind the Machine, positioning himself to hang on when it starts.

H.G. Wells, England, 1866–1946, creator of the science fiction genre, incorporating horror elements (photo by Alvin Langdon Coburn, 1905; Rare Book Division, The New York Public Library).

She pushes the lever, but groans, "Oh, dear me! It's stuck!" Sensing trouble, the Morlocks begin to advance in a threatening manner. In a suspenseful moment, King Morlock orders, "Kill! Kill Filby!" His men repeat, "Kill! Kill Filby!" and slowly move towards him. Filby cries, "Push, Mrs. Watchett, push!" She pushes the lever forward. Lights and sound effects indicate that The Time Machine is in motion.

Stagehands enter, remove the rocks, and replace the furniture in Filby's sitting room. Mrs. Watchett gets out of The Time Machine, and the machine is taken off stage. The characters from scene one resume their positions.

Filby relates his story, The guests look at one another and remain skeptical. It is only when they see the flower that Weena gave to Filby, and the Scientist says, "I've never seen a flower like this; it's like nothing I've ever come across," that doubts cease.

The play ends with Filby exiting to his workshop and activating The Time Machine. Amidst the sound and lighting effects, Mrs. Watchett says, "Mr. Filby's gone into the Future to see what he can do to help. He's such a considerate gentleman." The Physician wonders, "Will he ever come back?" Says the Scientist, "Time will tell." Curtain.

Acting Edition: Pioneer Drama Service.

Sem Benelli

The Jest (1909)
Adapted by Edward Sheldon (United States, 1886–1946)
From a play by Sem Benelli (Italy, 1877–1949)

La Cena delle Beffe (*The Supper of Jests*), a drama of revenge and murder, premiered on April 17, 1909, at the Argentina Theatre in Rome. It was a major success. On March 1, 1910, it opened in Paris under the French title *La Beffe*, starring Sarah Bernhard. The play was performed throughout Europe before the American playwright Edward Sheldon modified it for Broadway.

The plot is set in fifteenth-century Florence. The sadistic captain Neri Chiaramentesi and his brother Gabriello torture the artist Giannetto Malespini and throw him into the river bound in a bag. They then approach the father of his fiancée, Ginevra, and acquire her for 50 ducats, aiming to compel her to become Neri's mistress.

But Giannetto survives and pledges revenge. He sends word to Neri that he'll come to Ginevra's home at night. Neri sneaks through a window and hides behind a tapestry, observing as a man's silhouette appears, covered in Giannetto's white coat, his face hidden. Neri tails him into Ginevra's bedroom. A shriek is heard, then a tumble.

Waving a bloody sword, Neri laughs gleefully, but then beholds Giannetto, grinning at him in the doorstep. Neri has stabbed his brother, Gabriello, who disguised himself as Giannetto to spend the night with Ginevra.

Neri is crushed. Giannetto genuflects, makes the sign of the cross, and prays. Curtain.

* * *

Staged by Arthur Hopkins, *The Jest* opened at the Plymouth Theatre on April 9, 1919, starring John and Lionel Barrymore, respectively, as Giannetto and Neri. It played for 77 performances, took a summer break, then resumed on September 19, 1919, for a total of 179 showings. An operatic variant, with a libretto by Benelli and a score by Umberto Giordano, was produced at La Scala, Milan, in 1924, conducted by Arturo Toscanini. In 1926, the opera *La Gena delle Beffe* opened at the Metropolitan Opera House, New York, starring Beniamino Gigli as Giannetto; for following performances, Lawrence Tibbett vocalized the part of Neri. In 2004, a concert representation of the opera was presented at the Alice Tully Hall, New York.

Edward Brewster Sheldon wrote 15 Broadway plays, some with morbid components. *Lulu Belle* (1926, collaboration with Charles MacArthur) is the story of a Harlem prostitute who shuffles her men in order to enter high society until she is murdered by a betrayed lover. *Dishonored Lady* (1930, co-written with Margaret Ayer Barnes) is an Americanization of the well-known Madeleine Smith 1857 affair in Glasgow, Scotland—an elite Victorian lady accused of the fatal poisoning of a blackmailing beau.

W.W. Jacobs

The Monkey's Paw (1910)
Dramatized by Louis N. Parker (England, 1852–1944)
From a story by W.W. Jacobs (England, 1863–1943)

Dec. 3rd, 1904.   THE KING.   AND HIS

SEA-STORIES.

("*Dialstone Lane*," by W. W. Jacobs. Newnes. "*Men of the North Sea*," by Walter Wood. Nash. "*Under Tropic Skies*," by Louis Becke. Unwin.)

IN reference to Mr. Jacobs, the title of this article needs qualification. His stories are not really sea-stories at all. The sea, indeed, plays a very small part in them, both in space and in importance. He regards his skippers and mates as men, not mariners, and separates them almost entirely from their element. He knows them "backwards"; but he would have been just as funny if he had known some other class of men as well, and chosen lawyers or grocers or prime ministers for the expression of his humour. In "Dialstone Lane," indeed, he gets quite as much fun out of a lawyer, a contractor, and Mr. Chalk—who was emphatically not a mariner—as he does out of Captain Bowers himself, the retired skipper, whose idle word sent these three gentlemen to such a disastrous fate. The truth about Mr. Jacobs is that he has an uncommonly keen eye for all the little absurdities and eccentricities of conduct, the little meannesses and affectations, which most people leave unnoticed. Most of his new book is simply bubbling with humour, and the last chapter is one of the funniest scenes he has ever described in that sly, delicate style of his; but—oddly enough, at first sight—the part of the book that is the least amusing is just the part in which Mr. Jacobs does go to sea with Messrs. Tredgold, Stobell, and Chalk, and get them into a burlesque adventure after buried treasure on an island in the Pacific. The preparations for that adventure, their unceasing efforts to induce Captain Bowers to tell them exactly where the island lies, Mrs. Chalk's opinions of Mr. Chalk and Mr. Stobell's of Mrs. Stobell, Captain Bowers's relations with his male housemaid, and the male housemaid's with Miss Selina Vickers, the ruse by which Mrs. Chalk and Mrs. Stobell are left behind at the very moment of embarkation—all this is irresistibly funny. And what happened after the return of the three unsuccessful heroes is absolutely Mr. Jacobs at his best. The three daring adventurers have been "marooned" on an (though not *the*) island in the Pacific, and the traitorous skipper, Captain Brisket, has run off with their vessel. They are picked up and taken home; and once back in Binchester, they must, of course, invent a story of some kind to hide their ignominy. They invent one—and it serves, though they do not always agree—and the interested parties, especially Miss Selina Vickers, are not entirely convinced. The boat, they say, was wrecked—lost. But the boat was not lost, and in time it arrives in harbour again under the charge of the deceitful skipper. Now Messrs. Tredgold, Stobell, and Chalk must stick to it that

demand his pay. Anyone who knows Mr. Jacobs's inimitable slyness can understand what he makes of the scene of Brisket's return. But his literary origin is Dickens, not Hakluyt, and the more one reads of his work the easier it is to realise that Mr. Jacobs in person is not (as the portrait on this page will show) the bearded sea-dog one at first imagined. He has no great experience, perhaps no great love, of the sea. But he is one of the few writers who can actually make one laugh out loud while reading him, thanks to his instinct for the humour of a situation and his sense of fun, which contrives to be at once delicate and rollicking. Mr. Will Owen's clever illustrations exactly catch the spirit of his author.

MR. W. W. JACOBS   *Elliott and Fry.*

Author of the popular stories of skippers and mates of the Merchant Service. His new novel, 'Dialstone Lane,' has recently been published by Messrs. George Newnes, Limited.

With Mr. Walter Wood we are in the hands of one who sees his men first and foremost as mariners. His book should achieve a popularity, by no means undeserved, on account of its appearance within a few weeks of the date when the Baltic Fleet of Russia, passing the Dogger Bank, fired on the North Sea fishing fleet. For it is of that fleet that his stories tell, of the men who work in it, their smacks, their daily lives, and the sea they live on. The subject is not new in fiction. Mr. A. E. W. Mason, for instance, has touched it twice, once in a short story,

has seen the things of which he writes. He devotes a whole book to the various aspects of his subject; he does at length and fully what the author of the old song of "Caller Herrin'" did in a sketch. And if the effect of his able book is not to give a new significance to the ordinary breakfast-table fish—well, it should be. Even if one stands on the quay at Scarborough or Lowestoft and watches the smacks come in, goes over them and sees the accommodation, and pieces together the scraps of description that can be gained from these laconic toilers, it is hard to realise what a life theirs is; hard, indeed, to realise that such a life should be possible. Mr. Wood's book is a help towards that realisation. He tells of deadly cold, of great seas that sweep the trawlers from end to end, swamping the cabin and putting out the only fire on board, which cannot, of course, be lighted again till things are dry; he tells of food that nauseates even in imagination; of deliberate cruelty, of recklessness of life engendered by the too frequent spectacle of its loss; of mad orgies of drink; of constant and all but unendurable slavery, eight weeks at a time, for a miserably scanty reward. Mr. Wood writes in a straightforward, virile fashion, without sentimentalising or brutalising his subject; he extenuates nothing of the rogueries, sometimes humorous and sometimes tragic, of his characters, and he reveals their dumb heroism with a most appropriate reticence and restraint. These are fine stories, and all should read them. Mr. Wood is not, so to speak, a marine painter in words. It is the men, and not the sea, that he thinks of first, and he is not, like Mr. Joseph Conrad, one who loves (or hates) the sea for its own sake, and uses men merely as a vehicle for his own genius in translating the sea into words. But he knows what he is talking about, and is graphic and vivid in his descriptions.

Mr. Becke's book is mainly composed of what are clearly transcripts from life direct. These stories do not (most of them) read like fiction. There is little conscious art about them, no selection and no arrangement. They are not Mr. Becke at his best. But to read them is like listening to a traveller quietly telling stories of his own experiences. There is little literary pleasure to be gained from them, for Mr. Becke is often bald and clumsy in style; but there is a freshness and actuality, a sense of things seen, of truth and humanity, which will make them interesting to all who like stories with the warmth of life in them. Needless to say, Mr. Becke writes of the South Seas, the islands where men go to trade, taking their lives in their hands, where passions run high, where every prospect pleases, and man

William Wymark Jacobs, England, 1863–1943, author of mainstream fiction, occasionally wrote horror stories, notably "The Monkey's Paw" (ca. 1904; Print Collection, The New York Public Library for the Performing Arts).

"The Monkey's Paw" is a supernatural short story by the British author William Wymark Jacobs, first published in his collection, *The Story of the Barge*, in 1902. Notable dramatist Louis N. Parker adapted Jacob's story in 1910, a one-act version that became popular on both sides of the Atlantic.

The action occurs in an isolated house near Fulham, England. During a stormy evening, the elderly John and Jennifer White and their adult son, Herbert, host a friend, Sergeant-Major Thomas Morris, for dinner. Morris, who served with the British Army in India, exhibits a mummified monkey's paw. He relates that an old fakir placed a spell on the paw so that it will grant three men three wishes. The wishes are bestowed, says Morris, but always with hellish consequences as punishment for tampering with fate. Morris becomes agitated when recalling a horrible experience and throws the paw into the fire, but Mr. White retrieves it.

At Herbert's suggestion, Mr. White flippantly wishes for two hundred pounds, which will enable him to pay the final installment on the house. Herbert leaves for his night shift at the local factory. In the morning, a representative of the company comes to the White's house to report that Herbert has been killed in a machinery accident. Although the employer denies any responsibility for the mishap, the firm has decided to make a goodwill payment to the family of the deceased—two hundred pounds.

Ten days after their son's death and a week after the funeral, the grieving Mrs. White insists that her husband use the monkey's paw to wish Herbert back to life. He does so reluctantly; he has misgivings about their son's mutilated and now decomposing body. Soon there is a knock on the door. In a nerve-wracking climax, Jennifer White fumbles at a stubborn lock in a frantic attempt to open the door while her husband John, terrified at "the thing outside," retrieves the paw and makes a third wish: "I wish him dead. I wish him dead and at peace!" The knocking suddenly stops. Mrs. White opens the door to find no one there.

* * *

Dan Bianchi, a founder/artistic director of four international theaters, adapted W.W. Jacobs' 1902 story "The Monkey's Paw" in 2012 with a modern slant. In this version, John and Martha Walsh are visited by a former soldier, Jack McCarthy, who used to serve with their son Robert. As they chat, Jack shows the Walshes a mummified monkey's paw, which he received from a fortune teller in Paris. Supposedly, Jack says, it will grant three men three wishes each.

Jack relates that he does not know the first two wishes of the first man who owned the paw, but his third wish was for death. Jack himself was the second man, and while he doesn't want to go into details, it brought him more grief than happiness. Agitated, Jack throws the paw into the fireplace, but Mr. Walsh retrieves it. Jack warns him to be "careful with this thing" and leaves to catch a train.

Mr. Walsh jocularly makes a wish for a thousand dollars "for a new truck and a tractor" and places the trinket on the mantel as "sort of a curio." A knock on the door is followed by the entrance of Corporal Benjamin Farley of the Sixteenth Regiment, U.S. Army, who informs the parents that Private Robert Benjamin Walsh had been reported missing in action during the last battle, and his remains were discovered three days ago. His body will be shipped back within a week. Farley adds that he has been ordered to give them a package of Robert's belongings and a check for a thousand dollars which was left in his Army savings account. Farley regrets bearing such bad news but has to move along; he has more names on his list.

The parents are devastated. "To die so far off, away from us," wails Mrs. Walsh. Her eyes fall on the monkey's paw, and she exclaims, "We'll wish our boy alive again!" Her husband maintains that it's against the laws of God and nature, but his wife overpowers his objections. Mr. Walsh holds up the paw and says, "I wish my son … alive again,"

A clock ticks. A soft knock can be heard. Is it the shutter rattling in the wind? Louder knocking is heard. "It's my boy!" cries Mrs. Walsh. Mr. Walsh tries to stop her, but she passes by him. He snatches the monkey's paw and yells, "I wish … my dead son to return to the beyond!" Mrs. Walsh opens the door. No one is there. The wind howls. She sees footprints in the mud, leading up to the door. "He was here, George," she says. "But why did he go?"

Mrs. Walsh sees the monkey's paw clutched in her husband's hand. "You didn't!" she shrieks. He counters, "Now, Martha, think of it. It's not right. Not natural." Mrs. Walsh babbles, "You wished our son … away? Back, into the cold, dark, abyss? … How dare you?" In an entirely different ending from the original story, Mrs. Walsh stabs her husband fatally with a knife.

Henry James

The Innocents (1950)
William Archibald (Trinidad-born American, 1919–1970)
Adapted from *The Turn of the Screw* by Henry James

Henry James's 1898 horror novella, *The Turn of the Screw*, was adapted by Allan Turpin in 1946 for a short run in London, and by Mel Dinelli for an unsuccessful movie. A 1950 version by William Archibald, called *The Innocents*, became the first to perform on Broadway.

Archibald's play has little activity but bubbles with atmosphere. In 1880, the uncle of two orphans engages a young governess, Miss Giddens, to take care of them. She travels to an isolated country house in Essex, England, where she meets eight-year-old Flora and her twelve-year-old brother, Miles.

Mrs. Grose, an aged housekeeper, confides to Giddens that former governess Miss Jessel and valet Peter Quint are dead. The housekeeper hints that the late Quint had a strange hold

Henry James, United States, 1843–1916, writer of *The Turn of the Screw*, is considered by many to be among the greatest novelists in the English language (1889; Print Collection, The New York Public Library for the Performing Arts).

The Governess (Beatrice Straight) embraces the corpse of young Miles (David Cole) in the devastating climax of *The Innocents* **at the Playhouse Theatre, New York City, 1950 (photo by Friedman-Abeles, The New York Public Library for the Performing Arts).**

on the kids, and "he did what he wished" with Miss Jessel, driving her to suicide. Soon Giddens begins to observe dark figures of the dead servants lurking in corners.

Distressed, the governess dispatches Flora to her uncle and stays put with Miles, seeking to release him from Quint's evil influence. In a frightening finale, Giddens and Miles challenge the apparition of Quint. Quint steps toward Miles. The boy turns to Giddens, asking for help, and collapses. Quint disappears. Giddens crouches by the boy saying, "He is gone, Miles, dear Miles—he has lost you and you are free—you are free." A sudden wind blasts from the courtyard. The window's curtains flutter into the room. Moonlight pinpoints Giddens as she mournfully cradles Miles' body.

Acting Edition:
Samuel French, Inc.

The Innocents is also included in *10 Classic Mystery and Suspense Plays*, edited by Stanley Richards (New York: Dodd, Mead and Company, 1973).

The Turn of the Screw (1996)
Jeffrey Hatcher (United States, 1958–)

The American playwright Jeffrey Hatcher dramatized *The Turn of the Screw* in 1996. Hatcher utilizes only three actors—a nameless Narrator; The Man, British, who plays many male and female characters; and The Woman, who portrays the Governess (her name, Miss Giddens, is not mentioned in this adaptation)—on a spare set, with one Victorian chair in the center.

The curtain opens on The Man sitting in that chair, and a Narrator, most likely Henry James himself, presenting "a very agreeable, very worthy" governess who will relay to the audience "a story of terror … and horror … and death."

The Governess comes down stage and confides how, in 1872, she came to London to answer a job notice and met with a high society financier. The Man, in the role of The Uncle, informs her that a few years ago his brother and his sister-in-law died, and he gained custody of their two "delightful" children, eight-year-old Flora and twelve-year-old Miles. Consumed with business affairs, he requires a governess who will take charge of Miles and Flora.

The Governess relates how, after a long train trip, she arrived at Bly, a grand mansion with a Gothic tower surrounded by "a great lawn" and "a sparkling blue lake."

The Man meets her, a hand at his side as if he is gripping a small child. He identifies himself as Mrs. Grose, the housekeeper. The Governess reaches down, pats the invisible child, and conveys her delight at meeting Flora.

Mrs. Grose hands the Governess a letter. She reads that Miles has been expelled from school for "behaviors of a nature injurious to the other children" and that he's on his way home.

The Man is now the boy Miles, who at first appears to be courteous and well behaved. He amazes The Governess by playing Saint-Saens' "Introduction Et Marche Royale Du Lion" on the piano. Abruptly, Miles alters the music to Saint Saens' "Danse Macabre." The Governess then sees a face peeping in through the panes of the nursery's window.

The Governess whisks the children off to bed and queries Mrs. Grose if she has noticed a red-headed man with "a pale face, long, good features, and rather queer whiskers." Mrs. Grose believes the description fits Peter Quint, a former valet. When the uncle left, Quint stayed as Miles's tutor and had a strange hold on him. Miss Jessel, the former governess, also fell under Quint's influence. "She and Quint, they *did* things," sniffs Grose, who then adds that Miss Jessel drowned herself at the lake when she became pregnant. And when she drowned, Quint was overwrought. He abandoned the children and stayed inebriated, and then, one night, he was found at the foot of the tower, his head splintered from the fall.

The Governess dispatches Mrs. Grose and Flora by hansom cab to the girl's uncle. She is bent on ending Quint's hold over Miles and demands that the boy name his "villainous tutor." Miles finally gives into The Governess's persistent grilling, mumbles, "Peter Quint"—and falls dead. The Governess holds him in her arms and sings a soft melody.

*   *   *

Aspects of the macabre are scattered in many of Jeffrey Hatcher's plays. *Scotland Road* (first presented by Cincinnati Playhouse in the Park, 1993), was inspired by a newspaper item about a Titanic survivor discovered alive on an iceberg. The action unfolds in a sanitarium, where a sympathetic doctor and her malevolent employer quiz a woman found floating at sea. She is clothed in turn-of-the-twentieth-century apparel and says only one word: "Titanic." Her cross-examiners are relentless in unmasking her identity. By the final curtain, all three characters' singularity have been examined, and surprising skeletons in the closet are exposed.

Murder by Poe (The Acting Company, New York, 2004) blends Edgar Allan Poe stories into a spooky rendition set in 1840. A frail woman lost in the woods finds cover in an abode inhabited by characters from "The Black Cat," "The Tell-Tale Heart," "August Wilson," "The Mystery of Marie Roget," and "The Fall of the House of Usher." The intuitive French sleuth C. Auguste Dupin solves the enigmatic case of "The Murders in the Rue Morgue" and discovers the curiously missing "The Purloined Letter."

Hatcher's treatment of Robert Louis Stevenson's 1886 novella *Dr. Jekyll and Mr. Hyde* (Arizona Theatre Company, Phoenix, Arizona, 2008) takes place on the misty avenues in Victorian-era London. Dr. Henry Jekyll's testing has created his proxy—Edward Hyde, a fiendish voluptuary. The split personas collide to ascertain who shall be ruler. In Hatcher's knotty interpretation, the role of Hyde is played by four actors. The action unveils in several locales, including a laboratory, a morgue, a park, and a hotel room.

Acting Edition: Dramatists Play Service.

Awards and Honors: Jeffrey Hatcher's *Scotland Road* garnered the 1993 Lois and Richard Rosenthal New Play Prize in Cincinnati, Ohio. Hatcher's adaptation of Robert Louis Stevenson's *Dr. Jekyll and Mr. Hyde* was nominated for a 2008 Edgar Award by the Mystery Writers of America. *Sherlock Holmes and the Adventure of the Suicide Club*, a spin-off from Stevenson's *The Suicide Club*, was nominated for a 2012 Edgar.

Agatha Christie

And Then There Were None (1943)
Agatha Christie (England, 1890–1976)

Disappointed by several stage adaptations of her novels, Agatha Christie believed she could make "a perfectly good play" out of her 1943 novel *Ten Little Niggers* (aka *And Then There Were None*), by changing the outcome of two characters, who are found innocent and end up happily ever after.[48]

The manuscript of *Ten Little Niggers* was turned down by several producers who felt that it was impractical to stage; the accumulation of so many victims is liable to trigger laughs instead of anxiety among the viewers. But eventually impresario Bertie Mayer secured the performance rights. He engaged Irene Henscell to direct, and she cast a troupe of veteran actors. The production persevered to become a milestone in the genre of suspense.

A curious cluster of characters is isolated on an island off England's Devon Coast. The guests have been asked to show up for a diverting weekend by an anonymous host. A butler plays a phonograph record that blames each one of them for murder and getting away with it; now they are to receive their retribution.

Replicating the verses of a Victorian nursery rhyme, the visitors are dispatched one by one. An Oxford student who drove over two children suffocates on a drink blended with Cyanide; the cook who murdered her employer for a substantial inheritance sips on a deadly drug in her evening cocktail; the butler is decapitated with the stroke of an axe; an military general who ordered his wife's beau on a deadly mission is impaled in the spine; an old woman who drove her pregnant maid to suicide is killed with a syringe; a retired judge who condemned an innocent man to be executed is found on a sofa with a gunshot to the forehead; a doctor who operated when intoxicated and caused his patient to die is shoved off a steep rock; and a private detective who falsely incriminated a man is struck by a massive bronze statue.

As the guests are continuously dispatched, small sculptures of ten little Indians grouped on the fireplace mantelpiece are shattered.[49]

The vacationers are the only ones on the island, so it is clear that one of them is the avenging vigilante. The solution preserves Agatha Christie's ritual of a surprise ending.

Ten Little Niggers previewed at the Wimbledon Theatre and opened to the press at St. James's Theatre in London, on November 17, 1943. The notices were auspicious, and the play ran for 261 performances. In order to avoid controversy, the play's title was changed to *Ten Little Indians* when shown at New York's Broadhurst Theatre in 1944. Recent revivals of the play reverted to the original title of the novel, *And Then There Were None*.

Something's Afoot, a musical satire of *Ten Little Indians*, played at the American Conservatory Theatre of San Francisco, California, and at the Goodspeed Opera House, East Haddam, Connecticut, before moving to the Lyceum Theatre, New York City, on May 27, 1976, for 61 performances. Book, music, and lyrics are by James McDonald, David Vos, and Robert Gerlach, with additional songs by Ed Linderman.

Patricia D. Maida and Nicholas B. Spornick conclude in *Murder She Wrote* that *Ten Little Indians* defies the conventions of the genre: "All the players change positions so that 10 individuals play three distinct roles: victim, suspect and sleuth. One of the 10 also plays a fourth role, that of murderer."[50]

Ira Levin asserts that *Ten Little Indians* contains the "most dazzling of all Christie plots."[51]

A scene from the stage production of *Ten Little Indians*, Broadhurst Theatre, New York City, 1944. Sitting at center is Sir Lawrence Wargrave (Hallowell Hobbs), a key character. By the final curtain all but two murder suspects will themselves be dead (photo by Alfredo Valente, Billy Rose Theatre Division, The New York Public Library for the Performing Arts).

Acting Edition:

Samuel French, Inc. (under the title *And Then There Were None*).

Ten Little Indians is also included in *10 Classic Mystery and Suspense Plays of the Modern Theatre* edited by Stanley Richards (Dodd, Mead and Company, New York, 1973), and in *The Mousetrap and Other Plays* by Agatha Christie (Dodd, Mead and Company, New York, 1978).

Susan Hill

The Woman in Black
Adapted in 1987 by Stephen Mallatratt (England, 1947–2004)
From a 1983 novel by Susan Hill (England, 1942–)

Not unlike Bram Stoker's *Dracula*, in which a young lawyer, Jonathan Harker, travels to an isolated village in Transylvania and becomes immersed in a demonic venture, *The Woman in Black*, adapted by Stephen Mallatratt from a novel by Susan Hill, focuses on a young solicitor, Arthur Kipps, who is sent to a small market town on the east coast of England and gets embroiled in a supernatural phenomenon.

The Woman in Black begins in a mini-Victorian theater on a stage lacking scenery but piled with costumes, furniture, and props. The Actor, an aged man, enters and tells the audience a Christmas fable. He is disrupted by a character named Arthur Kipps, who warms up the audience for "a story, a true story, a story of haunting and evil, fear and confusion, terror and tragedy."

Kipps travels to Crythin Gifford, where he waits for low tide and crosses the causeway to Eel Marsh. His firm's assignment is to visit the home of a deceased widow, Alice Drablow, and review her official records and private correspondence.

The Actor is now a villager, Mr. Jerome, who guides Kipps to a church. Footsteps of the undertakers carrying a coffin are heard getting closer. Next to the center aisle sits the Woman in Black. Her face is hidden by a wide-brimmed hat, but she appears to suffer from a severe skin condition. Her flesh is tightly stretched over her bones, and her eyes are hollow. When he catches a glimpse of her, Kipps is taken aback, while Mr. Jerome seems unaware of her presence.

Kipps walks through the marshes and reaches Eel Marsh House. He switches on the lights and places parcels of documents on a dusty table. He spots a box of letters dated about 60 years ago and signed either "J," or "Jennet," written by a young woman who seems to be the sister of Mrs. Drablow. Further information reveals that "Jennet" was a single mother. She refused to hand over the child for adoption, insisting that they never be separated. But overtime she became desperate and legally bestowed her infant son to Morgan Thomas Drablow and his wife Alice.

It seems clear that at first Jennet stayed away, but the torment of separation from her son brought her back to Crythin. At first, Alice kept the boy away from her sister, but Jennet intimidated her, and she relented. Nathaniel, the boy, became fond of his mother, and she resolved to run away with him. But before leaving, an accident occurred. Nathaniel, his puppy, the babysitter, and its driver, all in the carriage, sank under the deceptive marshes and the concealed quicksand.

The bodies were found, and Jennet Humfrye began to lose her mind—with sorrow, wrath, and a hunger for retaliation. She held her sister responsible for allowing them to drive that day. She also caught an infection that caused her to weaken and ultimately die. Soon thereafter the spooky incidents began. She has been seen in various parts of town leaving behind a child who died in brutal fashion.

Kipps relates to the audience that "there is only the last thing left to tell." He came back home and married his girlfriend, Stella. A little over a year later, they had a son whom they called Joseph Arthur Samuel. On a sunny weekend, Kipps, Stella, and little Joseph drove to a nearby park. One of the popular events was a pony and cart ride. Because of limited seating, Stella and Joseph took a turn while Kipps stayed back joyfully to observe them. Suddenly, Kipps saw the Woman in Black, standing near, watching the ride. We hear the whinny of an alarmed horse, yells from the driver, a shriek of horror from a child, and finally a terrible smash. The illumination hitting the Woman in Black fades out and she vanishes.

Kipps ends his account by confiding that his son had been thrust against a fence and lay dead; a year later, Stella died from her injuries. The Actor thanks him for relaying his painful account, and Kipps confides that he wishes that the chronicle of the Woman in Black will now end. He ponders where the Actor discovered the actress to portray the part of a woman with such a damaged face. The Actor is baffled: "A young woman? ... I did not see a young woman." Curtain.

*   *   *

The Woman in Black was first produced at the Stephen Joseph Theatre-in-the-Round in Scarborough, England, on December 11, 1987, with the following cast: Jon Strickland (The Actor), Dominic Letts (Arthur Kipps), and Lesley Meade (The Woman). The play was staged by Robin Herford and designed by Michael Holt, who repeated their duties for a follow-up production offered at the Lyric, Hammersmith, London, on January 11, 1989. The show moved to the Strand Theatre in London's West End on February 15, 1989; to the Playhouse, London, on April 18, 1989; and to the Fortune Theatre, London, on June 7, 1989, where it has been running non-stop with a number of cast changes. *The Woman in Black* has been haunting London for more than three decades, the second-longest-running production in the West End, bested only by the 70-year-old *The Mousetrap*, a whodunit by Agatha Christie.

The Woman in Black has been translated into a dozen languages and shown in more than 40 countries, with notable success in New Zealand, Japan, and Mexico. In the U.S., the play was mounted by Blood Curdling Productions in Chicago, Illinois (1998), at Off-Broadway's Minetta Lane Theater (2001), at the Whitefire Theatre in Sherman Oaks, California (2009), at the Pasadena Playhouse, Pasadena, California (2018), and at New York's 6 (2020), directed and designed by Herford and Holt, the original creators of the show.

Acting Edition: Samuel French, LTD.

Stephen King

Misery
Adapted in 1992 by Simon Moore (England, 1958–)
from a 1982 novel by Stephen King (United States, 1947–)

First came the novel. Then the movie. And finally, the play.

Stephen King's psychological horror thriller, *Misery*, tells the story of Paul Sheldon, the author of a best-selling series of romance novels featuring the character of Misery

Chastain. Paul has recently published the series' final installment, wherein Misery is killed. In his Colorado hideaway, he has finished a new manuscript, a crime novel titled *Fast Cars*, which he hopes will launch his post–Misery career. Driving back to New York, Paul crashes his car in a freak blizzard. He awakens to find that he has been rescued by a woman, Annie Wilkes, a former nurse living nearby in a dilapidated farmhouse.

It turns out that Annie is an avid reader of Paul's *Misery* books, proclaiming herself his "number one fan." Although he has broken both of his legs, she refuses to take Paul to a hospital and nurses him with stockpiled food and codeine-based painkillers. Annie soon reveals herself to be mentally unstable, prone to bouts of unreasonable rage. When she reads *Misery's Child* and learns of the heroine's death, Annie deprives Paul of food, water, and medicine.

Annie soon forces a weakened Paul to burn the manuscript of *Fatal Cars* and presents him with an antique typewriter so he can write a new *Misery* novel that will resurrect the character. Paul begins *Misery's Return*, and, like Scheherazade, writes a new chapter every day simply to stay alive. On a few occasions, when Annie is out, he manages to leave his room in a wheelchair, searching for more painkillers and exploring the house. He finds a scrapbook full of newspaper clippings indicating that Annie is a serial killer who was charged and acquitted of murdering infants in a Boulder hospital maternity ward. When Annie discovers that Paul has escaped his room, she punishes him by cutting off his foot with an axe.

The authorities find Paul's Mustang buried in the snow, and soon Colorado state trooper Duane Kushner arrives at Annie's house in search of the missing author. When Paul attempts to alert him, Annie kills Kushner by running him over with a lawnmower. While she leaves to dispose of the body, Paul hides a can of flammable liquid. After he writes the final chapter, he douses a decoy with the fluid. Annie attempts to rescue the "manuscript" by putting out the flames, at which time Paul strikes her on the head with the typewriter. Annie dies. Paul is soon found by officers who have come to search for the missing Kushner.

Returning home to New York, Paul submits *Misery's Return* to his publisher, who has no doubt that it will become an international bestseller. Paul goes through a period of suffering from nightmares and alcoholism, but eventually gains renewed inspiration to write a new story.

Misery was published by Viking Press on June 8, 1987. It received positive reviews, won the Bram Stoker Award for Best Novel, and became a bestseller. Stephen King reveals that the image of Annie Wilkes came to him in a dream. He also notes a parallel with his own life. King successfully fought drug and alcohol dependency.[52]

In 1990, *Misery*'s 420 pages were adapted into a 107-minute film of the same name, scripted by William Goldman and directed by Rob Reiner. The two main roles were played by James Caan and Kathy Bates, who won an Academy Award for her performance, one of only three horror performances ever to receive that award. (The other two are Fredric March for *Dr. Jekyll and Mr. Hyde* and Anthony Hopkins for *Silence of the Lambs*). The movie is faithful to its source, with only minor alterations: in the movie's most harrowing scene, instead of using an axe, Annie puts a block of wood between Paul's legs and hits them with a sledgehammer; the name of the local sheriff is changed from Duane to Buster (played by Richard Farnsworth); in the final scene, Paul sits in a restaurant with his agent, Marcia Sindell (Lauren Bacall), when he mistakes a waitress (Wendy Bowers) for Annie in a haunting vision as she repeats Annie's line, "I'm your number one fan." Budgeted at $20,000,000, the cumulative worldwide gross of *Misery* amounted to $61,276,872.

Adapted and directed by Simon Moore, a stage version of *Misery* was mounted by the Carnival Company at the Criterion Theatre, London, on December 17, 1992. It is a two-character play, in which Paul Sheldon (Bill Paterson) and Annie Wilkes (Sharon Gless) are middle-aged antagonists playing a game of life or death. The basic plot and many of the novel's bizarre moments are captured in the play, preserving all the tension of the original and proving a *tour de force* for both actors.

In the first scene, Paul Sheldon is at an Annual Romantic Fiction Awards ceremony, standing in front of a giant cut-out of his novel *Misery's Child*. The canvas shows a nineteenth-century heroine with windswept hair, voluptuous but vulnerable, in the arms of a dashing young hero. There is huge applause as Paul approaches the microphone, lifts his winning statue, and relates that he'll be leaving immediately for a little hotel in Colorado to spend the winter writing a new novel.

The action shifts to a Colorado farmhouse. A stage note states, "It's still snowing heavily, and the overall effect is like a gingerbread cottage in a fairy tale." But what develops is a grim, cruel fairy tale as Paul, severely wounded by a car crash, finds himself in a small bedroom at the mercy of the unhinged Annie Wilkes. The proceedings generally follow the dictates of the novel, but the character of state trooper Duane Kushner is eliminated, as are the officers who come to search for him. Paul's publisher and agent do not appear either.

The play, directed by Alan Cohen, was revived in 2005 at the Kings Head Theatre in London, featuring Michael Praed and Susan Penhaligon. *Music OMH* reviewer Richard Ings wrote, "This is a brave attempt by some talented and experienced people to bring a powerful allegory to the stage. That it fails so spectacularly to convince or even entertain is a genuine disappointment."[53]

Another stage adaptation of *Misery*, written by William Goldman (who also penned the film's screenplay) and helmed by Will Frears, opened on Broadway on November 15, 2015. The play starred Bruce Willis as Paul Sheldon and Laurie Metcalf as Annie Wilkes. Willis's performance was savaged by most critics while Metcalf was nominated for a Tony Award as Best Actress in a Play. Goldman's adaptation received contrasting evaluations: *Variety*'s critic Marilyn Stasio believed that Goldman's version "lacks a stifling sense of claustrophobia,"[54] while Elizabeth Vincentelli of the *New York Post* opined, "the horror-tinged thriller *Misery* is popcorn theater—it's a carnival ride that piles on the twists and thrills…. The show is shameless, and that's what makes it so fun."[55] *Misery* closed on February 14, 2016.

Carrie
a 1988 musical adaptation from Stephen King's 1974 novel

Like *Misery*, Stephen King's *Carrie* went through the phases of print, screen, and stage. *Carrie* was King's first published novel, released by Doubleday on April 5, 1974. The story focuses on 16-year-old Carrie White from Chamberlain, Maine, a shy, misfit and bullied high-school girl who discovered her telekinetic powers. During the prom, one of Carrie's tormentors, the popular Chris Hargensen, dumps a bucket of pig blood on Carrie. It is the last straw for the victimized girl, and she retaliates by using her power to hermetically seal the gym where the prom takes place and ignite fuel tanks, causing a massive fiery explosion that destroys the school, killing Carrie's schoolmates and teachers. Still overwhelmed by a fit of rage, she smashes gas stations and cuts power lines on her way home. There Carrie confronts her domineering mother, Margaret, who stabs her with a kitchen knife, believing that killing Carrie is a sacrifice that will save her from damnation. Carrie slays Margaret by mentally stopping her heart. She then collapses, dying.

At the time of publication, King was working as a high school English teacher at Hampden Academy and barely making ends meet. Doubleday paid him a $2,500 advance against royalties. New American Library bought the paperback rights for $400,000. The 199-page hardcover sold a mere 13,000 copies; the paperback, released a year later, sold over 1 million copies in its first year.

A motion picture adaptation of *Carrie* was released in 1976, screen written by Lawrence D. Cohen and directed by Brian De Palma. The film starred Sissy Spacek as Carrie and Piper Laurie as Margaret, both receiving Academy Award nominations for their performances. Nancy Allen, Amy Irving, John Travolta, P.J. Soles, and William Katt played several of Carrie's classmates. The movie was budgeted at $1,800,000 and its cumulative worldwide gross reached $33,800,000. *Carrie* is regarded as a watershed film of the horror genre and one of the best adaptations of a Stephen King work.

A 1999 sequel, *The Rage: Carrie 2*, starring Emily Bergl, was based on the premise that Carrie's father had numerous affairs and had another daughter with telekinetic powers. A 2002 made-for-television film, *Carrie*, featured Angela Bettis in the title role and Patricia Clarkson as Margaret. In this version, Carrie survives at the end of the story. In 2013, a new film version scripted by Roberto Aguirre-Sacasa and directed by Kimberly Peirce, was less a remake of the earlier movies than a re-adaptation of the original novel. Chloë Grace Moretz portrayed Carrie, along with Julianne Moore as Margaret White. The picture received mixed notices and left many fans disappointed because much of the material from the book was eliminated. It was budgeted at $30,000,000 and made $84,790.678 worldwide.

According to Wikipedia, a stage musical adaptation, with book by Lawrence D. Cohen, score by Michael Gore, and lyrics by Dean Pitchford, was put on by the Royal Shakespeare Company in Stratford-upon-Avon, England, opening on February 13, 1988, for a four-week run. Act I begins in a high school gym, where the girls are going through a strenuous workout. After class, they head to the locker room, where they make fun of the klutzy Carrie White. The girls shower while gossiping about boys and their arrangements for the upcoming prom ("Dream On"). Carrie has her first period in the shower and, confused by what is happening, thinks that she is bleeding to death. Her classmates mock her mercilessly. Carrie is upset by the insults and dreams of gaining respect from her peers ("Carrie").

Carrie's mother, Margaret, is praying ("Open Your Heart") when Carrie arrives home. She relates what happened in the locker room, and Margaret decrees that the blood is a sign of Carrie's sins ("And Eve Was Weak"), forcing her into the cellar to pray for forgiveness. At school the next day, one of the teenagers, Sue Snell, feels remorse for teasing Carrie. To make up for what she's done, Sue asks her boyfriend, Tommy Ross, to take Carrie to the prom instead of her ("Do Me a Favor"). He reluctantly agrees. When Carrie tells her mother the news ("Invited"), Margaret forbids her to go, insisting that all men just want to take advantage of girls, including her own husband Ralph, who ran off with another woman ("I Remember How Those Boys Could Dance"). But Carrie is determined to attend the prom.

In Act II, Carrie leaves for the prom with Tommy, and everyone is surprised at how beautiful she is. Carrie is nervous about dancing with Tommy, but he finally convinces her to join him on the dance floor ("Heaven"). As the votes for the prom king and queen are cast, Tommy and Carrie are declared the winners. The envious Chris Hargensen, a student leader, dumps a bucket of pig blood on Carrie. Humiliated and incensed, Carrie unleashes her full telekinetic powers. She closes off the gym's exit and kills everyone present ("The Destruction"). After leaving the area, Carrie is met by her mother. Margaret stabs Carrie fatally, thinking it will save her soul. Carrie reciprocates, killing Margaret with her powers. Sue, the sole survivor of the school massacre, finds Carrie and comforts her as she dies.

Directed by Terry Hands and choreographed by Debbie Allen, the musical's cast included veteran cabaret singer Barbara Cook as Margaret and Linzi Hately, in her stage debut, as Carrie. A massive setting designed by Ralph Koltai plagued the production with technical problems, and the crew was unable to douse Hately with stage blood without causing her microphone to malfunction. *Carrie* received mixed reviews. Rewrites continued throughout the run. The show was transferred to Broadway's Virginia Theatre that same year,1988, opening on May 12, with Betty Buckley replacing the unhappy Cook. Hampered by scathing reviews, *Carrie* closed after sixteen previews and five performances, losing its entire investment of $8 million. It became notorious as one of the most expensive Broadway disasters but has gained a cult following in recent years.[56]

The musical was revived at Off-Broadway's Lucille Lortel Theatre, with book and score revised and many of the songs replaced. Directed by Stafford Arima and choreographed by Matt Williams, the show starred Molly Ranson as Carrie and Marin Mazzie as Margaret. It began previews on January 31, 2012, officially opened on March 1, 2012, and ran until April 8 for 46 performances. Well received, *Carrie* was nominated for several Drama Desk Awards, including Outstanding Revival of a Musical. The two lead actresses were nominated for a Drama League Award and a Lucille Lortel Award. An album was released on September 25, 2012.

The revamped musical came to London's Off-West End theater, the Southwark Playhouse, for a limited run in May 2015. Gary Lloyd staged the production with a cast that starred Evelyn Hoskins in the title role and Kim Criswell as Margaret White. The show opened to mostly positive reviews, congratulating the two lead actresses for their performances.

On March 18, 2015, a new environmental-immersive version, with revised book and score, re-titled *Carrie the Killer Musical*, received its Los Angeles premiere at the La Mirada Theatre for the Performing Arts. Directed by Brady Schwind and choreographed by Lee Marino, the cast was headed by Emily Lopez as Carrie and Misty Cotton as her terrifying mother. The production also featured Tiana Okoye as an alternative for Carrie, the first African American actress to play the part in a mainstream theater. The endeavor garnered supportive notices and five Ovation Award nominations from the L.A. Stage Alliance for actresses Lopez and Cotton, director Schwind, scenic designer Stephen Gifford, and Best Production of a Musical. After a short run, the show returned in October 2015 for a six-week engagement with the same cast.

The musical version of *Carrie* has been popular among young performers. It received its first licensed U.S. high school production at Sandia Preparatory School, Albuquerque, New Mexico, in February 2013. The next month, the show received its licensed collegiate premiere with Macabre Theatre Ensemble, Ithaca College, Ithaca, New York.

A non-musical production of *Carrie* debuted at Off-Off-Broadway's Performance Space 122 in 2006. It was adapted by Erik Jackson, directed by Josh Rosenzweig, and featured female impersonator Sherry Vine in the title role. Reviewer Anita Gates of the *New York Times* liked "the deliberately cheesy comedy version of *Carrie*," found most of the performances "joyously on target," and appreciated the insertion of puppets, notably "the adorable pig that closes Act I with a horror-movie-style death scene, perfectly played."[57]

Unofficial spoofs have been staged over the years, notably *Scarrie! The Musical!*, *Carrie White the Musical*, and *Carrie's Facts of Life*, which was a hybrid of *Carrie* and the American sitcom *The Facts of Life*.[58]

Acting Edition:

Misery—Samuel French LTD.

Carrie—Rodgers & Hammerstein Theatricals.

4

Musical Monsters

The Rocky Horror Show (1973)

Book, Lyrics, and Music by Richard O'Brien (England, 1942–)

The Rocky Horror Show, first produced at the Royal Court Theatre Upstairs on June 19, 1973, is a musical parody of the science fiction and horror B movies of the 1930s-1960s. The curtain rises on an usherette who works in a derelict cinema house and introduces tonight's "film" attraction in a song ("Science Fiction Double Feature"). She is joined by a chorus of four Phantoms, who enter through the audience dressed in black. The lyrics mention some of the era's actors: Fay Wray of *King Kong*, Claude Rains of *The Invisible Man*, Leo G. Carroll of *Tarantula*, Janette Scott of *Day of the Trifids*, Dana Andrews of *Crack in the World*, Anne Frances of *Forbidden Planet*, Michael Rennie of *The Day the Earth Stood Still*, and renowned genre producer George Pal.

A spotlight hits a Narrator, who promises to take the audience "on a strange journey." A newly engaged couple, Brad Majors and Janet Weiss, are leaving Denton (no state specified) to visit Dr. Everett Scott, a former science tutor from Boston. During a stormy night, their car has a flat tire, and they are forced to walk through the rain to seek help. They see a light coming from a castle ("Over at the Frankenstein Place"), where they are greeted by Riff Raff, a handyman, and his sister Magenta, a maid. Brad and Janet ask to use the telephone but become apprehensive as they hear Riff Raff, Magenta, and Columbia, a groupie, discuss the unfortunate fate of Eddie, a messenger boy who botched his delivery. The trio then performs the show's signature dance number, "The Time Warp."

Enter Dr. Frank N-Furter, a cross-dressing mad scientist, who introduces himself as "a sweet transvestite from Transsexual Transylvania" ("Sweet Transvestite"). Boasting that he has discovered the secret of life itself, Frank ushers Brad and Janet to his laboratory, where he unveils his creation—a well-built man named Rocky "with blond hair and a tan." Frank undresses Rocky while singing "The Sword of Damocles," and follows the number with a salute to muscle builders ("I Can Make You a Man").

The first act ends on a grim note. A Coca-Cola freezer in the laboratory is opened to reveal the ill-fated Eddie, whose face bears surgical scars and who has been rendered a brain-damaged zombie. Eddie exhibits signs of partially regaining his memory ("Hot Patootie") and Frank panics, forcing Eddie back into the freezer and hacking him to death with a pickax. Frank then tells Rocky—the recipient of half of Eddie's brain—that he prefers him over Eddie, who had no biceps.

Act 2 is raunchy. Brad and Janet are ushered to separate bedrooms for the night. Nonetheless, Janet enjoys Brad's advances in her darkened bedroom before realizing that it is Frank in disguise. She expresses shock but Frank convinces her, "There's no crime in giving yourself over to pleasure." After Janet asks Frank not to tell Brad, they resume their lovemaking. The scene moves to Brad's bedroom, where Brad makes love to Janet before discovering, once again, it is Frank in disguise. Frank promises not to tell Janet. Riff Raff interrupts on the television monitor with a message that Rocky has vanished.

Janet searches for Brad in the laboratory and finds Rocky hiding there. Checking the television monitor, she sees Frank kissing Brad. Overcome by sexual tension, Janet sings "I want to be dirty," and seduces Rocky.

Another visitor enters the castle—Dr. Everett Scott, the scientist who Brad and Janet planned to see. Columbia guides Dr. Scott's wheelchair into the laboratory. Frank accuses him of scheming with Brad to investigate the castle for the F.B.I. Dr. Scott assures Frank that he is looking for Eddie, his nephew ("Eddie's Teddy"); Brad's presence here has come as a complete surprise to him. Frank displays Eddie's remains in a bag of blood and gore, then reveals that the inhabitants of the castle are space aliens from the galaxy of Transylvania, led by him ("Planet Schmanet"). They abandoned their original mission of conquest in order to engage in kinky sex with Earthlings. Magenta suggests that they return to their home planet now that they have been discovered. Frank refuses and, instead, declares his plan to put on a "floor show."

Under Frank's instructions, Brad, Janet, Rocky, Columbia, and the Phantoms perform a song-and-dance routine wearing black stockings and black underwear ("Rose Tint My World"). Frank entreats them to lose all inhibition and give in to their carnal instincts. Dr. Scott appears in stockings and high heels and joins the group.

The "floor show" comes to an abrupt end when Riff Raff and Magenta enter wearing spacesuits and carrying ray guns. Riff Raff declares that he's the "new commander" and Frank is now his prisoner. Frank makes a final plea for sympathy, begging Riff Raff to understand his desire to spend the rest of his life making love to Earthlings ("I'm Going Home"). Riff Raff remains unmoved and shoots Frank, Columbia, and Rocky. He then orders Brad, Janet, and Dr. Scott to leave.

The survivors watch as the castle blasts off into outer space. At the show's end, the usherette returns to recount the night's events (reprise: "Science Fiction Double Feature").

* * *

As an out-of-work actor in London in the early 1970s, Richard O'Brien wrote *The Rocky Horror Show* to keep himself busy on winter evenings. A devotee of B science fiction and horror movies, he filled the work with portentous dialogue, schlock action, and stock characters. O'Brian took the still unfinished manuscript to Australian director Jim Sharman, who decided to direct it at the 63-seat experimental space Upstairs at the Royal Court Theatre, Chelsea, London, which was used for new work. Sharman brought Australian scenic designer Brian Thompson into the production. Tim Curry starred as Frank-N Furter and was supported by Christopher Malcolm (Brad Majors), Julie Covington (Janet Weiss), Paddy O'Hagan (Dr. Everett Scott), and the playwright as Riff Raff. The production opened on June 19, 1973, and transferred, three times, to bigger houses, amassing a total of 2,960 performances, receiving critical praise, and winning the 1973 Evening Standard Award for Best Musical.

Lou Adler, an American music impresario, was in London in the late winter of 1973 and attended a performance of the show. Sensing a hit, he met with the producers and within 36 hours he secured the American theatrical rights. *The Rocky Horror Show* opened at the Roxy Theatre in Los Angeles on March 24, 1974, running for nine months. The cast was all new except for Tim Curry. Curry also starred in the 1975 Broadway debut at the Belasco Theatre, but there the show lasted only three previews and 45 showings. Various international productions have since spanned six continents.

Rocky went on a United Kingdom national tour in 1979 and has toured the UK regularly since a 1990–1991 West End revival. A Broadway reincarnation of the show anchored at the Circle in the Square Theatre from October 2000 to January 2002. Dick Cavett played the Narrator, and when he went on vacation, his role was taken by several celebrities, including the magicians Penn & Teller, *New York Post* columnist Cindy Adams, and talk show host Jerry Springer. The production was nominated for several Tony Awards, including Best Musical Revival.

The Rocky Horror Show was adapted to the screen in 1975 as *The Rocky Horror Picture Show*, with Jim Sharman again directing and Curry and O'Brien reprising their roles of Frank and Riff Raff. Barry Bostwick and Susan Sarandon were cast as Brad and Janet. The movie was shot in the United Kingdom at Bray Studios and on location at a country estate named Oakley Court, best known for its earlier use by Hammer Film Productions. A number of props and set pieces were reused from the Hammer horror pictures.

Although critically panned, the movie has become a favorite midnight attraction, with audiences attending dressed as the characters and participating in the on-screen action. The phenomenon began at the now-defunct Waverly Theater in New York City in 1976 and developed into a standardized ritual across the country. By the end of 1979, there were twice-weekly showings at more than 230 theaters. *The Official Rocky Horror Picture Show: Audience Participation Guide* by Sal Piro and Michael Hess lists props and instructions for their use as the film progresses. Among the recommendations: "Newspapers—when Brad and Janet are caught in the storm, Janet covers her head with a newspaper. At this point, you should likewise cover your head." or: "Water pistols—these are used by members of the audience to simulate the rainstorm that Brad and Janet are caught in." And: "Rubber gloves—during and after the creation scene." Additional recommended props include candles, flashlights, noisemakers, confetti, party hats, bells, cards, hot dogs—and toilet paper.[1]

The Rocky Horror Picture Show was selected for preservation in the United States National Film Registry by the Library of Congress in 2005. A remake was aired on October 26, 2010, on the television series *Glee*. A modern-day reimagining of the film, titled *The Rocky Horror Picture Show: Let's Do the Time Warp Again*, premiered on October 20, 2016. It was directed and choreographed by Kenny Ortega and featured transgender actress Laverne Cox as Dr. Frank-N Furter.

Beyond its cult status, *The Rocky Horror Show* is also widely hailed, along other experimental works such as *Hair*, as an influence on the countercultural and sexual liberation movements.

Acting Edition: Samuel French, Inc.

Awards and Honors: In 2004, the Hamilton City Council in New Zealand honored Richard O'Brian's contribution to the arts with a statue of Riff Raff, the character from *The Rocky Horror Show*, on the site of the former Embassy Cinema.

Sweeney Todd, the Demon Barber of Fleet Street (1979)
Book by Hugh Wheeler (English-born American, 1912–1987),
Music and Lyrics by Stephen Sondheim (United States, 1930–2021)

In 1973, the British playwright Christopher G. Bond adapted the story of Sweeny Todd for the Theatre Royal, Stratford East, London. Stephen Sondheim, who attended this production, secured the rights to transfer the play into a musical. Sondheim wrote the melodies and lyrics, engaged Hugh Wheeler to write the book, and himself composed the score. *Sweeney Todd, the Demon Barber of Fleet Street* opened at New York's Uris Theatre on March 1, 1979. The show boasts 26 musical numbers, and there is little dialogue. The character of Todd is portrayed not as a greedy villain but as a wronged person sent to prison by a crooked judge who lusted after his wife. He returns to London to seek retribution.

The musical is set in Victorian London. The lights rise on an alley near the London docks. A small boat appears in the background. Sweeney Todd, a melancholy man in his forties, disembarks from a boat. A seedy female beggar offers herself to him, but he stalks away.

Todd stops outside a meat-pie shop. Inside, the proprietor, Nellie Lovett, "a vigorous, slatternly woman in her forties," at first assumes Todd to be a customer, but soon she confides in song that "these are probably the worst pies in London."

Todd takes interest in the room above Mrs. Lovett's shop. She tells him that a barber, Benjamin Barker, and his young wife, Lucy, used to live there. Judge Turpin and his associate, the Beadle Bamford, desired Lucy, so they had the barber exiled to a

Angela Lansbury (right) as Mrs. Lovett with cast in *Sweeney Todd, the Demon Barber of Fleet Street,* Uris Theatre, New York City, 1979 (photo by Martha Swope, The New York Public Library for the Performing Arts).

penitentiary in Australia, leaving Lucy behind with her infant, Johanna. As Mrs. Lovett sings "Poor Thing," the story is visualized on stage. We see a costumed festivity taking place at Judge Turpin's home. The Beadle ushers in a fearful Lucy, hands her a glass of wine, forces her to the floor and holds her there as the Judge assaults her.

Todd discloses that he is Benjamin Barker. Mrs. Lovett lets him know that his wife committed suicide with arsenic. Judge Turpin later adopted Johanna and raised her as his own. Todd pledges vengeance. Mrs. Lovett retrieves a set of razors that Barker had owned and tells him that she saved them in case he ever returned.

A competing barber, Pirelli, tells Todd that he recognizes him as Benjamin Barker; he won't tell his friend Beadle Bamford if the barber will hand him half his profits every week, Todd seizes the blackmailer and, after a fierce struggle, cuts his throat. Todd confesses his murder of Pirelli and its motive to Mrs. Lovett. There is the dilemma of discarding Pirelli's body. Lovett has a solution: with the price of meat so high these days, maybe she and Mr. Todd could be of mutual assistance? Todd comprehends her suggestion and accepts it with alacrity. Act I closes with the two of them brandishing "weapons"—he a butcher's cleaver, she a wooden rolling pin.

Act II begins at an outdoor garden beside the pie shop. Mrs. Lovett, in a showy dress, gives orders, accepts payments, and greets patrons.

Upstairs, Todd is setting in place an elaborate barber chair that tips at the pull of a lever and drops its occupant through a trapdoor to Mrs. Lovett's cellar. A customer enters. Todd leads him to the chair, lathers his face, and cuts his throat. He cranks the lever, and the man drops down the chute. A second customer comes in, and his outcome resembles that of the first. A cluster of smoke rises from the bake-house chimney. In a nearby alley, the Beggar Woman cries, "Smoke! Smoke! Sign of the devil." She climbs the stairs and goes into the barbershop, whining and rocking an imaginary baby.

Todd enters. He orders the Beggar Woman to leave just as down below Judge Turpin is knocking on the door, arriving to spruce himself up before asking his ward Johanna to marry him. Todd slices the Beggar Woman's throat and dispatches her down the chute. Todd and the Judge sing "Pretty Women," following which Todd reveals his identiry as Benjamin Barker, then ferociously slashes his throat and sends the body down the chute.

Todd descends and finds Mrs. Lovett cutting up the corpses of the Judge and the Beggar Woman. She opens the oven doors and the glow from the fire highlights the Beggar Woman's face. Todd is shocked to recognize his wife Lucy, whom he believed was dead. Todd quivers with rage at Mrs. Lovett's falsehood. She explains that by telling him that his wife poisoned herself, she meant to save Todd from the hard truth regarding Lucy's debasement.

Covering his ire, Todd embraces Mrs. Lovett gently and dances her toward the oven. He hurls her into the furnace and bangs the door shut. She shrieks, and black smoke spurts up.

Todd kneels, cuddles the body of the Beggar Woman, and sings "The Barber and His Wife."

Several constables burst into the bakehouse. Seeing the carnage, they freeze for a moment, then reprise "The Ballad of Sweeney Todd." The assorted victims—Pirelli, Judge Turpin, Mrs. Lovett, Beggar Woman, customers—sing: "Attend the tale of Sweeney Todd! He served a dark and a hungry god!"

*　*　*

Sweeney Todd, the Demon Barber of Fleet Street premiered at Broadway's Uris Theatre on March 1, 1979, marqueeing Len Cariou (Sweeney Todd), Angela Lansbury (Mrs. Lovett), and Edmund Lyndeck (Judge Turpin). It was directed by Harold Prince and designed by Eugene Lee. The critics gushed: "a staggering spectacle" (Douglas Watt),[2] "sensationally entertaining" (Clive Barnes),[3] "total theater, a brilliant conception and a shattering experience" (Howard Kissel).[4] Joel Siegel declared, "*Sweeney Todd* is more than a great musical. Like *West Side Story* 20 years ago; like *Oklahoma* 30 years ago, *Sweeney Todd* has cut a new boundary."[5]

Sweeney Todd ran for 557 performances. During the run, Denis Quilley portrayed the title role in a 1980 London production, George Hearn in a 1980–1981 tour of the U.S., and Timothy Nolen in 1984 showings presented by the Houston Grand Opera and by the New York City Opera. Leon Greene enacted the part in a 1985 London revival, Bob Gunton in a 1989 Broadway revival, and Alun Armstrong in a 1993 triumphant London revival. Timothy Nolen played Todd again at the Goodspeed Opera House, East Haddam, Connecticut, in 1996; Kelsey Grammer in a concert format at the Ahmanson Theatre, Los Angeles, California, in 1999; George Hearn again in a 2000 concert rendition offered by the New York Philharmonic at Avery Fisher Hall; and that same year Bryn Terfel slashed throats at the Lyric Opera of Chicago, Illinois. Brian Stokes Mitchell appeared as the avenging barber in a 2002 Kennedy Center, Washington, D.C., revival, and Paul Hegarty in a 2004 West End production, directed by John Doyle, unique for dispensing with the orchestra and instead, a ten-person cast brings on stage the musical instruments to play the score themselves. That show came to New York in 2005 with Michael Cerveris as a guitar-strumming Todd.

The Sondheim-Wheeler creation went on a U.S. and Canadian tour in 2007–2008 with David Hess in the lead. Irish tenor David Shannon portrayed Todd in an outstanding Dublin production in 2007, Jeff McCarthy in a 2010 performance in Pittsfield, Massachusetts, Franco Pomponi in a 2011 Paris engagement, and Michael Ball in a 2011 revival that played at the Chichester Festival and made it to the West End the following year. In 2012, London's Tooting Arts Club presented the musical at Harrington's Pie and Mash Shop, where audience members sat at tables and were served with pie and mash. The well-received endeavor crossed the Atlantic and came to Off-Broadway's Barrow Street Theater on March 1, 2017, garnering a tepid review from the *New York Times*. As in London, pie and mash were served before the show (at an additional cost of $22.50).

On January 19, 2019, *Sweeney Todd* was mounted by the South Coast Repertory in Costa Mesa, California. Online reviewer Tony Frankel esteemed Stephen Sondheim's score and lyrics as "rich with sophistication and droll wit," but felt that "director Kent Nicholson faltered at his post by not creating more humorous and scary bits.... And why do some actors have accents and others don't?"[6]

Sweeney Todd was presented on television by RKO/Nederlander and the Entertainment Channel on September 12, 1982, directed by Terry Hughes, starring George Hearn and Angela Lansbury. A 2002 made-for-television movie, *Tomorrow La Scala!,* directed by Francesca Joseph, depicted a small opera company undertaking to mount a production of the musical in a maximum security prison, cast by criminals sentenced to life imprisonment.

Sweeney Todd was adapted to the screen in 2007, scripted by John Logan, directed by Tim Burton, starring Johnny Depp and Helena Bonham Carter.[7]

Acting Edition: Applause, Theatre Book Publishers.

Awards and Honors: Winner of the New York Drama Circle Award for Outstanding Musical and titleholder of eight Tony Awards—for Best Musical, Best Book of a Musical (Hugh Wheeler), Best Music and Lyrics (Stephen Sondheim), Best Actor in a Musical (Len Cariou), Best Actress in a Musical (Angela Lansbury), Best Direction of a Musical (Harold Prince), Best Scenic Design (Eugene Lee), and Best Costume Design (Franne Lee). The British 1980 production earned the Laurence Olivier Award and the London Standard Drama Award for Best New Musical and Best Actor (Denis Quilley). A 1993 London incarnation won the Olivier Award for Best Musical Revival and Best Actor in a Musical (Alun Armstrong). A 2005 Broadway revival received Drama Desk Awards for Outstanding Revival of a Musical and Outstanding Director of a Musical (John Doyle).

Hugh Wheeler garnered the Tony Award and the Drama Desk Award for Best Book of a Musical in 1973 (*A Little Night Music*), 1974 (*Candide*), and 1979 (*Sweeney Todd*). He was nominated posthumously for a Tony for the book of *Meet Me in St. Louis* (1990).

Stephen Sondheim won seven Tony Awards, more than any other composer, winning Best Score for *Company* (1971), *Follies* (1972), *A Little Night Music* (1973), *Sweeney Todd* (1979), *Into the Woods* (1988), and *Passion* (1994), and a special Tony for Lifetime Achievement in the Theater (2008). Sondheim won the Pulitzer Prize for *Sunday in the Park with George* (1985) and an Oscar for Original Song, "Sooner or Later," in *Dick Tracy* (1991). With co-author Anthony Perkins, Sondheim received the Mystery Writers of America 1974 Edgar Award for Best Motion Picture Screenplay of *The Last of Sheila*.

In 1982, Sondheim was elected to The Theatre Hall of Fame and a year later was admitted into the American Academy of Arts and Letters. He was bravoed at the 1993 Kennedy Center Celebration of the Performing Arts. In 1996, President Clinton endowed Sondheim with the National Medal of the Arts. In 2010, a Broadway theater was named after him. In 2011, Sondheim was proffered New York City's top prize for accomplishments in the arts, The Handel Medallion.

Stephen Sondheim, 1930–2021, Broadway's most lauded composer-lyricist, at work (photo by Friedman-Abeles, ca. 1965–70; The New York Public Library for the Performing Arts).

Little Shop of Horrors (1982)
Book and Lyrics by Howard Ashman (United States, 1950–1991)
Music by Alan Menken (United States, 1949–)

The Howard Ashman-Alan Menken musical *Little Shop of Horrors*, based on a 1960 Roger Corman cult movie of the same name, has had countless revivals since its Off-Broadway debut in 1982. The latest incarnation was mounted in 2020 by the Weathervane Theater, Whitefield, New Hampshire, the nation's first indoor show since theaters were shuttered because of a coronavirus pandemic.

The protagonist, Seymour Krelborn, is a flower shop assistant in his mid-twenties—timid, insecure, sweet, and well-mannered. He is secretly in love with a co-worker, Audrey, a bleached-blond beauty, who in turn is enamored with Orin Scrivello, a tall, handsome, sadistic dentist.

The shop, Skid Row Florists, is located on the Lower East Side of Manhattan. Its proprietor, Mr. Mushnik, is a cranky middle-class Jew with Eastern Europe origins. On a stoop near the shop sit three Black female street urchins—Crystal, Ronnette, and Chiffon—who function as a Greek Chorus and occasionally sing to the audience directly. They open the show with a warning to be ready for "a creepy thing to be happening."

The lights come up on the interior of the shop. Mr. Mushnik is sitting at a table, reading the *Skid Row Daily News* and waiting for customers who do not arrive. At six o'clock, Mushnik tells Seymour and Audrey that he's closing this "customer forsaken place" for good. Audrey asks Seymour to go into the back and bring out the new plant he has been working on. She believes that it should be displayed and may attract business.

Seymour returns with a weird and sickly-looking plant. He hasn't been able to identify it in any of his books, so he gave it his own name—Audrey Two. He places Audrey Two on the window seat, and to their surprise, the doorbell chimes and a customer enters the shop. He is curious about "that strange and interesting plant," he says. "Where did you get it?" Seymour relates that a few weeks ago he was browsing the wholesale flower district where an old Chinese man sometimes sells him exotic cuttings. Suddenly, a total eclipse of the sun occurred, and when the light returned, the strange plant was just sitting there. The Chinese man sold it to him for a dollar ninety-five.

The customer finds it a fascinating story. While he's there, he will take $50 worth of roses. Audrey packs a handful of limp roses in a sheet of Mushnik's newspaper and presents the pathetic bundle to the customer. He thanks her and exits.

Mushnik orders Seymour to place the plant by the window and happily goes home. Audrey leaves for a date. Seymour stays behind, concerned about his ailing plant. He sings "Grow for Me," expressing his frustration about his inability to nurse Audrey Two to health. He accidently pricks his finger on a rose thorn, and, to his surprise, notices the plant opening its flytrap-like "mouth," which snaps at the drops of blood. As music builds, the plant begins to grow—and grow—and grow.

Scene 2 begins with Mushnik, backed by Crystal, Chiffon, and Ronnette, sitting on the stoop and singing "Ya Never Know," contemplating his amazing fortune since they put the plant on display.

Audrey enters, her arm in a sling. The girls press Audrey about her unsavory relationship and suggest that she get another guy, "the little botanical genius." But Audrey shrugs, "I could never be Seymour's girl. I've got a past," then exits to put on makeup. Orin walks in, wearing a black leather jacket and a smug expression. Crystal, Ronnette, and Chiffon descend upon him, blaming Orin for his cruel treatment of Audrey. Orin counters with a song, "Dentist," maintaining that his line of work requires a certain fascination with human pain and suffering. Audrey returns. Orin asks if she got the handcuffs, and Audrey assures him that she has them in her bag.

Lights come up to reveal the shop in the midst of renovation, Seymour empties a garbage can, and we see that he has band-aids on all ten fingers. Audrey Two is now over four feet tall and sporting dangerously spiked leaves. (A puppeteer is hidden inside the plant will maneuver its motions when called for.)

The plant suddenly reveals that it can speak. It opens its "snout" and demands, "Feed me! ... Feed me.... Feed me, Krelborn! Feed me now!" Audrey Two sings, "Git It," promising, if fed, it will make sure that all Seymour's dreams come true.

The plant promises a Cadillac, a room in the Ritz, a Harley motorcycle, and more. It goes as far as suggesting the murder of "folk who deserve to die," for their blood. Seymour is shocked; he does not know anybody who deserves to get chopped up and fed to a hungry plant. At this opportune moment, Audrey and Orin appear on the street and walk to the shop. "Stupid woman! Christ, what a friggin' scatterbrain!" scowls Orin. "Get the hell in there and pick up the goddam sweater, you dizzy cow!" Audrey apologizes profusely, exits into the workroom, and re-enters with a sweater. Orin slaps her, and they exit.

Seymour and Audrey Two exchange a dark look of mutual understanding.

Eerie organ music plays as a trapdoor opens, and an antique dentist's chair rises. It is the office of Orin Scrivello. Seymour nervously enters. He pulls a gun and levels it at the dentist. Orin easily takes the weapon away and pushes Seymour into the chair. Getting more and more excited about the punishment he intends to inflict on the little guy, Orin announces that he's gonna use his special gas mask and exits. Seymour picks up the gun and sings "Now, do it now!" but he cannot pull the trigger.

Seymour places the gun back on the tray. Orin, high on nitrous oxide, returns with a plastic gas mask over his head. He approaches Seymour, tries to remove the mask, but it is stuck. "Jesus Christ," Orin says in a panic. "I could asphyxiate here!" He asks Seymour for help. Seymour turns away. Orin sings, "It really is a rotten way to go," falls, and dies.

The lights come up in the shop to reveal Seymour gingerly lifting a severed hand from a blood-stained bucket and carrying it to the plant, which devours it. Seymour repeats the procedure with a string of intestines. The plant licks its chops and laughs hysterically. Terrified, Seymour runs off-stage.

Act Two begins with Mushnik, Audrey, and Seymour coping with a barrage of phone calls, taking orders for roses, daisies, violets, geraniums, camellias, magnolias— for proms, churches, funeral homes, and sporting events ("Call Back in the Morning").

In the evening, an exhausted Mushnik leaves. Seymour puts on a black leather jacket, hoping to impress Audrey, but she reacts with tears. Seymour apologizes; she must miss Orin since his mysterious disappearance. "Miss him?" says Audrey. "I never felt so relieved as when they told me he'd vanished." Seymour asks Audrey to leave all behind her and promises that he will protect and care for her from now on ("Suddenly Seymour").

Audrey is touched. When the music ends, Seymour and Audrey clutch in a passionate embrace. Mushnik enters, stares at them ominously for a moment, and asks Audrey to leave him alone with Seymour. He tells Seymour that he was called to the police station; they made a routine investigation into the disappearance of the dentist and found a Skid Row Florists bag in his office. Also, he's noticed the red dots all over the linoleum. Catching Seymour kissing the dentist's girlfriend looks like a motive.

Mushnik insists that Seymour accompany him to the police station. Prior to leaving, he wants to collect the day's receipts. Seymour tells Mushnik that he forgot the combination of the safe and deposited thousands of dollars in the plant. Mushnik shakes his head, crosses to the plant, and climbs inside to look for the money. Audrey Two chomps down mightily. Mushnik screams twice—and the lights fade.

In a succession of quick vignettes, Seymour is approached by a television producer with a proposal to host a weekly TV show; by a publisher offering a spot on the cover of Life Magazine; and by an agent waving a contract for a lecture tour. Seymour realizes that his bank account will thrive, but only as a result of "bloody, awful, evil things." He comes to a decision: he is determined to destroy the plant.

In the next scene, the plant now occupies most of the playing area—vines, leaves, tendrils, and, of course, its enormous jaws. A large portrait of Mushnik hangs prominently with a label, "Our Founder." Seymour is at the table, working on a speech for his lecture tour. The plant roars, "Feed me! Food! Foooood!"

Seymour leaves to buy a pound of roast beef. Audrey enters, obviously troubled, and sings "Sominex/Suppertime," expressing concern about Seymour's dark mood. The plant suddenly says, "Hey, little lady, hello," and rises to its full height. Audrey is shocked. "Your friendly Audrey Two," says the plant, and asks for a favor: "I need some water in the worst way. Come on and gimme a drink." Audrey hesitates, but her protective instincts get the better of her. She picks up a can from atop the refrigerator. When she moves closer to the plant, branches shove her into the its gaping maw. Seymour enters with the roast beef, but is too late.

The next day, Seymour sits outside the shop. Crystal leads in Patrick Martin, who introduces himself to Seymour as a representative of the World Botanic Enterprises. He comes with a "gilt-edged" proposition: "We take leaf cuttings, develop little Audrey Twos, and sell them to florists across the nation. Pretty soon, every household in America will have one."

Martin has a truck waiting outside. He and Crystal exit. Seymour turns to the plant: "We're not talking about a hungry plant here. We're talking about—world conquest!" He takes out his gun and fires. The plant laughs. Seymour keeps shooting, The plant smirks, "Give up, Krelborn." Seymour picks up a container from a shelf, cries, "Here! Rat poison!" and forces the liquid into the pod. The plant spits it out mocking, "Feh! Give up, small fry." Seymour rushes to the worktable and pulls a machete out from under it. He yells, "I'll hack you to bits," springs at the plant and dives inside. The pod slams shut, chews, and freezes. After a long pause, the plant spits the machete onto the floor.

Crystal, Ronnette, and Chiffon appear, wearing white lab coats decorated with green World Botanical insignias and carrying a carton of empty flowerpots. They enter the shop and begin to snip some of the smaller leaves, replanting them in the pots. The girls relate in song how other plants appeared across America, tricking vulnerable "jerks" into feeding them blood in exchange for fame and fortune.

Out of clouds of smoke, Audrey Two emerges bigger than ever, with four blood-red flowers appearing among the branches. In the center of each bloom is the face of a dead character: Orin, Mr. Mushnik, Audrey, and Seymour. The faces croon a warning to all: no matter the offer—don't feed the plants!

The massive plant start moving toward the audience, like a monstrous botanical crab. Vines come cascading down from the ceiling. The entire theater—stage and auditorium—has been taken over by Audrey Two.

* * *

Little Shop of Horrors had its world premiere Off-Off-Broadway on May 6, 1982, at the Workshop of the Players Art Foundation (WPA Theatre), playing there for a month. It opened Off-Broadway at the Orpheum Theatre in Manhattan's East Village on May 27, 1982. Howard Ashman, author of the libretto, directed, with musical staging by Edie Cowan, and Audrey Two puppets designed by Martin F. Robinson.

The cast included Lee Wilkof (Seymour Krelborn), Ellen Greene (Audrey), Hy Anzell (Mr. Mushnik), Jennifer Leigh Warren (Crystal), Sheilla Kay Davis (Ronnette), Marlene Danielle (Chiffon), Franc Luz (who played Orin Scrivello, customer, television producer, agent, and Patrick Martin), and Ron Taylor (Voice of Audrey Two).

The production was critically acclaimed and won several awards, including the New York Drama Critics Circle Award for Best Musical, the Drama Desk Award for Outstanding Musical, and the Outer Critics Circle Award. The show ran for five years, closing on November 1, 1987, after 2,209 performances. It spawned numerous productions by high school, college, and community theaters.

A London West End production opened on October 12, 1983, at the Comedy Theatre, produced by Cameron Mackintosh. It starred Barry James as Seymour with Ellen Greene reprising her role as Audrey, received the Evening Standard Award for Best Musical, and ran for 813 performances, closing on October 5, 1985.

In 2003, an $8 million revival of *Little Shop of Horrors* was planned for Broadway. A preview production debuted at the Miracle Theatre in Coral Gables, Florida, on May 16, 2003. Lee Wilkof, who originated the role of Seymour in 1982, was cast as Mr. Mushnik. The director was Wilkof's wife, Connie Grappo, who was the assistant to Howard Ashman during the original endeavor.

Critics complained that by expanding the show to fit a large theater, its intimacy was lost; they also judged several

Seymour (Craig Bond) feeds the plant, and it grows and grows, to the astonishment of Audrey (Katheryn Rudgers) and Mr. Mushnik (Bob Finley), *Little Shop of Horrors,* **Elmira College, Elmira, New York, 1991.**

actors as miscast. In June 2003, the production was cancelled. Nevertheless, within weeks the producers ousted Grappo in favor of veteran Broadway director Jerry Zaks, who fired everyone in the cast except Hunter Foster as Seymour and restaged the show from scratch. Fairly faithful to the original 1982 production, the musical made its Broadway debut at the Virginia Theatre on October 2, 2003, and ran for 372 performances.

On August 10, 2004, a U.S. national tour of the Broadway production began, closing April 16, 2006, in Columbus, Ohio. Two years later, on November 17, 2008, *Little Shop of Horrors* began previews at London's Menier Chocolate Factory, directed by Matthew White. The production was a critical and commercial success and transferred to the West End. It was nominated for a Laurence Olivier Award as Best Musical Revival.

A three-performance *Encores!* concert staging was offered at New York City Center in July 2015, directed by Dick Scanlan. The offering starred Jake Gyllenhaal (Seymour), Ellen Greene (Audrey), Taran Killam (Orin), Joe Grifasi (Mr. Mushnik), and Eddie Cooper (Voice of Audrey Two). Critic Ben Brantley wrote in the *New York Times*, "A confluence of alchemical elements was at work, converging in ways that made a perfectly charming but small musical feel like a major event."[8]

A 2016 Australian tour was nominated for ten Sidney Theatre Awards, winning eight, including Best Production of a Musical. Reviewer Cassie Tongue cheered in *The Guardian*: "Watching this show feels like a discovery, or a reaffirmation; to be reminded why musical theatre matters... And all this from a campy cult classic. What magic."[9]

The year 2019 was earmarked by four major revivals of *Little Shop of Horrors*. The Stratford Festival of Ontario, Canada, presented the musical as part of its repertoire from July through November, with André Morin as Seymour, Gabi Epstein as Audrey, and Frank N. Furter as Orin.

The Pasadena Playhouse, Pasadena, California, offered its production from September 17 to October 20, directed by Mike Donahue and featuring George Salazar (Seymour), Mj Rodriguez (Audrey), Kevin Chamberlin (Mr. Mushnik), Matthew Wilkas (Orin), and Amber Riley (Audrey Two). The show was lauded for its diversity. Mj is the first transgender woman of color to portray the role of Audrey in a major production of the show. George Salazar is of Ecuadorian and Philipino descent. Amber Riley is the first woman to voice Audrey Two. Critic Charles McNulty noted in the *Los Angeles Times* that "even when the staging goes Grand Guignol as the plant demands fresh human blood to sustain itself, a sweet vulnerability prevails.... Donahue's revival vibrates with virtuoso singing and authentic heart."[10]

An Off-Broadway revival at the Westside Theatre began previews on September 17, with an official opening on October 17. It was directed by Michael Mayer and choreographed by Ellenore Scott. *New York Times'* Ben Brantley found it "a delicious revival" featuring "a winningly cast that understands that camp is most successful when it's played with straight faced sincerity instead of a wink and a smirk."[11]

The Landmark Theatre Company of Long Beach, California, produced the musical on November 8 through 17, helmed by Megan O'Toole. The character of Mr. Mushnik was changed to Mrs. Mushnik, played by Michelle Chaho.

Actors Equity permitted Weathervane Theater of New Hampshire to cast members of the union in a 2020 revival of *Little Shop of Horrors* at a time when professional theater in America was paralyzed by a pandemic. Jorge Donoso portrayed Seymour, supported by Marisa Kirby (Audrey), Robert Fowler (Mr. Mushnik), and Ethan Paulini (Orin). Audrey II was played by actress Monica Rosenblatt who, as described in the *New*

York Times, was "cloaked in foliage and wearing an upturned hoop skirt designed to look like a maw."[12]

In 2022, *Little Shop of Horrors* was revived at Off-Broadway's Westside Theatre, directed by Micheal Mayer. A smash hit, the production starred two-time Grammy nominee Conrad Ricamora (Seymour), Emmy winner and Grammy nominee Tammy Blanchard (Audrey), and two-time Tony winner Christian Borle (Orin). The producers warned ticket buyers that upon attending the show, they would "Give up gardening for good!"

Howard Ashman wrote the screenplay of his musical for a 1986 feature, preserving the title *Little Shop of Horrors*. The movie was directed by Frank Oz and featured Rick Moranis (Seymour), Ellen Greene (reprising her role of Audrey), Vincent Gardenia (Mr. Mushnik), Steve Martin (Orin), and Levi Stubbs (Audrey Two). The 94-minute film was budgeted for $25 million and grossed worldwide more than $38 million. A 23-minute alternative ending, faithful to the stage version, was originally shot. In it, Audrey and Seymour are swallowed by Audrey Two, and, after the plant becomes a universal sensation, the world is taken over by various Audrey Twos. After two failed test screenings in San Jose and Los Angeles, in which the audiences rejected the ending, a Happy Ending was shot, wherein Seymour saves Audrey and then electrocutes the plant.

Acting Edition: Samuel French, Inc. (in manuscript form)

The Phantom of the Opera (1986)
Book by Richard Stilgoe (England, 1943–)
and Andrew Lloyd Webber (England, 1948–),
Music by Andrew Lloyd Webber,
Lyrics by Charles Hart (England, 1961–)

Gaston Leroux (1868–1927), a prolific French writer of detective stories and sensational melodramas, became known internationally with his 1907 thriller *Le Mystére de la Chambre Jaune* (*The Mystery of the Yellow Room*), in which "an impossible" murder is committed behind locked doors. Leroux dramatized *The Mystery of the Yellow Room* as a five-act whodunit.

Leroux reached his peak with *Le Fantôme de l'Opéra*, a 1909–1910 serialized novel. The title character, Erik, a masked musician, resides hidden in the catacombs of the Paris Opera and unleashes a reign of terror to achieve his goal—furthering the career of a lovely young singer, Christine Daaé. The story has been kept alive in movie adaptations, with Lon Chaney, Claude Rains, Herbert Lom, and Gerard Butler enacting Erik.

A milestone musical adaptation of *The Phantom of the Opera* was created in 1988 by Richard Stilgoe (book), Andrew Lloyd Webber (music), and Charles Hart (lyrics).

The plot's highlights include the Phantom dropping part of an opera set from the flies, nearly missing star Carlotta Gieudicelli; the disembodied voice of the elusive Phantom, coming from nowhere; an apparition wearing a half-mask becoming visible on the other side of a glass mirror in Christine Daaé's dressing room; the Phantom leading Christine deeper and deeper into the catacombs of the opera house, then climbing into a gondola that slowly glides across the misty waters of an underground lake; the garroted body of Buquet, the opera's prop master, falling to the stage floor, creating pandemonium; the Phantom far above the auditorium, releasing the massive chandelier and letting it crash on stage. Perhaps the most unnerving incident occurs when Christine, curious about her benefactor, tears the mask off his face, revealing Erik's horribly disfigured features.

* * *

Produced by Cameron Mackintosh and directed by Harold Prince, *The Phantom of the Opera* debuted at Her Majesty's Theatre, London, on October 9, 1986. The critics lauded the staging of the endeavor but some expressed misgivings about the quality of the book, score, and lyrics. Jack Tinker hailed "Andrew Lloyd Webber's triumphant re-working of this vintage spine-tingling melodrama,"[13] and Richard Barkle considered the show "a gorgeous operatic extravaganza that is a thrill to the blood and a sensual feast to the eye."[14]

Conversely, Nigel Williamson deemed the musical "a real load of old hokum,"[15] and Ros Asquith bewailed the absence of "tragedy, tenderness and terror."[16]

Michael Crawford as The Phantom and Sarah Brightman as Christine in *The Phantom of the Opera*, Majestic Theatre, New York City, 2000 (photo by Christopher J. Frith, The New York Public Library for the Performing Arts).

The play was very successful in the West End and went overseas to New York's Majestic Theatre, opening on January 26, 1988. The lead actors from the London production arrived with it: Michael Crawford (Erik, the Phantom) and Sarah Brightman (Christine Daaé). The production received a few rave reviews and several negative ones.

Despite the mixed reception, *The Phantom of the Opera* has had an astounding run. On January 9, 2006, *Phantom* played its 7,486th performance and was crowned as Broadway's longest-running show ever, overtaking *A Chorus Line* (13 years) and *Cats* (18 years). In October 2011, *Phantom* celebrated its 25th anniversary. On Saturday, February 11, 2012, the musical made theatrical history with the 10,000th Broadway performance. On January 26, 2019, *Phantom* commemorated its 31st anniversary, having played 13,000 performances. It was an $8 million production that grew into an $845 million smash in New York.

The Phantom of the Opera had a few lucrative touring ensembles across the U.S. The show ran for three years—1989 to 1992—at the Ahmanson Theatre, Los Angeles. In 2006, *Phantom* was condensed to 90 minutes by director Harold Prince for a $35 million Las Vegas production, a budget that exceeded any and all Broadway musicals of the era.

In 2019, while still going strong in New York, a revamped road production of *Phantom* was presented at the Hollywood Pantages Theatre of Los Angeles as part of a North

American tour. The show then embarked on an Asian trip, first to Manila, Philippines, then to Tel Aviv, Israel, with cast changes, and continued to Singapore and Abu Dhabi. By now, *Phantom* has played in more than 30 countries before more than 130 million people, earning $5.6 billion. The show finally closed in April 2023.

A 2004 motion picture based on the musical was co-produced by Andrew Lloyd Webber, who largely financed its $70 million budget. Directed by Joel Schumacher and starring Gerard Butler and Emmy Rossum as Erik and Christine, the film received devastating reviews. Lou Lumenick of the *New York Post* opined that Schumacher "has not so much directed the movie version as embalmed it … the falling chandelier, the signature moment of *Phantom*, has been moved from the end of the first act to climax the movie—by which point non-devotees may need to be roused from their sleep by their companions."[17]

In 1990, Andrew Lloyd Webber collaborated with author Frederick Forsyth on a sequel to the *Phantom of the Opera*. They set the plot in New York City at the turn of the 20th century. The endeavor fell apart, and Forsyth went on to incorporate some of their ideas in his 1999 novel *The Phantom of Manhattan*. Lloyd Webber came back to the sequel in 2006, working with several writers and directors. The title was altered to *Love Never Dies*.

After multiple delays, *Love Never Dies* debuted in London on March 9, 2010, directed by Jack O'Brien, and was panned by the critics. It ran for nearly eighteen

Harold Prince, 1928–2019, the distinguished Broadway director, staged, among other hits, *Sweeney Todd, The Demon Barber of Fleet Street* and *The Phantom of the Opera* (photo by Martha Swope, n.d.; The New York Public Library for the Performing Arts).

Andrew Lloyd Webber, 1948–, the renowned English composer whose credits include *The Phantom of the Opera* (1986), the longest running show in Broadway history; *Sunset Boulevard* (1993), a dark take on the classic film noir; and *The Woman in White* (2004), based on Wilkie Collins' eerie novel (photo by Martha Swope, 1982; The New York Public Library for the Performing Arts).

months with the loss of a $12 million expenditure. An Australian production opened on May 21, 2011, at Melbourne's Regent Theatre, directed and choreographed by local artists. The musical was revived in 2018 at the Hollywood Pantages Theatre but elicited a negative assessment in the *Los Angeles Times*: "*Love Never Dies* fails to capture the original's magic."[18] Lloyd Webber still hopes to bring *Love Never Dies* to New York someday. In the meantime, a DVD of the Australian show was released in the U.S. on the 25th anniversary of *The Phantom of the Opera,* and a UK tour commenced in 2020.

Awards and Honors: Winner of a 1988 Tony Award as Best Musical.

Andrew Lloyd Webber garnered the Drama Desk Award for Most Promising Composer—*Jesus Christ Superstar* (1972), and Outstanding Music—*Evita* (1980), *Cats* (1983), and *The Phantom of the Opera* (1988). Lloyd Webber received Tony Awards for Best Original Score—*Evita* (1980), *Cats* (1983), and *Sunset Boulevard* (1995). Lloyd Webber and lyricist Tim Rice won an Academy Award in 1997 for Best Original Song, "You Must Love Me," from the movie version of *Evita.* Lloyd Webber was knighted in 1992 and nominated a life peer in 1997.

Phantom (1991)
Book by Arthur Kopit (United States, 1937–)
Music and Lyrics by Maury Yeston (United States, 1945–)

The musical *Phantom*, with book by Arthur Kopit, music and lyrics by Maury Yeston, and based on the novel by Gaston Leroux, presents a humane interpretation of the title character, Erik, who in this version is obsessed by music, is enamored with a young singer, and has a love-hate relationship with his father.

Phantom begins with the arrival of Christine Daaé in Paris ("Melodie De Paris"), drawing the attention of handsome Philippe, Count de Chandon, who introduces her to Gerard Carriere, the kindly manager of the Opera House. The action shifts between the stage and the dressing rooms and a catacomb of shadows and mist, the domain of the masked Phantom and his Acolytes, a wretched-looking group that serve as henchmen. While the proceedings follow the original novel (the Phantom grooms Christine for stardom but resents her growing relationship with de Chandon), this version introduces several drastic innovations. Carlotta Gieudcelli, the opera's diva, offers Christine a goblet filled with questionable ingredients before curtain time on *The Fairy Queen,* and as a result the girl's voice cracks during the performance, raising cackles and boos from the audience. Enraged, the Phantom meets Carlotta in the hallway, pulls a cable from the wall, and touches it to the stairs. Sparks fly, smoke rises, and Carlotta is electrocuted.

In a twist, we learn that Carriere, the opera's manager, is Erik's father, and the Phantom's past is revealed. When Christine asks Erik to expose his face, the request takes his breath away, but she insists by singing "My True Love." Facing Christine, with his back to the audience, Erik removes his mask. She backs away, screams in horror, and flees. Shattered, Erik drops the mask. Towards the end, The Phantom, although in love with Christine, realizes that her heart is with the Count, and at a crucial moment saves the life of his rival.

In this version, Erik is fatally wounded by a volley of police bullets. Dying, he acknowledges that he has known "for some years" that Carriere is his father. He asks to be buried "deep," never to be found. Carriere promises to make sure that he will never be "on display." The Phantom softly touches Christine's face. She removes his mask and kisses his cheek. A production note states: "We still must not see his face; at most, we can see a small part of it."

Erik dies and Christine replaces the mask. Philippe takes her away. Carriere cradles his son's body in his arms. A slow curtain descends.

*   *   *

Arthur Kopit and Maury Yeston had previously collaborated on the 1982 hit musical *Nine*. The following year they were approached by actor/director Geoffrey Holder to write a musical based on Gaston Leroux's *The Phantom of the Opera*. Holder had obtained the rights to musicalize the novel in America from the Leroux estate. Initially, Yeston was skeptical of the endeavor: "I laughed and laughed.... That's the worst idea in the world! Why would you want to write a musical based on a horror story? ... And then it occurred to me that the story could be somewhat changed... [The Phantom] would be a Quasimodo character, an Elephant Man. Don't all of us feel, despite outward imperfections, that deep inside we are good? And that is a character you cry for."[19]

However, an announcement in *Variety* that Andrew Lloyd Webber planned a musical production of *The Phantom of the Opera* caused the Kopit-Yeston investors to back out, and the plan was scuttled. But when later they saw the Webber version, Kopit and Yeston realized that the approach they planned to take was fundamentally different and renewed their work on their own *Phantom*. Kopit rewrote the script outline into a teleplay for a four-hour miniseries offered in 1990 by NBC.

The Kopit-Yeston musical, titled *Phantom*, was finally produced by Theater Under the Stars, Houston, Texas, in 1991, with Richard White starring in the title role, supported by Glory Crampton (Christine Daaé), Jack Dabdoub (Gerard Carriere), Paul Schoeffler (Count Philippe de Chandon), and Patty Allison (Carlotta).

Though overshadowed by the success of Lloyd Webber's show, *Phantom* has played constantly by regional U.S. companies and internationally, amassing over 1,000 productions.

Acting Edition: Samuel French, Inc.

Jekyll & Hyde (1990)
Book and Lyrics by Leslie Bricusse (England, 1931–2021)
Music by Frank Wildhorn (United States, 1959–)

Musicals are generally considered family fare, but 1990's *Jekyll & Hyde* is not for the squeamish. In between its songs and dances, brutal murders are depicted on stage.

An Act I prologue begins in the dark, with ominous music in the background and a voice-over by Doctor Henry Jekyll concerning the duality of man, how we are torn between good and evil, "polar twins constantly struggling." A spotlight zeroes in on the lawyer Gabriel John Utterson, who informs us that in the autumn of 1880, his friend Jekyll embarked on a series of secretive—and perhaps dangerous—scientific experiments.

At St. Jude's Hospital, Jekyll presents a research proposal to the Board of Governors. Sir Danver Carew, Dr. Jekyll's future father-in-law, is chairman. Other members include The Right Honorable Sir Archibald Proops, Q.C. (Queen's Counsel), quick, methodical, all business; Lord Savage, very much a man-about-town; General Lord Glossop, elderly, formidable; Lady Beaconsfield, a pompous, well-dressed older woman; His Grace the Bishop of Basingstoke, in clerical purple; and Simon Stride, secretary to the Board, who is interested in Jekyll's fiancée, Emma Carew.

Jekyll shows them a vial encased in a protective container. The liquid inside the vial glows. In "Board of Governors," he sings of a world "where man wouldn't kill any more." Amidst cries of "Sacrilege," "Blasphemy," "Heresy," and "Lunacy," the Board votes six to one, with Sir Danvers' one abstention, to reject the proposal.

Later that night, the cream of society turns up at Sir Danvers' party to celebrate his daughter Emma's engagement to Dr. Jekyll. During a swirling waltz, the guests mention how worried they are about Emma marrying with a "madman." Simon Stride corners Emma and tries to persuade her to cancel the engagement, but she quickly turns him down ("Emma's Reason").

Jekyll arrives just as the party is ending. He shares a moment with Emma, warning her that he may always be busy with his work. Emma says, "Henry, I adore you," and vows she will be beside him through it all ("Take Me as I Am"). They kiss.

Jekyll enters his laboratory with determination ("This Is the Moment"). He turns levers and dials and lowers pulleys. The electrical process is colorful and dramatic, with smoke and sparks, bubble and fizz.

He picks up a glass beaker filled with brilliant red liquid, toasts the mirror, and gulps it down. He reaches for a pen to record his sensations, but he's soon writhing in agony. He looks in the mirror and sees himself becoming Hyde. A stage note describes the moment: "He staggers around the laboratory, totally out of control, knocking over equipment, growling and roaring furiously, like a wild animal."

In a spasm of rage, he seizes a thick, silver-headed cane from an umbrella stand, smashes a gas lamp, and exits into the night. He roams the streets of London with a "feeling of power and drive" ("Alive"), names himself Edward Hyde, and embarks upon a quest of revenge against the Governors who have rejected him.

On a shabby street near The Red Rat pub, an unlikely pair stroll—a young prostitute and the Bishop of Basingstoke, last seen with the St. Jude's Hospital Board of Governors. The Bishop pays the girl, who coquettishly walks away. Out of the shadows steps the terrifying figure of Hyde. The Bishop stops frozen with fear. Hyde grins cynically, calls the Bishop, "obscene, self-indulgent, malevolent, malignant *Hypocrite!*" and crushes the Bishop's skull with his cane. Then, drunk with power, he sings a reprise of "Alive":

Act 2 begins with the citizens of London gossiping about the Bishop's homicide ("Murder, Murder"). The Carews, the four remaining Governors, Stride, and Utterson attend the Bishop's funeral at St. Paul's Cathedral. Hyde hovers in the background. General Glossop, walking with two crutches, is the first to emerge from the service. Hyde appears from nowhere, knocks away Glossop's crutches, and breaks the general's neck.

Police whistles are heard in the blackout. When the lights are restored, newsboys are doing a brisk business. Their billboards read "War Lord Glossop Murdered," and "Second Slaying in Five Days."

The lights cross fade to a restaurant entrance—The Mayfair Club. A blind beggar carrying a tray of matches stands nearby. Lady Beaconsfield in full evening dress and ablaze with diamonds, staggers out of the club considerably worse for drink. She is escorted by Lord Herbert Savage and Sir Archibald Proops, who are also inebriated.

Hyde emerges from the darkness. "Well, well, well," he chuckles, "if it isn't Faith, Hope and Charity!" Savage prods Hyde with his umbrella and threatens to have him arrested. Hyde grins as he stabs Proops with a knife. He then tears off Lady Beaconsfield's tiara, necklace, and bracelet, and with the other hand snaps her neck, letting the lifeless body drop to the ground. He holds up the diamonds with a diabolical laugh and tosses them to the "blind" beggar, who catches them expertly and promptly examines their quality. Lord Savage seizes the opportunity to escape while Hyde, with another burst of maniacal laughter, is gone.

Amid the blowing of police whistles, the newsboys have another field day. Frantic, Lord Savage plans to flee London by train. At the railway station, Hyde steps out of a billow of steam. Lord Savage cries out, but he is cut short, as Hyde snaps his neck and tosses Savage's body onto the tracks. Hyde disappears in the steam and shadows. By now, all of the five Governors who rejected Jekyll's proposal are dead.

The last scene unfolds several weeks later at the ancient church where Jekyll and Emma are to be married. The minister starts the service when suddenly Jekyll doubles over in pain and quickly hurries down the aisle of the church, transforming into Hyde. Emma starts after him, followed by her father. Simon Stride rushes to confront Hyde. Stride brandishes his ebony walking stick, but Hyde is too fast for him. He snaps Stride's neck "as though he were a wooden puppet." Hyde then crosses toward Emma and drags her toward the altar. Emma reaches up and touches his contorted face. "Henry," she says, "I know that it is you … and you would never harm me … never." Hyde growls and holds her close, as though to crush her, but Jekyll is able to regain momentary control, and his arms drop wearily at his sides. Emma slides from his grasp and sobs at steps of the altar.

Hyde/Jekyll turns toward the lawyer Utterson, who served as best man: "John, do it now. I beg of you. Set me free. Set us all free!" Utterson understands and holds the blade at his friend's heart. Hyde/Jekyll looks into Utterson's eyes, pleading, then falls forward onto the sword. Emma kneels beside him and takes the dying man into her arms. She embraces him for a long moment, then rocks him, singing,

> Rest now … my tortured love….
> You are free now….
> You're with me now….
> Where you'll always be….

*　　*　　*

The world premiere of *Jekyll & Hyde* took place at the Alley Theatre, Houston, Texas, in May 1990. A substantially recast and revised version by the original creative team of librettist Leslie Bricusse, composer Frank Wildhorn, and director Gregory Boyd played at the Alley in January and February 1995. Reviewer Everett Evans of the *Houston Chronicle* reported that "gallows humor prevails as Hyde blithely dispatches Jekyll's adversaries" and praised Robert Cuccioli's "presence, powerful voice, and persuasive acting in the demanding title role(s)."[20]

Jekyll & Hyde undertook a national tour from August 1995 through April 1996, then opened at New York's Plymouth Theatre on April 28, 1997, starring Cuccioli. Here the critics were less than kind. "A leaden, solemnly campy musical," groaned Ben Brantley in the *New York Times*.[21] *New York Post*'s Clive Barnes called *Jekyll & Hyde* "a clumsy musical."[22] But the reviews had little effect on the box office. The show ran for 1,543 performances, closing on January 7, 2001, helped by fanatical fans known as Jekkies, as well as by CDs of the score. When the last curtain descended, the backers recouped only 75 percent of their $7 million investment.

The show garnered several Tony Award nominations for Best Book of a Musical (Leslie Bricusse), Best Actor in a Musical (Robert Cuccioli), Best Costume Design (Ann Curtis), and Best Lighting Design (Beverly Emmons). Cuccioli won both a Drama Desk Award and an Outer Critics Circle Award for Outstanding Actor in a Musical.

A 1997 Broadway Cast Album features Robert Cuccioli as Jekyll/Hyde and Christiane Noll as Emma. The most famous song is "This Is the Moment," which was performed at the Olympics twice and sung by The Moody Blues at various sports events.

The Broadway production was filmed live at the Plymouth Theatre in 2000 with actors-singers who by then had taken over key roles: David Hasselhoff (Jekyll/Hyde) and Andrea Rivette (Emma).

* * *

Leslie Bricusse wrote the book, lyrics, and score of *Sherlock Holmes—The Musical* (1988), in which a prologue depicts the Great Detective and his arch-enemy Professor Moriarty meeting face-to-face on a rocky cliff. They "grapple ferociously on the precarious precipice," and finally fall into the chasm of Reichenbach Falls, apparently to their doom. To the relief of Dr. Watson and the faithful Irregulars, Holmes returns to London alive and well. Bricusse adds a new wrinkle to the saga of Sherlock Holmes by introducing the character of Bella Spellgrove, the daughter of Professor Moriarty, who is bent on avenging her father's death. The musical was first presented at the Northcott Theatre, Exeter, England, in 1988. Retitled *The Revenge of Sherlock Holmes* and revised, the musical was mounted by Bristol Old Vic in 1993.

Following *Jekyll and Hyde*, Frank Wildhorn composed the music of *The Scarlet Pimpernel*, the story of an enigmatic, mysterious Englishman who helped Parisian aristocrats escape the guillotine during the French Revolution. The musical, adapted from a 1905 novel by the Hungarian-British Baroness Emmuska Orczy, opened at New York's Minskoff Theatre on November 9, 1997. It was snubbed by critics but, with Douglas Sills in the title role, managed to run until January 2, 2000, amassing 772 performances.

Widhorn's *Dracula*, with a book by Don Black and Christopher Hampton based on Bram Stoker's 1897 vampire novel, opened at the Belasco Theatre, New York, on August 19, 2004, featuring Tom Hewitt as the Count. The musical was pooh-poohed by the critics and struggled to run for 157 showings.

Wildhorn's latest Broadway offering was the score for *Bonnie and Clyde*, a $6 million musical about the infamous Bonnie Parker and Clyde Barrow, Depression-era outlaws and lovebirds who paved a bloody trail across the Southwest before being killed by Louisiana sheriff's deputies. *Bonnie and Clyde* arrived in New York's Schoenfeld Theatre on December 1, 2011, received unanimously negative reviews, and closed after sixty-nine performances.

Libretto: Cherry Lane Music Publishing Company.

Awards and Honors: Leslie Bricusse was awarded an O.B.E. (Officer of the British Empire) in 2001. Frank Wildhorn was nominated for a 1998 Drama Desk Award for *The Scarlet Pimpernel* in the category of Outstanding Music.

Evil Dead: The Musical (2003)
Book and Lyrics by George Reinblatt (Canada, 1977–)
Music by Frank Cipolla, Christopher Bond,
Melissa Morris, and George Reinblatt

Evil Dead is an American supernatural horror movie franchise consisting of four feature films and a television series. The original trilogy includes *The Evil Dead* (1981), *Evil Dead II* (1987), and *Army of Darkness* (1992), all written and directed by Sam Raimi. A 2013 reboot, *Evil Dead*, was directed by Fede Alvarez. The franchise has since expanded into other formats: video games, comic books, a stage musical, and a television series (*Ash vs. Evil Dead*, 30 episodes, 2015–2018). Bruce Campbell starred in the movies and on television as Ashley ("Ash") Williams, the leader of a group of students on a spring vacation. They stay in a secluded cabin located in a wooded area of Tennessee, where they find an ancient Sumerian "Book of the Dead," and inadvertently unleash evil demons.

Evil Dead: The Musical is a Canadian rock stage play based on the film series. The play's creators mixed concepts and characters from the movies, sprinkling horrific moments with gallows humor.

As the curtain rises, a spotlight hits a large book, titled *Book of the Dead*. It opens on its own, revealing pages filled with lines written in blood. A voiceover tells us that the text serves as a passageway to evil worlds beyond. In the year 1300 BCE, the book disappeared.

The book slams shut. Lights go up on Ash, Linda, Scott, Shelly, and Cheryl in a car. Cheryl is Ash's geeky sister. Scott is his brash best friend. Linda and Shelly are the guys' sexy, eager girlfriends. Ash stops the car at the end of a road, and they cross a bridge by foot. "It is the only way to the cabin," says Ash.

The group settles in, divides the bedrooms, and prepares for a relaxed evening. None of them hears a whispering voice saying, "Join us," but when a noise is heard in the cellar, Ash and Scott investigate. They return with several items they found: an axe, a gun, a dagger, a book, and a tape recorder, items that will play an important part in the upcoming proceedings.

Scott switches on the tape recorder. "This is Professor Raymond Knowby," says the recording. Knowby tells of his discovery of the Necronomicon, "Book of the Dead."[23]

The book speaks of something of evil roaming in the forest. A tree smashes through the window. Cheryl screams, "Shut it off!" Scott makes fun of her. Cheryl exits the cabin in a huff and walks through the forest. Actors dressed as trees follow her and attack her.

In the next scene, Ash, Linda, Scott, and Shelly are lounging around when Cheryl enters from the outside, beaten and bruised, her clothes ripped to shreds. She tells them, "The trees are alive." Naturally no one believes her. Suddenly, Cheryl is possessed by a demon. She sings, "Look Who's Evil Now." Scott and Ash grab Cheryl and throw her into the cellar.

Shelly screams from the bedroom and enters—she is also a demon. She sings, "Join Us, Join Us," then tells Scott that since he was kind enough to take her on this trip, she graciously decided that he's going to be the first one she'll take with her. Ash picks up the gun from a corner, throws it to Scott, who shoots Shelly. She falls dead. Scott, overwrought, exits.

Cheryl sings "Join Us" from the cellar, urging Ash to accept his fate and join the dark army of evil as they conquer "this land, and take over each and every soul of the living!"

Suddenly, the pictures, the books, the moose head on the wall—pretty much everything in the cabin—come to life. The Moose says to Ash, "Join our evil forces as we enslave all mankind, chew on their brains and bathe in their hot bubbling blood!" Blackout.

In the next scene, a bloody Scott barges in. He mumbles, "We're all going to die here.... Death is a bitch. A stupid bitch" and drops dead. Ash cries, "Nooooooo! What else can go wrong today?"—as Linda enters as a demon. But soon Linda returns to normal. She and Ash sing "Housewares Employee," recalling their first meeting while working part-time at S-Mart. The romantic moment ends abruptly when Linda changes back into a demon. Ash says, "I'm sorry, Linda, I've got to do this," and chops off her head with an axe. Blood splatters everywhere.

The cellar trap door swings open to reveal Cheryl holding the pages of *The Book of the Dead*. She cackles, "I'll kill you before you ever get your hands on them." Ash counters, "Cheryl, I'm getting sick of you trying to kill me," and shoots his sister.

The cabin becomes dark, and the demons—Cheryl, Scott, Linda, and Shelly—enter. They sing and dance "Do the Necronomicon."

Ash goes on the attack. He confronts and kills the demons one by one, His triumph is short lived. The demons return to life and sing,

> You must realize
> We will never die
> We're already dead.

Ashe yells the last passage of the book, "Condo Condo Nosperoto—Demonto!" The demons are sucked through the door on their way to Hell.

The last scene takes place in the housewares department of S-Mart. Ash, surrounded by random customers (played by cast members in wigs and moustaches), boasts how he sent evil Candarian demons back to hell. The customers react with chuckles of disbelief, poking fun at this savior of humanity who is working at S-Mart in a menial position.

However, one of the customers turns out to be Linda as a demon. She grabs a baby and tries to kill it. Ash snatches a gun off the shelf and shoots Linda three times. She flies in the air. Ash shoots her again, and the baby lands in his hand unharmed. "So," he says, "do you screwheads believe I can save you from Candarian demons now?" The members of the crowd sing with admiration "Blew That Bitch Away," and exclaim, "You're our hero!"

* * *

Evil Dead: The Musical first glimpsed the light of day in 2003 at the Tranzac Club, Toronto, Canada, where early workshop engagements played to capacity. The show then headed to Montreal, Canada, opening on July 2, 2004, at the Cabaret du Plateau as part of the 22nd Just for Laughs Festival. On October 2, 2006, *Evil Dead: The Musical* opened at Off-Broadway's New World Stages, directed by Christopher Bond and choreographed by Hinton Battle. Ryan Ward played the role of Ash. The show garnered rave reviews and ran until February 17, 2007. Since then, it has become a cult hit.

A notable revival of *Evil Dead: The Musical*, also featuring Ryan Ward, was mounted at Toronto's Diesel Playhouse starting May 1, 2007, extended its run four times, and lasted until September 6, 2008. It celebrated its 300th performance on June 26, 2008, which marked it as the longest running Canadian production in Toronto in twenty years.

Off-Strip Productions and RagTag Entertainment teamed up to present the musical at The Onyx Theatre, Las Vegas, Nevada, in 2011, winning critical kudos and returning to Sin City in January 2012 for another full-house run. Later that year, in June, Sirc Michaels Productions brought the play to Las Vegas Strip as a resident, open-ended offering at the V Theater. It encourages audience participation and utilizes multimedia elements. The venture moved to two other Las Vegas venues in 2015 and 2017 and is now officially the longest running production in the history of the show.

Over 150 productions of *Evil Dead: The Musical* have been staged by professional, amateur, and school theater groups throughout North America and in Seoul, Tokyo, Madrid, and other cities.

Acting Edition: Samuel French, Inc.

Re-Animator: The Musical (2011)

Re-Animator is a 1985 American horror movie loosely based on the 1922 H.P. Lovecraft novelette *Herbert West—Reanimator*. Co-scripted and directed by Stuart Gordon, the film stars Jeffrey Combs as Herbert West, a medical student at Miskatonic University in New England. He rents a room from fellow student Dan Cain (Bruce Abbott) and converts the basement into his own personal laboratory. West invents a concoction which can re-animate deceased bodies and, with Cain's help, plans to test the serum on human corpses. A conflict develops between the roommates and Dr. Carl Hill (David Gale), who wants to claim the invention as his own.

West and Cain sneak into a morgue. The dead man they inject comes back to life but in a violent zombie-like state. Dean Halsey stumbles upon the scene and is killed by the re-animated corpse. West injects Halsey with the reanimating fluid, and the dean returns to life, also in a psychotic state. West and Cain burrow deeper and deeper into uncharted territory, and soon the campus is brimming over with reanimated corpses.

Dr. Hill attempts to blackmail West into surrendering his experiment as well as his notes. West clobbers him with a shovel, then decapitates him. He reanimates Hill's head and body separately, and comic chaos ensues.

Stuart Gordon, who began his career by co-founding Chicago's Organic Theater Company, was initially inspired by the movie-to-musical adaptation of *Little Shop of Horrors* to bring Lovecraft's story to the stage. He turned it into a half-hour television pilot but ended up shooting an 86-minute feature with a budget of $900,000. The film received an X rating and was later edited to obtain an R rating. It was released to mostly positive reviews, spawning the sequels *Bride of Re-Animator* in 1990 and *Beyond Re-Animator* in 2003.

Gordon came back to his original idea and co-wrote the book of a stage musical, *Re-Animator: The Musical,* with lyrics and music by Mark Nutter. The show quite faithfully follows the grim-yet-humorous action of the 1985 movie. It first performed at the 99-seat Steve Allen Theatre in Los Angeles, California, March 5–27, 2011. Directed by Gordon and choreographed by Cynthia Carie, the cast included Graham Skipper (Herbert West), Chris L. McKenna (Dan Cain), George Wendt (Dean Halsey), and Jesse Merlin (Dr. Hill).

Re-Animator: The Musical won several honors, including Best Book from the Ovation Awards; Best Musical Score from the Los Angeles Drama Critics Circle; and the *L.A. Weekly* Award for Best Musical. Bob Verini, critic of *Variety*, wrote on March 9, 2011: "Not since *Little Shop of Horrors* has a screamfest tuner so deftly balanced seriousness and camp."

King Kong (2013)

In 1933, RKO Pictures released the motion picture *King Kong*, an adventure story about a film crew that travels to the uncharted tropical Skull Island for exotic location shots and discovers a gigantic ape who takes a shine to their female star, Ann Darrow. The ape is captured and brought to New York City for public exhibition. A tense climax depicts Kong on top of the Empire State Building, where he is shot by circling planes and dies. "The aviators didn't get him," says Carl Denham, the director of the film crew. "It was Beauty killed the Beast."[24]

Directed by Merian C. Cooper and starring Fay Wray and Robert Armstrong, *King Kong* was received with accolades (especially praise for Willie Obrien's stop-motion animation). It became a landmark horror film and spawned sixteen sequels or remakes, the best known of which are *Son of Kong* (1933), *King Kong vs. Godzilla* (1962), *King Kong* (1976), *King Kong* (2005), *Kong: Skull Island* (2017), and *Godzilla vs. Kong* (2021).[25]

The franchise is analyzed in Ray Morton's 2005 book *King Kong: The History of a Movie from Fay Wray to Peter Jackson*, and in the 2017 documentary, *Long Live the King*, by Frank Dietz and Trish Geiger.

The brainchild of an Australian animatronics company, a stage musical of *King Kong* premiered at the Regent Theatre, Melbourne, Australia, on June 15, 2013. Reportedly, the production took five years of planning and five months of rehearsals. It featured a score by Marius de Vries, lyrics by Michael Mitnick and Craig Lucas, and a book by Lucas. The director was David Kramer, and the choreographer John O'Connell.

A poster of the Great Ape fighting against surrounding airplanes on top of the Empire State building (printed in Italy by Rotolitografica, Rome, 1935).

A marquee of *King Kong* at the Broadway Theatre, New York, 2018 (photograph by the author).

Designed and built by Global Creature Technology in West Melbourne, the title role involved the largest puppet ever created for the stage—20 feet high, weighing 2,000 pounds. A group of 35 on-and-off stage puppeteers manipulated its motions. Several puppeteers were positioned on swinging trapezes ready to maneuver Kong's massive arm to strike at planes during the performance. The cast consisted of 49 actors, singers, dancers, and circus acrobats. The crew numbered 76. The visual effects included Kong's battle with a 40-foot snake puppet and the integration of a 90-foot video screen.

The producers announced that they were aiming for an immediate Broadway reprise of *King Kong*, but the notion was postponed several times before it materialized in 2018. During an extended planning period, many changes were made.

Directed and choreographed by Drew McOnie, Broadway's *King Kong* generally follows the outline of the 1933 movie but places the emphasis on a friendly relationship between the ape and Ann Darrow and paints the character of Carl Denham in villainous colors. The curtain rises on Ann (Christiani Pitts), a plucky farm girl arriving in New York City to realize her dream of appearing on Broadway and becoming "Queen of New York." She auditions for a show but does not make the cut ("Dance My Way to the Light"). To escape the cold weather, she takes refuge in a diner, where she meets Carl Denham (Eric William Morris), who introduces himself as a moviemaker in search of a leading lady. He keeps the details of the picture under wraps, aside from the fact that the filming location is accessible only by boat. Ann agrees to take the job, and the two set off on the steamship *S.S. Wanderer*, helmed by Captain Englehorn (Rory Donovan) and his crew ("Building the Boat/Sailing Sail").

Mid-voyage, tensions rise between Englehorn and Denham ("Pressure Up"), and after two months at sea, the crew is ready to snap. The captain pulls a gun on Denham and demands to know their destination ("The Mutiny") when Skull Island looms in the distance. On shore, Denham takes some shots of the island's jungle and suggests that Ann climb into some vines. Ann mounts a tree when suddenly heavy steps are heard. The vines tighten around Ann, and Kong appears. Ann thrashes wildly in a futile attempt to escape as the big ape sniffs at her. Denham tries to film the duo, but Kong smashes the camera to bits.

Kong grabs Ann and carries her away as she screams in terror ("Skull Island"). He brings the girl to a cliff overlooking the forest. Denham, angry about the destruction of his camera, suggests that he and the crew leave the island and let Ann fend for herself. But he changes his mind when it occurs to him that Kong will be the perfect tourist attraction back in New York. As Denham and the crew trudge through the forest, he sings about the potential profitable venture ("The World").

Meanwhile, Ann wakes up to face Kong in his cave. At first, she is frightened, but when the ape protects her from a giant snake ("The Cobra Fight"), Ann sees beyond Kong's harsh exterior, and the two form a bond ("Full Moon Lullaby"). Still, when Kong falls asleep, Ann, believing that she's still in danger, runs into the jungle. She hasn't made it too far before Kong realizes she's gone and chases after her. Ann encounters Denham, and he tells her of his plan. He asks that she scream for Kong, and Ann reluctantly does exactly that, bringing the ape right to where the ship's crew is waiting. Kong bursts through the trees and is gassed ("Kong's Capture").

The second act is set in New York. Denham advertises his upcoming show, in which he intends to present Kong to the audience. On opening night, Ann, feeling guilty and remorseful, disobeys Denham's demands to scream. She tells him that she won't "scream for the money." But when a stage crew drags her off stage, she screams. Kong reacts by breaking free from his shackles. He gestures for Ann to climb onto his back and off they go. Kong climbs to the top of the half-completed Empire State Building, Ann clinging to his back ("Empire Ascent"). Back at the theater, Denham is left alone, with the stage in shambles.

Army planes fly in to shoot at Kong ("Air War"). Kong destroys plane after plane, taking many bullets in the process. He gives Ann one last look and plummets to his death. Ann, grieving ("Empire Soliloquy"), reaches the street and spreads the word that Kong wasn't a monster, nor was he an attraction to be displayed. He was simply "a wonder" ("The Wonder").

King Kong came to New York's Broadway Theatre for previews on October 5, 2018, and opened officially on November 8. A technical marvel, with a stage crew dressed in black skillfully maneuvering a gigantic ape puppet, the musical was nonetheless greeted by critics more savage than the prehistoric creatures of Skull Island. "Kong is more clown than King," declared Charles McNulty in the *Los Angeles Times*. "One of the most ludicrous Broadway musicals in recent memory."[26] The *New York Times'* Ben Brantley and Jesse Green were unanimous in their distaste for the entire effort, finding Kong "the most expressive performer onstage" and the set of the Skull Island jungle looking "like green spaghetti with phlegm balls."[27] The show ran for 322 performances and reportedly lost the entire production budget of $36.5 million.

Nevertheless, *King Kong* won a Special Tony Award for Sonny Tilders and Creature Technology Company as well as Drama Desk Awards for Outstanding Puppet Design and Outstanding Projection Design.

5

Psychotics

Night Must Fall (1935)
Emlyn Williams (Wales, 1905–1987)

Actor-playwright Emlyn Williams was fascinated by the 1929 trial of Sidney Fox, a wide-eyed Englishman who burned his mother to death for insurance money. "For years I had been fascinated by real-life murders, and accounts of murder trials," tells Williams. "I found myself wanting to write a play in which the audience knew, as the curtain rose, that the murderer had not only 'done it,' but was to be hanged for his crime—I longed to go on from there."[1]

Night Must Fall begins with a verdict by the Lord Chief Justice that an inmate accused of a series of viscious murders is "to be taken from hence and hanged by the neck." The plot of the play reverts to 1935 and Mrs. Bramson's isolated country house in Essex, England.

Mrs. Bramson, an affluent hypochondriac in a wheelchair, is enchanted by the bellhop Dan, who captivates the old woman by stating, "You remind me of my mother." Dan has just lost his job with the widow Chalfort, whose body has been found, decapitated, in a nearby rubbish-hole. Mrs. Bramson hires him as a personal attendant. Dan moves in, carrying two worn suitcases and a frayed leather hatbox. It is disclosed later that the hatbox contains a severed head. A suspenseful scene concludes with Mrs. Bramson napping on the sofa, Dan picking up a cushion, and the lights fading out as he steps toward her. At the end, a Scotland Yard inspector accuses Dan of being a psychopath who delights in decapitating elderly women and fastens a pair of handcuffs on him. The murderer looks at himself in the mirror, grins, salutes his hatbox, and strolls out.

Actor-playwright Emlyn Williams, Wales, 1905–1987, peppered his plays with unnerving incidents (n.d.; The New York Public Library for the Performing Arts).

*   *   *

Staged by Miles Malleson, *Night Must Fall* debuted at King's Theatre in Edinburgh, on April 29, 1935, detoured to Newcastle and Glasgow, and officially opened at West End's Duchess Theatre on May 31 to rave reviews: "brilliant," "clever," "remarkable," "masterly," "absolutely first-rate theatre." Charles Morgan, in a telegram to the *New York Times*, opined, "From first to last, the play has maintained an extraordinary tension," and applauded the main actors: "Dame May Whitty gives an admirable performance as the old woman, and Emlyn Williams' portrait of the murderer brilliantly avoids melodrama and reveals by action and reference the whole personality of the man."[2]

Night Must Fall ran for 436 performances. Its British cast traveled to New York's Ethel Barrymore Theatre on September 28, 1936, but here the assessment was mixed. Richard Lockridge believed that audiences "will find the whole affair pleasantly upsetting."[3] Richard Watts, Jr., agreed: "Here at last is a good play to enliven the season in its amiably sadistic fashion."[4] Conversely, John Mason Brown sniffed at an "overslow, overcalculated show,"[5] and John Anderson sulked, "It is all so long drawn out, so labored in its elaborately sinister effect, that the fright wears off. You can't yawn and have your teeth chatter at the same moment."[6]

Night Must Fall lasted in New York for only 64 performances but became a favored offering on tour in the 1930s and 1940s. The play was shown in Millbrook, New York, with James Gregory as Dan; in Los Angeles, California, featuring Dwight Frye, *Dracula*'s Renfield, as Dan; and in Whitefield, New Hampshire, headlining David Wayne. Douglass Montgomery played Dan in New Jersey, New York, and Michigan. In 1946, Dame May Whitty reprised the role of Mrs. Bramson at the Boston Summer Theatre and the Cambridge Summer Theatre. The following year, Whitty brought the play to Mexico City. After World War II, the USO presented *Night Must Fall* for American soldiers in Germany, touting it as "a spine-tingling drama" and "The New York and London dramatic hit."

Night Must Fall was revived during the 1960s, 1970s, and 1980s at resident theaters across the U.S. New York showings of *Night Must Fall* took place Off-Broadway at the Cherry Lane Theatre, 1939; Equity Library Theatre, 1969; Manhattan Theatre Club, 1974; and the Greenwich Mews Theatre, 1975.

A Broadway revival of the play was presented at the Lyceum Theatre on March 8, 1999, running for 120 performances. Director John Tillinger added a short introductory scene showing the silhouette of a man digging a grave with a spade. The final moment depicts a handcuffed Danny splashing gasoline on the floor of the waiting-room and kindling it with a match. Reviewer Donald Lyons pouted that the play "belongs to a genre of thriller that has not worn especially well."[7]

London saw productions of *Night Must Fall* in 1936, 1947, and 1975. For a 1987 revival by the fringe Greenwich Theatre, Emlyn Williams compressed the play by ten minutes and reduced the number of intermissions from two to one. Critic Felix Barker disputed the choice of a "tired old shocker" but by the final curtain, acknowledged, "Despite all the cliché-ridden characters, stock situations, and blatantly signaled clues, we were compulsively held by Dan's cat-and-mouse game."[8]

Night Must Fall was welcomed in Paris, as *L'Homme qui se Donnait*, adapted by Jacques Deval, with Pierre Brasseur as Dan. Robert Montgomery portrayed the psychopathic killer in a tense 1937 MGM movie version scripted by John van Druten and

A tense scene from the stage production of *Night Must Fall*, in which handyman Dan (Emlyn Williams) prepares to strangle and decapitate his employer, Mrs. Branson (May Whitty), Ethel Barrymore Theatre, New York City, 1936 (photo by Alfredo Valente, Billy Rose Theatre Division, The New York Public Library for the Performing Arts).

directed by Richard Thorpe. Dame May Whitty repeated her stage role as Mrs. Bramson. The object in Dan's hatbox is never revealed, but we assume the gruesome worst. The scene in which the old woman is isolated and scared prior to her murder is artfully delineated. Whitty earned an Oscar nomination for Best Supporting Actress.

Directed by Karel Reisz, a remake of *Night Must Fall* was made in England in 1964 with Albert Finney (Dan) and Mona Washbourne (Mrs. Bramson). In this version, Dan plays sacrament games with the decapitated heads of victims. In 1964, William Drummond novelized the movie; it was published by Fontana in England and by Signet in the U.S.

* * *

Several plays by Emlyn Williams are flavored with eerie ingredients. *A Murder Has Been Arranged* (1930) is a supernatural thriller that unfolds on the stage of a London Theatre. In *Port Said* (1931), a city by the Suez Canal, Williams himself enacted an Egyptian vagabond who is fatally stabbed by a sinister Englishman, portrayed by Jack Hawkins. The plot of *He Was Born Gay* (1937) takes place in 1815, when Napoleon was vanquished at Waterloo. The play is stewing with conspiracy, as claimants to the throne keep emerging.

An unbalanced sixteen-year-old girl aims to break-up a happy family in *Guest in the House* (1946), adapted by Williams from a play by Hagar Wilde and Dale Eunson. A fortune teller is revealed as a pretender during a séance in *Trespass*, "A Ghost Story in Six Scenes" (1947). *Accolade* (1950) is a disturbing drama about a renowned author who has slept with an underage girl and is threatened with discovery. In *Someone Waiting* (1953), a father is on a mission to find the person who committed the crime for which his son was executed.

Acting Edition: Samuel French, Inc.

Night Must Fall is also included in *Famous Plays of Crime and Detection*, compiled by Van H. Cartmell and Bennett Cerf (Philadelphia: The Blakiston Company, 1946) and in *10 Classic Mystery and Suspense Plays of the Modern Theatre*, edited by Stanley Richards (New York: Dodd, Mead and Company, 1973).

Awards and Honors: In 1949, Emlyn Williams was given an honorary LL.D. by the Duke of Edinburgh. In 1962, Williams was designated Commander of the British Empire (C.B.E.).

Love from a Stranger (1936)
Frank Vosper (England, 1900–1937)

Frank Vosper, an English actor-playwright, dramatized Agatha Christie's short story "Philomel Cottage" in 1936. The play begins in the London apartment Cecily Harrington shares with her best friend, Mavis Wilson. As they chat, we learn that Cecily has some misgivings about her engagement to Nigel Lawrence. Cecily confides to her roommate that she wishes for more than the tedious middle class lifestyle Nigel promises.

The apartment is being rented. A potential tenant arrives—Bruce Lovell, who is "six feet in height, powerfully built, his appearance radiates health." The newcomer appeals to Cecily's restless nature, and following the meeting, she calls Nigel to delay the wedding.

She does not notice that Bruce pockets a newspaper page about "a tall, dark and handsome" serial killer.

Acts 2 and 3 unroll in a rural bungalow. Now married, Bruce requests that Cecily sign lease documents, and the glowing bride consents. Bruce installs a photography studio in the cottage and spends long hours reading criminology books. It is a homey, pleasant manner of living for Cecily. But soon ominous signs become apparent. Bruce is inclined to fits of fury, and we see him shaking frantically, ripping a handkerchief to tatters.

Cecily ultimately looks at pictures in a Notable Trials volume and discovers that Bruce is a serial killer who has disposed of several wives. Trapped in the remote bungalow, Cecily manages to outwit Bruce by "admitting" that she is an assassin who has done away with a few husbands and has just sprayed arsenic in his coffee.

The impact of the fabricated confession is lethal. Bruce's heart stops.

* * *

Love from a Stranger auditioned at Wyndham's Theatre in London, on February 2, 1936, then raised its curtain officially at the New Theatre on March 31, with Vosper himself playing Bruce Lovell. It collected positive reviews. "A brilliant terror play," said the *Daily Herald*. "Our blood was gloriously curdled."[9] The *Daily Telegraph* cheered, "Quite obviously it is going to hit the present state for cleverly manipulated horror."[10] Charles Morgan dispatched a mixed appraisal of the play to the *New York Times* but stated, "It leads to a genuinely exciting and ingenious denouement."[11]

Love from a Stranger ran for 149 performances. Vosper helmed a new cast that moved to the Erlanger Theatre in Philadelphia, on September 21, 1936, and later anchored at New York's Fulton Theatre eight days later. L.N. of the *New York Times* (identified by initials only) asserted that adapter Vosper had drawn out Agatha Christie's story "to dangerous length" and regretted the "interpretation of bluebeard as a head-holding, shoulder-straightening, partly ranting person, instead of a cool and calm characterization that would have seemed more dangerous."[12] The play lasted 31 performances.

Love from a Stranger was converted to the cinema twice—in 1937, starring Basil Rathbone as his wives' slayer and Ann Harding as his ill-fated bride; and in 1947, with John Hodiak and Sylvia Sidney.

The play was revived in 2001 by The Shaw Festival, Niagara-on-the-Lake, Ontario, Canada, and in 2020 by West Valley Playhouse, Canoga Park, California.

Frank Vosper's life ended puzzlingly in 1937, on a transatlantic voyage, when he disappeared from the boat. Several months later, his mutilated body surfaced on the coast of France.

Acting Edition: Samuel French, Inc. (in manuscript form).

Gas Light (1938)
Patrick Hamilton (England, 1904–1962)

Following his hit murder drama, *Rope* (1929), and his flopped blackmail play, *John Brown's Body* (1931), Patrick Hamilton wrote the Victorian chiller, *Gas Light*.

The non-stop action of Patrick Hamilton's *Gas Light* unfolds on a misty night in a London house during the 1880s. The lights fade up on Mr. Manningham—"tall, good-looking, about forty-five"—interrogating his wife, Bella—"about thirty-four, haggard, wan, frightened, with rings under her eyes"—about a missing picture. Bella Manningham vows that she doesn't know the whereabout of the picture, then, shattered, views her husband kissing the maid Nancy—"a pretty, cheeky girl of nineteen"—before he stalks out.

Bella collapses on the settee. Elizabeth, the housekeeper,—"stout, amiable, about fifty"—leads in a visitor, detective Rough—"over sixty, graying, short, wiry, brusque, friendly, overbearing." Bella relates to him that recently items have begun to vanish. Her husband goes out at night, and she thinks that he goes up to the attic, for the gas light quivers, as if someone has lighted an additional lamp.

Rough confides to Bella that more than a decade earlier, a wealthy old lady, Alice Barlow, was murdered for her possession of rubies. Barlow's home had been searched diligently. Obviously, she concealed the rubies skillfully. Rough then discloses that the murder was perpetrated in this house, and that Mr. Manningham, the possible killer, must have been looking in the attic for the Barlow rubies. The gaslight suddenly flickers.

Rough informs Bella that her husband's real name is Sydney Power and that he was a cousin of Mrs. Barlow. He also tells her that Power is still married to a woman in Australia and apparently has undertaken to send his second wife into insanity.

Rough hopes that there is some clue in the house to verify Manningham's real identity. He removes his hat and coat and smashes the lock on Manningham's desk. They find a market receipt, a watch, and a vase that have been missing. Bella tells Rough that she recently found some loose beads and placed them in the vase. The detective exclaims, "The Barlow rubies—complete, twelve thousand pounds' worth!" He puts the beads back in the vase.

They hear the front door open and hasten to the adjacent room. Rough leaves his hat behind, but—to the audience's relief—returns instantly to fetch it and departs again only seconds before Manningham's appearance.

Later that night, Manningham finds that the lock of his desk has been broken. He checks it carefully, scans his files, and then yanks the bell-cord for Nancy. He orders her to tell his wife to come down immediately.

Manningham questions Bella and her strength falters. She fears that the meeting with Rough was just an illusion. But the detective arrives, escorted by two uniformed police officers. After a struggle, Manningham is forced into a chair and safely tied.

Bella asks to talk with to her husband privately. Rough reluctantly agrees. Manningham says softly to Bella that there is a razor in the adjoining room. She walks to the door and for an anxious moment we believe that she will help Manningham escape. But then her conduct shifts. How weird, she says, the door is bolted. When he appeals for her to turn the key, she says that there is no key; she has lost it. After all, she is always losing things, and isn't she crazy? Bella keeps on mocking Manningham, then goes to the door, opens it, and calls Rough, "Come and take this man away!"

The police officers lead Manningham out. Rough offers condolences for what must have been the most terrible night of her life, but Bella retorts that it was "the most wonderful—far and away the most wonderful."

*   *   *

Gas Light previewed at the Richmond Theatre in Richmond, England, on December 5, 1938, and opened at London's Apollo Theatre on January 31, 1939, featuring Dennis Arundel in the role of Mr. Manningham, Gwen Ffrangcon-Davies as Mrs. Manningham, and Milton Rosner as detective Rough. The *London Times* critic lauded the first act but was less sympathetic to the second, when "the psychological tension vanishes into thin air, and there remains only one question: How may a cunning old detective ensnare a criminal maniac and crown his career by solving a mystery which baffled him in his youth?"[13]

Gas Light ran for 141 performances, returned to West End's Coliseum Theatre on August 19, 1939, for 12 more, and traveled to New York, where it opened at the John Golden Theatre on December 5, 1941. Directed by Shepard

Mr. Manningham (Vincent Price) plays a cruel game on his wife (Judith Evelyn) in *Angel Street,* John Golden Theatre, New York City, 1944 (photo by Friedman-Abeles, The New York Public Library for the Performing Arts).

Traube, and now called *Angel Street*, the three lead roles were played by Vincent Price, Judith Evelyn, and Leo G. Carroll. The critics were content. "It is guaranteed to chill the hottest spine and cause each particular hair to stand on end," wrote John Anderson.[14] "It is a tale of horror, terror, crime and suspense that is manipulated with masterful skill," cheered Richard Watts, Jr.[15]

Angel Street had a colossal run of 1295 performances. In 1947, Gregory Peck and Laraine Day starred at San Francisco's Curran Theatre. A year later, *Angel Street* played at the City Center of Manhattan for 14 presentations, with José Ferrer and Uta Hagen. In 1975, it returned to Broadway with Michael Allinson and Dina Merrill.

With its nerve-wracking plot, *Angel Street* became a fixture of summer stock and local theaters across the land. A burst of restored attraction to the play at the dawn of the 21st century led to the Off-Broadway presentation at the Blue Heron Art Theatre (2002); the showing by Actors Co-op of Hollywood, California (2004); and the production at the Sierra Madre Playhouse, Sierra Madre, California (2007).

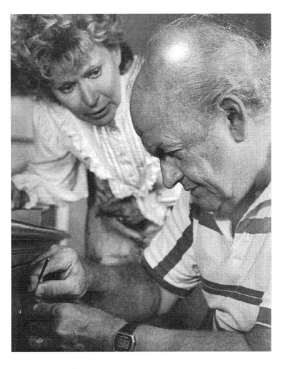

Police inspector Rough (Leon B. Stevens) aids the persecuted Mrs. Manningham (Lydia Bruce) in *Gaslight*, Elmira College, Elmira, New York, 1988.

Gas Light was adapted to the screen twice: in 1940, directed by Thorold Dickinson, with Anton Walbrook, Diana Wynyard, and Frank Pettingell, and in 1944, directed by George Cukor, marqueeing Charles Boyer, Ingrid Bergman (who garnered an Academy Award for this role), and Joseph Cotten. The movie was inducted into the Library of Congress's National Film Registry in 2019, in acknowledgement of its artistic merits.

* * *

Anthony Walter Patrick Hamilton's novels were flavored with ingredients of evil and the grotesque. The protagonist of *Hangover Square* (1941), George Harvey Bone, is a serial killer of women. Another murderer of women is Ernest Ralph Gorse, who shows up in *The West Pier* (1951), *Mr. Stimpson and Mr. Gorse* (1953), and *Unknown Assailant* (1955).

Hamilton was influenced by the notorious case of Leopold and Loeb when he wrote his first play, *Rope*, in 1929. Nineteen-year-old Nathan Leopold and eighteen-year-old Richard Loeb, students at the University of Chicago, kidnapped Loeb's cousin, Bobby Franks; killed him; then attempted to extract ransom from Franks' parents. Leopold and Loeb aimed to commit the perfect crime, but Leopold dropped his spectacles at the scene of the crime, and the police traced them. The two young murderers were tried, found guilty, and sentenced to life imprisonment.

The action of *Rope* takes place in an apartment inhabited by Wyndham Brandon and Charles Granillo, students and lovers. The curtain rises on the pair, kneeling by a chest in which they are placing the body of young Ronald Kentley, whom they have just strangled. With malicious audacity, Brandon and Granillo then throw a party, to which they have invited Ronald's father, his aunt, a former teacher, and several friends. At midnight, after the party, they will drive to Oxford, and that will be the end of the affair. "This is the complete story of the perfect crime," boasts Brandon. However, the proceedings evolve into a confrontation between Brandon and the teacher, Rupert Cadell, with a shaky Granillo gulping drink after drink and inadvertently disclosing the secret buried in the chest. Rupert, horrified, denounces the pair for killing an innocent young man and playing a sadistic jest upon his father, "Both of you! Hang!" he roars, then opens the window, and blows three loud whistles into the pitch-darkness.

Directed by Reginald Denham, a master of stage suspense, in 1929, *Rope* ran for 131 performances at West End's Ambassador Theatre and secured Patrick Hamilton's stature. The play, now called *Rope's End*, arrived in New York's Masque Theatre later that year, enduring 100 showings. Alfred Hitchcock transferred *Rope* to the screen in 1946, with John Dall and Farley Granger as the young criminals who are exposed by their former teacher, portrayed by James Stewart.

Hamilton's next play was *John Brown's Body*, the story of a world-famous scientist, Roger Aschenstein, who assaulted an under-age girl and when confronted, stabs her brother. With pangs of remorse, Aschenstein determines that his only way out is suicide. Directed by Reginald Denham, *John Brown's Body* had only one performance at London's Phoenix Theatre on January 11, 1931. It was savaged by the critics and never staged again.

However, in his next play, *Gas Light*, Hamilton arrived at the peak of his theatrical career. While his profession as a novelist and playwright thrived, he suffered from alcoholism and depression. He died of acute liver disease on September 23, 1962.

Acting Edition:

As *Gas Light*, Constable and Company, London.

As *Angel Street*, Samuel French, Inc.

Angel Street is also included in *Famous Plays of Crime and Detection*, compiled by Van H. Cartmell and Bennett Cerf (Philadelphia: The Blakiston Company, 1946); in *Great Melodramas*, edited by Robert Saffron (New York: The Macmillan Company, 1966); and in *Best Mystery and Suspense Plays of the Modern Theatre*, edited by Stanley Richards (New York: Dodd, Mead and Company, 1971).

Guest in the House (1942)
Hagar Wilde (United States, 1905–1971)
and Dale Eunson (United States, 1904–2002)

Evelyn Heath, a good-looking girl with a heart condition, is invited by her kind relatives, Ann and Douglas Proctor, to stay at their suburban Connecticut home. Their daughter, eight-year-old Lee, nicknames Evelyn "Snow White." Dan, a nephew, has a soft spot for her. None of them is aware that Evelyn is afflicted with a neurotic streak.

At first, Evelyn displays some harmless peculiarities—she chimes for the maid continuously, has a zeal for tidiness, and is scared of birds.

Steadily, Evelyn defiles the aura of a happy household. She ruins the rapport between Douglas, an artist, and Miriam Blake, his model; provokes the termination of the cook and butler; perverts the young daughter into neuroticism; causes strife between husband and wife; and finally, circles word in town that Douglas has sexually molested her.

Evelyn's downfall comes unexpectedly. When Lee enters through the French doors with an empty bird cage and sobs that her bird flew away, Evelyn begins to tremble. Conscious of the girl's deranged fear of birds, Aunt Martha warns that the bird is possibly in the room. Evelyn is petrified. She retreats slowly toward the dining room but stops when Aunt Martha points out that the bird could be there, too. Evelyn runs toward the sanctuary of her room only to halt when Aunt Martha announces that birds can fly anywhere. Evelyn rushes toward the French doors but stops in the doorway as Aunt Martha says, "There are thousands of birds outside." Aunt Martha gestures toward a corner and yells, "Look!" Evelyn utters a chilling scream and plunges through the door.

Ann enters hastily from the dining room. She gazes through the doorway and, shocked, sees Evelyn lying on the lawn, dead.

Ann's eyes come to rest on the empty bird cage. Aunt Martha is looking at it, too. Their eyes meet. Curtain.

* * *

Directed by Reginald Denham with Mary Anderson as Evelyn Heath, *Guest in the House* premiered at New York's Plymouth Theatre on February 24, 1942. Critic Brooks Atkinson found the drama "direfully engrossing" and added jokingly that the play, "crackling with terror and taking high rank as a heebie-jeebie show, has done more to destroy sympathy for invalids than psychoanalysis."[16]

Richard Lockridge called it "a sharply effective play,"[17] but John Anderson asserted that *Guest in the House* "shows laboriously how long it took the Proctors to find out what makes Evelyn scram. It took, I may add, too long."[18] Frank Farrell sneered, "But as the final curtain is rung down, one is positive that four patients really in need of a sanity commission are the producers and playwrights involved."[19]

Guest in the House ran for

The neurotic Evelyn Heath, played by Mary Anderson, attempts to destroy an entire household but is foiled unexpectedly because of her pathological fear of birds, in *Guest in the House*, Plymouth Theatre, New York City, 1942 (photo by George Karger, Getty Images).

153 performances. A touring company ensued, with Nancy Kelly as Evelyn. A 1944 motion picture version, directed by John Brahm, starred Anne Baxter in the role. Two years later, *Guest in the House* was produced in London, adapted and directed by Emlyn Williams.

The play was transferred to television by *Broadway Television Theatre* (1953), with Bonita Granville; by *Kraft Theatre* (1954), with Lenka Peterson; and by *Front Row Center* (1955), with Sally Forrest.

Guest in the House, like *Kind Lady* (1935), *Night Must Fall* (1935), and *Ladies in Retirement* (1940), delivers the message that kindness may backfire.

Acting Edition: Samuel French, Inc.

Hand in Glove (1944)
Charles K. Freeman (English-born American, 1900–1980)
and Gerald Savory (England, 1909–1996)

The curtain of the chiller *Hand in Glove* rises on the abandoned docks of Helsey, a Yorkshire town. Jenny Latham, a good-looking girl in her teens, is chatting with Charles Ramskill, a shipyard worker. As they converse, we learn that they just met at an inn owned by Jenny's father. Dad is rigid, she says, and thinks that she is out with a girlfriend.

Ramskill pulls Jenny into a hug. She slides her hands into his coat pockets, accidentally stabbing her hand with a sharp-edged object. She sees that the young man's demeanor has changed and, concerned, she begins to walk away. He stops her and puts on a pair of white suede gloves as the lights dim,

The following action unfolds in the kitchen of Aunt B.'s boarding house on Armitage Street. A middle-aged woman with an agreeable disposition, Aunt B. looks after her mentally impaired nephew, Hughie Roddis, who constantly strolls about at night. Among her boarders is Charles Ramskill. When Ramskill comes down the stairs for breakfast, Aunt B. hands him the paper. The headlines of the front page tell the story of Jenny Latham, a local girl who was discovered suffocated and mangled upon the rubble of the docks. Ramskill denotes his shock at the barbaric murder the audience knows he carried out.

A police sergeant enters and tells them that Hughie is a suspect. He then divulges that an inspector from Scotland Yard has arrived to join the investigation. Soon another body, that of 17-year-old Gwen Foley, is found strangled and disfigured.

A tense scene takes place when Ramskill enters softly and bolts the front door. He removes two white gloves from his pocket and walks to the staircase, dropping one of the gloves. He is about to fetch it when the London inspector enters through the back door. To Ramskill's dismay, the inspector paces about the room, articulating his theory that the unknown murderer is beset by schizophrenia; he desires girls but is petrified of them, so he kills them. And obviously he is impotent; that explains the omission of rape. During the scene, the glove is the core of attention: will the inspector spot it? He does not and leaves.

Later that day, Lily Willis, a neighbor's attractive daughter, enters and flirts with Ramskill. She hugs and kisses him, but steps back with terror as she sees him retrieve white gloves from his coat pocket and slowly slip them on. Lily understands that he is the murderer and collapses into a chair. "Yes, I done it," says Ramskill, and discloses that he never abused his victims sexually because he doesn't like females that way.

He grabs her. Lily fights back valiantly. The inspector and the sergeant enter in the nick of time and handcuff Ramskill. The sergeant takes him out, with Ramskill ranting. The inspector informs Aunt B. that he thought from the beginning that Hughie was never guilty, but he needed proof. Aunt B. demonstrates her esteem by pouring him tea "with a spot of brandy in it."

* * *

Helmed by notable movie director James Whale,[20] *Hand in Glove* premiered at New York's Playhouse Theatre on December 4, 1944, receiving mixed notices. Favorable appraisals came from Robert Garland: "If you're not too squeamish, too chicken-hearted or too young, you're pretty certain to get a kick out of *Hand in Glove* at the Playhouse,"[21] and Ward Morehouse, who believed the play was "Atmospheric and grimly fascinating."[22]

The skeptics included Howard Barnes, "*Hand in Glove* is ugly without being exciting,"[23] and Burton Roscoe, "The story is rather ghastly … a horror play with no horror in it."[24]

The cast, headed by George Lloyd (Charles Ramskill), Isobel Elsom (Aunt B.), Skelton Knaggs (Hughie Roddis), and Aubrey Mather (Scotland Yard Inspector), got lukewarm reviews as well. *Hand in Glove* lasted for 40 performances.

The Man (1950)
Mel Dinelli (United States, 1912–1991)

The Man begins when Mrs. Gillis, a widow, retains an apparently personable young man, Howard Wilton, as a caretaker for her Victorian home, which is located "in the unfashionable outskirts of a large American city." Wilton turns out to be a dangerous psychopath.

Mrs. Gillis's dog, Sarah, seems to dislike Howard and barks at him continuously. Howard strangles the dog and conceals the body in a closet. Soon Gillis realizes that Howard has locked the doors and ripped the telephone cables. Ruth, Gillis's niece, and Doug, the grocery boy, appear and it looks as if Howard will be revealed, but he manages to dismiss them.

By evening, the unhinged Howard has forgotten the day's happenings. He intends to leave quietly, but Mrs. Gillis clinches her fate when Howard overhears her requesting the telephone repair man to summon the police.

* * *

The Man premiered at the Fulton Theatre on January 19, 1950. The New York critics applauded the performances of Dorothy Gish—"a superb portrayal of sheer terror"—and Don Hanmer—"a bravura characterization"—as the two antagonists. However, the reviewers were split over the virtue of the play itself. "It is unquestionably more adult of Mr. Dinelli to make his murderer pitiful rather than villainous and not to permit the monster's victim to escape," wrote Richard Watts, Jr., "but it requires more skill than the play possesses to make such material moving and important."[25] Brooks Atkinson agreed: "This is obviously more learned than the old-fashioned melodramas. But it has a depressingly clinical attitude toward crime and it stacks the cards against casual enjoyment."[26]

Conversely, Howard Barnes perceived *The Man* as "a superior thriller, loaded with suspense,"[27] and Robert Garland designated it "a hair-raiser of a play."[28]

The Man ran for 92 performances. The thriller opened at London's Her Majesty's Theatre on December 30, 1952, with Joan Miller as Mrs. Gillis and Bernard Braden as Howard Wilton, playing 95 performances. Also in 1952, Mel Dinelli converted *The Man* to the screen, renamed *Beware, My Lovely*, with Ida Lupino playing the benevolent widow who is threatened by an insane handyman, enacted by Robert Ryan. Directed by Harry Horner, *Beware, My Lovely* is tight and thrilling, though the climax has been drastically altered.

Acting Edition: Dramatists Play Service.

The Spiral Staircase (1962)
F. Andrew Leslie (United States, 1927–2015)

F. Andrew Leslie's dramatization of *The Spiral Staircase* is based on a 1946 screenplay by Mel Dinelli, which in turn was based on a 1933 novel, *Some Must Watch*, by Ethel Lina White. All three versions feature an insane murderer who pledged to rid the world of the feeble and deformed.

The time is the early 1900s. The setting is a shadowy manor located in the suburbs of a Massachusetts city. The stage is divided into two rooms: a front salon and the small bedroom of the owner of the house, Mrs. Warren. The action progresses from the late afternoon of a stormy day into the following morning.

Mrs. Oates, the housekeeper, "graying and hearty-looking," unlocks the front door and admits the town's rain-soaked constable, Williams, a middle-aged man, into the house.

The constable relates to Mrs. Oates that there has been a third murder. "This time it was a crippled girl," says Williams. "It's always a girl—one with an imperfection of some kind." Mrs. Oates shares her apprehension for Helen Capel, the live-in attendant of Mrs. Warren. Helen, a young girl of twenty, has been mute ever since she watched her parents perish in a fire—just the sort of disability that may tempt the brutal assassin.

The constable asks Mrs. Oates to gather everyone in the house for emergency instructions. Enter Professor Albert Warren, a tall man with flowing white hair; Mrs. Warren, the professor's mother, a chronic invalid who stays in bed day and night; her nurse, Miss Barker, a capable woman in her late twenties; Stephen Rice, the professor's easy-going assistant; Dr. Parry, easy-going and likeable, who plans to drive to Boston the next day and would like Helen to accompany him and see an expert. He believes that Helen's condition was caused by shock and that advanced mental therapy can rehabilitate her voice.

The constable declares that there is reason to believe the murderer is in the neighborhood. He asks that they keep the house locked tight. If they see anyone suspicious, they should phone him right away.

In Mrs. Warren's bedroom, the old woman asks Helen to fetch a bundle from a desk drawer. Helen looks for the object in question and locates it—a revolver. She declines to give her the weapon, but Mrs. Warren snatches it and slips it under the pillow.

In the middle of the night, Mrs. Warren's face turns pale, and she falls back, her eyes closed. Helen is panic-stricken. She hurries to the salon and picks up the phone. The operator's voice is heard: "Number, please." Helen's lips move, but there's no sound. She hangs up the receiver.

Professor Warren comes out of his study. "What's the matter, Helen?" he asks. Helen turns fearfully at the sound of his voice, then relaxes and scrawls a note on a pad. He reads it, dispatches Helen to get brandy from the kitchen, and removes a pair of gloves from his coat pocket. He puts on the gloves. Helen returns. The Professor indicates a wall mirror: "Look at yourself, Helen ... you're imperfect, and there's no room for imperfection in the world ... it is my sacred duty to dispose of imperfect girls before they bring more of their own kind into the world."

Helen backs away, pursued by Professor Warren, when a shot is fired from across the room. The Professor staggers. There is a second shot, and the Professor collapses. Mrs. Warren stands in the bedroom door, pistol in hand. She mumbles, "I didn't want to believe it for a long time ... but I knew, I knew.... I made myself an invalid years ago, so I could be in the house near him, so I could watch him...."

Mrs. Warren lurches, then falls to the floor. Helen rushes to her and takes Mrs. Warren in her arms. The old woman is dead. There is a thumping on the door, and Dr. Parry's voice is heard, "Helen, are you alright?" Helen goes to the door, her lips quivering, and then she utters, "Yes, oh, yes, I'm all right, I'm all right!" She weeps with relief as the curtain descends.

*   *   *

Beginning in 1931, Ethel Lina White (Wales, 1877–1944) wrote 13 notable detective novels in as many years. "A writer with a Gothic touch," states Mary Groff in *Twentieth-Century Crime and Mystery Writers*, "Ethel Lina White wrote about the defenseless female.... They are wretched creatures trying to exist in gloomy situations, in decaying atmosphere full of unearthly threats, or earthy ones that are even worse, and trying bravely to cope with these real or imaginary terrors. The most horrifying story must surely be *Some Must Watch*."[29]

Along with *Some Must Watch* (which *The Spiral Staircase* is based on), two other books by White were converted into distinguished motion pictures. *The Wheel Spins* (1936) was filmed by Alfred Hitchcock two years later under the title *The Lady Vanishes*, the story of an abducted old woman who is hidden in a coffin aboard a train.[30] 1942's *Midnight House* (aka *Her Heart in Her Throat*), a haunted house tale distributed as *The Unseen* (1945), was scripted by Raymond Chandler and Hagar Wilde and directed by Lewis Allen.

During the 1930s and 1940s, White was celebrated as one of the genre's unequalled crime writers, but today her name draws a blank. However, White has obtained a resuscitation of sorts at the beginning of the 21st century, with a theatrical adaptation of *The Lady Vanishes* that toured England from March to July 2001, and was aired on BBC Radio 4.

*   *   *

Frederick Andrew Leslie dedicated himself to stage adaptations from screenplays and novels written by other hands. Leslie's 1962 *The Spiral Staircase* is perhaps his most notable accomplishment. In the 1980s, the play was presented by Vintage Theatre, under my direction, in various sites across the Finger Lakes area of central New York state. Other dramatizations by Leslie that are founded on films include *The Haunting of Hill*

House (1964), focused on the investigation of an old mansion by a crew of scientists, and *The People Next Door* (1969), the yarn of distressed parents of a drug-addicted daughter who hopelessly attempt to cure her. In 1978, Leslie adapted *The Hound of the Baskervilles*, a rendition loyal to Arthur Conan Doyle's Sherlock Holmes story.

Acting Edition: Dramatists Play Service.

The Collector (1998)
Mark Healy (England)

On December 8, 2005, the *New York Times* featured an obituary of the author John Fowles. Sarah Lyall wrote, "In *The Collector*, Mr. Fowles painted an early portrait of a plausible psychopath who kidnaps a young woman out of what he imagines is love, telling the story from the two characters' opposing points of view until, at the end, the narratives converge with a shocking immediacy."[31]

The 1963 novel became a bestseller. Two years later it was made as a movie, directed by William Wyler, featuring Terence Stamp and Samantha Eggar. Englishman David Parker adapted *The Collector* to the stage and debuted it at the King's Head Theatre Club, Islington, London, England, on February 8, 1971. An expanded rendition, by Mark Healy, opened at the Derby Playhouse, Derby, England, on October 2, 1998.

Frederick Clegg, a butterfly collector, decides to add Miranda Grey, an attractive art student, to his collection. After hitting the jackpot in a lottery, he buys an isolated cottage at a distance from the closest village. He stalks Miranda for a few days, studies her routine, and after a brief struggle, chloroforms her and drives her to his cottage.

Clegg promises to free Miranda in one month if she converses with him frequently and does not attempt to flee. He will provide her with food, books, and art supplies.

The relationship between Clegg and Miranda develops into a cat-and-mouse conflict. At some point, infuriated, she screams, "Bastard! Fucking little shithead! Pissing little son of a bitch!" At another instance she mellows and lets him take pictures of her. When he finds the courage to kiss her, she vigorously refuses him. Cunningly, one night she gasps in the dark, complains of a dreadful pain, and cries for a doctor. Clegg says that he cannot comply.

Gradually, Miranda evolves into a caged animal, throwing objects at him, flinging clothes all over the room, and blaming him of causing her to lose her mind.

The month is coming to a close. On day 27, Miranda dons a dress that Clegg has purchased for her and applies make-up. Clegg offers Miranda a present—a glittering diamond necklace, and says, "Marry me. Please." Miranda asserts that she does not love him. Then, sensing trouble, she kisses him on the lips. Clegg shoves her away and shouts, "Don't touch me!"

Miranda erupts and hurls a drink in his face. Clegg lunges at her. They struggle intensely. Miranda strikes Clegg over the head with a ceramic pan. She is about to deliver a decisive blow but hesitates. Clegg seizes her and knocks her out with chloroform.

In the final scene of the play, Miranda is physically ill. Clegg insists that she get out of bed and takes photographs of her. They'll launch his new collection. In the morning he finds her stretched on the floor. "I don't want to die," she murmurs and stops breathing.

Clegg addresses the audience: it took him three days to dig a hole for the body in a nearby orchard. He considered suicide by consuming sleeping pills, but then it crosses his mind that he picked the wrong girl. However, he has learned his lesson. He's already noted a girl in the next village who will be the perfect companion. Tomorrow he will clean the cellar thoroughly and make sure that it will be in pristine condition.

*   *   *

Directed by Mark Clements, Mark Healy's adaptation of *The Collector* debuted at the Derby Playhouse in 1998. It featured Mark Letheren (Frederick Clegg) and Danielle Tilley (Miranda Grey). Healy offers "Adapter's Notes" in the Acting Edition of the play, noting that designer Steven Armstrong "produced an extraordinary, operatic set with scene changes marked with huge butterflies lit up behind gauze walls."[32]

Healy's dramatization was also presented at the Arcola Theatre in Hackney, London, in 2008, and by the Vivid Theatre at the 2009 Edinburgh International Fringe Festival. In 2010, *The Collector* was shown at the Ruskin Group Theatre of Santa Monica, California; the Masque Theatre of Muizenberg, Cape Town, South Africa; and That Theatre Company of Copenhagen, Denmark.

Acting Edition: Samuel French Ltd.

6

Sherlock Holmes vs. Creatures of Horror

The Serpent

The Speckled Band (1910)
Arthur Conan Doyle (Scotland-born Englishman, 1859–1930)

In 1910, Arthur Conan Doyle found himself in financial straits. "After the withdrawal of my dramatization of *Rodney Stone* from a theatre upon which I held a six months' lease," he wrote in his autobiography, "...I shut myself up and devoted my whole mind to making a sensational Sherlock Holmes drama. I wrote it in a week and called it 'The Speckled Band' after the short story of that name."[1]

"The Adventure of the Speckled Band" was printed in the *Strand* issue of February 1892 and included later that year in *The Adventures of Sherlock Holmes*. Doyle considered it to be his best story, so naturally the author chose it for his redeeming project.

H.A. Saintsbury, who had already played the Great Detective in William Gillette's *Sherlock Holmes* (reportedly 1,400 times), reprised the part, with Claude King as Dr. Watson and Lyn Harding as Dr. Grimesby Rylott (in the original story, Roylott), a retired Anglo-Indian doctor with a yearning for his stepdaughters' holdings.[2]

During rehearsals, Doyle and Harding clashed over the concept of the role, with the author requiring a conventional melodramatic villain and the actor preferring a more nuanced characterization. Playwright J.M. Barrie was asked to attend a rehearsal, at the end of which he turned to Doyle and said, "Let Harding have his own way."

Harry Arthur Saintsbury, England, 1869–1939, a prolific interpreter of Sherlock Holmes (n.d.; Billy Rose Theatre Division, The New York Public Library for the Performing Arts).

"We had several snakes at different times," relates Doyle, "but they were none of them born actors and they were all inclined either to hang down from the hole in the wall like inanimate bell-pulls, or else to turn back through the hole and get even with the stage carpenter who pinched their tails in order to make them more lively. Finally we used artificial snakes, and everyone, including the stage carpenter, agreed that it was more satisfactory."[3]

Doyle's original story starts with the entry of Helen Stoner at 221B Baker Street, asking for help. In the play version, however, Doyle chose to eliminate Helen's lengthy exposition by going back in time and fading the lights on the "large, oak-lined gloomy hall" at her ramshackle mansion in Stoke Moran, on the western boundary of Surrey. Enid (as Helen is called in the play) is lying on a sofa, crying. A coroner's inquest is in progress concerning the sudden death of Enid's sister, Violet (in the story, Julia).

The coroner begins by asking Enid to relate the circumstances of the night of April 14. Enid states that she was awakened shortly after midnight by a scream. She ran into the hallway. As she reached Violet's door, she heard low music, then the key turned in the lock, and Violet rushed out in her nightdress, shrieking with terror. She uttered a few words and then fell. When Violet tried to lift her, she realized that her sister was dead. In an answer to the coroner's question, Enid says that she could hardly understand the final words mentioned by Violet. She thinks they were, "speckled ... band."

Enid asserts with certainty that Violet's bedroom door was locked prior to her exit into the hallway. The window, too, was secured. How could a sealed room be penetrated? The puzzle gets more complicated when Dr. John Watson, a new resident of the village, testifies that Violet's corpse showed no sign of violence or of poison—nothing to indicate the cause of her demise.

The jury's decree—"for unknown causes."

Act II, scene I takes place in Dr. Rylott's office at Stoke Place. It is two years later. Enid is now betrothed to Lieutenant Curtis, who will soon be leaving for duty in the Middle East.

The original story does not mention any of the mansion's servants. In the play, the household help includes Ali, an Indian attendant, who fulfills several unusual duties. He carries in milk and saucer on a tray, unlocks a cupboard, and retrieves a large basket; he then plays a tune on a wooden flute.

The proceedings transfer to Mr. Sherlock Holmes' flat on Baker Street. Dr. Watson, a former roommate, introduces Enid Stoner and informs Holmes of her sister's death two years earlier. Enid, shivering, says that her quarters are currently being renovated, so she now occupies Violet's bedroom. Last night she heard the sound of a flute that her sister feared before she died. Holmes is fascinated and takes the case.

Billy, the page, announces that "a very important gentleman" is at the door. Holmes tells the boy to guide Enid to the back exit. A raging Dr. Rylott barges in: "What do you mean by interfering with my lawful affairs? ... I'm warning you!" Rylott grasps the metal fireplace poker and warps it into a curve. "I was the strongest man in India once," he says. "I am not a safe man to play with, Mr. Holmes."

"Nor am I a safe man to play with, Dr. Rylott," says Holmes quietly, and cautions the visitor that "Lord help him" if he abuses his stepdaughter in any way.[4]

The third act unfolds in the hall of the Stoke Moran mansion. A new butler, Peters, enters with his young daughter, Amelia—Sherlock Holmes and Billy, disguised. Dr.

Rylott sends "Amelia" to the kitchen and tells "Peters," "I give good pay, but I expect good service."

At night, Peters/Holmes enters Enid's bedroom and helps Watson climb in through the window. They inspect the room. There are no hidden passageways. The bed is screwed to the floor. The bell-pull is out of commission. Above it there is a vent covered by a square of fabric. Holmes ponders if there could be an accomplice of Dr. Rylott "who can enter a room with locked doors, who could give a sure death which leaves no trace, who can only be attracted back by music."

They hear the flute. Holmes advises Watson to cover the lantern—"When I cry, 'Now!' turn it full blaze upon the top of the bell-rope." They linger in the dark. Suddenly flute music is heard, and the ventilator flap is pulled aside, revealing a small shaft of light. Holmes calls, "Now!" A snake is seen slithering through the ventilator opening. Holmes strikes at it with his cane. It departs backwards. The music stops. A scream is heard. Holmes throws open the door, exposing Dr. Rylott with the adder wrapped around his throat. "Save me," he sighs. Watson strikes at the serpent as it slithers around the hallway. "The brute is dead," he gasps at last. Holmes points at Rylott's corpse and says, "So is the other." They turn to the stunned Enid, and Holmes assures her that "there is no more danger for you under this roof."

* * *

The Speckled Band opened at London's Adelphi Theatre on June 4, 1910, and was transferred to the Globe on August 8, running 169 performances. The show's playbill listed among the characters the name C. Later in the role of Peters, a mischievous audience misdirection, as the butler was a charade assumed by Holmes, and was, of course, played by H.A. Saintsbury. A dispatch to the *New York Times* asserted, "Lyn Harding, as a half-mad Anglo-Indian villain, held the stage in a fashion evidently delightful to the gallery. Doyle responded to frantic calls with a bow."[5]

O.P. Heggie was cast as Holmes in a 1911 revival. A touring company featured Julian Royce as the consulting sleuth. Reginald Denham, ordained to become the principal stage director of thrillers, staged a road revival of *The Speckled Band* in 1914 with himself as Holmes. Denham duplicated the double

Lyn Harding, Wales, 1867–1952, who played Dr. Grimesby Roylott in *The Speckled Band*, specialized in portraying stage villains (n.d.; Billy Rose Theatre Division, The New York Public Library for the Performing Arts).

assignment during World War I, when serving as a lieutenant with the Tank Corps. The play was presented with a military cast.[6]

The American premiere of *The Speckled Band* took place at the Boston Theatre in Massachusetts, on October 24, 1910—a two-week engagement before heading to New York. The lead actors were Charles Millward (Holmes), Ivo Dawson (Watson), Edwin Stevens (Rylott), and Irene Fenwick (Enid). "C. Later" again was mentioned in the program as butler Peters.

The play came to Manhattan's Garrick Theatre on November 21. Most critics received *The Speckled Band* with chagrin. The *New York Times* perceived the play "tedious with talk,"[7] *The Sun* designated it "a virtually bad play,"[8] and the *Daily Tribune* jeered at "a manner that is childish and bland."[9] Positive comments came from *The Globe*:"The suspense is well built up, growing in intensity throughout,"[10] and the *Brooklyn Eagle*:"Much of the drama is tense and gripping."[11] Edwin Stevens was saluted as Dr. Rylott, while Charles Millward's Holmes collected lukewarm approvals. *The Speckled Band* ran for 32 performances.

The Speckled Band toured the U.S. in 1914, with H. Cooper Cliffe as Holmes. E.J. Davis portrayed the Great Detective at the Frivolity Theatre, Berlin, in 1915, and Edward Stirling wore the deerstalker at the Theatre Albert, Paris, ten years later. The play was revived in England by the Library Theatre, Manchester, 1970, and by the Nottingham Playhouse, 1974. In Canada, *The Speckled Band* performed at the Queen Elizabeth Theatre, Vancouver, 1975, and at the St. Lawrence Centre, Toronto, 1976. It reappeared at the Walnut Street Theatre, Philadelphia, Pennsylvania, in January 1990, the venomous adder rattling audiences for a month.

The Speckled Band was adapted to the screen thrice—a 1912 silent feature (produced by the Anglo-French company Éclair Films, directed by and starring Georges Treville, a Frenchman in an otherwise English cast; a 1923 silent (starring Eille Norwood); and a 1931 talkie (with Raymond Massey as the Great Detective, Athole Stewart as Watson, and Lyn Harding repeating his stage part of Dr. Grimesby Rylott).

* * *

Arthur Conan Doyle was born on May 22, 1859, in Edinburgh, Scotland. He moved to London to work in the medical field, but, enticed by the criminous plots of Émile Gaboriau and the deductive yarns of Edgar Allan Poe, he penned *A Study in Scarlet*, the first Sherlock Holmes novel. Doyle sold the rights of the book for 25 pounds, and the novel

Arthur Conan Doyle, 1859–1930, creator of Sherlock Holmes (n.d.; Print Collection, The New York Public Library for the Performing Arts).

was printed in *Beeton's Christmas Annual* of 1887. "I never at any time received another penny for it," confides Doyle.[12]

Doyle wrote a second Sherlock Holmes novel, *The Sign of Four* (1890), and a series of Holmes short stories for *The Strand Magazine* but always yearned to write historical novels. He devised the death of Holmes in "The Final Problem" (1893), in which the detective and his nemesis, Professor Moriarty, fall to their demise at the Reichenbach Falls. However, public demand compelled Doyle to restore Holmes in the novel *The Hound of the Baskervilles* (1902) and in a chain of stories. Altogether, Doyle wrote 56 tales and four novels (the fourth was *The Valley of Fear*, 1915), centered on Holmes and his chronicler, Dr. John H. Watson.

The Speckled Band (1910) was the only Sherlock Holmes play written exclusively by Doyle. But during the 20th century and up to the present time, many faithful disciples have transferred the Great Detective to the stage.

The Speckled Band, a Marionette show (1937)
Ruth Fenisong (United States, 1904–1978)

A marionette play of *The Speckled Band* by Ruth Fenisong was presented in July 1937 by the Federal Theatre Project, a program established to fund live artistic performances during the Great Depression.

Directed by Remo Bufano, the action of Feinsong's puppet play is split between "the office in the London apartment of Sherlock Holmes" and "a bedroom in Stoke's Manor—rural England." It begins with the arrival of Helen Stoner in 221B Baker Street, pale and shivery.

Helen confides that she is about to get married, at which time she will attain control of her money and will be able to pay the detective for his services. Her mother passed away in a train accident upon the arrival of the family in England from India, bequeathing her and her twin sister, Julia, the sizable amount of 3,000 pounds a year. The sisters live with their stepfather, Dr. Roylott, at Stokes Manor. Poor Julia died two years ago, at Christmas time, after becoming engaged. Helen describes the tragic circumstances that occurred that night at Stokes Manor.

The scene transfers to Julia's bedroom. A low whistle is heard. Julia turns off the lights and goes to bed. She suddenly shrieks, "Helen! Helen! Save me—save me." Helen hurries in as Julia exclaims, "The band—the speckled band." Dr. Roylott enters and announces Julia dead of "heart failure. Too much excitement."

Back in the present, Helen relates that two days ago, her stepfather decided repair her bedroom. She had to move into Julia's room. Last night, as she lay in bed, she heard a low whistle. She was petrified. As soon as it was daylight, she drove to the station—and here she is.

Holmes asks Ernestine, his housekeeper, to guide Helen out. Moments later Dr. Roylott rushes in, looking for Helen. Holmes tells him that he is determined to "discover the causes of Helen's fancied troubles," Dr. Roylott assaults him and ends up lying on the floor. He swears and strides out. Holmes and Watson load their guns and depart for Stoke's Manor. At the Manor, Holmes tells Helen to spend the night in another room.

Holmes and Watson linger in the dark. They hear a whistle. Holmes turns on the lights and strikes the bell-pull with his cane. It causes a snake—a speckled swamp adder—to crawl back through the ventilator flap. A scream is heard and Roylott reels in, dying of snake bite. Holmes jests that the snake demonstrated good judgment; that man was a devil incarnate. Watson adds a quip of his own, pointing out that his friend saved His Majesty the King the expense of a high-priced murder trial.

Four Sherlock Holmes Plays (1964)
Michael Hardwick (England, 1924–1991)
and Mollie Hardwick (England, 1915–2003)

Michael and Mollie Hardwick found their calling in adapting Sherlock Holmes stories for BBC radio and television. Believing that the Holmes and Watson cases also "translate themselves quite naturally into stage form, without mechanical difficulties, with compactness of setting and movement,"[13] the Hardwicks wrote a cycle of one-act plays inspired by their radio scripts—*The Speckled Band*, *Charles Augustus Milverton*, *The Mazarine Stone*, and *The Blue Carbuncle*.

The Speckled Band is partitioned into four short scenes and faithfully follows the happenings of the original story: Helen Stoner, an "attractive lady of 32," arrives at 221B Baker Street soliciting help. Her sister Julia died under puzzling circumstances two years ago, and Helen is worried that she is destined for the same fate. Holmes and Watson take the train to Stoke Moran and lock themselves in Helen's bedroom. Late at night, they are alarmed to see a snake sliding through a ventilation shaft and down a bell-rope. Holmes flogs the snake with his cane, and it withdraws. A shriek is heard from the hallway. Doctor Grimesby Roylott, the sisters' stepfather who desired their fortune, was himself bitten by his device of death.

Mollie and Michael Hardwick, Sherlockiana experts, in 1979 (photo by United News/Popperfoto, Getty Images).

*   *   *

Four Sherlock Holmes Plays was published by John Murray, London, in 1964. Five years later, the Hardwicks published *The Game's Afoot*, a collection of four more one-act plays based on Conan Doyle's stories. In 1973, the Hardwicks came up with *Four More Sherlock Holmes Plays*.

Life-long Sherlockians, Michael and Mollie Hardwick teamed on the reference books *The Sherlock Holmes Companion* (1962), *Sherlock Holmes Investigates* (1963), and *The Man Who Was Sherlock Holmes* (1964). They also penned the studies *World's Greatest Sea Mysteries* (1968) and *Dickens' England* (1970); novelized the movie *The Private Life of Sherlock Holmes* (1970); and collaborated on *The Upstairs Downstairs Omnibus* (1975).

The Adventure of the Speckled Band (1981)
Tim Kelly (United States, 1973–1988)

Tim Kelly dramatized "The Speckled Band" in 1981 for the North Hollywood Recreation Guild Youth Program, remaining faithful to the spine of the plot but inserting several new angles.

Among the characters created by Kelly are the youngster Kipper, who frequently collides with Dr. Roylott, and Morgana, an old Gypsy woman who tries to extort money from the doctor and ends up strangled.

The action unfolds in a decayed mansion at the dawn of the 20th century. Dr. Roylott engages a new gardener, Dirty Ned, a former seaman who wears an eye patch. Dirty Ned is assigned to feed the various animals that inhabit the grounds of the estate. Roylott does not know that Dirty Ned is in fact Sherlock Holmes, whose mission is to keep an eye on the doctor's niece, Helen.

The climax follows Conan Doyle's story—Roylott perishes of the snake's bite and his dastardly plot fails. Now that this case is behind him, the Great Detective is off to face Professor James Moriarty, "the Napoleon of crime."

*   *   *

It is rumored that Tim Kelly wrote well over 200 plays. Concentrating on melodramas, Kelly adapted to the stage works by Charles Dickens, Wilkie Collins, J. Sheridan LeFanu, Edgar Allan Poe, H.G. Wells, and Edgar Wallace, and converted for the theater the characters of Sweeney Todd, the Hunchback of Notre Dame, Frankenstein, Dracula, the Werewolf, and the Zombie—merging macabre components with dry humor.

Kelly's plays have been presented by colleges and rural theaters. He was the winner of several university prizes, and in 1991 defeated more than 300 entries to obtain the award of Elmira College Original Playwriting Contest with his drama *Crimes at the Old Brewery*. The play, portraying the crime ridden Five Points of Manhattan during the 1850s, debuted, under my direction, at the college's Emerson Theatre on March 7, 1991.

Conan Doyle's consulting detective was also the hero of the one-act *The Last of Sherlock Holmes* (1970) and *Beast of the Baskervilles* (1984); the full-length *The Hound of the Baskervilles* (1976) and *Sherlock Holmes* (1977); and the musical *Sherlock Holmes and the Giant Rat of Sumatra* (1987). Named after him, Shirley Holmes is the sleuth of Kelly's *If Sherlock Holmes Were a Woman* (1969). Sherman Homes, a private investigator, opposes a clique of monsters in *Bride of Frankenstein Goes Malibu* (1976). Arthur Conan Doyle himself shows up in the short play *The Adventure of the Clouded Crystal* (1982).

THE HOUND OF THE BASKERVILLES

The Hound of the Baskervilles, Sherlock Holmes' best known case, was serialized in *The Strand Magazine* during August 1901 and April 1902 and published in book form in 1902 by Newnes (London) and McClure, Phillips (New York). The tale unites elements of detection and the supernatural. Much of the action takes place at the bleak Grimpen Mire, where a wrong step may sink a person in misty swamps.

The Hound of the Baskervilles (1978)
F. Andrew Leslie
(United States, 1927–2015)

The 1978 dramatization of *The Hound of the Baskervilles* by F. Andrew Leslie divides the action between two locales: Sherlock Holmes' study at 221B Baker Street in London and Baskerville Hall in Dartmoor, Devonshire.

Dr. James Mortimer, an amiable fellow under 30, arrives in Holmes and Watson's flat and shows them an old document that chronicles the unusual annals of his neighbors, the Baskerville family. In 1742, the rash, uncontrolled Hugo Baskerville kidnapped the daughter of a neighboring farmer. The girl fled. Hugo hurried after her on horseback, followed by a few inebriated friends. On a rocky path, they discovered the corpses of both the maiden and her pursuer. Shocked, they saw an enormous, black dog biting into Sir Hugo's neck.

Dr. Mortimer relates that since that horrifying event, others of the Baskerville line have suffered death "sudden, bloody and mysterious." Sir Charles Baskerville is the most recent. He was found dead in the garden of his Dartmoor estate. There were no marks of physical brutality, says Dr. Mortimer. Sir Charles may have died of a heart attack, but that won't explain prints seen near the body—paw prints of a gigantic hound.

Young Sir Henry Baskerville, the heir, who has just returned from Canada, enters. He confides that a strange letter was delivered to his hotel that morning: "As you value your life or your reason keep away from the moor." He is also curious about two missing boots—one of a new pair he has just bought, the other of an old pair put out for brushing.

The Hound of the Baskervilles cigarette card (n.d.; George Arents Collection, The New York Public Library).

Sir Henry is anxious to return to his ancestral home. Holmes suggests that Dr. Watson escort Sir Henry to Dartmoor as he himself has undertaken a pressing assignment in London. He warns Watson to take his revolver with him.

The domestic staff at Baskerville Hall includes butler John Barrymore and his wife Eliza, a housekeeper. At midnight, Watson notices the Barrymores waving a candle at the window as if relaying a signal. Watson faces them, and they admit to sending a message to Mrs. Barrymore's brother, Selden, the Notting Hill murderer, an escaped convict. Mrs. Barrymore says that the light is a sign for her brother that they have food and clothing for him.

Wearing a coat owned by Sir Henry results in Selden's demise by the jaws of an enormous hound provoked by a scent matching that of an old boot. The beast was secretly trained to kill by the villain of the piece, the neighbor John Stapleton, who has taken advantage of the Baskerville myth. Stapleton splashed phosphorous on the dog's muzzle, giving it an abnormal and supernatural appearance.

Holmes notes a remarkable similarity between Stapleton and a portrait of Sir Hugo Baskerville. "He knew that two lives stood between him and the Baskerville estate," says the Great Detective, "Sir Charles and Sir Henry."

Stapleton dispatches his savage dog after Sir Henry and a rampant scene unrolls off-stage, complete with yells, barks, and revolver shots. The hound is killed, Sir Henry is rescued, and Stapleton flees into the misty swamps, from which he will never return.

Directed by Dr. Harry Farra, *The Hound of the Baskervilles* was first offered by the Frill and Dagger Players, Geneva College, Geneva, New York, on February 16, 1978, and ran for six performances. Jim Miller played Sherlock Holmes.

The Hound of the Baskervilles (1982)
Anthony Hinds (England, 1922–2013)

In 1959, Hammer Film Productions shot a motion picture of *The Hound of the Baskervilles*, starring Peter Cushing (Sherlock Holmes), André Morell (Dr. Watson), and Christopher Lee (Sir Henry Baskerville). Almost a quarter of a century later, one of the movie's producers, Anthony Hinds, wrote a stage adaptation of *The Hound*, placing the proceedings in two venues—Holmes' study in Baker Street and the hallway of Baskerville Hall—and incorporating several innovations. Each scene opens with intimidating chords of music, followed by booming thunder.

When Dr. Mortimer recounts the story of Sir Hugo, who coveted the daughter of a neighbor, a door at the rear of the auditorium opens, and a young girl in peasant costume dashes along the center aisle. She arrives at the stage, but halts at the view of a smirking Sir Hugo. The girl screams and hurries back the way she came. Sir Hugo rushes after her, exits, and the audience hears the clamor of hooves fading away.

In this adaptation, actors often enter and exit through the auditorium. Towards the end, Holmes proves that the culprit is Jack Stapleton, who then snatches Watson's revolver and leaps into the auditorium. Watson begins to follow, and Stapleton fires. Watson is saved by his watch—it is shattered by the bullet. Stapleton escapes through the rear of the theater. The sound of a barking hound echoes, first from a distance, then nearer and nearer. A dreadful shriek is heard, and Stapleton hobbles in and flounders down the aisle, groaning. He reaches the stage, turns around—revealing a red gash at his neck—and falls.

Anthony Hinds' *Hound* was produced by the Steeple Aston Players, Oxfordshire, England, in March 1982. The play was published by New Playwrights' Network in 1991.

*   *   *

Anthony Frank Hinds is the son of William Hinds, founder of Hammer Films, known for quality horror movies. Anthony began working at his father's company in 1946, mainly as writer and producer. Under the pseudonym John Elder, he penned *The Curse of the Werewolf* (1961), *The Phantom of the Opera* (1962), *The Kiss of the Vampire* (1963), *The Evil of Frankenstein* (1964), *Dracula: A Prince of Darkness* (1966), *The Mummy's Shroud* (1967), and *Taste the Blood of Dracula* (1970), in which he inverted Christopher Lee's vampire into a sympathetic character.

As a producer, Hinds worked on many forgettable suspense films before his smash hit *The Quatermass Experiment,* aka *The Creeping Unknown* (1955), based on the BBC-TV serial by Nigel Kneale. The following year, Hinds produced Hammer's first color film, *The Curse of Frankenstein,* selecting a team that would conceive what is now universally considered the golden age of horror filmmaking: screenwriter Jimmy Sangster, director Terence Fisher, cinematographer Jack Asher, production designer Bernard Robinson, composer James Bernard, and actors Peter Cushing and Christopher Lee. Hinds recruited the same artists for *Dracula* (1958) and *The Hound of the Baskervilles* (1959), the first Sherlock Holmes movie to be shot in color. His 1960s horror motion pictures include *The Stranglers of Bombay* (1960), *Paranoiac* (1963), *The Damned* (1963), and *Fanatic* (1965).

More on *The Hound of the Baskervilles*

At the end of the 20th century and the dawn of the twenty-first, some artful dramatizations of the *Hound* were produced in England.

An outdoor show by the Dukes Playhouse, Lancaster, in 1999, written by Simon Corble, used the exterior for an actual "chase" by a large dog pursuing escaped convict Selden, who ends up tumbling from the top of a hill to the rocks below.

Simon Williams dramatized *The Hound* for the Belgrade Theatre, Coventry, and portrayed the part of Sir Henry in a 2002 production that utilized an artificial dog designed by special effects virtuoso Andrew Deubert. It functioned by actors concealed inside a metal shell; camera pictures were forwarded to them so that they could maneuver around the stage. Julian Forsyth and Daniel Hill performed Holmes and Watson during the less-than-a-month run.

A Clive Francis adaptation of *The Hound,* offered by the Nottingham Playhouse and the Salisbury Playhouse in 2004, combined ingredients of fright and humor. Four actors enacted a dozen characters, among them Holmes and Watson, exchanging parts with precision. The production featured projections of misty moors and wild hounds. Critic Jeremy Lewis opined in the *Nottingham Evening Post,* "The complex technology has an integrated rather than bolt-on feel and comes into its own when the terrified Sir Henry Baskerville, lantern in hand, lurches between stalls rows L and M and is caught mid-auditorium by the phosphorescent gleam of the fast-closing hound."[14]

In the U.S., veteran playwright Ken Ludwig concocted a complex adaptation of Conan Doyle's novel, featuring over forty characters played by five actors. In the 2015 premiere at the Arena Stage, Southwest Washington, D.C., the two main roles, Sherlock Holmes and Dr. Watson, were portrayed by Gregory Wooddell and Lucas Hall. Actor Richard Glenn's parts included Daisy, a scullery maid; Scotland Yard Inspector Lestrade; and Sir Henry Baskerville. Ludwig infested suspense with comedy, saying, "You're not making fun of the genre—[but] at the same time, there's a lot of laughs, because they come out of the tension."[15]

The Vampire

The Adventure of the Sussex Vampire (1988)
Peter Buckley (United States)

"The Adventure of the Sussex Vampire" was published in the January 1924 issue of *Strand Magazine* and included in 1927's volume *The Case Book of Sherlock Holmes.* It is the only Conan Doyle story in which the Great Detective seemingly clashes with a mythical demon.[16]

Holmes rejects the concept of the undead: "Rubbish, Watson, rubbish," he exclaims. "What have we to do with walking corpses who can only be held in their grave by stakes driven through their hearts? It's pure lunacy."

The subject comes up when Watson's former schoolmate, Robert Ferguson, arrives at 221B Baker Street with a need for help. His wife, the stepmother of his fifteen-year-old son from a previous marriage and the mother of their one-year-old baby, was seen by the nurse hovering over the infant, evidently biting his neck. "There was a small wound in the neck from which a stream of blood had escaped," the nurse told him, but he brushed it off, because his wife has always been gentle and kind.

While the nurse and he were talking, relates Ferguson, they hear a cry. They hurried to the nursery. He explains, "I saw my wife rise from a kneeling position beside the cot and saw blood upon the child's exposed neck and upon the sheet." The wife's lips were stained with blood. Since that day the wife has confined herself to her room.

In his 1988 stage dramatization of *The Sussex Vampire*, playwright Peter Buckley deletes the 221B setting. Instead, the curtain rises on Ferguson's Sussex mansion, "a somewhat dark and foreboding place."

A woman is leaning over a bassinet, apparently struggling with the baby within. The door opens and a young boy, Jacky, guides in Mrs. Mason, the nurse. "You see?" he yells. "The baby! She's sucking the baby's blood!"

The woman, Mrs. Ferguson, turns. Jacky limps towards her[17]—"Look at her mouth! Blood! It's blood!" Mrs. Ferguson covers her face. Blackout.

In the next scene, Dr. Watson addresses the audience and relates that Robert Ferguson sent a letter asking for help. Watson enters the mansion. Loud knocks on the outer door are heard, and Dolores, a maid, faces a disheveled and gruff man who introduces himself as "a catcher of rats," curses the maid, and threatens Watson. The good doctor is flabbergasted until the Rat Catcher reveals himself as Sherlock Holmes.[18]

Holmes interrogates the members of the household one by one—the anxious Robert Ferguson; the ailing young son, Jacky, who is thrilled to meet the famous detective[19]; the sour nurse, Mrs. Mason; the middle-aged stable hand, Michael Ashton, whose dog has cultivated "some sort of paralysis"; the Peruvian maid, Dolores; and Mrs. Ferguson herself, an attractive, tormented woman.

Mrs. Ferguson augments the suspicion against her when she chases Jacky in the hallway, striking him with her fists, and it takes both Holmes and Watson to contain her. At night, she sneaks into the nursery and is thrust out by the nurse.

The ever-logical Holmes opines, "The idea of a vampire was to me absurd. Such things do not happen in criminal practice in England." When the detective perceives an empty quiver among the scattered weapons, he figures that the dog had been shot by a poisoned arrow, causing his paralysis, as a test for doing the same to the infant. Mrs. Ferguson must have identified the symptoms. When seen parting from the child with blood on her lips, she was actually extracting the poison out of the wound to save the infant's life. Concluding that her husband's son Jacky—envious and furious at the attention given to the baby—is the offender, she found herself in an awkward situation and was compelled, asserts Holmes, "into her wretched silence."

Ferguson kneels by his wife and asks her forgiveness. Holmes says, "a year at sea would be my prescription for Master Jacky," and murmurs to Watson, "This, I fancy, is the time for our exit." The Fergusons hold one other affectionately as the curtain descends.

*   *   *

The Adventure of the Sussex Vampire premiered at the Ferndale Repertory Theatre, Ferndale, California, in 1988. The story was adapted for radio but has seldom been seen on screen or television. *Sherlock Holmes en Caracas* (*Sherlock Holmes in Caracas*), a movie shot in Venezuela in 1992, is a spoof of "The Sussex Vampire." Sherlock Holmes and Dr. Watson voyage to Venezuela at the appeal of an old friend. He fears that his young wife is risking the lives of his children. The resolution changes the original story with Holmes deducing that the wife is, indeed, a vampire.

England's Granada Television aired on January 27, 1993, a color rendering called "The Last Vampyre," featuring Jeremy Brett (Holmes) and Edward Hardwicke (Watson). Adapted by Jeremy Paul and directed by Tim Sullivan, the plot deviates substantially from the Doyle story.

Clash of the Vampires (2006)
Frank J. Morlock (United States, 1941–)

The curtain of *Clash of the Vampires*, by Frank J. Morlock, rises on a misty London street where Sherlock Holmes encounters Count Dracula. The Count tells Holmes that he's looking for Lord Ruthven, who is "a disgrace to our vampire race."[20] Holmes consents to aid the Count, and they embark on a mission to capture Lord Ruthven.

A woman is sighted fatally stabbed in a Whitechapel alley; she clasps a calling card stamped with Count Dracula's name. Holmes believes that the Count is being framed by Ruthven. Holmes's opinion is validated when an elegant young man shows up in the Queen's Palace and introduces himself as Count Dracula. The caller confesses that he is enamored with the Queen and tries to kiss—or bite—her, but she calls for help, and the vampire vanishes.

In a sharp turnabout, Holmes concludes that it is not Lord Ruthven but Count Dracula who is the villain. He slashed the poor girl in Whitechapel and made it seem as if Ruthven attempted to frame him.

The Queen orders Dracula to depart from her domain at once. The Count complies.

Clash of the Vampires was published in 2006 by Black Coat Press, together with a few one-acts featuring Holmes, all by Frank J. Morlock, gathered in a paperback volume titled *The Grand Horizontals*. Among other adversaries, the Great Detective confronts the consummate mobster Professor Moriarty and the French king of the underworld, Fantomas.

Morlock, who retired from the legal profession in 1992 and lives in Mexico, has translated and/or adapted numerous plays from eighteenth- and nineteenth-century French originals, including Alexandre Dumas's *The Three Musketeers*, a translation of Dumas's dramatization of his own adventure tale; *The Count of Monte Cristo*, a translation of Dumas's stage version of his own classic novel; Eugène Sue's sprawling melodrama of the underworld, *The Mysteries of Paris*; and Émile Zola's psychological thriller *Thérèse Raquin*.

The Mummy

Sherlock Holmes and the Curse of the Mummy's Tomb (1994)
Book and Lyrics by Julian Harries (England)
Music by Pat Whymark (England, 1959–)

Sherlock Holmes is less of an armchair detective and more of a global adventurer in the melodrama *Sherlock Holmes and the Curse of the Mummy's Tomb*.

An introductory scene takes place in an ancient Egyptian temple. Lord Edward Brackishmere, a passionate archeologist, and his associate, Dorothy Hyde-Warren, admire the wall paintings. Suddenly Lord Edward clutches his throat and collapses. Dorothy tries to revive him, to no avail. She croons an "Opening Song," dedicated to Sherlock Holmes, whom she intends to see upon her return to England.

When Dorothy is kidnapped and cannot be found, Holmes suggests to Watson that they spend Christmas in Egypt. They are soon sailing through stormy seas. Cheerfully, Holmes relates to Watson that he "slept like a baby" while the poor doctor throws up over the railing. The action shifts to the dark Tomb of Atisu. Holmes is reading the inscriptions on the walls when a partition slides open and reveals a mummy on an altar. The mummy sits up, and arms outstretched, walks slowly up behind Watson and taps him on the shoulder. Watson turns, freezes, and faints. The mummy catches him, lifts him over his shoulder, and carries him off.

The next scene takes place in a temple in the desert. The mummy enters with Watson, covers his head with a sack, and draws a curtain to reveal an altar. There, bound and gagged, is Dorothy. A Priestess walks in with several attendants, followed by a figure wearing the jackal's head of the high priest Anubis. The Priestess tells Watson, "The god Osiris has chosen you to accompany him to the Underworld." She takes an attendant's sword. Holmes reveals himself under the jackal's head and whispers to Watson, "Don't worry, rescue is at hand."

The priestess orders Anubis-Holmes to raise his "mighty blade" and chop off the head of "this chosen one." However, when an attendant lifts the sack from Watson's face, the Priestess gasps. "Atisu! Oh, Great Queen, forgive us!" she says. "What is your will, oh

Fertile One?" Holmes whispers: "Well, Watson, luckily for us you seem to be the living image of the dead Queen."

Watson assumes a regal voice and orders the Priestess to release Dorothy. Holmes unties Dorothy, tears off his mask, and leads Watson and Dorothy away. The Priestess turns to the audience and confides that "all the exits are guarded. There is only one way out. The Labyrinth! No one has ever entered the Labyrinth and come out alive!"

In the maze of the Labyrinth, the Mummy approaches them. They scramble to escape, but Watson is cornered. The Mummy puts his arms round Watson and squeezes. Watson is confused: "He seems … rather affectionate." The Mummy leads Watson in a little dance and sings the "Mummy's Song."

Dorothy gives the Mummy a kiss. Overjoyed, the Mummy presses a panel in the wall, and a way out of the labyrinth is clear. He beckons to them and points. Shaking his hand, Holmes makes his way into the auditorium. Dorothy and Watson follow him. When they reach the back of the house, they turn and wave, "Goodbye!" The Mummy wipes away a tear.

Holmes concludes that in order to solve the case of the stolen artifacts, they should go back to England "as quickly as possible."

Brackishmere Hall has a desolate air. Dust sheets cover the furniture. Holmes announces to Watson, Dorothy, Lord Frederick Brackishmere (son of Lord Edward), and his assistant Marcia that he has solved the murder of the lord's father. The wheelchair-bound Lord Frederick has a coughing fit. Holmes asks Dorothy to cast her mind back to the last words uttered by Lord Edward. "Something about a tunnel," says Dorothy. "No," states Holmes. "No, not tunnel. It was indistinct, was it not? The word was 'funnel.' *Atrax robustus*. The funnel web spider. He was trying to tell you that he had been bitten by one of the most deadly creatures in the world. As the pain grew, he must have realized what had happened and recognized the symptoms."

Holmes walks behind Lord Frederick; describes the funnel web spider as large, brown, with long furry legs; and brings out from his pocket a toy spider. He places it on the lord, and says, "Rather like the one that, at this very moment, is perched on your shoulder."

The lord, terrified, leaps out of the wheelchair with a scream and raises his foot to stamp on the spider. He stops, looks at the toy, picks it up, and stares at Holmes. The detective chuckles, "A remarkable recovery, wouldn't you say, Watson?" Lord Frederick says quietly, "You seem to have all the answers, Mr. Holmes. Yes, I killed him. He was going to disinherit me and have me committed. He said I was mad. Me! Ha, ha, ha! … I had some sickness as a child. I fooled everyone into thinking I was the poor invalid. I discovered people did what I wanted. Out of pity. Fools!"

Holmes and Watson close in on him. Lord Frederick grabs Dorothy. "Stand back," he warns, "or I garrote her. A technique I picked up from the Bedouins in the Sudan." Dorothy elbows him in the stomach and karate-chops him in the neck, knocking him out. Dorothy says, "A technique I picked up from the nuns at Saint Augustine."

The last scene returns to Baker Street. On Christmas Day Holmes and Watson are expecting guests. Mrs. Hudson has prepared a feast. Watson is in high spirits, but Holmes is glum. Enter Marcia and Dorothy. They notice Holmes' dark disposition. Says Watson, "Pay no attention. One of his moods." Marcia gives Holmes a note that was pinned to the street door. He reads: "You have meddled in my affairs once too often. This time you will not stand in my way. Prepare to die. Signed Hee-Haw." Holmes explains that "Hee-Haw" is an alias, one of the many used by his arch-rival Professor Moriarty. Dorothy and Marcia are concerned and Watson sighs, "That this should happen on Christmas Day." But now the life of the party, Holmes says cheerfully, "The best Christmas present I could have wished for."

*   *   *

Produced by the Eastern Angles Theatre Company and directed by Ivan Cutting, *Sherlock Holmes and the Curse of the Mummy's Tomb* was first performed at Sir John Mills Theatre, Ipswich, England, on December 8, 1994. The playwright himself, Julian Harries, played Holmes, while Greg Wagland portrayed Doctor Watson. The rest of the cast consisted of three actors, each playing several characters.

Julian Harries is a British actor and playwright who works mostly in Suffolk, England. He and his associate Patricia Whymark collaborated on a number of plays for the Common Ground Theatre Company, including two other Holmes plays offered at Christmas: *Sherlock Holmes and the Mystery of the Missing Carol* (1990) and *Sherlock Holmes and the Hooded Lance* (2017). The former play sends Dr. Watson to Cambridge to join the preparations for the holiday ceremony to be held at the magnificent Kings College Chapel. But someone seems determined to sabotage it. Sherlock Holmes is summoned.

In *Sherlock Holmes and the Hooded Lance*, Holmes and Dr. Watson encounter a stiff challenge in the form of The Hooded Lance, their newest and deadliest adversary. The Hooded Lance is hell bent on spoiling everyone's Christmas. Can the intrepid duo save the festive season from the clutches of this dastardly demon? The main suspects are the mysterious residents of a lonely Suffolk manor house.

Ten years earlier, in 2007, Harries wrote, staged, and starred (as a werewolf) in *Mystery of the Blood Beast Horror of Wolfbane Manor Mystery*, with Pat Whymark serving as the show's musical director. The comedy-thriller traveled all year, then returned to its Ipswich home, Sir John Mills Theatre, for the Christmas season. Critic Timothy Ramsden welcomed "This year's yowl of the Werewolf, mixed with a frogspawn of witch's curse and a toenail-clipping of exotic travel," but felt, however, that the show needed tightening: "A dramaturgical hand (or claw) might have helpfully pruned some areas (Harries' Werewolf, for example, repeatedly paws the air just to fill time)."[21]

APPENDIX 1

Birth of the Gothics

Englishman Horace Walpole (1717–1797) launched the Gothic genre in book format with *The Castle of Otranto* (1764) and at the theater with *The Mysterious Mother* (1768), setting the action in a dilapidated castle and establishing standard gothic elements as listed by historian Bertrand Evans: "The atmosphere of mystery, the spiral staircase, the grated windows, the secret panel, the trapdoor, the antique tapestries, the haunted chamber, the subterranean passage, the gallery, the vault, the turret, the castle itself, the convent, the cavern, the midnight bell, the ancient scroll, the fluttering candle flame, the clank of chains, the gloomy tyrant, the persecuted maiden, the insipid hero, the emaciated 'unknown' locked in a dark dungeon."[1]

When *The Castle of Otranto* came out, Walpole was concerned about the novel's acceptance and published it under a pen name. The book, however, was acknowledged with elation, and Walpole admitted his authorship in ensuing editions, adding the subtitle "Gothic," a reference to his newly designed country house transformed into a full-blown medieval fortress. *The Castle of Otranto* narrates the story of Manfred, lord of an ancient castle, whose son is crushed to death by a gigantic helmet that falls from the banister of a staircase on the eve of his wedding. Manfred, concerned that his son's death signals the end of his line, resolves to marry the bride, Isabella. She is not happy with the idea, and complications arise, leading to imprisonment and murder. The novel was dramatized under the title *The Count of Navarone* by Robert Jephson in 1781.

The lead character of *The Mysterious Mother* is a nameless countess who lives in a decaying castle, in the South of France. We find out that 16 years ago, her husband died in a hunting mishap and that the countess exiled her son, Edmund, the next morning. Since then, the widowed countess has lived in isolation, and some unexplained dread envelops the castle. Edmund returns and, at the climax of the play, the countess reveals to him that in her grief at the death of her husband, she saw her son in "thy father's image," camouflaged herself, and entered her son's room at night posing as the maid. Edmund didn't notice that he had made love to his mother. Self-reproach and repentance caused her to exile Edmund. To top it all, the girl that Edmund has just married, Adeliza, is the daughter of this tryst; she is both his sister and his wife. Edmund pulls out his sword to kill the countess, but she grabs the weapon and stabs herself. Edmund urges Adeliza to join a convent; he himself will find death in war.

In 1797, M[atthew] G[regory] Lewis (England, 1775–1818) mastered the art of Gothic terror in *The Castle Spectre*. The action of the play unfolds in and around Conway Castle in Wales, "The most melancholy mansion and as to its master, Osmond Conway, he's the very antidote of mirth. He never smiles; and to laugh in his presence would be high treason." There's an ugly rumor that his dark mood emerged when the last owners of the castle, Osmond's older brother, his wife, and infant, were slain by bandits on a riverbank and their bodies thrown into the stream. Actually, it was Osmond who sent his four African henchmen to commit the murders in order to take possession of the family's estate. Much of the action unfolds in underground labyrinths and the castle's subterranean prison, where Osmond locks the earl, Percy, while pursuing Percy's beloved, Angela. Osmond's attempt to take Angela by force is interrupted by the appearance of the specter of a tall female figure whose white and flowing garments are spotted with blood; a large wound is visible upon her bosom. Osmond recognizes the murdered wife of his brother. Angela grabs Osmond's dagger and drives it into him. He falls moaning, and the ghost disappears.

The Captive (1803) by Lewis is a short play about a young woman shackled in the cell of an insane asylum. On a raised platform there are openings leading to various pathways. When the lights come up, a jailer opens the cell door, enters, refills a water jug, and puts a loaf of bread on the ground. The woman rises from her bedstraw. "I am not mad! I am not mad!" she cries out and raves that her husband forged a false accusation. The jailer detaches his hand from her grip and exits. The woman sighs, "My child! My child!" High-pitched screams are heard from above. A psychopath runs down and approaches the woman's cell. He begins to shove the door. She recoils in terror and shouts, "Help! Help!" *The Morning Mirror* said, "The effect of the moment was too strong for the feelings of the audience. The ladies fell into hysterics, the house was thrown into confusion."[2]

Intimidated by her howls, the psychopath hurries away. A jailer appears in the gallery with a lantern, leading the father, his youngest daughter, and two brothers. The jailer unlocks the door of the cell and withdraws. They approach the captive, who gazes at them in terror. They attempt to get her attention, but she cowers from them in fear. They seem helpless until an old maid guides in a child. The boy sees his mother, skips to her, and grabs her hand. She gazes at him with a blank expression, then joyfully cries, "My child!" She falls to her knees and presses him to her heart. Father, sister, and brothers close their eyes and thank the heavens while the curtain slowly falls. Harriett Litchfield was hailed in the challenging role of the captive.

The Irish writer Robert Charles Maturin (1782–1824) followed Horace Walpole and Matthew Gregory Lewis as a major contributor to Gothic drama. His most successful play, *Bertram, or, The Castle of St. Aldobrand* (1816), takes place in Sicily. In keeping with the Gothic tradition, the curtain opens on a rainy evening, with thunder roaring and lightening crashing outside the window of a convent. Monks escape in hysteria to the surrounding cliffs, where they see a shipwreck at shore. In the next scene, they carry in a drenched stranger who survived the raging waters. The action shifts to the nearby Castle of Aldobrand. The mistress, Imogene, is tense and restless, awaiting the return of her husband, Lord Aldobrand, from war. She pours out her heart to a maid, Clotilda, relating the story of an old love to a youth named Bertram, who had to flee for his life because of devices hatched by St. Aldobrand. After dark, in the yard of the castle, Imogene encounters the newcomer from the sea, who is none other than Bertram. At first, she is shocked then falls into his arms. Imogene informs Bertram that she had to marry St. Aldobrand to save her father from ruin and has a young son. He is upset and stalks out, but they meet again for a farewell assignation. The consequence of betraying her husband unhinges Imogene emotionally. In the convent, Bertram confesses to a priest that he's the head of a gang of thieves. A monk enters to report that "The brave St. Aldobrand" has returned home. Bertram rallies his men, and they attack the castle. While the band relieves the place of its costly possessions, Bertram duels the lord. Fatally injured, Aldobrand slumps at Imogene's feet and dies. In the finale of the play, Imogene, now totally deranged, dies in Clotilda's arms, and Bertram stabs himself.

The Grand Guignol

Paris, France, 1897–1962

Le Théâtre du Grand-Guignol was established in 1897 by Oscar Méténier, an assistant to the Police Commissioner of Paris. It offered more than 1000 plays of parody and horror over the next 65 years. Historian Mel Gordon relates, "Audiences came to the Theatre of the Grand Guignol to be frightened, to be shocked…. Here was a theatre genre that was predicated on the stimulation of the rawest and most adolescent of human interactions and desires: incest and patricide; blood lust; sexual anxiety and conflict; morbid fascination with bodily mutilation and death; loathing of authority; fear of insanity; an overall disgust for the human condition and its imperfect institutions."[1]

Among the more acclaimed authors whose stories were adapted and played at the Grand Guignol of Paris were Guy de Maupassant (*Le Retour*, 1902; *Héritiers!*, 1902); Henry-René Lenormand (*La Folie Blanche*, 1905; *La Grande Mort*, 1909); Gaston Leroux, author of *The Phantom of the Opera* (*L'Homme e Qui a Vu le Diable*,1911); Romain Rolland (*L'Anniversaire*, 1916); Englishman Alfred Sutro (*Le Triangle*, 1918); American Wadsworth Camp (*Prowling Death*, 1923); Henri-Georges Clouzot, director of *Diabolique* (*On Prendles Memes*,1941); Irishman Sean O'Casey (*Junon et le Paon*,1950); Englishman James Hadley Chase (*No Orchids for Miss Blandish*, 1950); Belgian Michel de Ghelderode (*La Farce du Tenébrèux*,1952); Georges Feydeau (*Dormez, Je Le Veux*, 1952); Sacha Guitry (*Le Renard et le Grenouille*,1954); and Boileau-Marcejac, the team that wrote *Vertigo* (*Muerte au Ralenti*, 1956).

André de Lorde, the son of a French count, was perhaps the most industrious of the Grand Guignol playwrights, writing more than 100 plays. Mary Elizabeth Homrighous confides that de Lorde led a dual existence: "During business hours he was a librarian … orderly, efficient, impersonal. In his leisure hours he wrote plays packed with primitive emotion and conflict…. In trying to explain his predilection for fear and terror in drama, de Lorde revealed that from infancy he had had an almost insatiable interest in the macabre."[2]

De Lorde collaborated with Henri Bauche on the full-length *The Cabinet of Dr. Caligari* (1925, based on the 1919 film) and the nightmarish one-act plays *The Mystery of the Black House* (1915), *The Castle of Slow Death* (1916), *The Laboratory of Hallucination* (1916), *The Coffin of Flesh* (1924), *The Red Nights of Tchéka* (1926), *The Burning Room* (1928), *The Horrible Passion* (1934), and *Black Magic* (1935).

De Lorde wrote on his own, or with other partners, *The Old Women* (1902), influenced by Maupassant; *The System of Dr. Tarr and Professor Father* (1903) and *The Murders in the Rue Morgue* (1936), both sparked by Poe; and *Jack the Ripper* (1934).

A scene from *Black Magic* by André de Lorde and Henri Bauche, produced by the Grand Guignol Theatre, Paris, France, in 1935 (photo by Roger-Viollet Collection, Getty Images).

Some of de Lorde's plays were filmed in the silent era, including *The Lonely Villa* (1909), directed by D.W. Griffith, and *The System of Dr. Goudron and Professor Plume* (1913), directed by Maurice Tourneur.

De Lorde's *Au Telephone*, written in 1901, was produced in London the following year at Wyndham's Theatre, ongoing for 36 performances. A French company came to London in 1914 with de Lorde's *Attaque Nocturne* (16 performances) and in 1915 with his *The Final Torture* (nine performances). In 1920–1922, a Grand Guignol span at London's Little Theatre marqueed Sybil Thorndike in de Lorde's *The Hand of Death*, *Private Room No. 6*, *The Vigil*, *The Old Women*, and *Fear*.

A prominent impresario, Jose G. Levy, produced in London de Lorde's *Private Room, No. 6* (Comedy Theatre, 1924, 38 performances) and *The Padre* (Lyceum Theatre, 1926, 194 performances). *The Old Women* was resurrected as part of a Grand Guignol repertory with the appearance of Russell Thorndike, Sybil's brother (Duke of York's Theatre, from June 16 to October 1, 1932).

During the 20th century, there were several efforts to found a Grand Guignol theater in the United States. One-act frights were produced on Broadway in 1913 and 1923, and Off-Broadway in 1927, 1958, 1990, and 1994. In 1999, Nowhere, A Company of Actors, mounted de Lorde's *The System of Dr. Goudron and Professor Plume* and *Lesson at La Salpretiers* at The Stella Adler Conservatory in New York City. In 2006, the Queens Players of Long Island City, New York, offered *Return to the Grand Guignol*, promoting it as "a unique evening of horror, suspense and eroticism." The bill consisted of three one-acts, including de Lorde's *At the Telephone*, in which a rural businessman on a trip to Paris hears on the newly invented telephone the dying screams of his wife and child as they are being strangled. Later that year, the Thrill Peddlers, a San Francisco company dedicated to plays of suspense, offered de Lorde's *The Laboratory of Hallucinations*, which ends with a mad patient stabbing his doctor with a pair of scissors.

In 2007, the Los Angeles company Moth rekindled the Grand Guignol practices, calling it *Grand Guignol du Paris*. The program consisted of ghastly puppet plays and chilling one-acts from the French repertoire: *A Crime in a Madhouse* by de Lorde, the story of a mental patient who is threatened by fellow psychopaths, and *The Final Kiss* by Maurice Level, which focuses on a man whose fiancée has scarred him dreadfully by hurling sulfuric acid in his face, and the shocking revenge he commits.[3]

The Cabinet of Dr. Caligari (1925)
André de Lorde (France, 1871–1933),
based on the 1919 film classic

Das Kabinett des Dr. Caligari, a 1919 German silent feature, is regarded a classic in the history of the silver screen. Written by Carl Mayer and Hans Janowitz and directed by Robert Wiene, the script presents a carnival hypnotist, Dr. Caligari (played by Werner Krauss), who sets loose his somnambulist Cesare (Conrad Veidt) on a deadly escapade in a desolate area of northern Germany. The film's expressionist style featured curved windows, jugged doors, and tilted furniture. The prologue and the epilogue unroll in an insane asylum, which suggests that the story is told from the point-of-view of a psychotic.

In 1925, André de Lorde, the prolific writer of Le Théâtre du Grand Guignol in Paris, teamed with Henri Bauche to dramatize *The Cabinet of Dr. Caligari.* "It is in plays dealing with the theme of madness that the Grand Guignol really shows its genius," stated Mary Elizabeth Homrighous in her doctoral thesis. "Simple folly is no longer enough. Now mental illness is combined with murder, linked with mystery, deceptively disguised as normality. An excellent example is *Le Cabinet du Docteur Caligari.*"[4]

The play is divided into seven scenes. The proceedings commence in the garden of a mental hospital. Further away, a fair is being constructed. Two patients, Alain and Francis, flee from the asylum to find Dr. Caligari, who they think can restore their sanity. Cesare does not participate in this adaptation; instead, it is Francis, under the hypnotic control of Dr. Caligari, who grabs his own fiancée, Jane, from her bedroom and hauls her to Caligari's hut. Police officers are confounded when the doctor exhibits a wax effigy of Francis, which they believe is the real man, asleep under hypnosis—proving there's no way Francis could have been Jane's abductor.

The police gone, Francis carries in Jane. When Caligari clasps her, she calls for help and abruptly dies. They bury her in a graveyard, and Francis and Alain go back to the asylum. Francis recognizes the chief medical director as Caligari and is tossed into a barren cell. There he is attacked by an apparition resembling Caligari. Blood drips from his mouth. He collapses and expires.

* * *

The Lorde-Bauche adaptation of *The Cabinet of Dr. Caligari* has not been seen in the U.S., but several other renderings of the horror movie were presented in New York: *The Alchemical Caligari,* a play by Michael Kirby (1981); a "stage version" by Susan Mosakowski, co-producer of the Creation Company (1987); and a burlesque musical with book by Richard Lawton and Douglas Hicton, music and lyrics by Hicton (2001).

Caligari, with libretto, music, and sound by John Moran, was offered by the American Repertory Theatre at the Loeb Drama Center, Cambridge, Massachusetts, in 1997, featuring Alvin Epstein as Dr. Caligari. In this presentation, the plot progresses in the format of a play-within-a-play, as the thespians of the Grand Guignol perform the musical in a rundown theater. In 2005, Chicago's Redmoon Theatre mounted a puppet show of *Caligari,* described by critic Hedy Weiss as "a magnificent piece of theatre, period."[5]

Chapter Notes

Introduction

1. Throughout the ages, the barbaric myth of the House of Atreus has enticed playwrights and composers. On the trail of Aeschylus's *The Oresteia*, Sophocles penned *Electra* in 409 BCE, and the Roman Séneca wrote *Agamemnon* in 60 CE. Also tackling the topic were Frenchmen Jean Racine in the 17th century and Voltaire in the eighteenth. The American Eugene O'Neill hinged his mighty 1931 drama *Mourning Becomes Electra* on the series of deadly events that unfolded at the House of Atreus. Almost a century later, in 2019, the Greek drama was adapted by Ellen McLaughlin with modern politics between the lines. Notable composers who were inspired by *The Oresteia* include Wolfgang Amadeus Mozart and Richard Strauss.

2. Sophocles' *Antigone* was revived often. In the 20th century, Jean Anouilh adapted the play during World War II as a call against the German occupation of France. The Nazi officials were not aware that the title character, by spurning domination, embodied the French resistance. The Anouilh version received its British premiere by the Old Vic Theatre Company in 1949, with Laurence Olivier directing and Vivien Leigh as Antigone.

3. *Oedipus the King* has historically been one of the most admired classic tragedies. Notable twentieth-century revivals of the play include innovative productions by famed directors Max Reinhardt in Berlin, Michel Saint Denis in Paris, and Tyrone Guthrie in Tel Aviv.

4. The ill-starred tale of Jason and Medea became fodder for many playwrights and composers, including the French dramatists Pierre Corneille, 1634, and centuries later, Jean Anouilh, 1946. In 1947 and 1949, Judith Anderson appeared in a rendering by Robinson Jeffers, which was a great success. Anderson won the Tony Award for Best Actress. Other actresses who garnered kudos in the role of Medea include Hanna Rovina, the First Lady of the Israeli stage (1955); Italy's Alida Valli (1959); Greece's Irene Papas (1972); Australian Zoe Caldwell (1982); and Britishers Diana Rigg (1993), Fiona Shaw (2001), and Helen McCrory (2014). In 2014, the Australian writer and director Simon Stone found a contemporary analogue to Medea in Debora Green, an American physician who in 1995 pleaded no contest to poisoning her husband with ricin and killing two of her children in a house fire. Stone took some aspects of her story—she had given up her career to raise her children and most likely suffered from postpartum depression—and grafted them to the original. He rehearsed the play for six weeks and presented it at the Toneelgroep Amsterdam, the largest repertory company in the Netherlands, in an all-white set—spare, clinical, a kind of laboratory for human experience. In 2020, Stone brought his *Medea* to the Brooklyn Academy of Music, starring Rose Byrne in the title role.

5. The Good and Evil angels are holdovers from medieval morality plays, abstract characters battling to influence inner-struggle souls.

6. Marlowe borrowed the idea of the seven deadly sins from the medieval morality plays. A classification of vices, the seven deadly sins are pride, avarice, envy, wrath, gluttony, lust, and sloth.

7. In the 20th century, American productions of *Faust* were staged almost every year from 1931 to 1941. Notable was a 1937 Federal Theatre presentation in New York, directed by Orson Welles, who also starred in the title role. In England, The Royal Shakespeare Company revived the play in 1961, 1968, and 1970, with smoke bombs, writhing devils, and a full range of comedy, including a custard pie routine in the Vatican scene. Adrian Nobel directed a 1981 Manchester production in which, by design, the pranks of Faustus fall flat, and a pair of devils rides around on bicycles. Based on a production by the Oxford University Dramatic Society, *Doctor Faustus* was filmed in 1966 with Richard Burton in the title role and Elizabeth Taylor as Helen of Troy.

8. Recruited assassins and executioners play a significant role in Elizabethan and Jacobean plays. Among the more fascinating henchmen of the era are Lightborn (*Edward II*, c. 1592); Black Will (*Arden of Faversham*, 1592); First and Second Murderers (*The Tragedy of King Richard III*, c. 1593); Aaron (*Titus Andronicus*, c. 1594); Hubert (*King John*, c. 1596); Brand (*The Death of Robert, Earl of Huntington*, 1598); Strozzo (*Antonio's Revenge*, 1600); Zarack and Baltazar (*Lust's Dominion*,

1600); Sir Pierce Exton (*Richard II*, 1601); Medic (*The Gentleman Usher*, c. 1603); First, Second, and Third Murderers (*Macbeth*, 1606); Borachio (*The Atheist's Tragedy*, 1611); Sergeant Ortuño and Captain Flores (*Fuente Ovejuna*, c. 1612); Lodovico (*The White Devil*, c. 1612); Bosola (*The Duchess of Malfi*, c. 1613); De Flores (*The Changeling*, 1622); again, Hubert (*King John and Matilda*, c. 1628); Vasques and his troupe of hired bandits (*'Tis Pity She's a Whore*, c. 1630); Osmin and Zarack (*Abdelazer, or, The Moor's Revenge*, 1676).

9. Richard Burbage, the most prominent thespian of Shakespeare's era, was the first to depict Richard III. Many distinguished actors undertook the call of enacting the mentally perverted king, including David Garrick (1741), Edmund Kean (1814), Edwin Booth (1849), Henry Irving (1877), and Richard Mansfield (1889). Among those who played the diabolic Richard in the 20th century were John Barrymore (1920), Emlyn Williams (1937), Laurence Olivier (1944), Alec Guinness (1953), Christopher Plummer (1962), Al Pacino (1973), and Denzel Washington (1990). And in the 21st century: Kenneth Branagh (2002) and Kevin Spacey (2011). *Richard III* was presented in the summer of 2022 at The Public Theater for Free Shakespeare in the Park, New York City, starring the actress Danai Gurira in the title role.

10. Even though the spurt of blood across the stage in *Titus Andronicus* has shocked scholars, the play was very successful in its day. Its earliest recorded performance, by Sussex's Men, on January 23, 1594, filled the Rose Theatre, and *Andronicus* remained a favorite for more than a decade. In the 20th century, *Titus Andronicus* was presented sporadically on both sides of the Atlantic. First, by London's Old Vic in 1923, featuring Wilfred Walter in the title role, directed by Robert Atkins with Elizabethan theatrical authenticity—a plain black backdrop and a minimum of props; and the following year in New Haven, Connecticut, at Yale University, staged by John M. Berdan and E.M. (Monty) Woolley with a stress on the play's ferocity and carnage. The best-known production of *Titus Andronicus* was directed by Peter Brook for the Royal Shakespeare Company in London in 1955 starring Laurence Olivier. This endeavor muted the violence; murders took place off stage while blood and wounds were symbolized by red ribbons.

11. Richard Burbage created the role of Hamlet for the Lord Chamberlain's Men around 1600. *Hamlet* continues to be staged, starring the Who's Who of world theater. In England: David Garrick (1742), William Charles Macready (1811), Edmund Kean (1814), Henry Irving (1892), Herbert Beerbohm Tree (frequently from 1897 to 1913), John Gielgud (1930, 1936), Leslie Howard (1936), Laurence Olivier (1937), Alec Guinness (1938), Paul Scofield (1948, 1955), Michael Redgrave (1950), Peter O'Toole (1963), Richard Burton (1964), Ian McKellen (1970–1971), Ben Kingsley (1975), Albert Finney (1976), Derek Jacobi (1977), Jonathan Pryce (1980), Kenneth Branagh (1988, 1992), Mark Rylance (1988–1989) , Daniel Day-Lewis (1989), Ralph Fiennes (1994), David Tennant (2009), Jude Law (2009), and again Ian McKellen (2021). In America: Edwin Forrest (1820s), Edwin Booth (1853 through 1881), Otis Skinner (1895), Walter Hampden (1920, 1925), John Barrymore (1922), Maurice Evans (1939), Martin Sheen (1968), Richard Chamberlain (1969), Stacy Keach (1972), Christopher Walken (1982), Kevin Kline (1986), and Keanu Reeves (1995). Among the two dozen women who played the role of Hamlet, the better known are Sarah Siddons, Charlotte Cushman, Sarah Bernhardt, Eva Le Gallienne, Judith Anderson, and Diane Venora. In 1990, Off-Broadway's Ridiculous Theatrical Company offered tween girl version called *Hamlette*. In 2013, the Los Angeles Women's Shakespeare Company presented an all-female *Hamlet*. In 2020, the Ethiopian-Irish actress Ruth Negga portrayed Hamlet for the Gate Theater at St. Ann's Warehouse in Brooklyn, New York.

12. Richard Burbage was the first to portray Othello in 1604. Over the years, many leading players took on the demanding roles of Othello (in blackface) and Iago. David Garrick played both, reportedly more assured as Iago. John Philip Kemble portrayed Othello alongside his sister Sarah Siddons as Desdemona. Englishman Henry Irving alternated the two roles with the American Edwin Booth at the Royal Lyceum Theatre, London (their Desdemona was Irving's customary costar, Ellen Terry). Tragically, during a performance of *Othello* at Covent Garden, London, 1833, Edmund Kean collapsed on stage into the arms of his son Charles, who was playing Iago, and died a few weeks later. The role was given to a young Black American actor, Ira Aldridge, whose performance was well-received and led to a successful career on the London stage. About 100 years later, in 1930, the American actor Paul Robeson played Othello at London's Savoy Theatre supported by Maurice Browne (Iago) and Peggy Ashcroft (Desdemona). Robeson reprised his role in a celebrated 1945 Broadway production, directed by Margaret Webster, the first time in America a Black actor played Othello with an otherwise all-white cast (José Ferrer as Iago, Uta Hagen as Desdemona). In 1951, Orson Welles directed and starred in *Othello* at London's St. James's Theatre. In 1956, Richard Burton and John Neville interchanged the parts of Othello and Iago at the Old Vic. John Gielgud played Othello at Stratford-upon-Avon in 1961. Laurence Olivier tackled the character three years later. His Othello was acclaimed as one of the greatest performances of all time. Other actors of note who enacted the Moor on both sides of the Atlantic include the African American actors Canada Lee, Earle Hyman, William Marshall, James Earl Jones, Paul Winfield, and Keith David. Still, white British actors continued to play Othello in blackface, among them Paul Scofield, Anthony Hopkins, Kenneth Haigh, Ben Kingsley, and Patrick Stewart. In September 2020, the Black actress Jessika D. Williams left Actors' Equity to take the role of Othello at the outdoor American Shakespeare Center

in Virginia's Shenandoah Valley. (Actors' Equity, the labor union representing performers and stage managers, barred its members from in-person performances around the country, citing safety concerns during a coronavirus pandemic.) Williams was surrounded by a non–Equity cast.

13. *Macbeth* first was presented by The King's Men, Shakespeare's company, on August 7, 1606. Richard Burbage, the chief tragic actor of the troupe, probably portrayed the title role. Among the renowned pairs who have played Macbeth and Lady Macbeth in England and the United States were David Garrick and Hannah Pritchard (1747), John Philip Kemble and Sarah Siddons (1778), Charles Kean and Ellen Tree (1850 to 1859), Henry Irving and Ellen Terry (1888), John Kellerd and Helena Modjeska (1900), Herbert Beerbohm Tree and Violet Vanbrugh (1911), E.H. Southern and Julia Marlowe (1909–1910), Walter Hampden and Gilda Varesi (1918), Lyn Harding and Florence Reed (1928), Charles Laughton and Flora Robson (1934), Maurice Evans and Judith Anderson (1941), Donald Wolfit and Patricia Jessel (1945), Michael Redgrave and Flora Robson (1948), Laurence Olivier and Vivien Leigh (1955), Roy Poole and Colleen Dewhurst (1957), John Clements and Margaret Johnston (1966), Ian McKellen and Judi Dench (1976), Albert Finney and Dorothy Tutin (1981), Jonathan Pryce and Sinead Cusack (1986), Christopher Plummer and Glenda Jackson (1988), and Alec Baldwin and Angela Bassett (1998). *Macbeth* productions saw no letup in the 21st century. Kelsey Grammer, of NBC sitcoms *Cheers* and *Frasier*, played Macbeth on Broadway alongside Diane Venora in 2000. Liev Schreiber portrayed the role for the New York Shakespeare Festival in 2006 with Jennifer Ehle as Lady Macbeth. Teller, the silent half of the magic team of famed Penn & Teller, codirected *Macbeth* in Red Bank, New Jersey, in 2008, with Ian Merrill Peakes and Kate Eastwood in a show that incorporated magic tricks, including the vanishing of some characters into thin air. Eastwood reprised her role later in 2008 at the Brooklyn Academy of Music, costarring Patrick Stewart interpreting Macbeth as an aging military man in a 1950s totalitarian dictatorship. In 2013, Kenneth Branagh starred in and codirected a highly praised *Macbeth* at the Manchester International Festival in England, mounted in a deconsecrated church with the audience seated in long pews. Alex Kingston played Lady Macbeth as a ripe beauty going to seed. In 2019, Loft Ensemble of Sherman Oaks, California, presented a version of the Scottish play that featured a female Macbeth (played by Bree Pavey) as a Viking warrior. Her relationship to Lady Macbeth (Jennifer Christina DeRosa) is an arrangement built on a desire to achieve the status and security that go with absolute power. Daniel Craig, known for his James Bond appearances, portrayed Macbeth on Broadway's Lyceum Theatre in 2022, playing opposite Oscar-nominee Ruth Negga.

14. *King Lear* was shown to James I at court in 1606. Notable interpreters of the role include David Garrick (1756), Edmund Kean (1815, 1823, 1826), William Charles Macready (1838), Samuel Phelps (1845, generally considered the finest Lear of his generation), Tommaso Salvini (Italy, 1884), Henry Irving (1892), John Gielgud (1931, 1940, 1950, 1955), Donald Wolfit (1944), Laurence Olivier (1946), Michael Redgrave (1953), Charles Laughton (1959), Paul Scofield (1962), Michael Hordern (1970), Michael Gambon (1982), Brian Cox (1990), John Wood (1990), and Ian Holm (1997). In America, the most celebrated nineteenth-century Lears were Edwin Forrest (1826) and Edwin Booth (1875). In 1892, Jacob Gordin wrote a *Jewish King Lear* in Yiddish, shifting the proceedings from a king's palace to the dwelling of a rabbi. Distinguished Lears who emerged in the 20th century were Fritz Leiber (1930) and Louis Calhern (1940). Orson Welles directed the play in New York in 1956, heading a large cast in the title role. Lears of distinction were enacted by Frank Silvera (1962), Morris Carnovsky (1963, 1965), Lee J. Cobb (1968), James Earl Jones (1973), Hal Holbrook (1990), and F. Murray Abraham (1995).

The first two decades of the 21st century were flooded with productions of *King Lear* in England and America, highlighted by stars Christopher Plummer (2002), Alvin Epstein (2006), Ian McKellen (2007), Stacy Keach (2007), Kevin Kline (2008), Derek Jacobi (2010), Sam Waterston (2011), and, in a busy 2014, Frank Langella, John Lithgow, and Simon Russell Beale. Also in 2014, Lear reversed gender in a production offered in Topanga, California, when Ellen Geer undertook the role of an aging queen who unloads royal responsibilities onto disloyal sons. Glenda Jackson, two-time Oscar winner, returned to the theater at the age of 80 to perform the challenging role of King Lear in a 2016 modern-dress production staged by Deborah Warner.

15. Following the rape and suicide of Lucretia, her husband, Lucius Tarquinius Collatinus, and her uncle, Lucius Junius Brutus, inflamed the citizens of Rome against the reigning family by exhibiting the grisly body of Lucretia to the Roman Council. They then led a revolt that forced Emperor Lucius Tarquinius Superbus out of Rome and changed the monarchy into a Republic.

16. An updated adaptation of *The Witch of Edmonton*, titled *Witch*, by Jen Silverman, directed by Marti Lyons, and starring Maura Tierney, premiered at the Geffen Playhouse, Los Angeles, California, on August 29, 2019.

17. In Sophocles' original *Oedipus the King*, Oedipus gouges his eyeballs with Jocasta's golden brooches. At the end of the play, he does not die, but is led away by attendants to perpetual exile from Thebes.

18. In 1935, Antonin Artaud, creator of the Theatre of Cruelty, adapted, directed, and starred in *Les Cenci* in Paris, France, a surrealistic staging that used highly graphic and disturbing images, especially during the murder scene.

19. Larry Stephens, *The Terrible Fitzball* (Bowling Green, Ohio: Bowling Green University Popular Press, 1993), 109.

20. In twentieth-century adaptations of the story—including a 1973 version by British playwright Christopher G. Bond and a 1979 musical created by Stephen Sondheim—the character of Sweeney Todd is painted with sympathy, a tragic figure bent on revenge instead of greed. Innocent, he was sent to prison by a crooked judge who coveted his wife, and he comes back to London for payback.

21. Mary Elizabeth Braddon, *Lady Audley's Secret* (New York: Barnes & Noble, 2005), ix.

22. *All the Year Round* was a weekly literary periodical, edited by Charles Dickens, that ran from 1859 to 1893.

23. In the original Dickens–Collins story of *No Thoroughfare*, Jules Obenreizer drugs and attacks George Vendale during a violent storm and leaves him for dead in a frozen ravine. Scholars point out that in the stage version, Collins tampered with the characterization of Obenreizer, transforming him from a cold-blooded swindler and murderer into a tragic figure.

24. In earlier versions of *Phaedra*, the ill-starred queen does not die by poison. In Euripides's *Hippolytus*, she was reported to have hanged herself; in Séneca's *Phaedra*, she stabs herself with the sword she had taken earlier from Hippolytus.

25. Quoted by Roe-Merrill Secrist Heffner, Helmut Rehder, and W.F. Twaddell in their Introduction to *Goethe's Faust* (Boston, Massachusetts: D.C. Heath and Company, 1954), 24.

26. In the original novel, *Uncle Tom's Cabin*, Simon Legree is not shot. He remains alone on his plantation, wasting away, drinking himself to death.

27. *An Octoroon* was resuscitated by Soho Rep in New York City on May 4, 2014, directed by Sarah Benson, with original music by César Alvarez, and set design by Mimi Lien. It won an Obie Award for Best New American Play.

28. Following calamitous previews in Newark and Atlantic City and trumpeted as "A Melodrama of the Orient," *The Shanghai Gesture* came to New York's Martin Beck Theatre on January 1, 1926. Mother God Damn was played by Florence Reed, surrounded by a cast of non–Asians. Guthrie McClintic staged the garish events with dazzle, integrating a sizeable cast of unskilled laborers, domestic help, ladies of the night, and their customers. Most reviewers rejected the play as vulgar and offensive. Even so, spectators attended in large numbers for 155 showings. *The Shanghai Gesture* was softened for a London production, but it still did not receive authorization for an opening. The play was given two private showings on May 12 and 13, 1929. The London critics described the play as repellent and unwholesome. Josef von Sternberg adapted and directed a movie version of the play in 1941. The script was sanitized by the Hays Office censors, and many plot changes were made.

Mother God Damn, portrayed by Ona Manson, became Mother Gin Sling, and her bordello was transformed into a gambling casino. Walter Huston played Sir Guy Charteris, and Gene Tierney was his unruly daughter, Poppy, who instead of a drug addict is a gambler in debt. Character actors from different countries—Albert Basserman, Maria Ouspenskaya, Eric Blore, Marcel Dalio, and Mike Mazurki—were among the colorful denizens of the casino. Upon its release, the movie was loudly derided, but over the years it has achieved cult status.

29. A grim drama of avarice, incest, and infanticide, *Desire Under the Elms* is considered one of Eugene O'Neill's major achievements, but when the play opened at New York's Greenwich Village Theatre on November 11, 1924, most critics scornfully dismissed it. However, the public disagreed, and the play's stars—Walter Huston as Ephraim, Charles Ellis as Eben, Mary Morris as Abbie—moved to Broadway for 420 performances. An attempt to produce the show in London was blocked by the Lord High Censor of Plays on moral grounds. Even as late as 1952, *Desire Under the Elms* had to overcome a flurry of censorship obstacles before it was presented in Cambridge, Massachusetts. A milestone revival of *Desire* took place at Off-Broadway's Circle in the Square in 1963, directed by José Quintero and featuring George C. Scott (Ephraim), Rip Torn (Eben), and Colleen Dewhurst (Abbie). It ran for 380 performances. *Desire* was transferred to the screen in the former Soviet Union in 1928, and was filmed in the U.S. in 1958, starring Burl Ives, Anthony Perkins, and Sophia Loren.

30. Ever since its initial 1941 Broadway presentation, *Arsenic and Old Lace* has become a staple of amateur and professional revivals. In May 1942, the comedy was presented at New York's Fulton Theatre by the dramatic club at Gallaudet University, a college for the deaf. It was the first sign language performance in the history of Broadway. In December of 1943, another special offering of *Arsenic and Old Lace* shook the boards of the Fulton, this one by the Professional Children's School. When the show returned to Broadway's 46th Street Theatre in 1986, some critics felt that the toxic elderberry wine had lost its kick. Despite the negative critical reception, however, *Arsenic and Old Lace* proved its potency by running for 221 performances and profiting the play's investors. In 1994, more than half a century after its inception, *Arsenic and Old Lace* scored again when presented in a Hebrew translation by Israel's Habimah National Theatre. No passage of time or language barrier can diminish the luster of this singular macabre comedy. One of the top-12, longest-running plays of all time, its latest incarnation took place in January–February 2020, at the La Mirada Theatre for the Performing Arts, La Mirada, California.

31. Margaret Lane, *Edgar Wallace: The Biography of a Phenomenon* (London: The Book Club, 1939), 323.

32. Benn Wolfe Levy contributed mightily to thrills in the cinema as screenwriter, dialogue doctor, and director. He collaborated with Charles Bennett on the plot of *Blackmail* (1929), directed by Alfred Hitchcock, England's first full-length talking picture. He also teamed with R.C. Sherriff on the movie adaptation of J.B. Priestley's novel *Benighted*, titled *The Old Dark House* (1932), directed by James Whale, featuring Boris Karloff, Charles Laughton, Melvyn Douglas, Raymond Massey, and Gloria Stuart. The film became the trailblazer for sensational adventures about castaway trekkers who obtain sanctuary in dark, isolated chateaux.

33. Quoted on the back cover of Clive Barker's *Coldheart Canyon* (New York: HarperCollins *Publishers,* 2001).

34. Clive Barker launched the popular *Hellraiser* film franchise with an adaptation of his horror novella *The Hellbound Heart,* published in November 1986 by Dark Harvest as the third volume of his *Night Visions* anthology series. The protagonist of the story, Frank Cotton, a hedonist who has devoted his life to the pursuit of sensual experiences, purchases and opens a puzzle box that is said to be a portal to a realm of unfathomable carnal pleasure. It turns out that the realm's inhabitants, the Cenobites, are members of a religious order devoted to extreme sadomasochism. Cotton is sucked into their realm, where he realizes that he will be subjected to an eternity of torture.

35. Conor McPherson's *The Weir* was first produced at the Royal Court Theatre Upstairs in London, England, in 1997. It opened on Broadway at the Walter Kerr in 1999, running 277 performances. The play received lofty reviews and won the 1998 Laurence Olivier Award for Best New Play. It was voted one of the 100 most significant plays of the 20th century in a poll conducted by the Royal National Theatre, London (40th place). *The Guardian* critic, Michael Billington, included *The Weir* in his 2015 book, *The 101 Greatest Plays: From Antiquity to the Present.*

36. *R.U.R.* premiered at the National Theatre, Prague, on January 25, 1921. An immediate success, the play was translated and performed around the world. It reached New York's Garrick Theatre on October 9, 1922, (184 performances) and London's St. Martin's Theatre on April 24, 1923 (127 performances). Lee Strasberg staged a revival of *R.U.R* at the Ethel Barrymore Theatre, New York, on December 3, 1942 (four performances). The word "robot" is derived from the Czech *robota,* which means "heavy labor." Karel Čapek's older brother, Josef, is credited with coining the term that made its way into the world lexicon. Čapek may have borrowed the idea of an artificial man from the old Jewish legend of the Golem of Prague. It is told that during the Middle Ages, the Kabbalistic Rabbi Judah Loew (1512–1609) created out of clay a giant-of-a-man, the Golem, to save his people from pogroms. Čapek also may have been inspired by Mary Shelley's story *Frankenstein*

(1818), Goethe's drama *Faust II* (1832), and H.G. Wells' novel *The Island of Dr. Moreau* (1896).

37. *Hollywood Gothique,* November 9, 2019.

38. Antonin Artaud's avant-garde theories, developed in the 1920s and 1930s, can be found in his 1932 manifesto about the Theatre of Cruelty and in his 1937 book, *The Theatre and Its Double.* In his lifetime, Artaud produced only one play that demonstrated his theories. In 1935, he staged *Les Cenci,* adapted from the drama of the same title by Percy Bysshe Shelley, at the Théâtre des Folies-Wagram in Paris. The production was snubbed by the critics and failed commercially, running for only 17 performances. Artaud's approach influenced many artists, including playwright Jean Genet and directors Jerzy Grotowski, Peter Brook, and Zombie Joe.

Chapter 1

1. Drake Douglas (a pseudonym: legal name, Werner Zimmerman), *Horror!* (New York: The Macmillan Company, 1966), 21.

2. A detailed account of vampire literature in folklore, prose, and poetry, 1687–1913, is provided in *Vampyres: Lord Byron to Count Dracula* by Christopher Frayling (London: Faber and Faber, paperback edition, 1992), 42–62.

3. William Godwin (1756–1836) wrote *Things as They Are, or, The Adventures of Caleb Williams* (1794), the very first novel about detecting a crime.

4. In addition to dramatizing John Polidori's *The Vampyre,* Charles Nodier also adapted for the Parisian stage the plays *Bertram ou le Pirate* (1822), based on the 1816 English thriller by Charles Maturin, *Bertram, or The Castle of St. Alobrand,* and *Le Montre et le Magician* (1826), an English melodrama by H.M. Milner, inspired by Mary Shelley's 1818 novel, *Frankenstein.*

5. The "Vampire-trap," so called because it gave well-timed entrances and exits for the vampire, operated on a mechanically innovative system.

6. *The Times,* London, August 10, 1820.

7. Alexandre Dumas, père, adapted by Frank J. Morlock, *The Return of Lord Ruthven* (Encino, California: Black Coat Press, 2004).

8. Michael Kilgarriff, *The Golden Age of Melodrama* (London: World Publishing, 1974), 62.

9. Reportedly, Horace Walpole, Mary Shelley, and Robert Louis Stevenson also dreamed, respectively, of *The Castle of Otranto, Frankenstein,* and *Dr. Jekyll and Mr. Hyde* before committing their masterpieces to paper. In Stoker's case, it is probably a myth. There is little doubt that he was well aware of the literary vampires who preceded his *Dracula*—Lord Ruthven in John Polidori's *The Vampyre* (1819), Sir Francis in *Varney the Vampyre, or The Feast of Blood* (1847) by James Malcolm Rymer, and the lesbian vampires in Sheridan Le Fanu's *Carmilla* (1872).

10. Stoker's attempts to interest Henry Irving in a full-scale production were rejected by the actor.

Irving also turned down an offer from Arthur Conan Doyle to play the role of Sherlock Holmes.

11. A second stage reading of Stoker's adaptation of *Dracula* took place exactly 100 years later, on May 18, 1997, at the Spaniards Inn, Hampstead, England. It is recorded that the presentation, by nine cast members, lasted six hours.

12. *New York Times*, March 11, 1927.

13. Roxana Stuart, *Stage Blood* (Bowling Green, Ohio: Bowling Green State University, Popular Press, 1994), 197.

14. The speech will also be delivered by Van Helsing—looking directly at the camera—in the fade-out of Universal's 1931 movie version of *Dracula*.

15. *New York Times*, October 6, 1927.

16. *New York Post*, October 6, 1927.

17. *New York Herald Tribune*, October 6, 1927.

18. As one who had the pleasure of directing *Dracula* twice—at Florida State University and Elmira College, New York—I can confirm that after more than nine decades, the vampire play has retained its vigor. At FSU my technical staff created such special effects as the flying of a mechanical bat onto stage from the back of the theater, causing a jolt similar to that of the sliding chandelier in the musical *Phantom of the Opera*; the swinging of an empty chair to indicate the Count's invisible presence; the appearance of *Dracula* out of nowhere, and his disappearing into thin air by means of a trapdoor. A fog machine and the sounds of howling wolves were incorporated for suspenseful aura. Like most modern approaches to *Dracula*, I, too, staged the play with tongue in cheek. Still, there are many dramatic moments: the Count sweeping Lucy in his arms, leaning down to bite her throat as the curtain falls on the second act; Lucy's attempt, in a Mr. Hyde-like daze, to entice Harker into yielding; the surrounding of the vampire by Van Helsing, Seward, and Harker, each holding a cross, ready to eliminate the creature at sunrise; Dracula's agonizing screams as the stake is thrust into his heart—a suitable climax to a thrilling play.

19. There are many other song-and-dance adaptations inspired by Stoker. *Dracula: The Musical* is a melodious show in which Dr. Sam Seward, Professor Hezekiah Van Helsing, and "peculiar patient" Boris Renfield sing and dance energetically as they defeat the king of vampires. In *The Dracula Spectacula*, sanatorium patients, village idiots, quicksand zombies, and the brides of Dracula partake in a whirlwind extravaganza. *Dracula Is Undead and Well and Living in Purfleet* (aka *Dracula or Out for the Count*) has the vampire flanked by an incompetent chorus of blonde Draculettes dressed in black lingerie. *Dracula: A Musical Nightmare* has the songs "The Bat," "Nosferatu," and "Renfield's Lament" presented by a low-grade English touring company in a cabaret-style. *Dracula*, in its 1976 London run, portrays the fly-eating Renfield singing a song while hanging upside down in a straitjacket. In *The Vampire and the Dentist*, Count de Cologne fixes his teeth with designs to bite into dental nurse Evelyn; this does not sit well with vampire Cristina. *I'm Sorry, the Bridge Is Out, You'll Have to Spend the Night* portrays mad scientist Dr. Frankenstein, his monster creation, Igor, his hunchbacked assistant, an ancient, bandaged mummy, Count Dracula, Renfield and a chorus of dancing Draculettes gathered during a stormy night for some madcap shenanigans. In *The Vampires Strike Out*, the Batt family purchases an old house on the edge of town, prove to be bloodsuckers, sing, "I'm an Old Fashioned Vampire at Heart," and are soon hounded by vampire hunters.

Miami Beach Monsters, a musical about the movie monsters of the 1940s and 1950s, including Dracula, Frankenstein, and the Wolfman, was directed and choreographed by Helen Butleroff in 2000 at Off-Broadway's Triad Theatre. *Dracula*—book and lyrics by Don Black and Christopher Hampton, music by Frank Wildhorn—opened on Broadway in 2004. It received mainly negative reviews but hung on for 154 performances. *Dracula: A Chamber Musical* premiered in Halifax, Nova Scotia, in 1997, and two years later became the first Canadian musical to be staged at the Stratford Shakespeare Festival. *Draculu—Entre l'amour et la mort* (*Dracula—Between Love and Death*) ran in Quebec throughout 2006. Also in 2006, *Dragula* premiered, a campy musical about a cross-dressing vampire who is on the prowl in gay London.

Children of the Night depicts a clash between author Bram Stoker and actor Henry Irving backstage at London's Lyceum Theatre, where Stoker desperately tries to interest Irving in playing Count Dracula. The *Los Angeles Times* found it "a curiously bloodless musical…. Despite rich source material, *Children* finally lacks teeth" (*Los Angeles Times*, February 20, 2009).

20. The Acting Edition of the play relays to us, "During the run of the New York City production of *Dracula*, the part of Professor Van Helsing was portrayed by three different actresses. The first was a tall Black woman who was quite heavy. She wore colorful satin gowns, with lots of ostrich feathers and jewels. Actress number two was an English lady in her sixties, barely over five feet tall, and she played the role as if in an Agatha Christie mystery. The third was a young model who displayed beautiful gowns. All three were most successful and convincing in playing the role of Professor Van Helsing" (*Dracula* by Crane Johnson, Dramatists Play Service, 1975, p. 4).

21. *New York Times*, January 17, 1974.

22. *Los Angeles Times*, October 30, 1995.

23. Arthur Conan Doyle, a crony of Stoker's and an admirer of *Dracula*, never involved Sherlock Holmes with the supernatural. "The Adventure of the Sussex Vampire" and *The Hound of the Baskervilles* contain ghostly elements, but the down-to-earth Holmes solves his cases through rational pursuits. Future Sherlockian authors could not resist the temptation and saw to it that the World's Foremost Consulting Detective and the King of Vampires meet face to face. Loren D. Estleman's *Sherlock Holmes vs. Dracula* (1978), Fred

Saberhagen's *The Holmes—Dracula File* (1978), David Stuart Davies's *The Tangled Skein* (1992), and Stephen Seitz's *Sherlock Holmes and the Plague of Dracula* (2006) are centered on a battle of wits between good and evil. A.L. Blake, in his article "Sherlock Holmes and the Vampire Connection" (*Sherlock*, issue 55, 2003, p. 3), reports that *Scarlet in Gaslight*, a comic book novel scripted by Martin Powell and drawn by Seppo Makinen, "featured a plot involving Holmes, Dracula and Moriarty. In a convoluted story, Moriarty secures the services of Dracula to spread a vampire plague in London."

24. *Chelsea Clinton News*, November 17, 1977.

25. In addition to *Dracula*, Tim Kelly dramatized Stoker's 1903 Victorian mystery-horror novel *The Jewel of Seven Stars* under the title *Who Walks in the Dark* (1987). Kelly also adapted to the stage the pioneering creature-of-the-night novels *The Vampyre*, from John Polidori's 1819 classic novella (1988), and *Varney the Vampire* by Thomas Preskett, an 1847 "Penny Dreadful" serial published in 220 segments (1990).

26. The gambit was previously used in the 1943 movie *Son of Dracula*, with Lon Chaney, Jr., as Count Alucard.

27. *New York Post*, December 10, 2002.

28. *New York Times*, December 10, 2002.

29. Anne Rice passed away on December 11, 2021, in New Orleans, Louisiana, at the age of 80 due to complications from a stroke.

30. *New York Post*, February 3, 2006.

31. *Village Voice*, August 21, 1969.

32. *Backstage*, October 9, 1970.

33. *Show Business*, October 10, 1970.

34. *New York Times*, April 18, 1971.

35. *Villager*, November 11, 1976. Years later, on April 21, 1994, a more seasoned Soho Rep Company, "dedicated to new non-naturalistic plays," presented for 20 performances another *Dracula*, by Mac Wellman, that was cited by Mel Gussow in *The Best Plays of 1993–1994* as "an outstanding Off-Off-Broadway production, both literate and bloodthirsty in its view of the liveliness of the undead."

36. *East Side Express*, February 16, 1978.

37. *Backstage*, May 4, 1984.

38. *New York Magazine*, July 22, 1985.

39. *New York Times*, June 6, 2000.

40. *Los Angeles Times*, July 31, 2007.

41. *Plays and Players*, January 1971, p. 48.

42. Quoted in *London Theatre Record*, March 13–26, 1985, p. 271.

43. In various dramatizations, Fritz is physically deformed, has a mental deficiency, and exhibits a sadistic pattern. The most memorable Fritz was enacted by Dwight Frye in the 1931 classic film.

44. London theaters of the era were provided with the means to exhibit volcanic explosions, storms, cruising boats, and galloping horses. The remarkable annihilation of the Creature at the end of the play became an important part of the plot during the following years.

45. Englishman Thomas Potter Cooke (1786–1864), an esteemed stage evildoer, was the first actor to be cast as both the Frankenstein monster and the vampire, Lord Ruthven. Cooke, who played Frankenstein's creation more than 350 times, became the symbol of the monster, not unlike Boris Karloff a century later. Paradoxically, Cooke and Karloff were refined and sophisticated gentlemen off the stage.

46. Jeffrey N. Cox, *Seven Gothic Dramas, 1789–1825* (Athens, Ohio: Ohio University Press, 1992), 386.

47. *Hideous Progenies* by Steven Earl Forry provides the contents and production data of *Frankenstein* adaptations from the 19th century to the 1980s (Philadelphia, Pennsylvania: University of Pennsylvania Press, 1990). *Frankenstein, A Cultural History* by Susan Tyler Hitchcock spotlights the myth of the Monster as recreated in literature, television, and motion pictures (New York: W.W. Norton & Company, 2007).

48. Donald F. Glut, *The Frankenstein Legend* (Metuchen, New Jersey: The Scarecrow Press, 1973), 39.

49. In the London production of *Dracula*, Hamilton Deane played Professor Van Helsing, and Raymond Huntley portrayed the vampire.

50. Donald F. Glut, *The Frankenstein Legend* (Metuchen, New Jersey: The Scarecrow Press, 1973), 44.

51. British-born James Whale (1889–1957) left a lasting impact in Hollywood with his prized horror films *Frankenstein* (1931), *The Old Dark House* (1932), *The Invisible Man* (1933), and *Bride of Frankenstein* (1935). The movie *Gods and Monsters* (1998), featuring Ian McKellen, is a fabricated life-study of Whale.

London-born Boris Karloff (1887–1969), whose real name was William Henry Pratt, became a household name as the Monster in *Frankenstein*. Karloff and Bela Lugosi partnered on some remarkable horror films, including *The Black Cat* (1934), *The Raven* (1935), *Black Friday* (1939), and *The Body Snatcher* (1944). Among Karloff's macabre movies are *The Mummy* (1932), *The Walking Dead* (1935), *The Devil Commands* (1941), *Isle of the Dead* (1945), *The Terror* (1963), *The Comedy of Terrors* (1964), and *Targets* (1967). He was also the target of offbeat shenanigans by Abbott and Costello in *Abbott and Costello Meet the Killer, Boris Karloff* (1949) and *Abbott and Costello Meet Dr. Jekyll and Mr. Hyde* (1953). On Broadway, Karloff played Jonathan Brewster, who turns maniacal when addressed as Boris Karloff, in the comedy *Arsenic and Old Lace* (1941).

52. *Scarlet Street* magazine No. 47, 2002.

53. David Campton, *Frankenstein* (London: J. Garnet Miller,1973), 6.

54. Pierre Biner, *The Living Theatre* (New York: Horizon Press, 1972), 123.

55. *New York Times*, October 3, 1968.

56. Donald F. Glut, *The Frankenstein Legend* (Metuchen, New Jersey: The Scarecrow Press, 1973), 51.

57. Biner, 53.

58. Renfreu Neff, *The Living Theatre: USA* (New York: The Bobbs-Merrill Company, 1970), 66.

59. *Show Business*, November 29, 1979.

60. Victor Gialanella, *Frankenstein* (New York: Dramatists Play Service, 1982), 64.

61. *New York Times*, January 5, 1981.

62. *Women's Wear Daily*, January 6, 1981.

63. Donald F. Glut, *The Frankenstein Legend* (Metuchen, New Jersey: The Scarecrow Press, 1973), 45.

64. *London Theatre Record*, December 11–15, 1984.

65. *New York Times*, November 2, 1986.

66. Otis L. Guernsey, Jr. and Jeffrey Sweet, ed., *The Best Plays of 1989–1990* (New York: Applause, 1990), 473.

67. *Royal Exchange*, Manchester, December 17, 1992.

68. Other stage plays of the 20th century influenced by Mary Shelley's novel include: *Frankenstein, a Melo-Drama*, book, music and lyrics by Gene Wright (1973); *Dr. Frankenstein and Friends*, a one-act play by Val R. Cheatham (1975); *Frankenstein Follies*, a Musical in Two Acts by Peter Walker and Katherine Jean Leslie (1977); *The Mary Shelley Play* by Mary Humphrey Baldridge (1978); *Frankenstein* by John Gardner (1979); *Ms. Frankenstein's Monster*, A Comedy in Three Acts by Albert Green (1979); *Frankenstein: The Monster Play* by Christopher O'Neal (1980); *Frankenstein*, a one-act play by John Mattera and Stephen Barrows (1981); *Frankenstein* by Alden Nowlan and Walter Learning (1981); *Frankenstein in Love, Or the Life of Death* by Clive Barker (1982); *Frankenstein's Centerfold*, a Two-Act Comedy by Eddie Cope (1984); *The Frankenstein Monster Show*, book by John Crocker and Tim Hampton, music by Ken Bolam, lyrics by Les Scott (1984); *The Curse of Frankenstein* by Robert S. Mulligan (1985); *Frankenstein* by Austin Tichenor (1990); *Frankenstein* by Philip Pullman (1990); *Frankenstein, The Modern Prometheus*, music and libretto by Libby Larsen (1990); *The Bride of Frankenstein* by David Yeakle (1992); *Genesis and Other Plays* (includes a monologue, *Frankenstein*) by Don Nigro (1992); Billy St. John's *Spook House*, subtitled *A Creepy Comedy* (1992), the story of ten friendly monsters who are bullied by tax assessor Abraham Van Helsing VI; *Frankenstein: A Dramatic Adaptation* by Arnold Ryan Bigler (1995); *Frankenstein Unbound*, Another Monster Musical by Sheldon Allman and Bob Pickett (1995); *Frankenstein 1930* by Fred Carmichael (1996); and *Frankenstein's Guests*, A Comedy by Martin Downing (1998).

69. http://www.oobr.com/top/volNine/seventeen/Frankenstein.html

70. *New York Post*, February 11, 2002.

71. *New York Times*, October 8, 2002.

72. *New York Times*, December 15, 2004.

73. *New York Times*, July 18, 2006.

74. *New York Post*, July 21, 2006.

75. *New York Times*, November 2, 2007.

76. *New York Times*, January 14, 2008.

77. *New York Times*, February 26, 2011.

78. *Time Out New York*, July 19–August 1, 2012.

79. *New York Times*, December 28, 2017.

80. *New York Times*, January 11, 2019.

81. Brad Steiger, *The Werewolf Book* (Farmington Hills, Michigan: Viable Ink Press, 1999), ix.

82. Ken Hill, *The Curse of the Werewolf* (London: Samuel French, 1978), unpaginated.

83. *The Independent*, February 11, 1994.

84. http//www.indielondon.co.uk/Theatre-Review/the-curse-of-the-werewolf-union-theatre-review

85. Billy St. John, *The Werewolf's Curse: Or Hair Today, Gone Tomorrow* (New York: Samuel French, Inc., 2002), 95.

86. The Maharal is an acronym for *Moreinu ha'ray Rabbi Loew* (our teacher the master Rabbi Loew).

87. The Habimah's *Golem* was directed by Boris I. Vershilov. The leading players were Baruch Tchemerinsky (The Maharal), Aharon Meskin (The Golem) and Hanna Rovina (The Messiah). Meskin and Rovina became prominent Israeli actors, and the Habimah Theatre in Tel Aviv has named its two main auditoriums after them.

88. *New York Times*, March 18, 1982.

89. *New York Times*, April 12, 2002.

90. German film maker Paul Wegener, who wrote, directed and starred in *Der Golem*, also conceived two silent sequels: *Der Golem und die Tanzerin* (*The Golem and the Dancing Girl*), 1917, and *Der Golem: wie er indie Welt* (*The Golem: How He Came into the World*), 1920. French director Julian Duvivier filmed the talkie *Le Golem* in 1936.

91. Drake Douglas, *Horror!* (New York: The Macmillan Company, 1966), 148.

92. Brian J. Frost, *The Essential Guide to Mummy Literature* (Lanham, Maryland: The Scarecrow Press, 2008), xii.

93. Douglas, 159.

94. Agatha Christie's little known and rarely performed three-act play, *Akhnaton* (written in 1937, first published in 1973), is set in ancient Egypt, a dramatic departure for the "Queen of Crime." The title character, who ruled Egypt from 1375 to 1358 BCE, is a young, rebellious pharaoh who undertakes a doomed mission to replace the old religion with one based on freedom and love. Christie, the wife of the distinguished British archaeologist Sir Max E.L. Mallowan, accompanied him on expeditions to the Middle East and used the experience in a number of mystery novels, notably *Death on the Nile* (1937), in which famous sleuth Hercule Poirot embarks on a pleasure cruise, only to get involved in a puzzling murder case, and *Death Comes as the End* (1944), a historical whodunit that unfolds in Ancient Egypt in 2000 BCE.

95. *Observer*, October 23, 2008.

96. Drake Douglas, *Horror!* (New York: The Macmillan Company, 1966), 178.

97. *Ibid*. 182.

98. *Ibid*, 188.

99. Jamie Russell, *Book of the Dead* (London: Titan Books, Revised edition, 2014), 9.

100. Russell, 12, 13, 14.

101. Russell, 14.

102. Burns Mantle, *The Best Plays of 1931–32* (New York: Dodd, Mead, 1932), 476.

103. Kenneth Seymour Webb (1885–1966), author of *Zombie*, became a writer and director of vaudeville sketches in 1910, a scenario writer for Vitagraph films in 1913, and a director for Vitagraph during 1918–1919. From 1919 to 1938, Webb was writer and director for several movie companies. He also wrote simultaneously for the stage and was a radio writer-producer beginning in 1933. Webb's Broadway credits include the hit musical *Gay Divorce* (1932), a team effort by the upcoming greats Cole Porter (music and lyrics), Howard Lindsay (direction), Jo Mielziner (scenic design), Raymond Sovey (costumes), and cast members Fred Astaire, Claire Luce, and Grace Moore. A movie adaptation was made in 1934.

104. Russell, 19.

105. *Variety*, April 11, 1996.

106. *Londonist*, October 27, 2009.

107. *Marcia*, July 20, 2015.

108. *Austin Chronicle*, October 27, 2017.

109. Additional zombie plays include *The Zombie* (1941) by Robert St. Clair, "A Mystery Comedy Drama in Three Acts," in which the action takes place in the sitting room of a mysterious old mansion overlooking the Atlantic Ocean. The zombie, dressed in a shabby, loose-fitting black suit and a black hat, his face made up to resemble a death's head, turns out to be a plant to scare people away. A dastardly gang intends to take possession of metal oil drums that fill the basement, material used to refuel foreign submarines. *The Zombie* (1980) by Tim Kelly unfolds in a cobwebbed manor situated in the Okefenokee Swamp of Northern Florida, where voodoo practices are accepted. A former carnival hypnotist and a crooked sheriff have joined forces to turn illegal immigrants and petty criminals into zombies and lease them out as farm laborers. In *Zombies from the Beyond* (1995), a musical by James Valcq, a flying saucer lands in Milwaukee, a craft piloted by Zombina, a buxom alien aviatrix on the prowl for human males, bent on procuring he-specimens to re-populate her planet (produced at Off-Broadway's Players Theater in October 1995, and at Los Angeles' Lex Theatre in 2014).

10 Ways to Survive the Zombie Apocalypse, a one-act comedy by Don Zolidis, was first mounted by White Knoll High School in Lexington, South Carolina, in 2013. A Production Note states: "A number of times in this play, zombies eat survivors. This should be cartoonish and ridiculous, not scary. Lots of loud eating noises, belches, ketchup. Dragging characters off-stage and eating them loudly in the wings is almost always funny."

Romeo and Juliet and Zombies, "a gory riff on the tragedy by the writer-performer Melody Bates" (*New York Times*, April 8, 2015), played at Off-Broadway's New Ohio Theater in April 2015.

Underneath, a ninety-minute monologue by Pat Kinevane, presented by Off-Broadway's Irish Arts Center in October 2015, starred the author as an undead woman who climbs out of her crypt and confides to the audience a story "about a life shaped and destroyed by deformity, beauty and cruelty" (*New York Times*, October 19, 2015). Off-Broadway's La Mama came up with *Zombie Asian Moms* in November–December 2018, an eighty-minute comedy by Kate Rigg, with music by Slanty Eyed Mama. The show's producers described it as "a multimedia mashup of killer electric violin, punk-ish spoken word, comedy, songs, storytelling, and video installation. And mom zombies." In April 2019, Celebration Theatre of Los Angeles, California, staged *Doctor Nympho vs the Sex Zombies*, a burlesque-style rock musical with book, music, and lyrics by Michael Shaw Fisher. It focuses on a shady pathologist who takes it upon himself to save humanity.

Chapter 2

1. Oxford, England: *Definition of Jack the Ripper* (Oxford University Press). *https://www.lexico.com/defintion/jack_the_ripper*

2. Josh Clark, "The Legacy of Jack the Ripper," *https:/history.howstuffworks.com/historical-figures/jack-the-ripper6.hi*

3. *Brooklyn Daily Eagle*, January 8, 1889.

4. *Galveston Daily News*, January 29, 1890.

5. *Brooklyn Daily Eagle*, October 4, 1891.

6. *The Two Republics*, Mexico, August 12, 1896.

7. *Variety*, April 26, 1999.

8. *New York Times*, January 9, 1917. Both Beryl Mercer (1882–1939) and Lionel Atwill (1885–1946) soon thereafter migrated to the West Coast for lengthy careers in the movies. Mercer established herself in unabashed weepy roles (notably James Cagney's long-suffering mother in 1931's *Public Enemy*), while Atwill found his niche in such horror films as *The Vampire Bat* and *Mystery of the Wax Museum*, both made in 1933 and co-starring Fay Wray of *King Kong* fame, one of the first "scream" queens.

9. Some true-crime writers—including Edmund Pearson, Donald Rumbelow, and Stephen Knight—criticized Leonard Matters' *The Mystery of Jack the Ripper* (1929) for being "almost certainly invented," and "based on unsupported and palpably false statements."

10. Additional plays about Jack the Ripper include *Jack the Ripper: A Musical Play* (1974), Book and Lyrics by Ron Pember and Denis de Marne, Music by Ron Pember; *Bloody Jack* (1981) by Tim Kelly; *Time After Time* (1983) by John Mattera, based on the 1979 book by Karl Alexander; *Jack the Ripper: Monster of Whitechapel* (1986) by Joe Dickinson; *Miller's Court* (2005) by James Jeffrey Paul.

11. The subject of causing the death of a gravely sick person by destroying medicine will appear six years later in Lillian Hellman's *The Little Foxes*.

12. *New York Times*, April 28, 1933.

13. *New York Evening Post*, April 28, 1933.

14. *Daily News*, April 28, 1933.

15. *New York World-Telegram*, April 28, 1933.

16. John Colton's Broadway credits include the steamy drama *Rain* (1922), in collaboration with Clemence Randolph, an adaptation of Somerset Maugham's short story "Miss Thompson," and the revenge melodrama *The Shanghai Gesture* (1926). Among several movies scripted by Colton are the horrific *Werewolf of London* (1935) and *The Invisible Ray* (1936). Carlton Miles (1884–1954) co-authored the tense play *Women in Prison* featuring the actress Dorothy Mackaye. Performed in Los Angeles, California, in 1932, it was based on Mackaye's imprisonment in San Quentin for her participation in a lethal love triangle. Miles penned a few suspense plays that were presented in New York. *Portrait of Gilbert* (1934) is focused on Anne Whitman, who is pressured to evade identifying the suspect for the slaying of her husband. *The Eldest* (1935), teamed with Eugenie Courtright, centers on Aurelia Janeway, who is condemned to life in prison for murdering her husband, gains a new trial, and is mistakenly acquitted.

17. *New York Herald Tribune*, February 10, 1959.

18. *New York Journal-American*, February 10, 1959.

19. *Daily News,* February 10, 1959.

20. Lillian de la Torre (1902–1993) wrote six plays that were produced in Colorado Springs between 1948 and 1966, including *Remember Constance Kent* (1949), focusing on the renowned English criminal who in 1860 cut the throat of her four-year-old half-brother with a razor. De la Torre, a graduate of Columbia and Harvard Universities, published several historical novels that borrowed from milestone factual crimes, including *The Truth About Belle Gunness*, 1955, which deals with a vicious murder case: in 1908, a dozen corpses were unearthed in the grounds of Gunness' estate in La Porte, Indiana. At first, it was thought that Gunness was one of the victims, but doubts were raised after the analysis of teeth and bridgework found in the debris. Had Gunness vanished and continued to live in obscurity?

21. James Reach (1910–1970), a graduate of Texas Christian University, was the prolific author of more than 200 plays written between 1935 and 1970, many of which are mystery melodramas. None were presented on Broadway; the plays have been produced by college clubs and little theaters throughout the country. Reach is best known for creating a young academic Chinese steward named Wing, who quotes from archaic scriptures when solving crime cases. Reach served as director of the literary department of Samuel French, Inc., publishers of acting editions, and was elected president of the Mystery Writers of America in 1968.

22. Lizzie Borden had a lesbian liaison with Nance O'Neill, a famous star of the stage.

23. *Mystery Scene Magazine*, Number 81, 2003.

24. Owen Haskell, a retired teacher and former bookstore owner, wrote the novel *Sherlock Holmes and the Fall River Tragedy* (1997), in which the great detective travels to the scene of the crime and solves the Borden case.

Chapter 3

1. John Ezard, *The Guardian*, October 24, 2000.

2. Reportedly, Mary Shelley and Bram Stoker also dreamed, respectively, of *Frankenstein* and *Dracula* before committing their masterworks to paper.

3. Irving S. Saposnik, *The Anatomy of Dr. Jekyll and Mr. Hyde* (1971), pp. 715–731.

4. Drake Douglas, *Horror!* (New York: The Macmillan Company, 1966), 198.

5. Martin A. Danahay and Alex Chisholm, ed. by *Jekyll and Hyde Dramatized* (Jefferson, North Carolina: McFarland & Company, 2005).

6. *Boston Post*, May 10, 1887.

7. *Boston Globe*, May 10, 1887.

8. In the original novel, Hyde bashes Sir Danvers to death with his walking stick, and then, "with ape-like fury," steps upon him. The broken half of a walking cane, discovered at the scene of the crime, is the clue that will steer the police to Mr. Hyde.

9. Danahay and Chisholm, 82.

10. *Ibid*, 83.

11. *New York Herald*, September 13, 1887.

12. Richard Mansfield is a persona in the celebrated 1988 English TV series *Jack the Ripper*. The series garnered mass audiences in both England and the U.S. The American actor Armand Assante enacted the role of Mansfield, receiving nominations for Best Supporting Actor at the Emmy and Golden Globe Awards.

13. *Daily Telegraph*, October 3, 1888.

14. "Jekyll and Hyde," 14 February 2015. *https://britishtheatre.com/review-jekyll-and-hyde-greenwich-theatre-then-uk-tour-3stars/*

15. *New York Times*, December 8, 1989.

16. Dawn B. Sova, *Edgar Allan Poe, A to Z* (New York: Checkmark Books, 2001), 24.

17. In the original Poe story, Montresor begins the narrative by relating to an unnamed friend the reasons for his hatred of Fortunato.

18. In addition to "The Cask of Amontillado," Edgar Allan Poe utilized the motif of burying a person alive in his stories "The Black Cat," "The Tell-Tale Heart," and "The Fall of the House of Usher." Other adaptations of "The Cask of Amontillado" are included in *Night Chills* (1992) by Billy St. John, one of five macabre Poe tales, and in *A Trio of Poe* (2000) by Paul Caywood, accompanied by "The Masque of the Red Death" and "Lionizing."

19. In the original Poe story, the unnamed narrator states that Roderick Usher and his sister Madeline are the last of the Usher bloodline.

20. The original tale ends with the narrator fleeing for his life, as the house splits in two and the fragments sink into an adjacent lake. L. Sprague de

Camp, the noted science fiction writer, theorizes in his *Lovecraft: A Biography* (Doubleday, 1975) that "Roderick Usher, his sister Madeline, and the house all shared one common soul." The theme of the crumbling, haunted mansion is a key feature of Horace Walpole's pioneering Gothic novel *Castle of Otranto* (1764) and may have been a source of inspiration to Poe.

21. G. R. Thomson, *Great Short Works of Edgar Allan Poe* (New York: HarperCollins, 1970), 36.

22. Thomas Woodson, ed., *Twentieth Century Interpretations of The Fall of the House of Usher* (Englewood Cliffs, New Jersey: Prentice-Hall, 1969), 99.

23. None of the characters appearing in this adaptation are in Poe's "The Tell-Tale Heart." The personae in the original tale are a nameless narrator, his victim, and three police officers. The motive for the murder is not greed but the killer's mad revulsion toward the old man's Evil Eye—"rid myself of the eye forever."

24. In the original story, the unnamed murderer suffocates the old man by placing a heavy bed over him. He then dismembers the corpse, cutting off head and legs, removes several planks from the floor of the chamber, deposits all underneath, then replaces the boards. It seemed like a fool-proof murder until the "louder-louder-louder" heartbeats instigate a confession.

25. Even though C. Auguste Dupin is considered the first fictional detective, historically he was preceded by Mlle. de Scuderi, the title character of E.T.A. Hoffman's *Das Fräulein von Scuderi* (1819), who establishes the innocence of a prime suspect in the murder of a jeweler. Another forerunner is Voltaire's *Zadig* (1748), with the main character performing feats of analysis, as is Honoré de Balzac's *Vautrin* (1840), who outwits the police in a number of instances. Poe himself was influenced by the real-life exploits of Eugene François Vidocq (1775–1857), who established the very first detective agency in Paris and in 1828 published four volumes of lively memoirs.

26. The "impossible" situation in a crime scene was invented by the father of the detective story, Edgar Allan Poe, in "The Murders in the Rue Morgue," 1841 (throttled bodies found in the chimney of a locked room). The technique was subsequently utilized by Israel Zangwill in *The Big Bow Mystery*, 1892 (a victim with a cut throat is discovered in a shuttered bedroom), and by Arthur Conan Doyle in "The Story of the Lost Special," 1898 (the disappearance of a train from a railroad line guarded at both ends). Among the better known, and fiendishly ingenious, practitioners of the hermetically sealed puzzles were English authors Edgar Wallace, Margery Allingham, E.C. Bentley, Anthony Berkeley, G.K. Chesterton, and Agatha Christie. American writers who concocted impossible predicaments include Melville Davisson Post, Ellery Queen, S.S. Van Dine, and John Dickson Carr/ Carter Dickson.

On stage, locked-room murders were depicted in *The Mystery of the Yellow Room* (1912), dramatized by Gaston Leroux from his 1907 novel of the same title; *In the Next Room* (1923), dramatized by Eleanor Robson and Harriet Ford from Burton E. Stevenson's 1912 novel, *The Mystery of the Boule Cabinet*; *The Canary Murder Case* (1928), adapted by Walton Butterfield and Lee Morrison from S.S. Van Dine's 1927 novel of the same name; *Alibi*, aka *The Fatal Alibi* (1932) by Michael Morton, based on Agatha Christie's 1926 novel, *The Murder of Roger Ackroyd*; *The Locked Room* (1933) by Herbert Ashton, Jr.; and *Busman's Honeymoon* (1936) by Dorothy L. Sayers and Muriel St. Clare Byrne.

27. In the original Poe story, Dupin is not an officer of the police department.

28. In the summer of 2009, a Boston antiquarian, Peter L. Stern, advertised a scarce first edition of *The Picture of Dorian Gray*, in dust jacket and a custom quarter-morocco slipcase, for $100,000.

29. John Osborne, *The Picture of Dorian Gray* (London: Faber and Faber, 1973), 12, 13.

30. *Ibid,* 14.

31. *Sunday Telegraph*, February 16, 1975.

32. *New Statesman*, September 24, 1976.

33. *New York Times*, August 18, 1956.

34. *New York Times*, August 29, 1963.

35. *Plays and Players*, September 1968.

36. *New York Times*, March 23, 2001.

37. *Los Angeles Times*, August 31, 2019.

38. Jack Sharkey and Dave Reiser, *The Picture of Dorian Gray* (New York: Samuel French, Inc., 1982), 9.

39. The playwrights propose that "The Monster" be played by a different actor, in either freakish makeup or a ghastly rubber mask, who switches places with Dorian when he conceals himself behind the curtain.

40. The Red Barn murder inspired plays, ballads, studies, and newspaper articles throughout the nineteenth and twentieth centuries.

41. Other plays that describe the trespass of a private residency by a threatening individual include *Blind Alley* (1935), *Kind Lady* (1935), *Night Must Fall* (1935), *Ladies in Retirement* (1940), *Arsenic and Old Lace* (1941), *Guest in the House* (1942), *The Man* (1950), and *The Desperate Hours* (1955).

42. Oscar Wilde, *Salomé and The Florentine Tragedy*, Preface by Robert Ross (London: Methuen & Company, 1908), xvii, xviii.

43. *New York Times*, July 30, 2007.

44. The Acting Edition of *The Invisible Man*, published by Samuel French LTD, outlines the effects of the illusions but does not specify the ways of achieving them as some of the gimmicks involved are closely guarded by The Magic Circle, a British organization dedicated to promoting the art of magic.

45. *Financial Times*, October 29, 1991.

46. *Time Out*, London, October 30, 1991.

47. A Production Note states: "The Time Machine is essentially constructed from a wheelchair. The actual design is left up to the resources of the individual production. But the more 'fanciful'

the better: lights, dials, levers, etc. Remember, it must be capable of being wheeled in and out."

48. Agatha Christie, *An Autobiography* (London: Collins, 1977), 471–472.

49. As well as *And Then There Were None*, nursery rhymes influenced Agatha Christie in concocting the novels *One, Two, Buckle My Shoe* (1940), *Five Little Pigs* (1943), *A Pocketful of Rye* (1953), *Hickory, Dickory, Dock* (1955), and the short story, "Three Blind Mice" (1950), which she adapted as her play *The Mousetrap* (1952).

50. Patricia D. Maida and Nicholas B. Spornick, *Murder She Wrote* (Bowling Green, Ohio: Bowling Green State University Popular Press, 1982), 81.

51. Ira Levin, Introduction to *The Mousetrap and Other Plays* by Agatha Christie (New York: Dodd, Mead and Company, 1978), viii.

52. "Stephen King, The Art of Fiction No. 189," *The Paris Review*, Fall 2006.

53. *Music OMH*, October 1, 2005.

54. *Variety*, November 15, 2015.

55. *New York Post*, November 15, 2015.

56. A 1999 book written by Ken Mandelbaum, which chronicles the history of flopped Broadway musicals, is titled *Not Since Carrie*.

57. *New York Times*, December 12, 2006.

58. "*Hell in a Handbag's Scarrie site.*" handbagproductions.org. Archived from the original on 2006-02-09. Retrieved 2008-02-27.

Chapter 4

1. Sal Piro and Michael Hess, *The Official Rocky Horror Picture Show: Audience Participation Guide* (San Bernardino, California: Binary Publications, 2012, updated reprint, 2015), 5.

2. *Daily News*, March 2, 1979.

3. *New York Post*, March 2, 1979.

4. *Women's Wear Daily*, March 2, 1979.

5. *WABC-TV7*, March 1, 1979.

6. *https://www.stageandcinema.com/2019/01/27/sweeney-todd-scr/*

7. Earlier motion pictures about the demon barber of Fleet Street were made in 1926 (a UK short directed by British pioneer George Dewhurst, with G.A. Baugham in the main role); 1928 (a UK silent feature, directed by Walter West, featuring Moore Marriott); 1936 (a UK talkie, directed by George King, starring Tod Slaughter); and 1970 (titled *Bloodthirsty Butchers*, with John Miranda).

8. *New York Times*, July 2, 2015.

9. *The Guardian*, February 24, 2016.

10. *Los Angeles Times*, September 28, 2019.

11. *New York Times*, October 18, 2019.

12. *New York Times*, October 15, 2020.

13. *Daily Mail*, October 10, 1986.

14. *Sunday Express*, October 12, 1986.

15. *Tribune*, October 24, 1986.

16. *City Limits*, October 16, 1986.

17. *New York Post*, December 22, 2004.

18. *Los Angeles Times*, April 9, 2018.

19. Paul Vitaris, "The Unsinkable Maury Yeston," *The Musical Theatre Magazine*, Spring, 1997, 17–23.

20. *Houston Chronicle*, January 29, 1995.

21. *New York Times*, April 29, 1997.

22. *New York Post*, April 29, 1997.

23. Necronomicon is a fictional text of magic appearing in stories by the horror writer H.P. Lovecraft and his disciples.

24. In 1932, during the movie's shooting and ahead of its distribution, a novelization of *King Kong* was published by Grosset & Dunlap. It was written by Delos W. Lovelace, who based the novel on an idea conceived by Edgar Wallace, the popular English writer.

25. A highly regarded 1949 film, *Mighty Joe Young*, tells the story of a twelve-foot African gorilla that is captured and taken to Hollywood, California, for a money-making exhibition. Produced by the same creative team responsible for *King Kong*, this movie is often mistaken as a sequel. (*Mighty Joe Young* was remade in 1998, directed by Ron Underwood.)

26. *Los Angeles Times*, November 9, 2018.

27. *New York Times*, November 9, 2018.

Chapter 5

1. Emlyn Williams, Introduction, *The Collected Plays*, Volume One (New York: Random House, 1961), xvi.

2. *New York Times*, July 7, 1935.

3. *New York Sun*, September 29, 1936.

4. *New York Herald Tribune*, September 29, 1936.

5. *New York Evening Post*, September 29, 1936.

6. *New York Evening Journal*, September 29, 1936.

7. *New York Post*, March 9, 1999.

8. *Plays and Players*, February 1987.

9. Quoted in Peter Haining's *Agatha Christie—Murder in Four Acts* (London: Virgin Books, 1990), 26.

10. *Ibid.*

11. *New York Times*, April 26, 1936.

12. *New York Times*, September 30, 1936.

13. *London Times*, December 6, 1938.

14. *New York Journal-American*, December 6, 1941.

15. *New York Herald Tribune*, December 6, 1941.

16. *New York Times*, February 25, 1942.

17. *New York Sun*, February 25, 1942.

18. *New York Journal-American*, February 25, 1942.

19. *New York World-Telegram*, February 25, 1942.

20. James Whale (1889–1957) directed the horror classics *Frankenstein* (1931), *The Old Dark House* (1932), *The Invisible Man* (1933), and *The Bride of Frankenstein* (1935).

21. *New York Journal-American*, December 5, 1944.

22. *New York Sun*, December 5, 1944.

23. *New York Herald Tribune*, December 5, 1944.

24. *New York World-Telegram*, December 5, 1944.

25. *New York Post*, January 20, 1950.

26. *New York Times*, January 20, 1950.

27. *New York Herald Tribune*, January 20, 1950.

28. *New York Journal-American*, January 20, 1950.

29. John M. Reilly, ed., *Twentieth-Century Crime and Mystery Writers* (New York: St. Martin's Press, 1980), 1473.

30. George Axelrod scripted and Anthony Page directed a pale remake of *The Lady Vanishes* in 1979.

31. *New York Times*, November 8, 2005.

32. Mark Healy, *The Collector* (London: Samuel French Ltd, 2006), unpaginated.

Chapter 6

1. Arthur Conan Doyle, *Memories and Adventures*, Second Edition (London: John Murray, 1930), 120.

2. Englishman H.A. Saintsbury (1869–1939) was a prominent actor and director from the 1890s to the 1930s. Following *The Speckled Band*, he reprised the role of Sherlock Holmes in the British silent motion picture *The Valley of Fear* (1916) and in the stage parody *You Know My Methods, Watson*, written by Malcolm Logan, which had its single performance on December 4, 1932, at the Shaftesbury Theatre, London.

3. Doyle, 121.

4. In the original story, Holmes takes the bent poker and, "with a sudden effort, straightens it out again." Doyle omitted this demonstration of strength, because, as biographer Daniel Stashower states, "no sufficient pliable prop could be obtained," (*Teller of Tales*, Henry Holt and Company, New York, 1999, p. 271). However, Holmes' robust reaction had been used in later stage and film adaptations of "The Speckled Band."

5. *New York Times*, June 5, 1910.

6. Reginald Denham came back to the Great Detective in 1953 when directing a Broadway production of *Sherlock Holmes*, by Ouida Rathbone, starring her husband Basil in the title role. The production was greeted with mixed reviews, and its run was short.

7. *New York Times*, November 22, 1910.

8. *New York Sun*, November 22, 1910.

9. *New York Daily Tribune*, November 22, 1910.

10. *The Globe*, November 22, 1910.

11. *Brooklyn Eagle*, November 23, 1910.

12. Doyle, 91.

13. Michael and Mollie Hardwick, *Four Sherlock Holmes Plays* (London: John Murray, 1964), Foreword.

14. *Nottingham Evening Post*, September 9, 2004.

15. *The Washington Post*, January 18, 2015.

16. A few disciples of Conan Doyle united the Great Detective and the King of Vampires in satirical novels: Fred Saberhagen, *The Holmes-Dracula File* (1975); Loren D. Estleman, *Sherlock Holmes vs. Dracula* (1978); T.A. Waters, *The Probability Pad* (1993); Roger Zelazny, *A Night in the Lonesome October* (1993).

17. In the original story, young Jack walks with "a curious shambling gait, suffering from a weak spine." The play made Jack a cripple who walks with the aid of a metal tipped walking stick and drags his right foot.

18. Holmes' disguise is not part of the Doyle yarn and provides no logical motive—except for an entrance of grandiosity.

19. In the original tale, notices Watson, "the youth looked at us with a very penetrating and, it seemed to me, unfriendly gaze."

20. Lord Ruthven was originated by John William Polidori, a physician for Lord Byron, in the novella *The Vampyre*, published in the April 1819 issue of *New Monthly Magazine*.

21. *Reviews Gate*, December 7, 2007

Appendix 1

1. *Gothic Drama from Walpole to Shelley* (Berkeley, California: University of California Press, 1947).

2. *The Morning Mirror*, April 15, 1803.

Appendix 2

1. Mel Gordon, *The Grand Guignol: Theatre of Fear and Terror*, Revised Edition (New York: Da Capo Press, 1997), 2.

2. Mary Elizabeth Homrighous, *The Grand Guignol* (Evanston, Illinois: Northwestern University Press, 1963), 152–153.

3. Like André de Lorde, Maurice Level (1875–1926) was a French writer who specialized in eerie short stories and one-act plays that were produced by the *Théâtre du Grand-Guignol*. Twenty-six of his stories were collected in *Curses, Tales of Mystery and Horror* (1920), translated into English by Alys Eyre Macklin, a British editor, and introduced by actor H.B. Irving. "In allowing his stories to take an English form," wrote Irving, "M. Maurice Level is courting comparison with some very remarkable writers in his own peculiar line of output. Reminding one of Edgar Allan Poe more than any other, he employs the methods of O. Henry in the service of the horrible.... But his stories are more real than those of Poe, terser, more concentrated in their horror; they bear a closer relation to life; and in certain of them there is a genuine pathos of which Poe was incapable" (*Curses*, published by Erskine Macdonald, London, 1920, page iii).

4. Mary Elizabeth Homrighous, *The Grand Guignol* (Evanston, Illinois: Northwestern University Press, 1963), 96.

5. *Chicago-Sun Times*, March 14, 2005.

Bibliography

Balfour, Graham. *The Life of Robert Louis Stevenson*. New York: Charles Scribner's Sons, 1912.

Biner, Peter. *The Living Theatre*. New York: Horizon Press, 1972.

Compton, David. *Frankenstein*. London: J. Garnet Miller, 1973.

Conan Doyle, Arthur. *Memories and Adventures*, Second Edition. London: John Murray, 1930.

Cox, Jeffrey N. *Seven Gothic Dramas, 1789–1825*. Athens: Ohio University Press, 1992.

Danahay, Martin A., and Alex Chisholm, eds. *Jekyll and Hyde Dramatized*. Jefferson, NC: McFarland, 2005.

Dickens, Charles, ed. *All the Year Round*. 1859–1893.

Drake, Douglas. *Horror!* New York: Macmillan, 1966.

Evans, Bertrand. *Gothic Drama from Walpole to Shelley*. Berkeley: University of California Press, 1947.

Forry, Steven Earl. *Hideous Progenies*. Philadelphia: University of Pennsylvania Press, 1990.

Frayling, Christopher. *Vampyres: Lord Byron to Count Dracula*. London: Faber & Faber, 1992.

French, Sean. *Patrick Hamilton: A Life*. London: Faber & Faber, 1993.

Frost, Brian J. *The Essential Guide to Mummy Literature*. Lanham, MD: Scarecrow, 2008.

Glut, Donald F. *The Frankenstein Legend*. Metuchen, NJ: Scarecrow, 1973.

Gordon, Mel. *The Grand Guignol: Theatre of Fear and Terror*, revised edition. New York: Da Capo Press, 1997.

Guernsey, Otis L., and Jeffrey Sweet, eds. *The Best Plays of 1989–1900*. New York: Applause, 1990.

Haining, Peter. *Agatha Christie—Murder in Four Acts*. London: Virgin Books, 1990.

Heffner, Roe-Merril Seerist, Helmut Rehder, and W.F. Twaddell. *Goethe's Faust*. Boston: D.C. Heath, 1954.

Homrighous, Mary Elizabeth. *The Grand Guignol*. Evanston: Northwestern University Press, 1963.

Kilgarriff, Michael. *The Golden Age of Melodrama*. London: World Publishing, 1974.

Lane, Margaret. *Edgar Wallace: The Biography of a Phenomenon*. London: The Book Club, 1939.

Macklin, Abys Eyre, ed. *Curses, Tales of Mystery and Horror*. London: Erskine Macdonald, 1920.

Maida, Patricia D., and Nicholas B. Spornick. *Murder She Wrote*. Bowling Green, OH: Bowling Green State University Popular Press, 1982.

Mantle, Burns, ed. *The Best Plays of 1931–1932*. New York: Dodd, Mead, 1932.

Morlock, Frank J. *The Return of Lord Ruthven*. Encino, CA: Black Coat Press, 2004.

Neff, Renfreu. *The Living Theatre*. New York: Bobbs-Merrill, 1970.

Piro, Sal, and Michael Hess. *The Official Rocky Horror Picture Show: Audience Participation Guide*. San Bernardino, CA: Binary Publications, updated reprint, 2015.

Reilly, John M., ed. *Twentieth-Century Crime and Mystery Writers*. New York: St. Martin's Press, 1980.

Russell, Jamie. *Book of the Dead*, revised edition. London: Titan Books, 2014.

Sova, Dawn B. *Edgar Allan Poe, A to Z*. New York: Checkmark Books, 2001.

Stashower, Daniel. *Teller of Tales*. New York: Henry Holt, 1999.

Steiger, Brad. *The Werewolf Book*. Farmington Hills, MI: Visible Ink Press, 1999.

Stephens, Larry. *The Terrible Fitzball*. Bowling Green, OH: Bowling Green State University Popular Press, 1993.

Stuary, Roxana. *Stage Blood*. Bowling Green, OH: Bowling Green State University Popular Press, 1994.

Thomson, G.R. *Great Short Works by Edgar Allan Poe*. New York: HarperCollins, 1970.

Woodson, Thomas, ed. *Twentieth Century Interpretations of the Fall of the House of Usher*. Englewood Cliffs, NJ: Prentice-Hall, 1969.

Index

Abbott, Bruce 210
Abbott, George 106
Abbott, Richard 142
Abdelazer, or, the Moor's Revenge 21
Abley, Sean 148
Abraham, F. Murray 116, 253
Accolade 217
Ackland, Rodney 61
Adam the Creator 117
The Adding Machine 49
Adler, Lou 189
The Adventures of Sherlock Holmes 230
The Adventure of the Clouded Crystal 236
The Adventure of the Speckled Band 236
The Adventure of the Sussex Vampire 240, 241, 256
Aeschylus 1, 3, 51, 63, 251
The African Millionaire 61
After Dark 42
After Mary Shelley 109
After You, Mr. Hyde 142
Agamemnon 51, 251
Agatha Christie Made Me Do It 166
Agnes of God 57
Aiken, George L. 40
Ajax 4
Akhnaton 258
Alas! Alack! Zorro's Back! 159
Albert, Brian 100, 107
The Alchemical Caligari 250
Aldridge, Ira 252
Alias Jack the Ripper 130, 131
Alias Jimmy Valentine 45
All the Year Round 29, 30, 254
Allen, Debbie 186
Allen, Lewis 227
Alvarez, César 42
Alvarez, Fede 208
Amendt, Matthew 92
And Then There Were None 52, 179, 180, 262
Anderson, John Stuart 156
Anderson, Judith 17, 251, 252, 253
Anderson, Loni 54
Anderson, Mary 223
Anderson, Maxwell 54, 70
Andrews, Dana 188

Angel Street 219, 220, 221
Another Piece of Presumption 98
Anouilh, Jean 251
Antigone 4, 5, 251
Antonio's Revenge 8, 10
Anzell, Hy 198
Aphrodite 3
Archer, William 45
Archibald, William 177
Arden of Faversham 9
Arias, Alfredo Rodrigues 94
Arima, Stafford 186
Armadale 31
Armstrong, Alun 193, 194
Armstrong, Paul 45
Armstrong, Robert 211
Armstrong, Steven 229
Army of Darkness 208
Arrah-na-Pogue 42
Arsenic and Old Lace 53, 254, 257, 261
Artaud, Antonin 73, 253, 255
Arundel, Dennis 219
Ash vs. Evil Dead 208
Ashcroft, Peggy 252
Asher, Jack 239
Ashman, Howard 195, 198, 200
Ashton, Herbert, Jr. 62, 261
Assante, Armand 260
Assassins 72
Asselstine, Robert George 107
At the Telephone 249
At the World's Mercy 44
Atkins, Robert 252
Attack of the Pom-Pom Zombies 125, 126
Atwill, Lionel 129, 259
Austen, Jane 160
Austin, Elizabeth 98
The Axe 136
Ayckbourn, Alan 95, 101

Bacall, Lauren 183
The Bacchae 4
Bad Seed 54
Balderston, John L., 79, 81, 82, 85, 86, 93, 94, 95, 99, 100
Baldwin, Alec 253
Baldwin, James 55
Ball, Michael 193
Balzac, Honoré de 261
Bang Bang You're Dead 59

Bangs, Donald 92
Barker, Clive 64, 160, 255, 258
Barnes, Peter 129
Baron, Mark 107
Barras, Charles M. 43
Barrie, J.M. 230
Barrows, Stephen 109
Barrymore, Ethel 216, 217, 255
Barrymore, John 10, 173, 238, 252
Barrymore, Lionel 173
Bassett, Angela 253
The Bat 45, 46
Bates, Kathy 183
Bates, Melody 259
Battle, Hindon 209
Bauche, Henri 248, 249, 250
Baugham, G.A. 262
Baxter, Anne 224
Beale, Simon Russell 253
Bean, Orson 143
Beard, Mark 146
Beast of the Baskervilles 236, 237
Beck, Julian 101
Beebe, Dick 92
Behn, Aphra 21, 22
Beim, Norman 90
Bell, Neal 107, 108
The Bells 31
Benavente, Jacinto 67
Bene, Carmelo 142
Benelli, Sam 173
Bennett, Charles 255
Benson, Sarah 42, 254
Berdan, John M. 252
Berg, Alban 129
Bergl, Emily 185
Bergman, Ingrid 221
Bernard, James 239
Bernhardt, Sarah 32, 36, 37, 91, 160, 173, 252
Berry, Stephanie 109
Bertram, or The Castle of St. Aldobrand 246, 255
Bettis, Angela 185
Beware, My Lovely 226
Beyond Re-Animator 210
Bianchi, Dan 175
The Big Bow Mystery 261
Billy Budd 55
The Birds 67
Bishop, John 56
Black, Don 207, 256

Black, William Electric 106
The Black Abbot 56, 61
The Black Cat 148, 179, 257, 260
The Black Crook 43
Black Magic 249
Black Waters 46
Blackmail 255
Blanchard, Tammy 200
Blaney, Charles E. 44, 45
Blood Poetry 106
Blood Relations 135
Bloodthirsty Butchers 262
Bloody Jack 130
The Blue Ghost 48
Blues for Mr. Charlie 55
Bogdanov, Michael 90
Boker, George Henry 41
Bond, Christopher G. 95, 191, 208, 209, 254
Bond, Craig 198
Bonnie and Clyde 207
Booth, Edwin 252, 253
Booth, Eric 143
Borden, Abby 132
Borden, Andrew 132
Borden, Lizzie 1, 132, 260
Borle, Christian 200
Bosco, Philip 5
Bostwick, Barry 190
Boucicault, Dion 41, 42, 77
Bowers, Wendy 183
Bowman, David 130
Boyd, Gregory 206
Boyer, Charles 221
Boyle, Danny 108
Braddon, Mary Elizabeth 29, 95, 160
Braden, Bernard 226
Brahm, John 224
Branagh, Kenneth 252, 253
Brasseur, Pierre 216
Brett, Jeremy 81, 156, 241
Bricusse, Leslie 143, 204, 206, 207
The Bride of Frankenstein 99, 104, 106, 113, 257, 287, 262
Bride of Frankenstein Goes Malibu 103, 236
Bride of Re-Animator 210
Brightman, Sarah 201
Bristow, Gwen 52
Broadhurst, George 46
Brome, Richard 20
Brome, Robert 150
Brontë, Charlotte 29, 160
Brontë, Emily 160
Brook, Peter 252, 255
Brooks, Mel 108
Brothers 62
Broughton, John 28
Bruce, Lydia 221
Buckley, Betty 186
Buckley, Peter 240
Bufano, Remo 234
Bujold, Geneviève 49
Bumgarner, Burton 153
Burbage, Richard 15, 252, 253
Burch, Tom 170
The Burglar's Daughter 45

Buried Child 57
Burton, Richard 14, 251, 252
Burton, Tim 193
Busch, Charles 91
Bush, Catherine 107
Butler, Gerard 200, 202
Butleroff, Helen 256
Byrne, Rose 251

Caan, James 183
The Cabinet of Dr. Caligari 248, 249, 250
Cable, Eric 148
Cain 23
Cains, Frederick 92
Calderón, Pedro 21
Caldwell, Zoe 251
Calhern, Louis 253
Caligari 250
The Call of the Banshee 47
Camp, L. Sprague de 260
Campbell, Bruce 208
Campton, David 95, 100, 101, 148
Čapek, Karel 68, 117, 255
The Capeman 88
The Captive 246
Carie, Cynthia 210
Cariou, Len 193, 194
Carmilla 95, 101, 255
Carnovsky, Morris 253
Carr, John Dickson/Dickson, Carter 261
Carrie 88, 184–187
Carris, Colston 143
Carroll, Leo G. 188, 221
Carter, Helena Bonham 193
The Case of the Frightened Lady 62
The Cask of Amontillado 114, 147, 260
The Castle of Otranto 245, 255, 261
The Castle of St. Aldobrand 246
The Castle Spectre 245, 246
The Cat and the Canary 45, 47, 56, 79
Cavanaugh, Kenneth 92
Cavett, Dick 190
The Cenci 23, 24, 253, 255
Cerveris, Michael 193
Chaho, Michelle 199
Chamberlain, Richard 252
Chandler, Mark 119
Chandler, Raymond 227
Chaney, Lon 200
Chaney, Lon, Jr. 110, 257
Chapman, George 8
Chapman, Robert 55
Chase, James Hadley 64, 248
Chase, Lucia 137
Chatterley, W.H. 76
Chepulis, Kyle 91
Children of the Night 256
Child's Play 56
Chodorov, Edward 61
Chong, Ping 91
Christie, Agatha 52, 150, 179, 182, 218, 219, 256, 258, 261, 262

A Christmas Carol 160
Chuzzlewitt, Martin 161
Cinderella Meets the Wolfman! 114
Cipolla, Frank 208
City of Angels 72
Clark, Mariande 128
Clarkson, Patricia 185
Clash of the Vampires 241, 242
Clement, John 253
Clements, Mark 229
Cliffe, H. Cooper 233
Clifford, Jo 144
Clive, Colin 99
Clunes, Alec 160
The Clutching Claw 48
Cobb, Lee J. 253
Coffey Pott Meets the Wolf Man 114
Cohen, Alan 184
Cohen, Lawrence D. 185
Cole, Eric 150
Cole, David 177
The Collector 64, 228, 229
The Colleen Bawn 42
Collins, Wilkie 29, 30, 31, 70, 73, 160, 202, 236, 254
Colton, John 47, 133, 260
Colton, Misty 186
Combs, Jeffrey 210
Compton, David 95
Compulsion 54
Conan Doyle, Arthur 150, 153, 193, 194, 228, 230–234, 236, 237, 239, 240, 241, 256, 261, 263
Cone, Jack 128, 129
Conte, Scott 129
Cook, Barbara 186
Cooke, Thomas Potter 25, 26, 76, 98, 257
Cooper, Eddie 199
Cooper, Merian C. 211
Cope, Eddie 166, 167
Corble, Simon 239
Coriolanus 15, 183
Corman, Roger 195
Corneille, Pierre 32, 251
The Corsican Brothers 42
Cotten, Joseph 221
Cotton, Misty 186
Count Dracula 82, 83
The Count of Monte Cristo 77, 160, 242
The Count of Navarone 245
The Count Will Rise Again 94
Countess Dracula 86
Courting Vampires 94
Courts, Randy 131
Cowan, Edie 198
Cox, Brian 253
Cox, Constance 95, 159, 160
Cox, Laverne 190
Coxe, Louis O. 55
Crack in the World 188
Craig, Daniel 253
Crawford, Michael 88, 201
The Crazy, Mixed Up Island of Dr. Moreau 170, 171

The Creature Creeps! 121, 159
A Crime in a Madhouse 249
Crimes at the Old Brewery 236
Criswell, Kim 186
Cross, Felix 143
The Crucible 55
Cry of the Werewolf 110
Cuccioll, Robert 143, 206, 207
Cukor, George 221
Culliman, Ralph 47
Curran, Kelley 92
Curry, Tim 189, 190
The Curse of Frankenstein 239
Curse of the Werewolf 111, 112, 114
*Curses, Tales of Mystery and
    Horror* 263
Curtis, Ann 207
Cusack, Sinead 253
Cushing, Peter 238, 239
Cushman, Charlotte 252
Cutting, Ivan 244
Cymbeline 16

Dall, John 222
Daly, Augustine 44
The Danaid Tetralogy 3
Dance of the Vampires 72, 88
Dark Dark Ride Ride 73
Dark Shadows 110
Da Silva, Howard 142
David, Keith 12, 252
Davies, David Stuart 257
Davis, E.J. 233
Davis, John Henry 107
Davis, Owen 44, 45, 46, 52
Dawson, Ivo 233
Day, Laraine 221
Day of the Trifids 188
The Day the Earth Stood Still 188
Day-Lewis, Daniel 95, 252
The Deadly Game 70
Dean, James 105
Deane, Hamilton 77, 78, 79, 81,
    82, 84, 85, 86, 93, 94, 95, 99, 257
Dear, Nick 108
Death Comes as the End 258
Death on the Nile 258
de Balzac, Honoré 32, 35
Decker, Thomas 19
de la Torre, Lillian 134, 260
de Lorde, André 129, 263
de Lorenzo, Barl 157
de Maupassant, Guy 248
Deming, Dan 93
Dempsey, John 124
de Mille, Agnes 137, 138
de Molina, Tirso 21
Dench, Judi 253
Denham, Reginald 63, 223, 232,
    263
Denis, Michael Saint 251
de Palma, Brian 185
Depp, Johnny 193
Derleth, August 123
Desire Under the Elms 49, 50, 254
Deubert, Andrew 239
de Vega, Lope 21
Deval, Jacques 216

The Devil aka *The Devil Passes* 63
The Devil Among the Players 99
Devlin, Graham 143
Dewhurst, Colleen 50, 52, 253,
    254
Dewhurst, George 262
Dial "M" for Murder 54
Diamond Lil 52
Dickens, Charles 29, 30, 72, 160,
    236, 254
Dickey, Paul 45, 46, 52, 99
Dickinson, Thorold 221
Dietz, Steven 87
Dillman, Valerie 129
Dine, Jim 156
Dinelli, Mel 176, 225, 226
Dishonored Lady 173
Doctor Death 121
Doctor Faustus 251
Doctor Frank's Styne 109
Dr. Jekyll and Mr. Hyde 1, 43, 44,
    139–146, 179, 183, 255
*Dr. Jekyll and Mr. Hyde: A Love
    Story* 143
Doctor Jekyll et Mister Hyde 142
*Doctor Nympho vs. The Sex
    Zombies* 259
Donahue, Mike 199
Donner, Clive 156
Donoso, Jorge 199
Donovan, Gene 93
Donovan, Rory 213
Dorian 156
A Double Door 53
Douglas, Melvyn 255
Douglas, Timothy 109
Downing, Martin 96, 106
Drac's Back! 93
Dracula 59, 76, 78–81, 83, 85–88,
    90, 92, 95, 96, 99, 109, 112, 123,
    152, 207, 216, 239, 255, 256, 257,
    260
Dracula (novel) 77, 78, 89
Dracula: A Chamber Musical 256
Dracula, A Modern Fable 90
Dracula: A Musical Nightmare
    256
*Dracula, A New Enviromental
    Ritual* 92
Dracula, Baby 81, 82
Dracula, Darling 94
Dracula in Paradise 94
The Dracula Kidds 86
Dracula, Lord of the Undead 94
Dracula, or A Pain in the Neck 90
Dracula, or The Un-Dead 31, 77,
    78, 79
Dracula Sabath 90
The Dracula Spectacula 256
Dracula: The Death of Nosferatu
    94
*Dracula: The Journal of Jonathan
    Harker* 92
Dracula: The Musical 97, 256
Dracula: The Twilight Years 86
Dracularama 91
Dracula's Treasure 92
Dracula's Widow 94, 114

Drake, Alfred 142
Drayton, Mary 56
The Dreamy Kid 51
Drivas, Robert 92
Driving Wilde 157
Druten, John van 216
Dryden, John 22
Du Brock, Neal 86
The Duchess of Malfi 8, 19, 110
The Duchess of Padua 160
Dürrenmatt, Friedrich 69, 70
Duffield, Brainerd 54
Duke, Vernon 62
Du Maurier, Daphne 67, 70
Dumas, Alexandre père 34, 42,
    77, 158, 160, 242, 255
Dunlop, William 40
Durazo, Drina 73
Duse, Eleonora 91
The Dust Heap 46
Dutchman 55
Duvivier, Julian 160, 258

Earl the Vampire 93
Eastwood, Kate 253
Edgar, David 143
The Edgar Allan Poe Show 150,
    153
Edna, the Pretty Typewriter 45
Edward II 9
Eggar, Samantha 228
Ehle, Jennifer 253
The Eldest 260
Electra 251
Ellis, Charles 254
Ellstein, Abraham 116
Elsom, Isobel 225
Emmons, Beverly 207
The Emperor Jones 51
End and Beginning 62
Engelbach, Jerry 90
Epstein, Alvin 250, 253
Estleman, Loren D. 256, 263
Eulo, Ken 106
Eunson, Dale 217, 222
Euripides 1, 4, 63, 254
Evans, Maurice 17, 252, 253
Evelyn, Judith 220, 221
An Evening with Edgar Allan Poe
    147–150
The Evil Dead 208
Evil Dead: The Musical 208, 209,
    210
Evil Dead II 208
Evil Doings at Queen Toot's Tomb
    153
Extremities 58, 59

Fairchild, Robert 108
The Fall of the House of Usher 114,
    147, 148, 179, 260, 261
*The Fall of the House of Usher and
    Other Plays* 148
Fall River Legend (ballet) 137, 138
Fallon, Thomas 46
Fantastical Friends 152
Farnsworth, Richard 183
Farra, Harry 238

Farren, Nellie 99
Farrow, Michael Kodi 157
The Fatal Deception 40
Faust 37, 38, 251
Faust II 116, 255
Fawcett, Farrah 58
The Fearless Vampire Killers 88
Fenisong, Ruth 234
Fenwick, Irene 233
Ferrer, José 221, 252
Ffrangcon-Davies, Gwen 220
Field, Barbara 106
Field, Crystal 90
Fielding, Henry 22
Fiennes, Ralph 252
The Final Kiss 250
"The Final Problem" 234
Finch, Jon 164
Finley, Bob 198
Finney, Albert 207, 252, 253
The First Men in the Moon 163
Firth, Peter 156
Fisher, Michael Shaw 259
Fisher, Terence 239
Fitzball, Edward 27, 28, 110
Flagrantle, Eddie 124
Flesh and Fantasy 160
Fletcher, Lucille 54
Flood, Marty 112
Floyd, John 47
The Flying Squad 62
Foch, Nina 110
Fog 46
Forbidden Planet 188
Force and Hypocrisy 130
Ford, John 19
Foreman, Richard 116
Forrest, Edwin 40, 252, 253
Forrest, Sally 224
Forrester, Bill 87
Forsyth, Frederick 202
Forsyth, Julian 239
Foster, Hunter 100
The Fountainville Abbey 40
The Four of Hearts 54
Fowles, John 64, 228
Frances, Anne 188
Francesca da Rimini 41
Francis, Clive 239
Francoeur, Bill 114
Frankenstein 16, 59, 92, 99, 104,
    101–107, 109, 112, 116, 255, 257,
    260, 262
Frankenstein! 107
Frankenstein: A New Musical 108
The Frankenstein Affair 106
*Frankenstein: An Adventure in the
    Macabre* 99, 100
Frankenstein ... Do You Dream?
    107
*Frankenstein in Love, or The Life
    of Death* 64
Frankenstein (Mortal Toys) 108
*Frankenstein, or The Man and the
    Monster* 26
*Frankenstein, or The Modern
    Prometheus* 24, 75, 97
The Frankenstein Summer 107

Frankenstein: The Gift of Fire
    100, 101
Frankenstein: The Musical 107
Frankenstein: The Rock Musical
    106
Frankenstein Unbound 106
Frankie 106
Franklin, David 130
Frears, Will 184
Freeman, Charles K. 224
Frye, Dwight 216, 257
Fuente Ovejuna 21

Gable, Clark 49
Gaboriau, Émile 233
Gale, David 210
Gallienne, Eva Le 252
Galsworthy, John 59, 60, 70
Gambon, Michael 253
The Game's Afoot 236
Garber, Victor 72
Gardenia, Vincent 200
Garrick, David 252, 253
Gas Light 219–222
Gay Divorce 259
Gaywood, Paul 260
Geer, Ellen 93, 253
Geiser, Janie 108
Genet, Jean 70, 255
Germain, Mark St. 131
The Ghost Breaker 45
Ghost Detective 153
Ghost of Dracula 91
The Ghost of Jerry Bundler 32
The Ghost Train 59, 60
Gialanella, Victor 59, 104, 105
Gielgud, John 156, 252, 253
Gigli, Beniamino 173
Gilbert and Sullivan 77, 163
Giles, Ian 119
Gillett, William 230
Gilmore, William 106, 107
Giordano, Umberto 173, 193
Giraldi, Giovanni Battista 8
The Girl and the Detective 45
Gish, Dorothy 225
Gish, Lillian 133
*Glass Guignol: The Brother and
    Sister Play* 108
Gleason, William K. 114
Glenn, Richard 240
Gless, Sharon 184
Godber, John 96
Goddard, Charles W. 45, 99
Godfrey, Thomas 39, 40
Gods and Monsters 257
The Gods of the Mountain 65
Godwin, William 75, 255
Godzilla vs. Kong 211
Goethe, Johann Wolfgang von
    37, 75, 117, 255
Gold 51
Gold, Blaise 100
Goldberg, Eyal 116
Goldman, William 183, 184
Goldstein, David 87
Der Golem 115, 117, 258
Le Golem 258

The Golem 115, 116, 117, 258
Gonzales, Mario 143
Goodbye, Miss Lizzie Borden
    134
Goon with the Wind 105
Gordin, Jacob 253
Gordon, Barry 157
Gordon, Stuart 210
Gore, Michael 185
Gorey, Edward 80
The Gorilla 47
Gould, Morton 138
Graham, Martha 33
Grammer, Kelsey 193, 253
Granach, Alexander 115
The Grand Guignol 37, 248, 249
Granger, Farley 222
Granville, Bonita 224
Grappo, Connie 198, 199
The Green Archer 56
The Green Beetle 46
The Green Goddess 45
The Green Pack 62
Greene, Graham 160
Greene, Leon 193
Gregory, James 216
Greif, Michael 107
Griffith, D.W. 249
Grotowski, Jerzy 255
Gruber, H.K. 107
Guest in the House 217, 222, 223,
    224, 261
Guild, Blaise 107
Guinness, Alec 252
Gulley, John 143
Gunton, Bob 193
Guthrie, Tyrone 9, 251
Gyllenhaal, Jake 199

Hackett, Peter 87
Hagen, Uta 15, 221, 252
Haigh, Kenneth 252
Hall, Bob 84
Hall, Lucas 240
Halperin, Edward 123
Halperin, Victor 123
Hamill, Kate 92, 109
Hamilton, Patrick 219, 221, 223
Hamlet 8, 13, 14, 15, 52, 63, 77,
    252
Hamlette 252
Hammer, Don 225
Hampden, Walter 252, 253
Hampton, Christopher 207, 256
Hand in Glove 224, 225
Hands, Terry 186
Hangover Square 221
Harding, Ann 219
Harding, Lyn 230, 232, 233, 253
Hards, Ira 79
Hardwick, Michael 235, 236
Hardwick, Mollie 235, 236
Hardwicke, Edward 241
Hare, David 156, 160
Harries, Julian 242, 244
Hart, Charles 200
Haskell, Owen 136, 260
Hasselhoff, David 207

Hatcher, Jeffrey 59, 143, 144, 148, 177, 178, 179
Hately, Linzi 186
Hatfield, Hurd 157
The Haunted House 6, 46
The Haunting of Hill House 54, 227
Have I Got a Girl for You! 106
Hawkins, Jack 217
Hawkins, Joy 124
Hayes, Hanna 63
Hazlewood, Colin Henry 29
He Was Born Gay 217
Healy, Mark 64, 94, 228, 229
Hearn, George 193
Heatherley, Frank 130
Heckart, Eileen 57
Hegarty, Paul 193
Heggie, O.P. 232
The Hellbound Heart 255
Hellman, Lillian 70, 259
Hellraiser 255
Helsinger, Jim 92
Hendrix, Suzy 56
Henning, Timothy 144
Henry, Martha 5
Henry, O. 263
Henschell, Irene 179
Hepenstall, W.D. 47
Herbert West—Reanimator 210
Herford, Robin 182
Herod and Miriamne 34
Herod the Great 8
Hess, David 193
Hewitt, Tom 207
Heywood, Thomas 18, 20
Highsmith, Patricia 64
Hill, Daniel 239
Hill, Ken 95, 111, 118, 119, 164, 167
Hill, Robert 156
Hill, Susan 64, 181
Hillhouse, Larry 109
Hinds, Anthony 238, 239
Hippolytus 254
The History of the Devil 64
Hitch, Geoffrey 92
Hitchcock, Alfred 222, 227, 255
The Hitch-Hiker 54
Hobbs, Hallowell 180
Hodiak, John 219
Hoffman, Alice 117
Hoffman, E.T.A. 261
Holbrook, Hal 253
Holcroft, Thomas 23
Holder, Geoffrey 204
Hollow Man 164
Hollow Man 2 164
Hollywood and Hyde 144
Holm, Ian 253
The Holmes-Dracula File 257, 263
Holnquist, Paul S. 170
Holt, Michael 182
Hooray for Hollywood 152
Hopkins, Anthony 183, 252
Hopkins, Arthur 173
Hoppe, Gip 148
Hopwood, Avery 45

Hordern, Michael 253
Horner, Harry 226
Horrors of Doctor Moreau 167, 168
Hoskins, Evelyn 186
The Hound of the Baskervilles 62, 228, 234, 236, 237, 238, 239, 256
The House in the Magnolias 123
The House of Dracula 96
The House of Frankenstein 96, 106
Howard, John 110
Howard, Leslie 252
Hughes, Terry 193
Hugo, Victor 32, 34, 35
Hulbert, Claude 160
Hulbert, Jack 160
Hull, Henry 110
Humphrey, Harry E. 48
Huntley, Raymond 79, 80, 257
Huston, Walter 254
Hyland, James 144
Hyman, Earle 252

I Was a Teen-Age Dracula 93
I Was a Teenage Jekyll and Hyde 142
An Ideal Husband 160
If Sherlock Holmes Were a Woman 236
I'm Sorry, the Bridge Is Out 105, 256
The Importance of Being Earnest 160
The Incredible Murder of Cardinal Tosca 163
Inflatable Frankenstein 108
The Innocents 177
The Invisible Host 52
The Invisible Man 70, 163–167, 188, 257, 261, 262
The Invisible Thief 163
Irving, H.B. 142, 263
Irving, Henry 31, 77, 142, 252, 253, 255, 256
The Island of Dr. Moreau 163, 168, 169, 255
Ives, Burl 254

Jack the Ripper 1
Jack the Ripper 128, 129, 248
Jack the Ripper (TV series) 260
The Jack the Ripper Show 130
Jack the Ripper: The Final Solution 130
Jack's Holiday 131, 132
Jackson, Glenda 253
Jackson, Jeffrey 107
Jackson, Shirley 54
Jacobi, Derek 252, 253
Jacobs, W.W. 32, 33, 174, 175
Jakes, John 81
James, Barry 198
James, Henry 176, 178
Jane Eyre 28, 70, 152, 160
Janowitz, Hans 250
Jeffers, Robinson 251
Jekyll & Hyde 72, 143, 144, 204, 205, 206
Jekyll and Hyde Follies 143

Jekyll Hides again! 143, 159
Jephson, Robert 245
Jessel, Patricia 253
The Jest 173
The Jew of Malta 9
The Jewel of Seven Stars 257
Jochim, Keith 104
Joe, Zombie 73
Johann, Zita 49
John, Elton 73, 88, 89
John Brown's Body 217, 222
Johnsen, Daniel 91
Johnson, Crane 83
Johnston, Margaret 253
Jonathan Bradford, or The Murder at the Roadside Inn 27
Jones, James Earl 14, 252, 253
Jones, LeRoi 55
Jones, Michael G. 119
Jones, Robert Edmond 10
Jordan, Tom 94
Jory, Victor 80
Joseph, Francesca 193
Joseph, Stephen 101
The Judas Kiss 160
Jukes, Bernard 80
Julia, Raul 81
Jumbee 123
Justice 59, 60

Kanor, Seth 87
Kaplan, Mark 168
Karloff, Boris 53, 54, 96, 99, 255, 257
Katz, Leon 90
Kaufman, Moses 160
Kauzlaric, Robert 168, 170
Kaye, Adi 56
Kaye, Nora 137
Keach, Stacy 252, 253
Kean, Charles 42, 252, 253
Kean, Edmund 252, 253
Keeley, Robert 97, 98
Kehret, Peg 94
Keller, Tedy 93
Kellerd, John 253
Kellman, Jon 93
Kelly, Nancy 224
Kelly, Tim 56, 77, 85, 103, 106, 114, 130, 135, 143, 148, 164, 167, 170, 236, 257, 259
Kemble, John Philip 252, 253
Kemp, Lindsay 162
Kennedy, Arthur 55, 57
Kent, David 135
Kerr, John Atkinson 98
Kesselring, Jodeph 53, 54
Kettering, Ralph Thomas 48
Killam, Tarran 199
Killer Joe 59
The Killing of Abel 8
Kind Lady 61, 224, 261
Kinevane, Pat 259
King, Claude 230
King, George 262
King, Stephen 64, 182–185, 262
King Kong 62, 73, 91, 188, 211–214, 259, 262

King Kong vs. Godzilla 211
King Lear 11, 15, 253
King Richard the Third 10, 11, 12, 25
Kingsley, Ben 252
Kingston, Alex 253
Kirby, Michael 250
Kirschner, Lowell 168
Kitchen, Michael 156
Klein, Charles 45
Kline, Kevin 252, 253
Knaggs, Skelton 225
Knott, Frederick 54, 56
Koch, George C. 136
Koltai, Ralph 186
Kondoleon, Harry 90, 91
Kong: Skull Island 211
Kopit, Arthur 203, 204
Kornfield, Larry 90
Krauss, Werner 250
Krieger, Gus 73
Kunza, Michael 88
Kuznetsov, Misha 93
Kyd, Thomas 8, 9

The Laboratory of Hallucinations 249
Ladies in Retirement 63, 224, 261
Lady Audley's Secret 29, 70, 71, 95
The Lady Vanishes 227
Lady Windermere's Fan 169
Laine, Cleo 71
Lambert, Carol 63
The Lancashire Witches 20
Landau, Martin 81
Landis, Joseph C. 116, 117
Langella, Frank 80, 81, 253
Lansbury, Angela 157, 191, 193, 194
The Last Laugh 45, 99
The Last of Sheila 194
The Last of Sherlock Holmes 236
The Last Vampyre 241
The Last Warning 46
The Late Lancashire Witches 20
Laughton, Charles 62, 96, 253, 255
Laurie, Piper 185
Law, Jude 252
Lawrence, Reginald 134
Lazarov, Yehezkel 157
The League of Extraordinary Gentlemen 157
LeClerc, Jean 81
Lee, Canada 252
Lee, Christopher 238, 239
Lee, Eugene 193, 194
Lee, Franna 194
Lee, Nathaniel 21, 22
Le Fanu, Sheridan 95, 236, 255
The Legend of Lizzie 134
Leiber, Fritz 253
Leigh, Vivien 251, 253
Leivick, Halper 115, 116, 117
Lermontov, Mikhail 38
Leroux, Gaston 159, 200, 203, 204, 248, 261
Lescot, Mario 83

Leslie, F. Andrew 54, 55, 226, 227, 228, 237
Leslie, Fred 99
Lessing, Gotthold Ephraim 37
Lestat 73, 88, 89
Letheren, Mark 229
Letts, Dominic 182
Letts, Tracy 59
Level, Maurice 250, 263
Levin, Ira 56, 57, 180, 262
Levin, Meyer 54
Levy, Benn Wolfe 60, 63, 255
Levy, Jose G. 249
Lewin, Albert 157
Lewis, Brenda 138
Lewis, Leopold 31
Lewis, Matthew Gregory 245, 246
Lewisohn, Alice 65
Lewton, Randall 142
Like Totally Weird 59
Lind, Gillian 62
Linney, Romulus 59
Lionizing 260
Litchfield, Harriett 246
Lithgow, John 253
The Little Foxes 259
Little Shop of Horrors 72, 124, 195–199, 210, 211
Liveright, Horace 99
The Living Theatre Ensemble 101, 102
Lizzie! 136
Lizzie Borden (chamber opera) 138
Lizzie Borden of Fall River 135
Lloyd, Gary 186
Lloyd, George 225
Lockhead, Liz 95
The Lodger 129, 130
The Lodger (opera) 130
Logan, John 193
Logan, Malcolm 263
Lola 45
Lom, Herbert 200
London, Frank 116
The Long Voyage Home 51
Lopez, Emily 186
Lorca, Frederico Garcia 70
Lord Arthur Savile's Crime 95, 159, 160
Lord Arthur Savile's Crime and Other Stories 160
Lord Byron 23, 24, 75, 106, 107, 109
Lord Dunsany 65, 66
Lorde, André de 129, 248, 249, 250, 263
Loren, Sophia 254
"The Lottery" 54
Lounsbery, G. Constant 156
Love from a Stranger 218, 219
Love Never Dies 202, 203
Lovecraft, H.P. 210, 261, 262
Lovelace, Delos W. 262
Lowndes, Marie Belloc 129
Lucie, Doug 130
Lucretia, Borgia 34, 35

Ludlam, Charles 56, 91
Ludwig, Ken 239, 240
Lugosi, Bela 80, 81, 257
Lulu 129
Lulu Belle 173
Lunt, Alfred 69
Lupino, Ida 226
Lust's Dominion 21
Luz, Franc 198
Lyndeck, Edmund 193s
Lyons, Marti 253

Macbeth 15, 17, 253
Machinal 49, 50
Mackaye, Dorothy 260
Mackintosh, Cameron 198, 201
Macready, William Charles 252, 253
Mad Hercules 6
Madame Conti 63
The Maid's Revenge 20
Malcontent 8
Malina, Judith 101
Mallatratt, Stephen 64, 181
Malleson, Miles 216
Mama, Slanty Eyed 259
The Man 225, 226, 261
The Man and the Monster 98
Man-Made 108
The Man Who Changed His Name 62
Manfred 23
Mann, Terence 72
Manning, Bruce 52
Mansfield, Richard 44, 128, 139, 141, 142, 252, 260
Manson, Ona 254
Marasco, Robert 56
Marcello, Vince 125
March, Fredric 183
Margie and the Wolf Man 110, 111
Maria Marten, or The Murder in the Red Barn 28
Marino, Lee 186
Marlowe, Christopher 9, 21, 37, 251
Marlowe, Julia 253
The Marriage of Mr. Mississippi 69
Marriott, Moore 262
Marshall, William 252
Marston, John 8
Martin, Steve 200
Masefield, John 59, 62
Mason, Robert 147, 148, 150
The Masque of the Red Death 260
Masquerade 38
Massey, Raymond 233, 255
Mastrantonio, Antonio 100
Mastrosimone, William 58, 59
Mather, Aubry 225
Mattera, John 59, 109
Maturin, Charles Robert 110, 246, 255
Maugham, W. Somerset 70, 260
Mayer, Carl 250
Mayer, Michael 199, 200

The Mayor of Zalamea 21
Mazurek, Camille 63
Mazzie, Marin 186
McCarthy, Jeff 193
McClintic, Guthrie 254
McCrory, Helen 251
McDonald, James 180
McDowell, Malcolm 157
McElvain, Richard 148, 150, 153
McFadden, Elizabeth 53
McGillis, Howard 71
McGuinness, Frank 96
McKellen, Ian 252, 253, 257
McKenna, Joseph 116
McKinley, Philip William 124
McMahon, Luella E. 150
McNulty, William 93
McOnie, Drew 213
McOwen, Bernard J. 46
McPherson, Conor 66, 67, 255
Meacham, Anne 134
Mead, Ralph 92
Meade, Lesley 182
Medea 4, 6, 251
Meehan, Thomas 108
Melville, Herman 55
Menken, Alan 195
Mennie, Michael 188
Mercer, Beryl 129, 259
Mérope 34
Meskin, Aharon 258
Metamora, or The Last of the Vampanoags 40
Metcalf, Lauri 184
The Meteor 70
Meyer, Nicholas 163
Meyrink, Gustav 117
Miami Beach Monsters 106, 256
Mid-Life Dracula 94
Middleton, Thomas 20
Midnight House 227
Mighty Joe Young 262
Migliaccio, Rene 91
Miles, Carlton 133
Miles, Joanna 81
Miller, Arthur 55
Miller, Jim 238
Miller, Joan 226
Miller, Kathryn Schultz 153
Miller, Peter 142
Miller's Court 130
Mills, Alex 144
Millward, Charles 233
Milner, Henry M. 26, 98, 255
Miranda, John 262
Misery 182, 183, 184
Miss Gwilt 31
Miss Sara Sampson 37
Mitchell, Brian Stokes 193
Mitchell, Robert 107
Mitchell, Thomas 160
Mixon, Alan 50
The Model Man 99
Modjeska, Helena 253
Molloy, Kenneth 91
Moncrieff, W.T. 77
The Monkey's Paw 152, 175s
Monster 107, 108

The Monster and the Magician 98
Montgomery, Douglass 134, 216
Montgomery, Elizabeth 134
Montgomery, Robert 216
The Moonstone 31, 70
Moore, Julianne 185
Moore, Simon 182, 183, 184
Moorehead, Agnes 54
Moran, John 250
Moranis, Rick 200
Morino Faliero 23
Morlez, Chloë Grace 185
Morlock, Frank J. 77, 241, 242, 255
Morell, André 238
Morrell, Charles 79
Morris, Eric William 213
Morris, Mary 254
Morris, Melissa 208
Mosakowsky, Susan 108, 250
Mourning Becomes Electra 49, 51, 52, 251
The Mousetrap 56, 182, 262
The Mouthpiece 62
Mozart, Wolfgang Amadeus 251
Mulgrew, Kate 12
The Mummy 56, 257
The Mummy's Claw 119–121
The Mummy's Tomb 70, 118–122
Murder By Poe 148, 179
A Murder Has Been Arranged 217
Murder in the House of Horrors 113, 114, 153
Murder Most Foul 129
The Murder Room 122, 159
Murder Takes the Stage 134, 135
The Murders in the Rue Morgue 114, 148, 150, 151, 152, 179, 248, 261
Murnau, F.W. 91
Murphy, Hugh M. 124
Murphy, Karen 124
Murray, Stephen 125
The Musical Comedy Murders of 1940 56
The Mysteries of Paris 35, 242
The Mysterious Mother 245
The Mystery of Edwin Drood 71, 72
The Mystery of Irma Vep 56
The Mystery of Jack the Ripper 130, 259
The Mystery of Marie Roget 146, 150, 179
Mystery of the Blood Beast Horror 114, 244
The Mystery of the Yellow Room 261, 200

Nagy, Phyllis 64
Negga, Ruth 252, 253
Nellie, the Beautiful Cloak Model 44
Nero, Emperor of Rome 21
Nevermore 153
Neville, John 252
A New Case of Jekyll and Hyde 144

New Faces of 1952 137
Newes, Tilly 129
Nichols, Christopher 94
Nichols, James W. 143
Nicholson, Kent 193
A Night at an Inn 66
Night Chills 114, 148–153, 260
Night Must Fall 62, 215–218, 224, 261
Night of the Living Dead 73
Nightfall with Edgar Allan Poe 148, 150
Nine 204
Nine Pine Street 133, 134
The Ninth Guest 52
No Orchids for Miss Blandish 64, 248
No Thoroughfare 29, 254
Nobel, Adrian 251
Nodier, Charles 24, 42, 76, 77, 255
Nolan, Timothy 193
Northanger Abby 160
Norwood, Eille 233
Nosferatu 91
Nosferatu: Angel of the Final Hour 93
Not About Nightingales 58, 59
Not the Count of Monte Cristo? 158
Nuenz, Richard 124
Nutter, Mark 210

O'Brien, Adale 47
O'Brien, Jack 202
O'Brien, Michael 167
O'Brien, Richard 188, 189, 190
O'Brien, Willie 211
O'Bryne, Joe 156
The Octoroon 41, 42, 254
Odle, Robert L. 92
Oedipus the King 4, 22, 251, 253
Oklahoma 193
Okoye, Tiana 186
The Old Dark House 255, 257, 262
The Old Ladies 61
The Old Man 62
Old Sleuth 44
Olivier, Laurence 251, 252, 253
On the Spot 62
One Autumn Evening 70
O'Neil, Nance 68, 260
O'Neill, Eugene 49, 50, 51, 70, 251, 254
Orbecche 8
Orczy, Emmuska 207
The Oresteia 3, 4, 51, 251
Orlando, Dominic 153
Oroonoko 22
Oroonoko, or the Royal Slave 22
The Orphan of China 34
Ortega, Kenny 190
Osborne, John 153, 154, 156
Oscar Wilde 160
O'shea, Chris 125
Osterman, George 143, 144, 146
Othello 11, 14, 16, 252
O'Toole, Megan 199

O'Toole, Peter 252
Oz, Frank 200

Pacino, Al 252
Page, Patrick 87
Pal, George 188
Palmer, Betsy 86
Panaro, Hugh 89
Pancella, Phyllis 138
Papas, Irene 6, 251
Par for a Corpse 159
Parker, David 228
Parker, Louis N. 175
The Passion Flower 67, 68
The Passion of Dracula 84, 85
Paterson, Bill 184
Pathé, Charles 164
Paul, James Jeffrey 130
Paul, Jeremy 241
Pavey, Bree 253
Payton-Wright, Pamela 52
Peake, Richard Brinsley 25, 97, 99
Pearson, Anne 95
Peck, Gregory 221
Peirce, Kimberly 185
Penn & Teller 190, 253
The People Next Door 228
Percy, Edward 63
Pericles, Prince of Tyre 15
Perkins, Anthony 194, 254
Persons Unknown 62
Peters-Lazaro, Sebastian 109
Peterson, Dorothy 80
Peterson, Lenka 224
Pettingell, Frank 221
Phaedra 6, 32, 254
Phaedra (ballet) 33
Phantom 203, 204
The Phantom of Manhattan 202
The Phantom of the Opera 1, 72, 88, 200–204, 248
Phelps, Samuel 253
"Philomel Cottage" 218
The Physicists 70
The Picture of Dorian Gray 59, 153, 154, 156, 157–160, 261
Pielmeier, John 57
Pierre Patelin 75, 76
Piewerts, J.P. 48
The Pinchpenny Phantom of the Opera 122, 159
Pirkis, Claude 129
Pitchford, Dean 185
Pitt, George Dibdin 28
Pitts, Christiani 213
Pitts, Zasu 46
Planché, James Robinson 24, 25, 76
Plautus, Titus Marcius 6
Playing with Fire 106
The Playroom 55
Plummer, Christopher 14, 252, 253
Poe, Edgar Allan 114, 146, 147, 149, 150, 153, 179, 233, 236, 248, 260, 261, 263
Poe-Dunked 153

Poe! Poe! Poe! 153
Poe's Midnight Dreary 148
Polanski, Roman 88
Polidori, John William 24, 75, 77, 106, 107, 255, 257, 263
The Polish Jew 31
Politian 146
Pollock, Sharon 135
Pomponi, Franco 193
Poole, Michael 119
Poole, Roy 253
Port Said 217
Portrait of a Man with Red Hair 60, 61
Portrait of Gilbert 260
The Power of Darkness 38, 39
Preskett, Thomas 257
Presumption, or The Fate of Frankenstein 25, 26, 97, 98, 99
Price, Vincent 163, 220, 221
Pride and Prejudice 160
Priestley, J.B. 70, 255
Prime Evil 143
Prince, Harold 193, 194, 201, 202
Prince of Parthia 39
The Prince of the World 44
Pritchard, Hannah 253
The Private Life of Sherlock Holmes 236
The Probability Pad 263
Problem Potion 143
Prometheus Bound 3
Prosky, Robert 116
Pryce, Jonathan 252, 253
Pulaski, Charles 89
The Purloined Letter 114, 150, 152, 179

Quaid, Randy 116
Queen, Ellery 54
The Queen's Enemies 65, 66
Quilley, Denis 193, 194
Quintero, José 254
Quinton, Everett 143, 146

Rabe, David 57
Rachel 32
Racine, Jean 32, 251
The Rage: Carrie 2 185
The Rage of Frankenstein 103
Raimi, Sam 208
Rain 260
Rains, Claude 164, 188, 200
Ranson, Molly 186
The Rape of Lucretia 18
Rathbone, Basil 219, 263
Rathbone, Ouida 263
Rattigan, Terence 70
Reach, James 134, 260
Re-Animator: The Musical 210, 211
Recklessness 50
The Red Falcon 46
Redgrave, Michael 252, 253
Redmond, Barbara 143
Reed, Florence 253, 254
Reeves, Keanu 252
Reid, Hal 44

Reinblatt, George 208
Reinhardt, Max 90, 251
Reinking, Megan 89
Reiser, Dave 122, 156, 157, 261
Reisz, Karel 217
The Reluctant Vampire 93
Remember Constance Kent 260
The Return of A.J. Raffles 160
The Return of Lord Ruthven 77, 255
Return of the Maniac 121
Return to the Grand Guignol 249
Revenge of Busy D'Ambois 8
The Revenge of Sherlock Holmes 207
The Revenger's Tragedy 18
Ricamora, Conrad 200
Rice, Anne 73, 88, 89, 257
Rice, Elmer 49, 52, 70
Rice, Tim 203
Richard III 10, 12, 15, 252
Richmond, David 84
Ridley, Arnold 59, 60
Rigg, Diana 251
Rigg, Kates 259
Riley, Amber 199
Rinehart, Mary Roberts 45
The Ringer 61
Ripper! 130
The Rise of the House of Usher 148, 153
Rivette, Andrea 207
Roberts, Adam 125
Robeson, Paul 15, 252
Robin, Don 164
Robin Hood 159
Robinson, Bernard 239
Robinson, Edward G. 160
Robinson, Martin F. 198
Robinson, Meghan 91
Robson, Flora 253
Rock, Charles 32
The Rocky Horror Picture Show 70, 190
The Rocky Horror Show 188, 189, 190
Roland, Richard 124
Rolands, Betty 142
Romanoff, Dimitri 137
Romeo and Juliet and Zombies 259
Romero, George A. 73
Ronald, Bruce 81
Roos, Audrey 54
Roos, William 54
Rope 219, 221, 222
The Rope 6
Rope's End 222
Rosa, Dennis 80
Rosenblatt, Monica 199
Rosenzweig, Josh 187
Rosner, Milton 219
Ross, Andrew 126
Ross, Bertram 33
Rossum, Emmy 202
Roth, Robert Jess 88
Rovina, Hanna 251, 258
Rowe, Dana P. 124

Rowley, William 19, 20
Royce, Julian 232
Ruddigore 77
Rudgers, Katherine 198
RuPaul 125
R.U.R. 68, 69, 117, 255
Ryan, Mark 143
Ryan, Robert 226
Rylance, Mark 252
Rymer, James Malcolm 255

Saberhagen, Fred 256, 263
Sacharow, Lawrence 116
St. Clair, Robert 110, 259
St. John, Billy 94, 112, 114, 148, 150, 152, 153, 260
Saintsbury, Harry Arthur 230, 232, 263
Sal, the Circus Gal 45
Salazar, George 199
Salomé 160, 162
Salvini, Tommaso 253
Sánchez, Luis Rafael 48
Sanders, Donald 108
Sanders, George 157
Sangster, Jimmy 239
Santana, Victor 83
Sarandon, Susan 190
Sardou, Victorien 35, 36
Saunders, Dudley F. 92
Sauver, Jason St. 91
Savory, Gerald 224
The Scandalous Case of Dr. Jekyll and *Mr. Hide* 144
Scanlan, Dick 199
Scarlet in Gaslight 257
The Scarlet Pimpernel 207
Schreiber, Liev 253
Schulman, Susan H. 132
Schulusselberg, Eleanor 168
Schumacher, Joel 202
Scofield, Paul 252, 253
Scotland, Road 178, 179
Scott, Ellenore 199
Scott, George C. 254
Scott, Janette 188
The Seafarer 67
Seitz, Stephen 257
Séneca, Lucius Annaeus 1, 6, 7, 9, 10, 251, 254
Seven Brides for Dracula 86
Seven Wives for Dracula 86
Sh! The Octopus 48
Shadwell, Thomas 20
Shakespeare, William 8, 10, 11, 13, 14, 15, 174, 182, 183
The Shanghai Gesture 47, 254, 260
Shannon, David 193
Sharkey, Jack 114, 119, 121, 122, 143, 156, 157, 261
Sharman, Jim 189, 190
Shaw, Fiona 251
Shaw, George Bernard 163
Sheen, Martin 252
Sheldon, Edward 173
Shelley, Mary 24, 25, 59, 75, 97, 98, 99, 101, 103, 105–109, 116, 255, 258, 260

Shelley, Percy Bysshe 23, 24, 75, 106, 107, 255
Shepard, Sam 57
Sherlock Holmes 230, 236, 263
Sherlock Holmes and the Adventure of the Suicide Club 179
Sherlock Holmes and the Curse of the Mummy's Tomb 242, 243, 244
Sherlock Holmes and the Fall River Tragedy 260
Sherlock Holmes and the Giant Rat of Sumatra 236
Sherlock Holmes and the Hooded Lance 244
Sherlock Holmes and the Mystery of the Missing Carol 244
Sherlock Holmes and the Plague of Dracula 257
The Sherlock Holmes Companion 236
Sherlock Holmes in Caracas 241
Sherlock Holmes—The Musical 72, 207
Sherlock Holmes vs. Dracula 256, 263
Sherriff, R.C. 255
Sherwood, George 123
Shining City 67
Shirley, James 20
Siddons, Sarah 252, 253
Sidney, Sylvia 219
The Sign of Four 153, 234
Silence of the Lambs 183
Sills, Douglas 207
Silvera, Frank 253
Silverman, Jen 253
Simon, Stephen 157
Simonson, Lee 68
Simpson, Susan 108
Skinner, Otis 252
The Skull 48
Slaughter, Tod 262
Slaughter on Second Street 135, 136
Sleep in Chains: Jekyll's Nightmare 143
Slout, William L. 143
Smith, Corinna 118
Smith, Joseph Lindon 117
Smith, Noah 143
Smith, O. 27
Smoky Cell 62
Snee, Dennis 94
So Frightful an Event is Single in the History of Man 107
The Sob Sister 52
Sodaro, Craig 93, 167
Some Must Watch 227
Someone Waiting 217
Somerano, Frank 93
Something's Afoot 180
Son of Dracula 257
Son of Kong 211
Sondheim, Stephen 95, 191, 193, 194, 254
Sophocles 1, 3, 4, 22, 63, 251, 253

Sorry, Wrong Number 54
Southern, E.H. 253
Southerne, Thomas 22
Spacek, Sissy 185
Spacey, Kevin 252
The Spanish Tragedy 8, 9
Speaking of Murder 54
The Specked Band 230–235, 263
Spence, Ralph 47, 48
The Spiral Staircase 55, 226, 227
Spitzer, John 92
Spook House 114, 153
Springer, Jerry 190
The Squeaker 62
Stafford, Kate 146
Stamp, Terence 81, 228
Stanczyk, Laura 56
Stanley, Robert J. 123
Stanwyck, Barbara 54
Starke, Pauline 123
Stedman, Eric 100, 107
Steinman, Jim 88
The Stepmother 35
Sternberg, Josef von 254
Stevens, Edwin 233
Stevens, Leon B. 221
Stevenson, Robert Louis 43, 44, 139, 140, 143, 144, 179, 255
Stewart, Anna Burt 142
Stewart, Athole 233
Stewart, James 222
Stewart, Patrick 252, 253
Stilgoe, Richard 200
Stirling, Edward 233
Stoddart, Joseph M. 153
Stoker, Bram 31, 32, 59, 77, 78, 85, 86, 87, 89, 91, 92, 95, 96, 97, 99, 109, 114, 163, 181, 207, 255, 256, 257, 260
Stone, Joel 167, 168
Stone, John Augustus 40
Stone, Rodney 230
Stone, Simon 251
The Story of the Lost Special 261
Stowe, Harriet Beecher 40
Straight, Beatrice 55, 177
Strange Case of Dr. Jekyll and Mr. Hyde 144
The Strange Case of Dr. Jekyll and *Mr. Hyde* 143
Strasberg, Lee 255
Strauch, Claire 81
Strauss, Richard 160, 251
Streamers 57
Street Scene 52
Strickland, Jon 182
Stridhan, Ari 150
The String of Pearls, or The Fiend of Fleet Street 28
Stroman, Susan 108
Stuart, Gloria 255
Stubbs, Levi 200
A Study in Scarlet 233
Sue, Eugène 35, 242
The Suicide Club 179
Sullivan, Thomas Russell 44, 139
Sullivan, Tim 241
The Summer People 54

Sunset Boulevard 202, 203
The Supper of Jests 173
Svoboda, Karel 96
Swamp Pirate Zombies 126, 127
Swartz, L. Don 153
Sweeney, Matt 109
Sweeney Todd, the Demon Barber of Fleet Street 70, 95, 191–194, 202
Swoop 91

Tait, Lance 148
A Tale of Mystery 23
A Tale of Two Cities 160
The Talented Mr. Ripley 64
Tales of Mystery and Imagination: The Edgar Allan Poe Show 153, 263, 264
Tamburlaine the Great 9
The Tangled Skein 257
Tate, Phyllis 130
Taupin, Bernie 89
Taylor, Elizabeth 251
Taylor, Kenneth Alan 112
The Tell-Tale Heart 114, 148, 149, 150, 179, 260, 261
Tellegren, Lou 156
Ten Little Indians 180
Ten Little Niggers 179, 180
$10,000 Reward 45
Tennant, David 252
Terfel, Bryn 193
The Terror 61, 257
Terry, Ellen 252, 253
Théodora 35
Thérèse Raquin 35, 36, 70, 242
The Third Degree 45
Thirst 50
The Thirteenth Chair 45
Thomas, Augustus 44, 45
Thomas, Eberle 143
Thomas, Tom 92
Thompson, Brian 189
Thorndike, Russell 249
Thorndike, Sybil 249
Thornton, Jane 96
Thorpe, Richard 217
The Three Musketeers 242
Thyestes 1, 7, 8, 10
Tibbett, Lawrence 173
Tierney, Gene 254
Tierney, Maura 253
Tiller, Ted 82, 83
Tilley, Danielle 229
Tillinger, John 216
Time Lock Number 776 44
The Time Machine 163, 171, 172
Titus Andronicus 8, 11, 12, 13, 251, 252
Tolaro, Robert 92
Tolstoy, Leo 38
Tom Thumb 22
Tomorrow La Scala! 193
Torn, Rip 254
La Tosca 36
Tosca, Jules 143
Toscanini, Arturo 173
La Tour de Nesle 34

Tourneur, Cyril 18
Tourneur, Maurice 249
Townsend, Stuart 157
The Tragedy of Frankenstein 106, 107
The Tragedy of Julius Caesar 11, 13
The Tragedy of Nan 59
The Tragical History of Doctor Faustus 9, 37
Traylor, Gene 130
Treadwell, Sophie 50
Tree, Ellen 253
Tree, Herbert Beerbohm 252, 253
Trespass 63, 217
Treville, Georges 233
The Trial of Dr. Jekyll 143
The Trials of Oscar Wilde 162
The Trickster of Seville and the Stone Guest 21
A Trio of Poe 260
True Crimes 59
The Truth About Belle Gunness 260
Tucker, Duane 90
The Tumbler 63
The Turn of the Screw 1, 59, 176, 177, 178
Turney, Matt 33
Turpin, Allan 177
Tutin, Dorothy 253
The Two Mrs. Carrolls 53

Uncle Tom's Cabin 40, 254
Under Jekyll's Hyde 143
Under the Gaslight 44
Underneath 259
Underwood, Ron 262
The Undying Monster 110
The Unseen 227
Usher 101, 148
Usher: A Totally Teen Comedy 148

Vachell, Horace Annesley 129
Vale, Martin 53
The Valley of Fear 234, 263
Valli, Alida 251
The Vampire 42, 56, 77, 95
The Vampire and the Dentist 256
The Vampire Bat 259
The Vampire Chronicles 73, 88
Vampire Cowboy Trilogy 93
Vampire Freako 90
Vampire Lesbians of Sodom 91
The Vampire, or The Bride of Death 95
The Vampire, or The Bride of the Isles 24, 25, 76, 77
Vampire! or, The Spectre of Mount Snowden! 77
A Vampire Reflects 93
The Vampire Show 89
The Vampire Strikes Out 256
Vampire Valley 92
The Vampires 90, 91
Vampires in Kodachrome 92
The Vampyre 24, 75, 77, 255, 257, 263

Vanbrugh, Violet 253
Van Dine, S.S. 261
Van Sloan, Edward 80
Varesi, Gilda 253
Varney the Vampire 257
Varney the Vampyre, or The Feast of Blood 255
Veidt, Conrad 250
Veiller, Bayard 45
Venora, Diane 252, 253
Vera, or the Nihilists 160
Verhoeven, Paul 164
Verone, Doug 166
Veronica's Room 56, 57
Vershilov, Boris 258
Vidocq, Eugene François 261
Vigoda, Abe 47
The Visit 69, 70
Voltaire 32, 34, 75, 251, 261
Vonnegut, Kurt 142
Vosper, Frank 218, 219

Wagland, Greg 244
Wait Until Dark 56
Wakefield Master 8
Walbrook, Anton 221
Walken, Christopher 252
The Walking Dead 257
Wallace, Edgar 56, 61, 62, 236, 261, 262
Wallack, James 98
Walpole, Horace 245, 246, 255, 261
Walpole, Hugh 60, 61
Walter, Wilfred 252
The War of the Worlds 163
Ward, Joseph 130
Ward, Ryan 209
Warner, Deborah 253
Washbourne, Mona 207
Washington, Denzel 252
Watanabe, José 48
Waters, T.A. 263
Waterston, Sam 252
Watson, Lucille 46
Wayne, David 216
We Have Always Lived in the Castle 54
The Web 50
Webb, Kenneth 123, 259
Webber, Andrew Lloyd 73, 200–204
Webber, Julian 91
Webling, Peggy 99, 100
Webster, John 8, 19, 110
Webster, Margaret 252
Wedekind, Frank 129
Weekend 152
Wegener, Paul 258
Weigall, Arthur 117
Weigall, Hortense 118
The Weir 66, 255
Welch, Sean Michael 93
Welles, Orson 54, 251, 252, 253
Wellman, Mac 91, 257
Wells, H.G. 163–167, 172, 236, 255
Werewolf? 114
The Werewolf of London 110

The Werewolf's Curse 112, 11
West, Mae 52
West, Matt 88
West, Walter 262
The West End Horror 163
West Side Story 193
Whale, James 99, 105, 164, 225, 255, 257, 262
Whannel, Leigh 164
The Wheel Spins 227
Wheeler, Hugh 54, 191, 194
While the Lights Were Out 159
White, Courtney 80
White, Ethel Lina 55, 227
White, Matthew 199
White, Richard 204
The White Devil 19
White Zombie 123
Whitehead, Henry 123
Whitty, Dame May 216, 217
Who Is He? 129
Who Walks in the Dark 257
Whymark, Patricia 242, 244
Wiene, Robert 250
Wilde, Hagar 217, 222, 227
Wilde, Oscar 59, 84, 95, 153, 154, 156, 157, 159, 160, 162, 163, 261
Wildhorn, Frank 143, 256, 204, 206, 207, 256
Wilkof, Lee 198
Willard, John 46
Williams, Emlyn 62, 63, 70, 215–218, 224, 252

Williams, Jessika D. 252
Williams, Matt 186
Williams, Simon 239
Williams, Tennessee 58, 59, 109
Willis, Bruce 184
Wilson, Jessica-Snow 124
Wilson, Snoo 95
Winfield, Paul 252
Winkler, Henry 92
Winters, Shelley 54
Wiseman, Joseph 116
Witch 59, 253
The Witch of Edmonton 19, 253
The Witching Hour 45
Wolf, Leonard 91
The Wolf Man 56, 110, 112
Wolff, Ruth Rehrer 116, 117
Wolfit, Donald 9, 253
The Woman in Black 64, 181, 182
The Woman in White 29, 30, 73, 160, 202
A Woman of No Importance 160
Women Beware Women 20
Women in Prison 260
Women of Trachis 3
Wood, Mrs. Henry 70
Wood, John 253
Wood, Peter 143
Wooddell, Gregory 240
Wooden Kimono 47
Woods, Phil 90
Woolley, E.M. (Monty) 252
Woolverton, Linda 88

The World That We Knew 117
Wray, Fay 4, 188, 211, 259
The Wrecker 60
Wuthering Heights 160
Wyler, William 228
Wynyard, Diana 221

Yaffe, James 70
The Yellow Mask 62
Yeston, Maury 203, 204
A Yorkshire Tragedy 18
You Know My Methods, Watson 263
Young, Robert 80
Young Dracula, or The Singing Bat 85, 86
Young Frankenstein 108
Yours Truly, Jack the Ripper 130

Zadig 261
Zaire 34
Zaks, Jerry 199
Zangwill, Israel 261
Zelazny, Roger 263
Zola, Émile 32, 35, 36, 70, 242
Zombie 123, 259
Zombie Asian Moms 259
Zombie Joe 255
Zombie Prom 72, 124, 125
Zombies from the Beyond 259
Zwerling, Joseph 168